Further Praise for Clive James's translation of

THE DIVINE COMEDY

"Clive James's translation of *The Divine Comedy* is a remarkable achievement: not a scowling marble Dante of sublime set pieces but a living, breathing poet shifting restlessly through a dizzying succession of moods, perceptions and passions. Under James's uncanny touch, seven long centuries drop away, and the great poem is startlingly fresh and new." —Stephen Greenblatt, Harvard University, author of *The Swerve*

"This is the translation that many of us had abandoned all hope of finding. Clive James's version is the only one that conveys Dante's variety, depth, subtlety, vigor, wit, clarity, mystery and awe in rhymed English stanzas that convey the music of Dante's triple rhymes. This book lets Dante's genius shine through as it never did before in English verse, and is a reminder that James's poetry has always been his finest work." —Edward Mendelson, Columbia University

"Seeking to preserve Dante's 'infinitely variable rhythmic pulse,' James makes an inspired metrical choice. . . . The greatest virtue of James's translation is his gift for infusing poetry in the least likely places. . . . James's austere volume achieves something remarkable: It lets Dante's poetry shine in all its brilliance." —Joseph Luzzi, *New York Times Book Review*

"James gives us something sublime: a new way of reading a classic work. James' version is not merely a mirrored word, but a trans-figured word. As such, it will no doubt enter the essential Dante canon, and remain there for years to come." —Earl Pike, *Cleveland Plain Dealer*

"As with [Seamus] Heaney, the telling choices in his diction are dis-creet in themselves, but overwhelming in their impact. . . . James has translated the meaning along with the words, so that his *Divine Comedy* is, for the twenty-first-century English speaker, something very close to reading Dante in 1317." —Deirdre Serjeantson, *Dublin Review of Books*

"The poem flows magnificently. . . . The speeches are magnificent. . . . As for the later books . . . I know of no English versions that come near James's. . . . Easily the best introduction to Dante for the general reader." —Peter Goldsworthy, *The Australian*

"James's *Divine Comedy* . . . is an impassioned, impressive, some-times dazzling piece of work. . . . James has written a remarkable contemporary version of Dante—stately, colloquial, full of move-ment and fire and light. . . . [It] is a remarkable tour de force—brave, sparkling, encyclopedic and with a tremendous forward momen-tum as it traverses the vast space of life and death and eternity." —Peter Craven, *Sydney Morning Herald*

"An outstanding achievement. . . . He restores the sense of drama, the colours and music of Dante's vision. . . . Clive James has now given us a translation worthy of this and any other time, and a great piece of literature in its own right." —Robert Fox, *London Evening Standard*

"At his best James balances complexity and forward impetus in a way no other contemporary version manages."

—Peter Hainsworth, *Times Literary Supplement*

"A vigorous, poetic paraphrase of the *Comedy*." —*Library Journal*

"Daring. . . . Deciding that Dante's terza rima is too strained in English, [James] uses robust, rollicking quatrains. . . . James' revitalizing translation allows this endlessly analyzed, epic, archetypal 'journey to salvation' to once again stride, whirl, blaze, and sing. Anyone heretofore reluctant to pick up *The Divine Comedy* will discover that James' bold, earthy, rhythmic and rhyming, all-the-way live English translation fulsomely and brilliantly liberates the profound humanity of Dante's timeless masterpiece." —*Booklist*

"Do we really need yet another translation of Dante's world-famous journey through the three parts of the Catholic afterlife? We might, if the translator is both as eminent, and as skillful, as Clive James. . . . It is a wonder to see the light cast by the whole."

—*Publishers Weekly*

"A translation for readers who are culturally engaged, willing to follow lengthy narratives, and curious about free will and the soul. A Dante for fans of *Mad Men*?" —Camila Domonoske, NPR.org

"Perfect for the Don Drapers in your life." —Megan O'Grady, Vogue.com

Autobiography

The Blaze of Obscurity

Unreliable Memoirs

Falling Towards England

May Week Was in June

North Face of Soho

Fiction

Brilliant Creatures

The Remake

The Man from Japan

The Silver Castle

Verse

The Book of My Enemy: Collected Verse 1958–2003

Opal Sunset: Selected Poems 1958–2008

Angels over Elsinore

Nefertiti in the Flak Tower

Criticism

Reliable Essays: The Best of Clive James

The Metropolitan Critic (new edition, 1994)

Visions Before Midnight

The Crystal Bucket

First Reactions

At the Pillars of Hercules

From the Land of Shadows

Glued to the Box

Snakecharmers in Texas

The Dreaming Swimmer

On Television

Even as We Speak

As of This Writing

The Meaning of Recognition

Cultural Amnesia

The Revolt of the Pendulum

A Point of View

Travel

Flying Visits

DANTE

THE DIVINE COMEDY

A NEW VERSE TRANSLATION BY
CLIVE JAMES

LIVERIGHT PUBLISHING CORPORATION

A DIVISION OF W. W. NORTON & COMPANY

NEW YORK • LONDON

TO PRUE SHAW

without whom this book, like all my other books,

would never have existed

For information about permission to reproduce selections
from this book, write to Permissions, Liveright Publishing
Corporation, a division of W. W. Norton & Company, Inc.,
500 Fifth Avenue, New York, NY 10110

For information about special discounts for bulk purchases,
please contact W. W. Norton Special Sales
at specialsales@wwnorton.com or 800-233-4830

Manufacturing by RR Donnelley Harrisonburg
Book design by JAMdesign
Production manager: Julia Druskin

Library of Congress Cataloging-in-Publication Data

Dante Alighieri, 1265–1321.
[Divina commedia. English]
The divine comedy / Dante ; a new verse translation by Clive James. — First
edition.
     pages cm
ISBN 978-0-87140-448-0 (hardcover)
I. James, Clive, 1939– translator. II. Title.
PQ4315.J36 2013
851'.1—dc23

                              2013003584

ISBN 978-0-87140-741-2 pbk.

Liveright Publishing Corporation
500 Fifth Avenue, New York, N.Y. 10110
www.wwnorton.com

W. W. Norton & Company Ltd.
Castle House, 75/76 Wells Street, London W1T 3QT

1 2 3 4 5 6 7 8 9 0

Mouth, do what you can . . .
—*Heaven*, 14, 79

CONTENTS

THE DIVINE COMEDY

INTRODUCTION

Many people, not all of them outside Italy, think that the *Divine Comedy* is a rather misshapen story. And indeed, if it were just a story, it would be back to front: the narrator has an exciting time in Hell, but Purgatory, when it is not about art, is about theology, and Heaven is about nothing else. What kind of story has all the action in the first third, and then settles back to stage a discussion of obscure spiritual matters? But the *Divine Comedy* isn't just a story, it's a poem: one of the biggest, most varied and most accomplished poems in all the world. Appreciated on the level of its verse, the thing never stops getting steadily more beautiful as it goes on. T. S. Eliot said that the last cantos of *Heaven* were as great as poetry can ever get. The translator's task is to compose something to suggest that such a judgement might be right.

This translation of the *Divine Comedy* is here today because my wife, when we were together in Florence in the mid-1960s, a few years before we were married, taught me that the great secret of Dante's masterpiece lay in the handling of the verse, which always moved forward even in the most intensely compressed of episodes. She proved this by answering my appeal to have the famous Paolo and Francesca episode in *Inferno* 5 explained to me from the original text. From various translators including Byron we can see what that passage says. But how did Dante say it? My wife said that the *terza rima* was only the outward sign of how the thing carried itself along, and that if you dug down into Dante's expressiveness at the level of phonetic construction you would find an infinitely variable rhythmic pulse adaptable to anything he wanted to convey.

One of the first moments she picked out of the text to show me what the master versifier could do was when Francesca tells Dante what drove her and Paolo over the brink and into the pit of sin. In English it would go something like:

> We read that day for delight
> About Lancelot, how love bound him.

She read it in Italian:

> Noi leggevam quel giorno per diletto
> Di Lancialotto, come amor lo strinse.

After the sound *"-letto"* ends the first line, the placing of *"-lotto"* at the start of the second line gives it the power of a rhyme, only more so. How does that happen? You have to look within. The Italian eleven-syllable line feels a bit like our standard English iambic pentameter and therefore tends to mislead you into thinking that the *terzina*, the recurring unit of three lines, has a rocking regularity. But Dante isn't thinking of regularity in the first instance any more than he is thinking of rhyme, which is too easy in Italian to be thought a technical challenge: in fact for an Italian poet it's *not* rhyming that's hard.

Dante's overt rhyme scheme is only the initial framework by which the verse structure moves forward. Within the *terzina*, there is all this other intense interaction going on. (Dante is the greatest exemplar in literary history of the principle advanced by Vernon Watkins, and much approved of by Philip Larkin, that good poetry doesn't just rhyme at the end of the lines, it rhymes all along the line.) Especially in modern times, translators into English have tended to think that if this interior intensity can be duplicated, the grand structure of the *terzina*, or some equivalent rhymed framework, can be left out. And so it can, often with impressive results, each passage transmuted into very compressed English prose. But that approach can never transmit the full intensity of the *Divine Comedy*, which is notable for its overall onward drive as much as for its local density of language.

Dante is not only tunnelling in the depths of meaning, he is working much closer to the surface texture: working within it. Even in the most solemn passage there might occur a touch of delight in sound that comes close to being wordplay. Still with Paolo and Francesca: in the way the word *"diletto,"* after the line turning, modulates into *di Lancelotto*, the shift from *-letto* to *-lotto* is a modulation across the vowel spectrum, and Dante has a thousand tricks like that to keep things moving. The rhymes that clinch the *terzina* are a very supplementary music compared to the music going on within the *terzina*'s span.

The lines, I found, were alive within themselves. Francesca described how, while they were carried away with what they read, Paolo kissed her mouth. *Questi* (this one right here), she says, *la bocca mi basciò, tutto tremante* (kissed my mouth, all trembling). At that stage I had about a hundred words of Italian and needed to be told that the accent on the final *"o"* of *basciò* was a stress accent and needed to be hit hard, slowing the line so that it could start again and complete itself in the alliterative explosion of *tutto tremante*. An hour of this tutorial and I could already see that Dante was paying attention to his rhythms right down to the structure of the phrase and even of the word.

The linked rhymes of the *terza rima* were a gesture towards form, marking the pulse of the onward surge of the great story, which was driven by its poetry; and would be infinitely less great without its poetry, just as Wagner's *Ring* cycle would be infinitely less great without its music. But Dante's formal requirements for himself went down to the very basics of the handling of language. It was all very precise, and yet it all added up. Though it was assembled from minutely wrought effects, the episode really did have rhythmic sweep. My wife, clearly touched by my sudden impersonation of a proper student, said all the rest of the poem was like that too, including the supposedly colourless theological bits. Every moment danced, and the dance was always moving forward.

Over the next year or so, while I was reading Dante in the original to satisfy the requirements of the English tripos at Cambridge, I looked at several rhymed translations and found them strained. On the other hand the translations done in prose had whole chunks that were too dull to read, especially in the second and third books. The total effect of looking at so many translations was to be convinced that the job was thankless. One thing I could see clearly, however, was that any even halfway successful translation would have to rhyme, although the question was how, especially in those long stretches, later on in the poem, where not a lot seemed to be happening.

You could see easily why Byron went no further than his Paolo and Francesca; he couldn't keep up the excitement if there was nothing for the excitement to bite on, as it were. Starting from the level of incident, he, or any other translator, couldn't get down to the level of language. They could raise themselves to the level of thought: some of the translators were, *mutatis mutandis*, as educated as Dante was, who was one of the most educated men of his time even in the conventional sense, quite apart from the proto-scientific sense in which he was original without parallel. But they couldn't, or wouldn't, get down to the level where syllables met each other and generated force. That had to be the aim, impossible as it seemed; to generate the force, both semantic and phonetic: the force of both meaning and sound. Indeed, in the original, some of the meaning was *in* the sound. Unless a translator did something to duplicate how the poem sounded, he, or she, wouldn't get near what it meant.

So the task, if task it was, went on the back burner and stayed there for about forty years. I was barely aware that I was even thinking about it. Helping me to be diffident on the topic were my memories of what my wife had said about the Dorothy Sayers translation. Back at Sydney University, when we first met in the late 1950s, she was studying Italian: the beginning of what would turn out to be a distinguished lifelong career of teaching and editing Italian literature, with particular attention to Dante. As part of the course, she had been required to produce a substantial paper; and she had made her subject the Dorothy Sayers translation, which was famous at the time and indeed is still well-known now: the total amount of money it has made for Penguin must be colossal. But my wife, always the closest of readers, was able even then to detect that Sayers had simultaneously loaded her text with cliché and pumped it full of wind.

Finally, not long after I retired, I thought I could see how a translation might work. I started by drawing the necessary conclusions from my knowledge of what to avoid. The first thing I had learned was that a strict *terza rima* was out of the question. Even Louis MacNeice, one of the great verse technicians of modern times, had resorted to half-rhyme in order to sustain a long poem in *terza rima*. And the sad truth about *Autumn Sequel* is that it is simply terrible. Its predecessor, *Autumn Journal,* had been a triumph—it should be ranked, in my view, as the great long poem of its time—but for that work he had allowed himself access to his vast stock of classical metres. In *Autumn Sequel* he stuck himself with the *terza rima*, and with a not very attractive version of it. I tried writing a longish poem in strict *terza rima* and could see that it was creaking with strain the longer it went on, thereby accomplishing the opposite of the desirable effect of a narrative form, which is to get you into the swing of the thing. With the dubious exception of Shelley's *The Triumph of Life,* nobody has ever written a *terza rima* poem in English that makes you forget the form in which it is composed, and a *terza rima* translation of Dante like Laurence Binyon's makes a feature of Binyon's virtuosity rather than Dante's mastery.

So if it couldn't be in strict *terza rima*, and if a loosely rhymed *terza rima* wasn't worth writing, what regular measure would carry the freight? Over the years I had written thousands of couplets and although I enjoyed using them for comic effect I knew that they wouldn't fit this task. The *Divine Comedy* isn't comic. A few couplets might come in handy to clinch each canto but on the whole the couplet suffers the drawback that Johnson spotted in the work of Pope: in a rhyme-starved language like English, the same rhyme sound keeps cropping up too early. Even if the words that rhyme are kept deliberately different each time—night/bright, light/sight, etc.—the sound is the same, and calls the wrong kind of attention to itself. And yet I wanted the rhyming words to be close enough together to be noticed.

Finally I realised that I had been practising for this job every time I wrote a quatrain. In my poems, ever since I started writing them in the late 1950s, the quatrain was the most common measure unless I was writing in free verse. Decades of practice had made the quatrain so natural to me that it had become a mode of thought. For this project, if the quatrain could be augmented with extra lines whenever the occasion demanded or opportunity offered, it would yield the ideal combination of strictness and ease. To reinforce the strictness, I would avoid feminine rhymes. When writing couplets, one veers inexorably towards feminine rhymes, and the effect, though often usefully flippant, is always in danger of recalling Gilbert and Sullivan. To match Dante's gravitas, a strong, solid dignity would be required. Well, I had had plenty of practice in writing quatrains with masculine rhymes. So really I had spent all this time—the greater part of a lifetime—preparing my instruments.

Quietly I got the project under way, starting with the first line of the first canto. It would be a mistake to do the famous passages and then join them up: the welds might show. If my modified quatrain measure was to justify itself, it would have to work from the beginning, and be still working at the end—because the *Divine Comedy* ends as it begins, with the same feeling of exuberance that has been maintained throughout. Dante registers this exuberance even in his most desperate moments. He doesn't stop singing just because something dreadful is happening. What he says is: something dreadful is happening *even as I sing*. It's an interplay of form and content: the most ambitious that any literary artist ever attempted. Dante's torrential cascade of poetic effects adds up to a claim. No poem could be equal to my subject: no poem except this poem.

I wanted my translation to provide parallels for such effects while maintaining all of Dante's sense of economy. No poet, not even Shakespeare, could say quite so much so quickly, so the translator must know how to be brief. But there are things he can add without slowing the pace. (Or, indeed, taking more space: since English needs less room than Italian, there is latitude for adding things while keeping to the same length as the original.) Dante had barely finished the poem before the first commentaries began appearing. Commentary was thought necessary because Dante had composed every canto of his poem as if it were a weekend article based on news that had only just happened, and whose details did not need to be outlined. There must have been readers who, not having heard the news about who robbed whom and which pope double-crossed which prince, were puzzled even at the time.

Since then, the chances of being puzzled have multiplied, and there is also the increasingly pressing matter of making even references to the Gospels clear to readers who might not be familiar with them. The first commentaries inaugurated seven hundred years of scholarship and criticism which have gone on to this day, and the summary of all that knowledge and informed speculation is there at the foot of the page in any scholarly edition. But this translation would be for non-scholars in the first instance. Footnotes would be a burden to it. Ideally, the thing itself should carry all the information it would need. How to do this?

The reservoir of material at the foot of the page of a scholarly text (sometimes there are five lines of text and fifty of apparatus) provides the translator of the poem with an ideal opportunity to upload salient facts into the verse narrative and make things clear. There are stretches in all three books when it really helps to be told who belongs to which family; whether one family is at war with another; and what precisely happened to which city when it was betrayed. On the vexed question of theology—this crops up especially in the third book, *Heaven*—it can help to be told that a certain scholar represents a certain position. Almost always the relevant information is there on the page, down at the bottom. In numerous instances I felt justified in lifting it out of the basement and putting it on display in the text. It might seem bold to assume that Dante, if he thought the reader might not know, would have explained which features of a certain scholarly dispute he was referring to, but we can also assume that he didn't want the reader to be presented with an insoluble puzzle. Dante wanted to be read. Every stratagem he employed tells us that. He was talking about the whole of creation at once but he wanted to glue the reader to the bench.

To help him do it for the present age, I opened up a way to make simple, sparing but sufficiently wide-ranging use of what we might call the basic scholarly heritage. My aim, when importing an explanatory detail, was to make the text more readable instead of less. Also I have cut back on his lists of names here and there, when a list is all it is. Perhaps boldly, I would say that all the reader needs to know is in the poem as I have presented it. As Dante, in Heaven, travels all over the sky, some of the references to the Zodiac might seem obscure, but they probably seemed so at the time: and really that's all you have to know, that the references sounded learned. Dante's first readers could take the more obscure points for granted while they followed the main points. My job was to make some of the main points more self-clarifying by putting in some of the explanations that had been accumulating at the bottom of the page for the best part of a millennium, but to do so without slowing the tempo. The result one hopes for is a readily appreciable outline of Dante's Christian vision. Is it possible, though, in an age without belief?

Well, how much does Dante believe? The truth is that he didn't want to believe anything if he couldn't test it. As we trace the story through one hundred cantos, three regions and every shade of emotion from despair to bliss, we find that he believed in his journey to salvation. But if his belief had been without its doubts, there would never have been a journey; and at the very end we find ourselves concluding that the great poet, setting out the reasons for his faith, has reached conclusions that will eventually make blind faith impossible. Dante could ask questions about theology because he was in love with questioning itself; he was in love with the design of the divinely inspired universe because he was in love with design, which he could see in a fold of cloth and a fallen leaf.

Dante had a scientific mind: one of the first scientific minds we know of in the modern age, for which, indeed, he can be said to have built the foundations. His poem stands at the dawn of modern science, and therefore of the times we live in now: its essential moment is in its final vision, when Dante the traveller, at the apex of heaven, looks into the source of creation and sees the imprint of a human face. The *Divine Comedy* is the precursor of the whole of modern history, and I hope this translation conveys enough of its model to show that he forecast the whole story in a single song: a song of lights. The joy of discovery is what drives the poem, and if my translation gets some of that exultation into English verse then it will have done its work.

For all his majestic weight, there is also a lightness to Dante, and I hope to have got that in. Finally but essentially, tempo is one of the two main poetic elements in play. The other is texture. What we have, in this miraculous work of art, is a mutually reinforcing balance of tempo and texture, of a kind that had never been heard before over such a distance: fourteen thousand lines of it. Much as he worshipped Virgil, Dante was better at it than his master. If he could have read Homer, he would have found that he was better at it than Homer too. In the original Italian, you can hear it. But most of us will never read Dante in the original Italian. It's a pious wish that translators are always making: they hope that the reader, intrigued by the translation, will be driven to learn Italian, etc. Common sense tells us that it will seldom happen.

To know a foreign language thoroughly is a big task, and to know its literature is a full time job. For more than fifty years, my wife's scholarship, her tenacity and seriousness of purpose, have been there to remind me of what it means to be dedicated to Dante and to help pass on the body of knowledge associated with his name. Her work culminated first with her gold-medal-winning edition of Dante's *Monarchia* for the Società Dantesca Italiana, the only national edition of any work of Dante edited by a non-Italian, and a labour of love that took her thirty years. It culminated all over again with the completion of her digital edition of the *Divine Comedy*'s manuscript tradition, a tool for all Dante scholars, and a thing of extraordinary beauty and utility. I hope she will forgive me for straying onto her territory, but really there is no contest. Beside her lucid and scrupulous scholarship, a translation counts for very little. But I have done my best with it, always encouraged by the memory of how, in Florence, she first gave me an idea of what it meant to be in the service of her great poet.

—LONDON, 2012

TRANSLATOR'S NOTE

For Dante it was a strict rule not to rhyme the word "Christ" with any other word except itself. I have followed him in that, as in any other matter of decorum. But when it comes to vocabulary, the translator needs a decorum of his own. Dante, the man on the spot, never had to think about whether his words were apt to the age, whereas the translator, if he is not careful, will find himself thinking of nothing else. Not wanting to get between the reader and the original, I have tried to avoid anachronistic language except when it could hide itself in the blur of time. I used the word "*bastille*" only after checking that it might—just might—have reached Florence from Paris in time for Dante to hear it. "Breaker's yard" is no doubt a modern term, but for a long time there have been ships and there were always places where they were broken up, so I thought a term like that might be slipped in, whereas one could not possibly use, say, "napalm," a word which would have been very employable in the lower regions of Hell. Such a modern coinage would stand out like a phrase of recent slang in one of those television dramas where millions have been spent on the look of the thing but the whole effect is dissipated by an untimely phrase coming out of an actor's mouth. Down among the Evil-Claws, however, I used modern low-life filth because a shock effect is exactly what such scatological language is always after.

As I mentioned in the Introduction, on numerous occasions I thought it useful to employ the time-honoured consensus of the scholarship in the interests of clarity, and lift a name, as it were, from the footnotes to the text. Let one instance stand for many. For hundreds of years it has been more or less agreed among the scholars that one of the animals Dante meets early in the poem is a symbol for Avarice. So I put that in. On the other hand, I have left some of the mysteries unsolved because there has never been an answer to them. Who was the Veltro? Scholars are still wondering, so the reader of this translation will have to wonder too. Such a question will soon become recognizable as a Dantesque puzzle. The renowned German scholar Karl Vossler once said that Dante was a great mystifier. And so he was, but not as much as he wasn't. Really he was a great clarifier. The *Divine Comedy* is a vast act of illumination. Even for Hell, Gustav Doré was too dark an illustrator, and by the time we get to Purgatory the whole universe is lighting up, so that you can see, in fine detail, everything that the poet refers to. I may have taken a liberty, towards the very end, in making Dante seem to intuit the space-time continuum. Nobody ever intuited that before Einstein. But one of the tributes we must pay Dante's great poem is that all subsequent human knowledge seems to unfold from it.

As to my chosen stanza form, there are no puzzles at all. The form is a quatrain, either simple or augmented, and any augmentations use the same rhymes, so *abab* might grow to *ababa* or *ababab* or sometimes more. The aim is an easy-seeming onward flow, except at the end of the canto, where a couplet closes the action with a snap. In every other formal respect, the layout is established by Dante himself. It was his idea to have one hundred cantos divided into three lots of thirty-three, with a single canto to start things off. These three groupings of cantos are known to scholars as canticles, but it is perhaps less ponderous to call them books. Dante ends each book with the word "stars." It would be nice if the translator could do the same, but in English the word "stars" has very few words with which to rhyme. Rather than write a strained couplet to close each book, I wrote a final line in which the stars indeed show up, but not as the last word.

In the poetic world of Dante, things happen in a certain order;

with the words, from start to distant finish, always sounding inevitable. Therein will lie the translator's most daunting obstacle. Some of the phrases, known by heart to every educated person in Italy, sound more wonderful in Italian than they ever can in English. It was bound to happen, because different languages have different words for the same thing. In Italian, for example, there is the beautiful word *"sinistra."* In English we just say "left": nothing like as sinuous. By extension, there will be Italian phrases that the translator can't hope to equal for their sonority. But working on such a large scale, there will be other Italian phrases that will offer opportunities to be rendered in English words as resonant as he knows how to make them. Finally, then, it will come down to what he can do with verse. The poet will be on his mettle. Part of his consolation, as he cudgels his brains through the long nights, is that Dante thought the same about himself.

ACKNOWLEDGEMENTS

My thanks are due to both of my publishers, Robert Weil at Liveright in New York, and Don Paterson at Picador in London. Each of them saw the text before it was finished and to neither of them did it occur that I might be overambitious for wanting to press on to a conclusion: or if it did, they didn't say so. In America, Dennis Looney agreed to vet the text: not necessarily a comfortable offer from my angle, because his standards of scholarship are high. His numerous corrections on points of fact have all been incorporated into the text, and his remarks about interpretation have been listened to at the very least: sometimes, after thinking it over, I simply decided he was right, and sat down to recast a line or even more. I should insist, though, that any moments of excess or carelessness are my responsibility. For his scrutiny of my versification, once again I thank Don Paterson, who has supervised my last two books of verse for Picador: to have his fine ear on the case is a great privilege. An even greater privilege was to have my family looking after me when I fell ill. The actual translation was already done, but the whole business of finalizing the text has taken place during the period of my bad health, and if I had not been looked after I would not have lived to see the book made ready for the press. In that regard, my particular thanks should go to my elder daughter, Claerwen, who made crucial suggestions about the order of events in the preliminary pages.

A NOTE ON THE TRANSLATION

In this new translation of the *Divine Comedy*, Dante speaks through Clive James with a strong voice in English we haven't heard before. The translator makes the unusual choice of recasting the original Italian into quatrains (not the tercets of Dante's *terza rima*), which he meticulously constructs with keen attention to rhythm and rhyme. The poetic metre imbues the narrative with a drive that propels the pilgrim on his journey from Hell to Heaven. And with it James develops and sustains an impressive periodic syntax—see, e.g., Adam's appearance in Canto 26 of *Heaven*—that pulls the reader in and pushes him along the poem's course too. Unsuspecting readers will find themselves snagged, and happily so, even in the poem's dense doctrinal passages, where often the most devoted fall by the wayside or simply skip ahead to what they imagine is the next good bit of poetry. Consequently, the Beatrice we hear speaking in these Jamesian quatrains (not to mention Thomas Aquinas, Bonaventure and Peter Damian, among others) may be the most convincing in English verse. In this translation there are no lulls when scholastic doctors or purging souls or prolix demons hold forth. Like the pilgrim, you too, good reader—*lettor*, Dante calls you in more than one direct address—move swiftly to the ultimate destination at the end of the poem.

James also makes the laudable decision to flesh out the more obscure references in Dante's poetry by incorporating into the translation explanatory details culled from commentaries, which are often necessary to understand fully Dante's point in a given passage. The translator decides where and when to add these for the sake of clarity. These additional bits, tipped in judiciously, actually bring the reader closer to the original by removing the necessity of having to consult notes. Some scholars may balk but the typical reader needs help in negotiating Dante's elaborate network of references and will appreciate not having to search it out in footnotes, endnotes or notes in an accompanying volume. Anyone comparing this translation with the original may wonder at times why Dante didn't do this himself. Clive James has given us a new Dante, a forceful Dante, a Dante who deserves to be heard.

—*Dennis Looney*

Dennis Looney, a professor of Italian and classics at the University of Pittsburgh, is the author of *'My Muse will have a story to paint': Selected Prose of Ludovico Ariosto* (2010) and *Freedom Readers: The African American Reception of Dante Alighieri and the* Divine Comedy (2011).

DANTE

THE DIVINE COMEDY

BOOK

I

———

HELL

CANTO 1

At the mid-point of the path through life, I found
Myself lost in a wood so dark, the way
Ahead was blotted out. The keening sound
I still make shows how hard it is to say
How harsh and bitter that place felt to me—
Merely to think of it renews the fear—
So bad that death by only a degree
Could possibly be worse. As you shall hear,
It led to good things too, eventually,
But there and then I saw no sign of those,
And can't say even now how I had come
To be there, stunned and following my nose
Away from the straight path. And then, still numb
From pressure on the heart, still in a daze,
I stumbled on the threshold of a hill
Where trees no longer grew. Lifting my gaze,
I saw its shoulders edged with overspill
From our sure guide, the sun, whose soothing rays
At least a little melted what that night
Of dread had done to harden my heart's lake—
And like someone who crawls, half dead with fright,
Out of the sea, and breathes, and turns to take
A long look at the water, so my soul,
Still thinking of escape from the dark wood

I had escaped, looked back to see it whole,
The force field no one ever has withstood
And stayed alive. I rested for a while,
And then resumed, along the empty slope,
My journey, in the standard crofter's style,
30 Weight on the lower foot. Harder to cope
When things got steeper, and a mountain cat
With parti-coloured pelt, light on its feet,
In a trice was in my face and stayed like that,
Barring my way, encouraging retreat.
Three beasts—was this the leopard, Lechery?—
Were said to block the penitential climb
For sinners and for all society,
And here was one, sticking to me like lime.
Not only did it hamper me, it made
40 Me think of turning back. Now was the time
Morning begins. The sun, fully displayed
At last, began its climb, but not alone.
The stars composing Aries, sign of spring,
Were with it now, nor left it on its own
When the First Love made every lovely thing
The world can boast: a thought to give me heart
That I might counter, in this gentle hour
Of a sweet season, the obstructive art,
Pretty to see but frightful in its power,
50 Of that cat with the coloured coat. But wait:
If fear had waned, still there was fear enough
To bring on Pride, the lion, in full spate:
Head high, hot breath to make the air look rough—
As rocks in summer seem to agitate
The atmosphere above them without cease—
So rabid was its hunger. On its heels
The wolf appeared, whose name is Avarice,
Made thin by a cupidity that steals
Insatiably out of its own increase,
60 Obtained from many people it made poor.

This one propelled such terror from its face
Into my mind, all thoughts I had before
Of ever rising to a state of grace
Were crushed. And so, as one who, mad for gain,
Must find one day that all he gains is lost
In a flood of tears, a conscience racked with pain,
Just so I felt my hopes came at the cost
Of being forced, by this unresting beast,
Little by little down towards that wood
70 Whose gloom the sun can never in the least
Irradiate. But all at once there stood
Before me one who somehow seemed struck dumb
By the weight of a long silence. "Pity me,
And try to tell me in what form you come,"
I cried. "Is it a shade or man I see?"
And he replied: "No, not a man. Not now.
I was once, though. A Lombard. Parents born
In Mantua. Both born there." That was how
His words emerged: as if with slow care torn,
80 Like pages of a book soaked shut by time,
From his clogged throat. "Caesar was getting on
When I was young. That's Julius. A crime,
His death. Then, after he was gone,
I lived in Rome. The good Augustus reigned.
The gods were cheats and liars. As for me,
I was a poet." He grew less constrained
In speech, as if trade-talk brought fluency.
"I sang about Anchises' son, the just
Aeneas, pious, peerless. When proud Troy
90 Was burned to ashes, ashes turned to dust
Which he shook off his feet, that marvellous boy.
He did what any decent hero must:
Set sail. But you, you turn back. Tell me why.
Why not press on to the delightful peak?
The root cause of all joy is in the sky."
Almost too shocked and overawed to speak—

For now the one who fought for words was I—
I asked him, just as if I didn't know:
"Are you Virgil? Are you the spring, the well,
100   The fountain and the river in full flow
Of eloquence that sings like a seashell
Remembering the sea and the rainbow?
Of all who fashion verse the leading light?
The man of honour? What am I to say?
Through learning you by heart I learned to write.
My love for your book turned my night to day.
You are my master author. Only you
Could teach me the Sweet Style that they call mine.
I could go on. But what am I to do
110   About this animal that shows no sign
Of letting me proceed? It scares me so,
My veins are empty, all the blood sucked back
Into the heart. There's nothing you don't know,
My sage, so tell me how this mad attack
Can be called off." Then he: "You need to choose
Another route." This while he watched me weep.
"This way there's no way out. You're bound to lose:
Bound by the spell of this beast pledged to keep
You crying, you or anyone who tries
120   To get by. In a bad mood it can kill,
And it's never in a good mood. See those eyes?
So great a hunger nothing can fulfil.
It eats, it wants more, like the many men
Infected by its bite. Its catalogue
Of victories will be finished only when
Another dog arrives, the hunting dog:
The Veltro. As for now, it's hard to see
Even his outline through the glowing fog
Of the future, but be assured by me—
130   The Veltro will make this thing die of shame
For wanting to eat wealth and real estate.
The Veltro's diet will be bigger game:

Love, wisdom, virtue. It will operate
In humble country, eat the humble bread
Of that sad Italy where Trojans fought
Our local tribes: the Latium beachhead.
The brave Princess Camilla there was brought
To death in battle, and Prince Turnus, too—
Killed by Aeneas, of whose Trojan friends
140 Euryalus and Nisus died. The new
Great Dog will harry this one to the ends
Of that scorched earth and so back down to Hell,
From which, by envious Lucifer, it was
First sent forth. But by now I've pondered well
The path adapted best to serve your cause,
So let me be your guide. I'll take you through
The timeless breaker's yard where you will hear
The death cries of the damned who die anew
Each day, though dead already in the year—
150 No dated stones remain to give a clue—
The earliest sinners died, when time began.
And you'll see, in the next eternal zone,
Those so content with purging fire they fan
The flames around them, thankful to atone,
Hopeful of being raised to join the blessed.
If you would join them too, we'll reach a stage
When only someone else shows you the rest:
Someone more worthy, though of tender age
Beside me. I can't tell you her name yet,
160 But what I can say is, the Emperor
Who reigns on high vows he will never let
A non-believer—though I lived before
Belief was possible—see where he sits
In judgement and in joy with the elect."
Sad and afraid, but gathering my wits,
"Poet," I said, "I ask you to effect,
In the name of that God you will never see,
An exit for me from this place of grief,

And then an entry to where I would be—
170 Beyond the purging flames of which you tell—
In sight of Peter's Gate, though that relief
Demands for prelude that I go through Hell."
And then he moved, and then I moved as well.

CANTO 2

The day was dying, and the darkening air
Brought all the working world of living things
To rest. I, only, sweated to prepare
For war, the way ahead, the grind that brings
The battler to hot tears for each yard gained:
To bitter tears, and memories more real
Than what was real and which is thus retained
Unblunted, edged with even sharper steel.
My Muse, my schooled and proven gift, help me:
10   It's now or never. Fortify my mind
With the vivifying skills of poetry,
For what I saw needs art of a great kind.
I saw great things. Give them nobility.
Thus I began: "Poet I call my guide,
Judge first my powers. Will they serve so high
A purpose? Would you rather step aside
Than put me to this road? For you, not I,
Have told the world Aeneas, mortal still,
Went to another world, and not to die.
20   But if the Adversary of All Ill
Saw fit to let him live, thinking of who
And what he was—princely progenitor
Of everything that Rome would be and do
In times to come—who could deserve it more?

A man of intellect, the soul of Rome
And all its empire, he was singled out
There where the light eternal has its home,
At the Highest Level. Also, what about
That city? Though the world fell at its feet,
30   Rome was created first so that one day
Great Peter's followers might have their seat,
Enthroned by the divine will. When you say
Aeneas sailed to victory, what he heard
Along the way ensured not only that,
But the papal mantle. So the Holy Word,
Sent backwards into time, aimed only at
Your hero, hit the mark. And then Paul's ship,
The Chosen Vessel, came to Rome as well—
The vessel, in a sense, that Faith might sip
40   Renewal from, and did. But now, pray tell,
Why me? Who says that I get to go there?
Do I look like Aeneas? Am I Paul?
Not I nor anyone I know would dare
To put me in that company at all.
Therefore, if I persuade myself to go,
I trust I'll not be punished as a fool.
Wise man, what I have not said, you must know."
Just so, obeying the unwritten rule
That one who would unwish that which he wished,
50   Having thought twice about what first he sought,
Must put fish back into the pool he fished,
So they, set free, may once again be caught,
Just so did I in that now shadowy fold—
Because, by thinking, I'd consumed the thought
I started with, that I had thought so bold.
"If I have understood your words aright,"
Magnanimously the great shade replied,
"Your soul is crumbling from the needless blight
Of misplaced modesty, which is false pride
60   Reversed, and many men by this are swayed

From honourable enterprise. One thinks
Of a dreaming beast that wakes with temper frayed
And finds the prowler into whom it sinks
Its teeth does not exist. Upon that head,
That you be free of fear, I'll tell you why
I came and what I felt when I was led
First to your quaking side by your far cry.
Along with all those caught between desire
To see the One Above and sheer despair
That they will never even see hellfire,
I was in Limbo. Out of the open air
She stepped, and stood, and then she called my name:
A woman beatific, beautiful.
Her scintillating eyes outshone the flame
Of stars. To disobey? Impossible.
I begged her to command me. She gave voice.
It was an angel's voice, restrained and sweet.
'Courteous soul of Mantua, rejoice:
Your fame lives on, exalted and complete,
And will throughout the world, from end to end,
Until the world ends. But I need you now.
In a deserted hillside field, my friend
Is fortune's enemy, and can't see how
To make his way. Terror could turn him back.
I'm not sure if he's not already dead
Or if I've come in time to clear the track
That leads him, as in Heaven I've heard said,
To salvation. So if you would obey,
Go to him, and with all your verbal art,
With anything it takes, show him the way.
Do this for me, for I am sick at heart.
My name is Beatrice. Now you know your task.
Where I come from, and long to be restored,
Love rules me. It determines what I ask.
When I am once again before my Lord,
Then I to Him, whom all praise, will praise you.'

Her melody was done. Then I to her:
'Woman of quality, know this is true:
One look at you and I knew who you were.
100 For only through that quality, the race
Of men raised by that quality, Virtue,
Can hope to set their eyes on the high place
Beyond any contentment they enjoy
Under the lower sky ruled by the moon.
So glad am I to be in your employ
I'd not have carried out my task too soon
If I'd already done it. Enough said:
I was persuaded even as you spoke.
But tell me this. Why do you feel no dread
110 Coming down here into this pall of smoke,
This ball of fire that pulses at the core
Of the higher world to which you would return?'
She spoke again: 'A little, but no more,
To satisfy a mind still keen to learn,
I'll tell you why to come here holds no threat
For me. Your Aristotle gets it right:
All fearful things we safely can forget
Except those which, allowed their freedom, might
Cause harm to others. God in mercy made
120 Me such that all your miseries touch me not,
Nor do the flames of this condemned arcade
Scorch one hair of my head. But now to what
Most matters. Take due note of this, great shade:
There is a woman in the sky laments
For the unfortunate I send you to.
Her pain at his entrapment is intense.
She is the Virgin, and, like me to you,
She told Lucy—the spirit of all Grace,
Grace that illuminates like the spring sun
130 The soul within: you see it in her face—
She told Lucy: "Right now your faithful one
Has need of you. You are my choice to go."

Lucy, beside whom cruelty has none
To match her as an enemy, did so,
And came to where I sat with dear Rachel,
The soul of contemplation, as you know:
You loved your books and candlelight so well.
"Beatrice," said Lucy. "Hear me. You that are
The picture of God's praise, why do you not
140 Bring help to him whose love for you so far
Exceeded that of all the common lot
Who loved you too? Do you not hear his screams
Of agony? Do you not see the death
He battles on the river of bad dreams
Deeper than any ocean?" In a breath—
For never was one quicker in the world,
Whether to gain a point or flee his fate,
Than I was when I heard those words—I hurled
Myself from that serene, unhurried state
150 Like a thrown stone down here, putting my trust
In you, your honest tongue that draws to you
Honour from all who listen, as truth must.'
Thus Beatrice. Then she turned away, a new
Lustre appearing in her shining glance:
Her tears, which spurred me quickly to your side,
As she asked, lest this beast should seize its chance
To cut the straightest road, and you abide
Far from the lovely mountain. So then, why?
Why falter, weakling? Why so faint a heart?
160 Why doubt there is a highway in the sky
That leads to where all doubts are set apart?
Where is your courage, where your inner steel?
Three women loved in Heaven do their best
To make you loved there too, and still you feel
No shame at shrinking down inside your nest,
Afraid of your first flight. This isn't real.
And what of me, who promised you much good?
Much good it did. Claiming to like my book!

Does the hero's story shame you? So it should."
170 Catching the firmness in his still fond look—
As the little flowers, bent by the night's cold
And closed and smooth on the outside like gems,
When sunlight lights them straighten and unfold
And open opulently on stiff stems—
So did I find in my depleted strength
The strength of mind to lift my heart again.
I thanked them both at last, if not at length:
"Would she were here who came to my aid when
I was most lost. My thanks can have no end:
180 This is the start. And you, my guiding light—
Who listened to her like a loving friend,
Of mine as well as hers—with second sight
You saw into my soul, and said the things
That needed to be said for a return
To my first purpose. Thank you for what brings
My will and yours together: what I learn
From my teacher, master, leader." So I said.
On the high, hard road, I followed, and he led.

CANTO 3

TO ENTER THE LOST CITY, GO THROUGH ME.
THROUGH ME YOU GO TO MEET A SUFFERING
UNCEASING AND ETERNAL. YOU WILL BE
WITH PEOPLE WHO, THROUGH ME, LOST EVERYTHING.

MY MAKER, MOVED BY JUSTICE, LIVES ABOVE.
THROUGH HIM, THE HOLY POWER, I WAS MADE—
MADE BY THE HEIGHT OF WISDOM AND FIRST LOVE,
WHOSE LAWS ALL THOSE IN HERE ONCE DISOBEYED.

FROM NOW ON, EVERY DAY FEELS LIKE YOUR LAST
10 FOREVER. LET THAT BE YOUR GREATEST FEAR.
YOUR FUTURE NOW IS TO REGRET THE PAST.
FORGET YOUR HOPES. THEY WERE WHAT BROUGHT YOU HERE.

Dark both in colour and in what they meant,
These words incised above a city gate
I read, and whispered: "Master, the intent
Of this inscription makes me hesitate."
And he to me, reading my secret mind,
Said: "Here you must renounce your slightest doubt
And kill your every weakness. Leave behind
20 All thoughts of safety first, or be shut out.
We have arrived where all those who have lost

The sum of intellect, which is the Lord,
Bewail their fate and always count the cost,
Forever far more than they can afford.
I told you of this place." He held my hand,
And even smiled, which gave some comfort when
He led me through the gate to a strange land
Where sighs and moans and screams of ruined men,
Filling the air beneath a starless sky,
30 Resounded everywhere, and everywhere
Was there inside me. I began to cry,
Stunned by the sound of an unseen nightmare.
Inhuman outcries in all human tongues,
Bad language, bursts of anger, yelps of pain,
Shrill scrambled messages from aching lungs,
And clapped hands, self-applause of the insane:
All this was whipped by its own energy
Into a timeless tumult without form—
Dark as a whirlpool in a dead black sea
40 Or a whirlwind sucking sand into a storm.
Ears ringing to the centre of my brain
From horror, "Master, what furore is this?"
I asked, "Who are they, so distraught with pain?"
Then he: "Their pride to have no prejudice,
Seeking no praise for fear of taking blame,
They were for nothing, nor were they against:
They made no waves and so they made no name.
Now their neutrality is recompensed,
For here there is no cautious holding back:
50 Voices once circumspect are now incensed
And raised to make each other's eardrums crack.
Thus they are joined to that self-seeking squad
Of angels fitted neither to rebel
Against, nor put their heartfelt faith in, God—
Hunted from Heaven and locked out of Hell
Because the perfect sky would brook no blur,
And in the lower depths the rebels prized

The glory won from being what they were,
Not the nonentities that they despised."
60 And I: "But Master, what could grieve them so,
To make them not just so sad, but so loud?"
And he: "To put it briefly, they have no
Death to look forward to. Their only shroud
Will be this darkness. They're condemned to live
In envy always, even of the damned.
The world that gives fame to a fugitive
Gave none of that to them. Instead, it slammed
The door on them, and as for Him on high,
His mercy and His justice He withdraws.
70 They never even get to see the sky
That will not have them. But we should not pause
So long for wastrels weeping for what's gone.
Enough of this. All that there is to see
You've seen. It's nothing. Time that we moved on."
But I, wide-eyed in that cacophony,
Saw something that my gaze could fix upon
At last: an ensign, twisting without rest
Because it knew no victory or defeat,
And fast behind it ran a crowd I guessed
80 No frightened city taking to its feet
To flee an earthquake could outnumber. So
Many there were, I would not have believed
Death had undone so many. There was no
Obstruction now to vision. Those who grieved
Were in plain sight, and some I recognised:
Among them Celestine, of heart so faint
He made the Great Refusal. If he prized
The papal throne—and some call him a saint—
So much, he should have sat on it, and not
90 Left it to be usurped by Boniface,
Who ruined Florence. Rooted to the spot,
I saw and knew for certain that this race
Of never-living sprinters were the ones

Who once believed fence-sitting no disgrace,
But now they sit no more. The whole bunch runs
Naked, with flies and wasps to stimulate
Their actions at long last, and their scratched cheeks
Spill blood that joins with tears to satiate—
A soup lapped from their footsteps as it leaks—
100 The mass of squirming worms that forms their track.
And when I looked beyond, I saw the bank
Of a mighty river, and another pack
Of people. I said, "Master, whom I thank
For secret knowledge, let me be allowed
To know who these ones are and why they seem
So ready, with a single mind endowed,
To cross in this grim light so great a stream."
And he: "This matter I will speak upon
When you and I, like them, come to a halt
110 At that sad river called the Acheron."
My gaze cast down in shame, fearing my fault
Of curiosity stuck in his throat,
I kept my silence until we were there—
Where suddenly an old man in a boat
Headed towards us, tossing his white hair
As he cried "Woe to you and to your souls!
Give up your hopes of Heaven! I have come
To take you to the other side. Hot coals
And ice await, to brand you and benumb
120 In everlasting shadow. As for you,
You living one, this route is for the dead:
Leave it to them." But when I did not do
His bidding: "By another way," he said,
"Through other ports and to a different shore
Your passage will be worked, but not through here.
For you a lighter boat than mine's in store."
And then my Leader: "Charon, never fear:
All this is wanted there where what is willed
Is said and done, so more than that don't ask."

130 At these hard words the bristling jaws were stilled,
And the eyes blinked in the wrinkled, flame-red mask,
Of the ferry pilot of the pitch-black marsh:
But all those naked souls unhinged by fate
Changed colour when they heard that speech so harsh.
Clicking their bared, chipped teeth in hymns of hate,
They cursed their parents, God, the human race,
The time, the temperature, their place of birth,
Their mother's father's brother's stupid face,
And everything of worth or nothing worth
140 That they could think of. Then they squeezed up tight
Together, sobbing, on the ragged edge
That waits for all who hold God in despite.
Charon the demon, with hot coals for eyes,
Herds them yet closer with time-tested signs.
To anyone who lingers he applies
His oar, and as the autumn redefines
A branch by taking off its dead leaves one
By one until the branch looks down and knows
Its own dress, falling as it comes undone—
150 So Adam's bad seed, grain by bad grain, throws
Itself from that cliff not just at a run
But flying, as the falcon to the glove
Swoops home when signalled. Out across the black
Water they flock, whereat the heights above
That they have left, without a pause go back
To being thick with people, a dark spring
Filling the branch for its next emptiness.
"My son, from many countries they take wing,"
My Master said, "but just the one distress
160 Collects them here. God's wrath, in which they died,
Came from His justice, which now turns their fear
Into desire to see the other side.
No soul worth saving ever comes through here,
So Charon's anger you can understand,
And understand why he spoke in that tone."

At which point the dark ground we stood on heaved
So violently the shock wave still can soak
My memory with sweat. As if it grieved,
The earth wept while it moved, and plumes of smoke
170 Went sideways with the wind. A red light shone.
My reeling senses gave out. I was gone.

CANTO 4

Into my soundly dreaming head there broke
A sudden thunder so loud that I shook
Like one shaken awake. When I awoke
With sight restored, I rose and took a look
Around me, keen to know where I might be:
I and my Guide, the man who wrote the book
On quests and questions, doubts and destiny.
And true it was that I was on the edge
Of the great pit of the piteous abyss
10 Where sad cries have the dubious privilege
Of gathering in perpetual synthesis,
And griefs already infinite are by
Their own great number multiplied, to swell
Uproar to an eruption. It was Hell.
And as it sounded, so it looked: all bad.
Even the clouds were dark. I couldn't tell
How far it went down. It was deeply sad.
"Now we descend into the sightless well,"
My Poet said, and paused. His cheeks were pale.
20 "First me, then you." And I, at having seen
Him seem to flinch, said: "How shall I not fail,
If this scares you when usually you've been
The one to calm my fears?" And he to me:
"It is the anguish of those locked below

That paints my face with pity. What you see
As fear is something else. It's time to go:
A long road calls." And thus compelled by him
Who had compelled himself, I took a breath
And entered the first ring around the rim
30 Of that great well-head's endless wall of death.
I was in Circle One. To the extent
That I could hear at all, all cries were sighs.
The air without end shook to the lament
Not just of men and women: with surprise
I saw young children too. Why were they sent?
I thought, and once again my Master saw
Into my mind, and said: "You do not ask
Who these ones are, why here, and by what law?
I'll tell you, before we resume our task,
40 Of pain without a sin. But though they be
Ever so virtuous, no unbaptized
Souls are exempted from this penalty,
And if they lived before His Son, they prized
God insufficiently. And I was one
Of those. For such defects, and for no crime
More grave, we're lost: for something left undone
We're doomed to live without hope for all time."
When I heard this a great grief seized my heart,
Because I knew that people of much worth
50 In ancient sciences and every art
Had been sent down by accident of birth
To Limbo. "Tell me, Master, for I must
Know this," I begged him, needing to be told
My faith was not just powerful but just:
"Has even one, of all this place can hold,
Ever got out—by merit of his own
Or someone else's grace—to join the blessed?"
And he, aware of the doctrinal bone
I picked at, said: "I had not joined the rest
60 Down here for long when someone of true power—

Crowned with a blaze of glory—came to choose
From this tremendous garden, flower by flower,
The lucky few from all He would refuse.
Plucked from the dark and lifted to the light
Were Adam, Abel, Noah, Moses—he
Who gave the law and kept the law in sight—
And Abraham the patriarch was free;
King David, Jacob, Isaac and their seed,
And Rachel, for whom Jacob forty years
70   Worked out the price and thereby proved his need;
And there were many others left their tears
Behind and went to be beatified,
But never before them was human soul
Delivered out of here." So said my Guide,
But saying so, did not pause in his role
Of leader. We continued passing through
The forest thick with spirits. Not so far
From where I'd slept, I noticed something new:
Ahead of us, beginning as a bar
80   Of light, it swelled to form a hemisphere
Of fire that through the shadows burned a dome—
And from a good way off I guessed that here
Some honourable people had their home.
"My Sage so honoured in all fields of art
And science, who are these that by such light
Are honoured too, all others set apart?"
And he to me: "Divine grace shines its bright
Approval on them for the fame they earned
And still have in the world by what they made.
90   Here glory burns again as there it burned."
A voice inside the radiant arcade
Responded with a ringing antiphon:
"All hail the greatest poet, for his shade
Returns, that we had thought was gone."
When silence had come back to fill the space
The voice had left when it went still, I saw

Four great shades come towards us, and each face
Was neither glad nor sad. My Guide said more:
"Behold the one with upright sword in hand:
He walks by right before the other three,
For he is Homer, who put his Greek brand
On all the Romans, not excluding me.
If you could read him, you would understand
Why we, who can, verge on idolatry
In praising him. Horace the satirist
Is that one there, then Ovid. Lucan last.
Because that voice put my name on its list
With these, it did me honour unsurpassed."
So I saw gathered the immortal school
Of him who sang below the walls of Troy,
And over all who write shall always rule
Like a watchful eagle in its high employ,
Spreading its wings on winds we know are there
Only because it glides across the sky
So easily, as if born in the air,
And never to descend, even to die.
And after they had talked a little while
They turned, with signs of fellowship, to me:
Whereat I saw my Master broadly smile.
And, still more honour from that company,
They said that I was with them from now on,
Sixth of their school, the college of the wise.
And so it was, until the light was gone,
We walked and talked of what I must surmise
Were best left unsaid now, but when said then
Was fit, and, dare I say it, flattering:
Such words I hardly hope to hear again
But just to hear them once meant everything.
Surrounded seven times by one high wall
Inside another, plus a pretty stream
As moat, a castle noble, strong and tall
Now stood before us. As if in a dream
We walked across the water. Seven gates

I passed through with my five wise ones, until
We reached a fresh green lawn. The ancient greats
Awaited us: their eyes were grave and still,
Their features full of calm authority.
Sparely they spoke, in voices sweet and soft.
They were so many that, to count them, we
140 Withdrew to a well-lighted place aloft.
From there, above the green enamel, I
Looked down on each and every face of fame,
The sight of which I'd been exalted by
Already, only now I heard the name:
Electra, whose beloved son built Troy,
And whose companions saw it end in flame
Or died defending it. I heard with joy
That this was Hector, this Aeneas. There,
Just as essential for a later age,
150 Was Caesar with his griffin's fiery stare.
Princess Camilla stood at centre stage
With Penthesilea, the war-like Queen
Of the Amazons, she whom Achilles slew,
And the King of Latium was on the green
As was Lavinia, his daughter. Who
Would not be moved to know this was the first
Brutus, the one who laid proud Tarquin low?
Lucrezia, wife of Collatine, well versed
In grace; and Caesar's daughter whom we know
160 As wife to Pompey, the chaste Julia,
And Marcia, Cato's wife. Cornelia too,
Daughter to Scipio of Africa
And mother of the Gracchi. Names I knew
Only from books, without reserve revealed
How they had looked—except the Saladin,
Sadly by robes of shadow part concealed:
He helped our age of learning to begin,
But had another faith. Lifting my gaze
A little, one I saw who sat in state
170 Among the family of philosophers—

Their father, of all thinkers the most great:
Aristotle. Looking up to him in praise
Like all the others, even Socrates
And Plato, who preceded him, were each
Lost in their awe of his abilities
At amplifying what they'd had to teach:
The moral law. There was Democritus,
Who said the world is made of tiny parts
That interact by chance, unseen by us.
180　Diogenes and Anaxagoras,
Thales, Empedocles were side by side,
And Heraclitus who said any mass,
Even if still, still moves. There in his pride
Was Zeno, stoicism's founding voice,
And next to him was Dioscorides
The herb collector. I was spoiled for choice:
Where next to look, among these prodigies?
190　And I saw Orpheus and Cicero,
Linus, and Seneca the moralist,
Euclid and Ptolemy. There in a row
Were famous adepts first to get the gist
Of modern medicine and help it grow:
Hippocrates and Galen, with the two
Arabs who led the world in this respect:
Avicenna, then Averroës, who
Wrote down what both could conjure and confect
In his Commentary that none doubts to be true.
200　And these and all those others on the lawn—
So many giants of the intellect—
Were like the first sunrays that build the dawn.
I can't speak fully of them all. My theme
Is vast, and drives me on so that the facts
Often exhaust my words. Again a team
Of two, we entered into cataracts
Of trembling air, all quietness left behind—
Where no light shines and all who see are blind.

CANTO 5

So we descended out of Circle One
To Circle Two: the less in measurement,
The greater in its sad cries fit to stun
The senses. Here, deciding who'll be sent
To which reception, the Selector looms
Whose name is Minos. Horrible to see,
He's worse to see in action. Separate dooms
For separate deeds, betokened by how he
Runs rings around himself with his long tail,
So many turns for such and such a fault.
The tortured souls, confessing without fail,
Are thus assigned to that drawer in the vault
This connoisseur of turpitude may deem
Appropriate, while to his platform comes
Another load to share the same wild dream.
They watch his living bull-whip do its sums
Always for others, not for them. Not yet.
And then it's their turn, as they count the loops
That weigh the crimes they hoped he might forget—
And down they go, sad army, naked troops,
To find their level. "You that come to stay
At this unlucky lodge, watch where you tread
And whom you trust," Minos was moved to bray.
"The width of Hell's mouth doesn't mean the dead

Who get in ever get to go away."
My Leader spoke for me: "Shout till you drop:
His travel papers bear a sacred seal.
This thing is wanted where the moot points stop
And certainties begin. There's no appeal."

30 Here, after Limbo, as I had before,
I heard the countless outcries of lament
Combine to strike me as a constant roar.
This was a place where every light was spent.
It ranted as the sea does in a storm
That splits its own winds to go left or right,
Shrieking in all directions. Thus the form
Of the infernal tempest: day and night
The same, forever shapeless, without rest
It rends and roils the spirits with its force.

40 They are the smeared signs of how it is blessed:
Their cries can testify to its remorse.
And when they come to where the rocks are cracked
By background pressure, and a fissure gapes
Before them, then we hear the law attacked
That brought them to this pass so none escapes,
As all yell their complaints at that brute fact.
I understood this was the punishment
For carnal sinners, who let appetite
Rule reason, and who, once drawn, are now sent—

50 Like winter starlings by their wings in flight—
Across the bleak sky in a broad, thick flock:
Here, there, now up, now down, the winds dictate
Their track. Small hope of pausing to take stock
Of whether anguish might not soon abate
At least a little, and no hope at all
Of peace. And as the cranes sing when they fly,
In a long line attracting with their call
Our eyes to them as they move through the sky,
Just so I now saw souls borne on the wind

60 Trailing their cries of grief towards the spot

Where we stood. "Who are these? How have they sinned?"
I asked my Master. "Dare to tell me what
Dooms them to be so harshly disciplined."
"The first of those of whom you would have news
Was empress of many peoples." So explained
My Master. "Willing neither to refuse
Demands from her own lust, nor to be stained
By rules against it, she rewrote the law
To make praiseworthy what had been her vice
70 And vicious what was virtuous before.
Her name is Semiramis. More than twice
As bad as her hot blood was her incest:
She married her own son so they could rule
The Sultan's lands, Egypt and all the rest.
The next is Dido, Queen of Carthage, cruel
To the ashes of her husband when she slew
Herself because of love: not love for him,
But for Aeneas. Cleopatra, too—
That dark one there—desire led to a grim
80 Reckoning. Behold Helen, in whose name
A sea of trouble came to Troy in ships,
And Paris knew it was a sea of flame,
The fire that started when he kissed her lips.
And there's Tristan . . ." A thousand more at least
He named, the shades who left our life for love:
The gentle women of a time long ceased
To be, and all their cavaliers. Above
My head, the waves of fear closed and increased
Their turbulence, and I was almost lost.
90 Then I to him: "My Poet, I would speak
With those two—by the ill wind swept and tossed
As light as dead leaves on a mountain creek—
Who do not fly alone, but as a pair."
And he to me: "Call out, when they can hear,
In the name of love that leads them through the air,
And they will come to you." When they drew near

I spoke: "Tormented spirits, come to us,
If Someone Else does not forbid you to.
You fly for love, and love we should discuss,
100 Though it stir shades into a witch's brew."
And as when doves that long for their sweet nest
See it, and with their stiffened wings spread wide,
Moved only by desire come home to rest,
So these from Dido's squadron turned aside
And down through the malignant atmosphere
They came to us in an unerring glide,
So deeply had my summons to appear
Touched them. "O Being gracious and benign—
Visiting us in air whose darkness is
110 Tinged by the blood of all in our long line—
If the Emperor of the Universe in His
Great mercy were our friend, then we would pray
For your repose, because of your distress
At our sad fate. What you would have us say
Let's hear about, now that the wind blows less,
So we may speak before it howls once more."
So she began, he silent in assent.
"Born where the Po descends to the seashore
To meet its followers and rest content,
120 I was a beauty. Love, in gentle hearts,
Strikes quickly, and the fair form I once had
Before I cruelly lost it—by dark arts
That still offend me—quickly drove him mad.
Love pardons no one loved from Love, and I
Was drawn to him with what force you can see:
It still holds me beside him as we fly.
Love gave two lives one death for destiny.
As for who killed us, Cain will help him die."
Those stricken souls, through her we heard them speak:
130 And when I understood the full import
Of what was said, as if my neck grew weak
I hung my head. My Guide said: "Lost in thought?"

I was indeed. When I could breathe, I said:
"Alas, so many sweet shared thoughts and things
Brought them this fate they think unwarranted."
Thus I to him. To them: "Your sufferings,
Francesca, make me weep for grief and more.
But tell me, in that time of your sweet sighs,
In that first flush, how love made you both sure
140 Of what you half saw in each other's eyes."
And she to me: "Life brings no greater grief
Than happiness remembered in a time
Of sorrow; and he knows that well, your chief,
Who now walks in a world of dust and grime
When once he took bright laurels as his due.
But if to know the one true origin
Of our Love means so very much to you,
Then even as I weep I will begin.
Reading together one day for delight
150 Of Lancelot, caught up in Love's sweet snare,
We were alone, with no thought of what might
Occur to us, although we stopped to stare
Sometimes at what we read, and even paled.
But then the moment came we turned a page
And all our powers of resistance failed:
When we read of that great knight in a rage
To kiss the smile he so desired, Paolo,
This one so quiet now, made my mouth still—
Which, loosened by those words, had trembled so—
160 With his mouth. And right then we lost the will—
For Love can will will's loss, as well you know—
To read on. But let that man take a bow
Who wrote the book we called our Galahad,
The reason nothing can divide us now."
One spoke as if she almost might be glad,
The other wept as if forgetting how
To stop. And I? I fainted dead away,
And went down as if going down to stay.

CANTO 6

When I came round, and was no longer blind—
My pity for that self-deluding pair
Gave me much grief, and grief had closed my mind—
I saw new types of torment everywhere
Around me, so no matter where I turned
Were the tormented. This was Circle Three,
And here there was no fire, and nothing burned.
Instead, a dark cold rain falls heavily
Forever. At a rigidly fixed rate
10 And steady density, the muck descends
Through shadowed air already dark as slate.
The fall of dirty water never ends,
With hail and snow mixed in. The soaked earth reeks.
The people stuck in it have Cerberus
To guard them. Overhead, that creature shrieks
In anger with three mouths, each hideous
As a mad dog's. Beards greasy black, eyes red,
Big belly, fingers well supplied with nails,
He scores and scrapes and tears them to a shred—
20 Those that the rain already hardly fails
To make howl—and they turn from side to side
As if they could keep something unbesmirched
By his paws, though they have no goods to hide,
No house but this remaining to be searched.

When Cerberus the hulking worm got wind
That he was not alone—he never is,
In view of how he's made—he turned and grinned.
His hungry mouths displayed those teeth of his
In six rows. Every limb was quivering.
30 My Leader spread his hands and, to his wrists,
He dug down through the slop so he might fling
The loads of firmer sludge caught in his fists
Into those gulping throats, and like three hounds
That yelp for greed but shut up when they eat,
The monster made the small contented sounds
It doesn't make for souls spread at its feet.
Those we passed over, where they lay prostrate,
Gripped by the mud and held down by the rain.
We trod on ghosts as if their actual state
40 Were human and they did not flinch in vain.
Supine or prone, they all lay stretched out flat,
Except for one who sat up when he saw
Us pass, and said: "You that I'm looking at
Instead of through, because no fatal flaw
Yet sends you here to stay: do you know me?
You should, for you were born before I died."
And I to him: "Perhaps my memory
Aims at the mark you set but wanders wide
Through air unsettled by your agony.
50 But tell me who you are, and why sent here
To such a punishment that none more great
Could well be worse, so much it fills with fear
A visitor not marked for the same fate."
And he to me: "Our city, then as now
A sack of envy stuffed to spill its load,
I spoke for in the world, where I knew how
To put myself about, my sharpest goad
The supper I sang for. 'Ciacco,' they said,
'Sit down and eat.' And now it's here I sit,
60 Wrecked by the rain because of broken bread,

Like anyone too fond of eating it—
Like all those here now. See how we are fed."
And I replied: "Ciacco, your moans of pain
Meet mine, and I am—almost—moved to tears.
But if there is foreknowledge you retain,
Then tell me if just one Just One appears,
To save the city. What becomes of them,
The disunited Florentines? And how
Did all this start? What snapped the diadem
70   That once encircled the untroubled brow
Of Santa Reparata? Diplomat
You were. You know things. Give me what you know."
Then he to me: "At first, the usual spat
Or two, then drawn-out tension, then the blow
By blow expansion, then the all-out fight
Between the Blacks and Whites. With due offence
The Whites drive out the Blacks. Day follows night,
And in three years the Blacks come back. Immense
Success, with help from Boniface. In tears,
80   The Whites find out the hard way that their shame
Is just the start of payment in arrears
For the crime of losing. Two men have the name
Of being just, but no one listens. Three
Real motives: Envy, Avarice and Pride—
Fires of the Florentines, as you will see."
And I to him, although I knew my Guide
Grew restive: "Still there's something I would know
Ahead of time. Those men who wished no ill—
Tegghiaio, Farinata, Jacopo
90   Rusticucci and Arrigo, Mosca—will
I find they rose to grace? Or do they weep?"
And he to me: "The whole bunch rot in Hell,
Black souls that different faults have driven deep.
Go down that far, you'll see how far they fell.
But if it's true you're going all the way
Back to the sweet world, tell them who you met.

They might remember. That's all I can say."
Whereat, his gaze still fixed on mine, he bent
His head and lay back down to join the blind.
100 My Leader said: "Until the air is rent
By the angel's trumpet—and the dead shall find
Their graves, take fleshly form, and hear resound
The eternal echoes, as shall be decreed
By the Last Judge—this one, held by his ground,
Will never wake again. Shall we proceed?"
And so, with slow steps, fording the foul blend
Of shades and rain, we moved, our speech concerned
With life beyond the tomb. "After the end,
What starts?" I asked. "Will all those who have earned
110 Their place down here feel less pain from the Day
Of Judgement on, or just the same, or more?"
And he to me: "What does your science say?
The more a thing's more perfect than before
The more it takes delight, or feels despair?
Although these damned will never know a true
Perfection, they'll be closer to it there,
Beyond that Day. So: much more than they do
Must be the answer to your question." We
Had walked the inner edge of that great ring
120 With much more talk about theology
That I have room or time for rendering.
We reached the entrance to a lower zone,
But first the fearsome Plutus stood alone.

CANTO 7

"The Pope pops Satan, Satan pips the Pope,"
Plutus barked raucous nonsense, while my Guide,
Who knew all things, to give me back my hope
Said: "Don't let fear of him turn you aside.
Whatever power he has will never stretch
To stopping your descent to the next stage."
And, turning to the fat lips of the wretch,
"Wolf, shut your mouth," he said. "Swallow your rage
And let it eat your guts. He goes with cause
10 Into the depths, for it is willed on high
Where Michael the Archangel planned the wars
Against the rebels." As when all winds die
And sails, once swollen, flap and fall in folds,
Just so the beast lay flat. We left it so,
And down to Circle Four—and what it holds
For its share of the universe of woe
Contained in the immeasurable pit—
We went. Merciful God! Who gets it in,
This wretched harvest? What accounts for it?
20 And why to such pain are we led by sin?
For just as waves above the clashing jaws
Of Scylla and Charybdis rush to fight
Each other, so these shades danced without pause,
More of them than had so far met my sight.

From either side damned souls let out a shout
And roll weights with their chests until they crash
Together, whereupon they turn about
And shriek "Why pile it up?" and "Why waste cash?"
And work in a half-circle to the point
30 Opposed, still giving out their spiteful yell,
And turn to joust again. Heart out of joint,
I said: "My Master, who are these, pray tell:
And were these tonsured ones here to the left
Once clerics?" He to me: "Yes, all of them
In their first life were so of sense bereft
They spent like wastrels, and thus they condemn
Their madness, barking every time they find
Themselves returned to either of the two
Opposing points at which their faults of mind
40 Divide them. One and all were clerics who,
Head sticking through their hair, were ruled by greed.
There are popes here, and cardinals." And I:
"My Guide, should I not then in such a breed
See faces that I can identify,
Famous for sins of avarice and waste?"
My Master answered thus: "That thought is vain.
In life for their dim sight they were disgraced:
Here they are dimly seen, and must remain
Forever split into two charging teams:
50 Those money-grubbing ones who from the grave
Arise with grasping fists and foolproof schemes,
And these with hair close-cropped to show they gave
As those took—a two-sided robbery
That stole the world from both and set them here
In this unprepossessing scrum that we
Lack words to dignify. You see it clear,
My son: the squalid fraud as brief as life
Of goods consigned to Fortune, whereupon
Cool heads come to the boil, hands to the knife.
60 For all the gold there is, and all that's gone,

Would give no shred of peace to even one
Of these drained souls." "Master," I said,
"Finish the lesson you have just begun:
Tell me who Fortune is. How has she spread
Her arms to seize the world's wealth?" A sharp glance:
"Half-witted mortals, how is it you know
So little even of the ignorance
That starves you? That you not continue so,
Now feed on news of how I estimate
70   The Understanding that transcends all things,
And made the heavens, and gave each heavenly state
The luminous intelligence that brings
Light from each part to every other part
In perfect measure. Just so, on the Earth,
Fortune, his minister, with timely art
Endlessly portions out, for what they're worth,
The riches of the world from man to man
And race to race—and none can even guess,
Because no human sense can know her plan,
80   Why one has power, another powerlessness—
According to her judgement where she lies
Unseen, just as the grass conceals the snake.
Your mortal judgement shrivels up and dies
Compared with hers, perpetually awake,
Providing, weighing, balancing. She rules
Her realm the way the lofty ones rule theirs.
Unceasing alterations make her tools
Invisible, so quickly her affairs
Must be arranged and rearranged. She, then,
90   Who is so often cursed by those who should
Praise her, thinking themselves forsaken men,
Although, by breaking them, she brought them good—
She, then, although she hears no human word
Of her true value, happy like the rest
Of those first creatures—who have always heard
Their praises sung—nevertheless is blessed,

The world her wheel. And so much for your doubt,
For now we must descend to deeper grief,
As all the stars that rose when I set out
100 To meet you, start to fall. Even a brief
Pause in our course is not permitted. Move."
We cut across the circle to a ledge
Above a fountain spurting in its groove
And spilling back, swamping the precinct's edge
With water more a turgid grey than black;
And we, in company with that grim flood,
Picked our way down an ankle-turning track
Into the place beneath, where sliding mud,
Spread thickly from the foot of those dark slopes,
110 Became the sad, slow river called the Styx.
While I stood doing nothing except look,
I thought at first my eyes were playing tricks
As these slime-covered naked people shook
With anger. Not with sticky hands alone
They hit each other, but with heads, chests, feet
And teeth. They bit each other to the bone.
And my great Guide to me: "Son, here you meet
The souls of those who gave way to their rage.
But know, too, there are those who lurk below
120 The surface—from the bubbles you can gauge
Their number—who could let no anger flow,
Or any feeling else. Stuck in the mud,
They croak: 'In that sweet world the sun made glad,
Our hearts were stopped with a slow, smoking flood.
In these dank depths we work at being sad.'
This is the chorus their clogged throats emit:
The best that they can do." Thus we traversed
A great arc of that filthy, festering pit,
Walking between the dry bank and the cursed
130 Wet edge that sighs to suck you into it,
Always our eyes on those lost to its power—
Until we faced the foot of a tall tower.

CANTO 8

Just to go back a bit, I should have said
That long before we reached the tower's base
We saw two lights set on its lofty head,
To which a third light, from a far-off place,
Sent back a pinpoint signal. Turning to my
Attendant sea of wisdom, I asked: "What
Does this mean? And that other fire's reply,
What is it? And who tends that flame?" "Let not,"
He said, "the foul fumes of the marsh deceive
10   Your eye, for what's to come, no longer there,
Is almost here." When did an arrow leave
A bowstring and run whistling through the air
More quickly than this little boat skimmed in
Across the sludge? "Caught you!" the oarsman cried.
"Guilty as charged!" "Flegias, cut the din:
This time it counts for nothing," said my Guide.
"You get to keep us only while we cross
This swamp." As one who knows that some great fraud
Is practised on him, and resents the loss,
20   So Flegias in his bottled rage. My lord
Stepped down into the boat, and then made me
Step after him, and only after I
Was on board did the craft appear to be
Laden. Thus, then, the ancient prow, less high

Than usual since its cargo weighed much more
Than shadows, moved off, cutting all too deep
Into the muck, from which there rose, before
Our gaze, a man-shaped darkly streaming heap
Of that same stagnant stuff we rowed through. "Who
30 Are you that come before your time?" And I
To him: "If so, it's not to stay. But you,
Who are you, to be such a mess?" "I cry,"
He said, "as all the damned do." Me again:
"Cry all you like, mud crab. Thicken your mask.
I still know who you really are." Just then
He reached with both hands for the boat, his task
To turn us over, but my wary chief
Warded him off, and said "Get back down there
With the other dogs." And then, to my relief,
40 My Master's anger turned to loving care,
His arm around me as he kissed my cheek.
"Disdainful one," he said, "blessed was the womb
That held you. In the world, he was the peak
Of arrogance, and now, beyond the tomb,
With not one good word to adorn his name,
He rages at his own inanity.
And there are others up there of the same
Persuasion they are kings. They, too, will be
Pigs in this filthy sty, and leave behind
50 Nothing but curses rained upon the hole
Their swelled heads filled." And I: "I have a mind,
Before we leave this festering soup bowl,
To see it swallow him." My Master said:
"Before we reach the other shore, your wish
Will be fulfilled." And soon, as if they fed
A hunger, we saw men like muddy fish
Surround him, and I thanked God as they cried
"So, Filippo Argenti! Not so great!"
While even he sank teeth in his own hide,
60 That tortured Florentine. Such was the state

We left him in. I have no more to tell,
Save of the sound of grief that struck my ears
As I gazed forward. "Son, you should note well,"
My Master said, "that now the city nears
Called Dis, home of a thoughtful populace
And mighty garrison." I in my turn:
"Master, already I can see its face.
The mosques within its ramparts seem to burn
As red as iron new-drawn from the fire."

70 Then he: "The fire eternal makes them glow
So red. Here Hell becomes the funeral pyre
That burns in Circle Six and burns below."
Between the outworks and the walls that showed
Their fever of that city sad and vast,
The moat was deep, and through it ran the road
We followed far around, until at last
We came to where the boatman bellowed "Out!
Now we get out of here and go in there!"
His cry was nothing to the angry shout

80 Of a thousand angels, fallen from elsewhere
Like rain to make the door a thing of dread.
"Who's this," they yelled, "who dares to go while still
Alive into the kingdom of the dead?"
By signs my silent guide expressed his will:
A wish to speak in secret. They cut back
A little on their uproar of bad grace.
"Just you, then," said the leader of the pack,
"And let your friend, the unfitting one, retrace
The false steps that have boldly brought him here

90 On a mad road. Leave him alone to face
His journey home. He might have known more fear
Had you, his sponsor, not shown him the way.
Now let him tremble. Lose him. You, draw near."
Think, reader, of the depth of my dismay
At these forbidding words. They were a curse:

Never, I thought, would I be here again.
I to my Master: "Nothing could be worse
For me now than to be as I was then,
Without you. You have seven times and more
Saved me from danger and rebuilt my heart.
If I'm denied the path that lies before,
Then let's go back together to the start."
"Fear not," said he who had brought me this far,
"For nobody can interrupt a course
Mapped for us from on high. Stay where you are,
And with the food of hope restore the force
Of your weak spirits. Never would I leave
You on your own down here." And so he goes,
And leaves me half convinced that I deceive
Myself that this is not what I suppose.
Am I betrayed? What he said to unman
Those sentinels I couldn't hear, but he
Was not long there with them before they ran
A race to go back in, and instantly
They shut the door against him. He began
With pensive steps the slow walk back to me,
Eyes on the ground and brow bereft of all
Serenity. And as he went, he sighed:
"Who are they who presume to guard the wall
That keeps me from where sufferings reside,
Its weeping houses?" Then to me: "Be not
Dismayed that I should grieve. In this contest
Of wills I shall prevail, no matter what
That gang in there come up with. For the rest,
There's nothing new in their intransigence.
They used it once before to bar a gate
Less secret, which still stands without defence,
Its locks and bolts undone by Someone Great.
You saw, above its head, the mortal text,
Yet came through to the slope, and since have come

Down through the circles, first one, then the next,
As far as this, and I am the whole sum
Of your protection. Therefore, why be vexed?
To lay this city open, we need no
Sanction beyond what sent us. Shall we go?"

CANTO 9

Seeing how his reverse had paled my face,
My Leader summoned up the means to drive
The same pallor from his. He checked his pace
And stopped to listen, as a man would strive
To make up with his ears for his dimmed eyes
In dark air and thick fog. "Nevertheless,"
He said, "We're bound to win, or otherwise . . ."
He paused, and then: "But no. That's idleness.
We have such help. But why is it so late
In coming?" I saw clearly how the first
Thing that he said the next would mitigate
To calm my fear. From that, I feared the worst:
Perhaps these fragments had a common source
In some deep theme too terrible to tell.
I said: "Does anyone in the long course
Of time descend into the hellish well
This far whose proper place is Circle One,
Where none are damned but all hope is cut short?"
I questioned, he gave answer. "Almost none
Of us have made a journey of the sort
That I make now, though I did once before,
Through the magic of Erichtho, who recalled
Souls to their bodies. Seeing how I wore
My flesh no longer, that fell Sybil hauled

Me through the wall of Dis and down to fetch
A spirit from the lowest circle, where
Judas resides. You've seen only a sketch
So far of what this pit is like down there
At the bottom of the dark: far out of sight,
30 The crystal sky that makes the world turn. I
Know well that journey to the end of night,
Although condemned too soon to live and die.
But rest assured that it is just for now
We are debarred from the sad city which
Adds such unholy rage—we've just seen how—
To its protection by this stinking ditch."
And more in the same vein, but I forget;
My gaze was focused on a bastion
The ruins of whose high rim were beset
40 In an instant by the triple power, close-drawn,
Of three infernal furies, stained with blood.
In form and manner female, they were clad
With snakes, and smaller snakes, as if from mud,
Rose from their hair, and their fierce temples had
Snake-spawn with little horns for diadems.
My Guide, who knew full well the coiled intent,
And the foul taste for such hissing, writhing gems,
Of Proserpine, Queen of the Long Lament,
Said: "Look! Eumenides! There on the left,
50 Megaera. On the right, Alecto weeps.
Tisiphone is she who fills the cleft
Between them. A Greek nightmare never sleeps."
I shook for fear against my Poet's side.
"Bring on Medusa! With her aid we'll make
This man a stone!" So, looking down, they cried.
"With Theseus we made a big mistake.
Now for revenge!" My Master: "Turn your back.
Hands over eyes. Tight fingers. Stay that way.
Just one glimpse of the Gorgon through a crack—
60 Goodbye forever to the light of day."

And he himself turned me around, nor did
He trust my own hands, adding his as well
To guard my eyes. You of sound mind, I bid
You look beneath the strange, veiled way I tell
This story to the struggle in the soul
Of one who seeks redemption. Now, across
The turbid waves, there came a thundering roll
Of fearful sound, with both banks at a loss
To stay still, trembling at the violent roar
70 Of such a summer wind as heat propels
Into the woods when, fallen to the floor,
Split branches fly away, and dizzy spells
Of dust are driven by its boastful pride,
And even the wild beasts and shepherds flee.
"Now train your gaze across that scum-skinned tide,"
He said to me as he set my eyes free,
"To where the fog is thickest." As the snake,
Their enemy, sends frogs down fading through
The water to the bottom of the lake
80 To squat and wait, so I now had in view
More than a thousand dead souls fleeing. One
Who passed dry-shod across the Styx had come,
Clearing its thick air from his face. This, done
With his left hand, and often, was the sum
Of all the sufferings that sapped him: no
Compassion and no fear. I could well see
That he was Heaven-sent. I made a show
Of turning to my Guide, but he told me,
With just a sign, to shut my mouth and bow.
90 Disdainful angel! Who now faced the gate
And with a little sceptre touched somehow
Its secret spring. Not even with its weight
Did it resist. The way was open now.
"You outcasts from the sky," the angel cried
On the ghastly threshold. "You rejected race,
Where did you get your overweening pride?

Why fight against the will none can outface
And which so often has increased your pain?
By flouting the decrees of providence
Some call the fates, what can you hope to gain?
Remember Cerberus and get some sense.
Those wounds he carries at his throats and jaws,
Chains made, when he was dragged out of the way
Of Hercules in Hades. There are laws."
Thus having said what he had come to say,
Without a word to us, and with the air
Of one with other business on his mind
More pressing, he turned back and left us there
To watch him take that filthy road. Confined
No longer, by his holy words set free
From doubt, we could take certain steps towards
The city, and without a struggle we
Went in, and I, agog to see the hordes
Held there, and how, took one quick look around
And there they were, broad fields on either hand
Of pain and cruelty: the sight, the sound.
Just as the Rhone at Arles dissolves the land
Into a swamp, just as at Pola near
Quarnero where the bounds of Italy
Are set and bathed, just so I saw it here,
But far worse: the uneven territory
Of graveyards, and among the tombs were fires
That made them glow with more intensity
Of heat than any forge or stove requires.
The lids were lifted. Such cries of lament
Came out of them as only the despised
And desperate could make. "Who has been sent,"
I asked my Guide, "to lie here paralysed
In open boxes? Whose groans do we hear?"
"Arch-heretics," he said, "and every sect
That followed them. And more than might appear
Roast in these glowing ovens, which collect

100

110

120

130

Their occupants according to what sort
Of error they espoused, and so assign
The fitting heat to which they should be brought
And kept at, as forever they repine."
Then we turned right, and passed between all this
Destruction and the lofty wall of Dis.

CANTO 10

My Master, by a hidden path, now made
His way between the city and the plain
Of torment. As I followed him, I stayed
Close to his shoulder. "You by whom I gain
Access," I said, "to all these rings of sin,
My Height of Virtue, could you stoop to tell
Me this much? These tombs. Those who lie within,
Can they be seen? The lids are off. As well,
No one keeps guard." And he to me: "They all
10 Will be locked down when, from Jehoshaphat,
They come back with the bodies they let fall
On Earth. In this part you are looking at
Lie Epicurus and his followers
From ancient times until the present day—
All who believe that death for souls concurs
With death for flesh. Your question? Let's just say
That soon it will be answered there inside,
Along with the desire that you conceal."
"Master," I said, "the reason that I hide
20 My heart is just to answer your appeal,
Made several times, that I say less to you."
"Tuscan who earned on earth by fitting speech
The right to walk invulnerable through
This city's fire, one moment, I beseech,

Of your time. By your accent, you were born
In that same noble country which I left—
Perhaps because of my ideals—more torn
Than mended." I, of bravery bereft
By this abrupt voice from the tomb, now drew
30 A little closer to my Guide. And he
To me: "Come on, what's wrong with you?
Look where he rises so that you can see
His whole form from the waist up. Know him now?
It's Farinata." I had turned my eyes
To his. I knew him. Proud in chest and brow,
He rose like one who only can despise
All Hell can do. The sure hand of my Guide
Steered me to him between the sepulchres,
With this advice: "Make your words dignified."
40 I stopped at the tomb's foot. There was a pause.
The shade surveyed me. Then, in scorn almost,
He asked: "Your ancestors, what was their cause?"
Keen to obey, I told him. If a ghost
Can raise an eyebrow, his did. Then, his voice:
"Your people were fierce enemies to me
And mine, and to my clan. I had no choice:
Twice, they were scattered." "You mean made to flee,"
I said, "And if they did, they twice returned
From every haven they took refuge in,
50 An art you Ghibellines have never learned."
Another shade, on view from crown to chin
Only, now rose beside him. On its knees,
I think, it looked around me where I stood,
As if I had not come alone to these
Extremes, and then, its last hopes not made good,
It spoke through tears: "If you for your great skills
In poetry are led here through this blind
Bastille, where is my son, he who fulfils
The same description. Is he left behind?"
60 And I: "Not just my own worth brings me here,

And He who waits for me where I might go,
Your Guido could have held Him much more dear."
His words and form of pain had let me know
His name already, hence my full reply,
At which he jerked straight. "What is that you say?
'Have held,' not 'holds'? You use the past tense. Why?
Does he not live? Does not the light of day
Still sweetly wound his eyes?" When he had seen
How slow I was to answer, he fell back

70 And disappeared. As if this had not been,
That other great one who had checked my track,
His face unchanged, his neck unbent, still straight
His body, spoke to what I'd said before:
"If it be true they failed to learn, my fate
In this bed hurts me less than that thought. Nor
Will you be spared, for fifty moons from now—
The moon which is her face, the one who reigns
Down here—you White Guelphs will be taught just how
Hard it can be to come back. It remains,

80 If ever you return to that sweet air,
For you to tell me why the Florentines
Conspire to drive my kindred to despair
In all their laws." And I: "Our senate means,
By what it speaks, to recollect the rout
And massacre of Montaperti. Red
With blood the Arbia flowed." For once in doubt,
He sighed and shook his head, and then he said:
"It wasn't me alone, nor, with the rest,
Would I have moved unprompted. But alone

90 I was, when all agreed it would be best
To wipe out Florence. I was on my own
In a defence with open helm professed."
"So that your faction might at last know peace,"
I begged, "assist me to untie a knot
From which my tangled judgement craves release.
Is what I'm told a fact, that you have got

The secret of foreseeing what time brings,
But only at a distance, and not now?"
"Like those with faulty sight, we can see things
Only far off," he said. "For that is how
Much light the Lord still grants us. Things more near,
Or here, leave our minds helpless, and unless
The news is brought by others, nothing's clear
About the human state. Thus you may guess
That all we know will lie dead on the Day
Of Judgement, when the future will be sealed."
Then sorrow for my fault moved me to say:
"Could you now tell that other one who reeled
And fell back, that his son yet lives? And let
Him know that if my answer was so slow
Before, it was because I was beset
With that doubt you have settled." Keen to go,
My Master was recalling me. In haste
I begged the shade to read the roll of those
There with him. He to me: "Here lie encased
More than a thousand. Fiery tombs enclose
The second Frederick, sensual emperor,
And Cardinal Ottaviano who
Boasted of his lost soul, and many more
Of whom I will say nothing." Back into
His crucible he vanished, and I turned
Towards my ancient Poet, thinking still
Of what I had just heard, and how it burned
With such hostility. "And what thoughts fill
Your head?" he asked as we walked. I replied.
"What he has said against you, you should hold
In memory," he said. "But that aside,
You must attend to what you see unfold
As we proceed." He pointed, and spoke on:
"When you are bathed in the sweet radiance
Of her whose fair eyes leave the sun outshone
And see all, then the full significance

Of your life's journey you will learn from her."
He turned left, and the wall was at our back,
And downward, even further than we were,
We worked towards the centre on a track
Into a valley which, even as high
As where we strode, still stank to make you cry.

CANTO 11

On the edge of a high rim of broken rock—
Boulders that formed a mighty circle's arc—
We came upon a crowd I saw with shock
Were even more tormented. Here the stark
Force of the stench that welled like a wound's pus
Drove us to shelter in behind a vault
Inscribed: "I hold Pope Anastasius,
Led by Photinus to the grievous fault
Of scorning all belief in the straight way."
10   "Here if we pause in our descent awhile
So that our senses can adjust, we may
Proceed with less revulsion at this vile
Breath from Hell's throat." So said my Guide. And I:
"How can we make up for the time we lose?"
And he: "My thoughts exactly. Bounded by
These cliffs, my son, are three more circles whose
Diameters, like those we've left behind,
Decrease as they go down. All three are packed
With blighted spirits. You should bear in mind—
20   So the mere sight will be enough, in fact,
For you to understand—how they're confined
And why. Crimes Heaven hates have for their end
Injustice, and that end afflicts someone
Either by force or fraud, and must offend

The Lord, for fraud is human, and ills done
By humans please Him least, and therefore they,
The tricksters, lie low down and suffer more.
In the first circle here, which is to say
The seventh if you count all those before,
30 The violent lie in three zones. And why three?
Violence is done to three: to God, the man
Who does it, and the neighbour. It can be
For what they are—a crime whose only plan
Is hatred—or else for their property.
You're looking puzzled. Let me make it plain.
By force, death and cruel damage can be dealt
To someone in himself, and the same pain,
If what he has is hurt, is sorely felt:
Ruin, extortion, burning. Thus it is
40 That murderers and all who would inflict
Damage from malice, all the plunderers
And pillagers, for this first zone are picked
To suffer, each to his due squad assigned.
And since a man may violate by force
Himself and what he has, so we must find
It fit that in the second zone remorse
Without relief assails him who deprives
Himself of your sweet world, gambles away
His gifts, and here is joined to the lost lives
50 Who must shed tears forever and a day
For joy they might have had. Then, the third zone:
Violence to God, done in the secret heart
By doubt, or done not just through thought alone
But outright blasphemy, negates the part
God plays in nature. Thus the smaller ring
Stamps with its seal both Sodom and Cahors
(That is, the usurers) and all who bring
Contempt against God from behind closed doors.
Fraud eats the conscience, whether used against
60 Those who trust us or those who trust us not.

In the latter case, the bonds of love dispensed
By nature are undone. Thus you have got,
In Circle Eight, toadies and hypocrites,
Magicians, forgers, thieves, thugs, dealers in
Holy preferment, everything that fits
The definition of sheer filth. The sin
Arising from the former case? Still worse.
With natural love forgotten, added trust
Is ruined too. When this sad universe
70 Draws to the tightest ring, when it is just
A central point where Lucifer resides
In Circle Nine, the traitors are consumed
Forever." I said: "Master, your report
Thus far is clear. How this pit of the doomed
Is portioned out to hold them you've made plain.
But tell me why those of that stygian slime,
Those driven by the wind, lashed by the rain,
And their own tongues, must serve their endless time
Like that and not like this, here in this red
80 Metropolis. Is not the wrath of God
Upon them too? If not, why are they led
To suffer?" He to me: "How your wits nod
And wander aimless! Can't you concentrate?
Don't you recall how Aristotle shows,
In the *Ethics*, that three different kinds of state
In humans breed all crimes that can oppose
Themselves to heaven's will? Incontinence,
Malice and brutishness? And of those three,
Incontinence is held the least offence
90 By God, and so is punished less? You see,
Or ought to, how this basic teaching yields
The reason that all those we left outside
And higher up in their respective fields
Are separate from the wicked who reside
Down here. These were more guilty. Hence, divine
Justice assails those less than it does these."

"Bright sun," I said, "you calm these doubts of mine
As you heal any troubled sight. Such ease
You bring me that to question pleases me
Like being answered. But could you just touch
100 Again on one point? You said usury
Offends the holy goodness. Why so much?
Turn back a little and untie that knot."
"Philosophy," he said, "to him who reads
It well, speaks more than once of what
Dictates the course of nature. It proceeds
According to the holy mind and art.
And from the *Physics*, a few pages on,
You'll find your own art a dependent part
Of nature's, as a pupil draws upon
110 His teacher's principles to the extent
That he can grasp them. Thus your industry
Is God's grandchild. By this twin element
Of nature's force and human effort—see
The book of Genesis, near the beginning, where
Men are enjoined to earn their bread by sweat—
Humanity needs must accept its share
Of effort to advance. The trade in debt
Ignores that pact. His course set otherwise,
The usurer holds nature in contempt
120 Both in herself and in her human guise,
Simply by how he holds himself exempt
And sets his hopes elsewhere. But time for you
To follow me, for here we can't remain.
On the horizon's rim they shine like dew,
The quivering fish of Pisces. The great Wain
Lies over Caurus. Soon the dawn will break,
And the cliff give us a downward path to take."

CANTO 12

The place we came to for our next descent
Was alpine, and because of what it held
No eye would seek it. As, downstream from Trent,
By either earthquake or weak ground impelled,
The landslide struck the Adige's left bank
So that the shaken peak now joins the plain
Through one steep slope the traveller might thank
For steps of broken rock, the same again
Was this path downward into the ravine,
And on the chasm's edge outstretched there lay
The infamy of Crete, by whom I mean
The Minotaur, conceived on the sad day
When Pasiphae wore the cow of wood,
And when he saw us he began to eat
Himself, as one whose rage would, if it could,
Consume him, hungry for the nearest meat.
My wise one cried: "Perhaps you think that I
Bring you the Duke of Athens, Theseus,
Who in the living world taught you to die?
Beast, get away. This man will not discuss
Plans with your sister. He is on the road
To see the suffering in the realm you guard."
As a bull that breaks loose when the final goad
Delivers the death stroke, but is debarred

From running, lunges here, there, anywhere,
So did the Minotaur, and when my Guide
Saw this, he cried: "That passage over there!
Run for it while he's still preoccupied
With his own fury, and start down!" And so
We picked our way down those piled rocks, which moved,
Because they felt a weight they did not know,
Often beneath my feet, and thereby proved
That I was mortal. As I went, I thought.
And he: "You think about this ruined cliff,
Guarded by that wild beast whose rage I brought
To heel just now? You'd not have seen it if
You'd been with me the first time I came here
Into the depths of Hell. None of this rock
Had fallen then. Love caused it to appear
When He who took his pick from Limbo's stock
Came down to the top circle. Then Love shook
This putrid valley to its depths. I felt
The universe feel Love. (Some others look
On Love as causing chaos that can melt
The world entire, and has, repeatedly.)
That was the moment when this rock was thrown
Down thus, both here and elsewhere. But now see,
Below, that river. Made of blood alone,
It holds and boils all those whose violence
Has injured others." Blind greed! Brainless rage!
In our brief lives they drive us beyond sense
And leave us misery for a heritage
Throughout eternity! I saw a wide
Moat, curved, just as my Escort had outlined,
To frame the level. Here on the near side,
Between the moat's edge and the cliff behind,
A line of archer centaurs ran, as they
Had done on Earth when chasing game. They saw
Us coming down, and stopped. Three broke away,
Bringing their best-made arrows. "Lest I draw

30

40

50

60   My bow," one cried from far off, "tell us what
       Torment you come to. Why descend the slope?
       Tell us from there." My Master: "You we'll not
       Taunt with an answer. Chiron, there, can cope:
       Your hasty will was always your disease."
       Then he touched me, and said: "The one who shouts
       Is Nessus. For the wife of Hercules,
       Fair Deianira, he died, and the gouts
       Of blood that soaked his shirt avenged him. He's
       Nothing beside great Chiron. That's him there
70   In the middle, looking down at his own chest.
       He had the young Achilles in his care.
       The other one is Pholus, so possessed
       With rage. And this is just the one patrol
       Of the centaur army. Round the moat they go
       In thousands, loosing shafts at every soul
       That lifts itself out of the blood by so
       Much as an inch more than its guilt permits."
       Now we were near to those quick beasts, Chiron
       Pulled back his beard with where the notched bolt fits
80   Into the string. Mouth bared, "Keep your eyes on
       That second one," he told his friends. "His feet
       Shift what they step on. Dead feet never do."
       At Chiron's breast, where his two natures meet,
       My Master said of me: "He lives, it's true.
       And he's alone. It is for me to show
       This clouded valley to him. He is brought
       Here by necessity, not pleasure. So
       Someone instructed me who had cut short
       Her hallelujahs. He is not a thief
90   And nor am I, but by the Power that steers
       My steps on this road wild without relief,
       Choose from your ranks, to be our eyes and ears,
       One who can find the ford, or take a man
       Across the bloodstream on his back, for men
       Cannot fly through the air as spirits can."

Chiron turned to his right, and "All right, then,"
He said to Nessus. "You can double back,
Show them the ford, and scare off any band
Like ours that you might meet." Off down the track
100 We moved with our new guide, on the last land
Before the bubbling red, in which the boiled,
Up to their eyebrows, screamed. "Tyrants who dipped
Their hands in blood, they never then recoiled,"
Said the great centaur. "Lust for plunder gripped
Them once, and how it got them where they are
They now regret, as you can hear. But see,
That's Alexander, called, by Seneca,
The Cruel and not the Great. And Sicily
Suffered from that man, Dionysius,
110 For long years. And that brow with the black hair
Belongs to Ezzelino, tortured thus
For tortures given. That one is the fair
Obizzo d'Este, smothered by his son
Up there. Down here, what takes his breath away
Flows from the things he did, and not those done
To him." I turned to hear my Poet say
"That last news will make certain what you guess."
We moved on. When the centaur stopped once more,
There was a crowd below us who were less
120 Deeply immersed than those we'd seen before.
Mere murderers, they had caused less distress
And so their heads, as far down as the throat,
Stood out above the blood like flesh and bone
While Nessus, pointing, bade us both take note
Of one shade who appeared to stand alone
Even among the alone. "That one is Guy
De Montfort, who in God's house took a life,
And now the heart he stabbed sits in the sky
Above the Thames, and still it feels the knife
130 And still drips blood." And after that I saw
People who stood with head, neck and whole chest

On view, and I knew many. More and more
The blood grew shallow. Leaving raw the rest,
It cooked only the feet. Here we could cross.
"On this side you may see the blood run thin,"
The centaur said, "But there is no real loss,
For on the other side more blood flows in
To fill a bed which goes on deepening
Until it reaches where the tyrants groan
140 As Holy Justice puts the sacred sting
To Attila, Scourge of Earth. In the same zone
Are Pyrrhus, Rome's inveterate enemy,
And Sextus, likewise. Justice milks the tears,
Let loose by steam the boiling gore sets free,
From Rinier da Corneto. Recent years
Have seen the high roads made a battlefield
By him and Rinier Pazzo. Same first name,
Same ruthlessness. But time forced them to yield—
And when their world died, this was where they came."
150 The centaur turned. We watched his head-high stride
Back through the ford across the crimson tide.

CANTO 13

Nessus was not yet back to the far bank
When we set out into a forest void
Of any pathway. No green leaves, but dank,
Discoloured. No smooth boughs, but cloyed
With knots, warped. No sweet fruits, but just the blank
Stems and envenomed thorns. Beasts who despise
The cultivated land that lies between
Cecina and Corneto would not prize
A home this thick and harsh. Here can be seen
The nests of loathsome Harpies that once chased
The Trojans from the Strophades with dire
Warnings of woe. Wide-winged and human-faced,
Clawed feet, big feathered bellies, a strange choir
Sobbing from stranger trees their sad ill will.
And my good Master: "You should understand
Before you go on, that from here until
You reach the Third Zone's horrifying sand,
You travel in the Second Zone. So fill
Your eyes with things of which I could not speak
And be believed." I heard from every side
Crying, but saw none cry. My spirits weak,
I stopped. I think he thought I thought, my Guide,
That all these voices from the trees belonged
To people hiding from us. He to me:

"To prove that in your thoughts the truth is wronged,
Break off a little branch from any tree."
I reached to pluck a twig from a great thorn
Whose trunk cried: "Who are you to tear me so?"
The trunk turned dark with blood as if more torn
30 Than barely touched, and went on: "May I know
Why you assault me? Pity can't mean much
To one like you. We who were men are now
Dead wood. You might have shown a gentler touch
Had we been serpent's souls." And then somehow
The twig, too, cried. Just as a green brand weeps
Both sound and sap when it burns from one end
And, from the other, hissing liquid seeps,
So my torn trophy bubbled forth a blend
Of blood and words, at which I let it fall
40 And stood afraid. My Sage said: "Wounded soul,
Had he believed what he, before, in all
His life, saw only in my lines, then whole
You would have stayed. Thought would have stayed his hand.
But such things were so far beyond belief
Even to me, I failed to understand
The consequences you would pay in grief
Were I to urge him on, and I grieve, too.
But tell him who you were, so he can make
Some restitution by restoring you
50 To worldly fame, for he has leave to take
The road home, by a heavenly remit."
The trunk said: "You so charm me with your speech
I too must speak, so please put up with it
If I should prattle trying not to preach.
Know me for Piero della Vigne, who
Kept both the keys to Emperor Frederick's heart.
So smoothly did I lock and unlock, few
Men saw into his secrets. To the part,
So glorious, of chancellor, I brought
60 Such faithfulness I lost both strength and sleep.

Envy, that common bane of any court,
The harlot who haunts Caesar's house to keep
Her shameless eyes on all that happens, set
Men's minds against me. My Augustus, fired
By rumour's flames, was driven to forget
All honours due to me. Soon I was mired
In misery, accused of treason, lost
My eyes. Then, in my cell, my scornful mind,
Despising scorn from others, paid the cost
70   By making me, the just man, yet more blind,
Even to justice, when myself I slew.
But by the new roots of this tree, I swear
That to my dear Lord I was always true,
True to his well-earned honour. When you're there,
Should either of you get back, please rebuild
My memory, that still, from envy's blow,
Lies wrecked, a worse death than the one I willed."
My Poet waited, then addressed me so:
"Now that he's silent, seize your chance to ask
80   What further questions you might have." Then I
Gave answer: "Once more I give you the task
Of seeking what you think might satisfy
My doubts. I can't, so much does pity fill
My heart." And so my Guide began again:
"That this man freely answer to your will,
Imprisoned shade, say more of how and when
A soul is tied in knots, and, if you can,
Tell us if ever any is set free."
The trunk blew hard, and quickly what began
90   As wind became a voice: "These points can be
Quite briefly answered. When the violent soul
Uproots itself and leaves a corpse, Minos
Sends it to Level Seven. Protocol
Decrees that it not mitigate its loss
By choosing where it falls into the wood.
It falls where thrown by chance, and then, a grain

Of grief, it sprouts. Then, where a sapling stood,
There's suddenly a savage tree, whose pain,
When Harpies come to eat its leaves, must find
A vocal outlet. Like the rest, one day
We'll go to fetch the flesh we left behind,
But it will never clothe us in the way
It did, for Justice would be undermined
If one who robs himself should own once more
The thing he stole. So we will drag them here,
Those bodies, and the thing he was before
On each tree in this wood will hang, so near
Yet so far from its murderous soul." We were
Still listening, in case the trunk was not
Through talking, when we heard a sudden stir.
As one who, waiting in his chosen spot,
Is still surprised to hear the boar-hunt charge
Towards his post—the beasts, the crashing through
Of branches—we were stunned to see at large,
There on our left, two naked runners, two
Scarred runners, and they fled so fast they snapped
The tangle-wood. "Come now!" the first one cried,
"Come quickly, death!" The other, looking sapped
Of winning speed, yelled: "Lano, why the pride?
You ran at Toppo but you still got killed."
He crouched, perhaps because his breath was short,
Close to a bush. The woods behind them filled
With black bitches, ravenous for the sport
And swift as unleashed hounds. They chose the one
Who squatted there to get their teeth into,
And bit by bit tore him apart. That done,
They took the suffering pieces beyond view.
My Escort took me by the hand and led
Me to the bush, which sobbed: "O Jacopo
Da Sant Andrea"—anywhere it bled
From wounds, they vainly whined—"why stoop so low?
How did it profit you to make a screen

Of me? Your guilty life was not my blame."
My Master stooped above it. "You that keen
Both blood and bitter tears, what was your name?"
It said to us: "O souls who come to see
The shameful damage that has stripped my leaves,
Gather them up and bring them back to me,
Heaped at these roots to comfort one who grieves.
140 My city once chose to set Mars aside
For John the Baptist as its patron. Thus
The scorned, discarded one will always guide
Its path to civil war, us against us:
And were it not that near our bridge still stands
A shard of his old statue, those who raised
The city once again from the black brands
And ash left when Attila's wrath once blazed
Would have worked uselessly. I know. I made
My house my gibbet. Here, I am repaid."

CANTO 14

Compelled by love of home, I gathered in
His scattered leaves for him, who spoke no word,
His voice gone. We moved out. Now I begin
To speak of where the Second and the Third
Zones meet, and where the fearful art is seen
Of Justice. To show clearly these new things,
I have to say we reached a plain swept clean
Of every plant, so that the dark wood rings
A desert, as the sad moat rings the wood.
10 Here, at the edge's edge, we paused. The ground
Was dry, deep sand, as where once strode and stood
Cato in Africa, not to be bound
By Empire. Holy Vengeance, how you must
Be feared by all who read what now I saw!
Herd after herd of naked souls were just
Weeping the one lament, although the law
By which they suffered differed. Some lay flat
Face up, some sat knees high, and there were some
Who kept on moving. Those who moved like that
20 Were most in number but were largely dumb
Compared with those who lay in pain. Pain turned
Their tongues loose. Over that great stretch of sand
Slowly broad flakes of fire fell while they burned,
As snow falls in the mountains when not fanned

By any wind. Just as, in India,
When Alexander marched to that hot land
And saw his army, having come so far,
Assailed by falling flames that reached the ground
Unbroken, he told all his troops to tread
30 The soil free of those fires which had been found
To have, if not quenched, deadly fumes to spread,
Just so the eternal fire fell through the air,
Kindling the tinder sand like the flint's spark
To multiply the pain. Hands, in despair,
Unsleeping in their dance, hit first that mark,
Now this, as if they hoped to beat away
The burning flakes. And I: "My Master, you
Who overcome all things that say us nay
Save stubborn imps who would not let us through
40 The gate, name me that great one there who seems
To think the fire means nothing, and in scorn
Lies scowling, as if these hot drops were dreams
That could not melt him." He himself was torn
From his aloofness by what he'd heard said
By me about him. He cried: "What I was
When living, I am now when I am dead.
My fire within outdoes these flames, because,
Though Jove wear out the forge from which in rage
He seized the deadly bolt that skewered me
50 On that last day—though he should stage by stage
Wear down his crew to immobility—
At that black forge on Etna, shouting 'Help,
Good Vulcan, help!' as once on Phlegra's field,
And try to shaft me with the victor's yelp,
He'll not have vengeance, for I will not yield."
My Guide then spoke with force I had not heard
From him before. "Capaneus, your pride,
Undimmed, brings you worse punishment: absurd
Ravings like yours alone could match your tide
60 Of anger." Then, with gentler look and word,

He turned to me again. "That was the king,
One of the seven kings, who once laid siege
To Thebes, and held God for a paltry thing
And still does, but to match his sacrilege
He has, as I just told him, his sad bleat.
Follow me now, and keep on walking near
The wood, or else the sand will scorch your feet."
In silence we approached a point where—fear
Still makes me shudder—gushes forth a small
70 Red stream. The Bulicame rivulet
Shared by Viterbo's harlots one and all
Is similar. So this creek's course was set
Across the sand. Its bed and banks were stone
With footways alongside, from which I saw
The passage. "Of all things you have been shown,"
My Guide said, "since we entered by that door
Whose threshold is denied to none, you've seen
Nothing like this. This stream can cancel out
All of the flames above it." These had been
80 My Leader's words: but what were they about?
I begged him satisfy the appetite
He'd given me. "Out in the sea lies Crete,
A waste land which once bathed in perfect light
Under its king. Mount Ida was replete—
When Saturn ruled, although he ruled by fright—
With leaves and water, but is now bereft
Of both, worn out. Queen Rhea hid her child
For safety in the cradle of a cleft
And when he cried, she made the crowd go wild,
90 To block off Saturn and his murderous theft.
Inside the mountain sits a grand old man.
Back to Damietta, face to Rome, gaze fixed
As to his mirror: head of fine gold, span
Of chest and arms pure silver, brass betwixt
His breast and fork, choice iron from there down
Except for his right foot made of baked clay

On which most weight rests. And save for his crown
Of gold, there is no part not split asplay
By tracks of tears, which gather and descend
100   By force into that cavern there, and take
Their course from rock to rock unto this end.
They make the Acheron, the Styx, they make
The Phlegethon, and here, where they're confined
To this tight channel and no further fall
Is possible, Cocytus forms. What kind
Of pond that is, you'll see, so all in all
I'd rather skip that subject." But then I:
"You say this stream flows from our world. But here,
And only here, is where we see it. Why?"
110   And he: "It's not the trick it might appear.
You know this place is circular, and you,
Although you have come far, veer left always
As you go down, and have not yet turned through
A full rotation. Let it not amaze
You then, if we encounter something new:
No need to look stunned." I again: "Where flow
The Phlegethon and Lethe? On the one
You're silent, and the other—now I know—
Comes from this trough of tears." He: "You have done
120   Me proud with all your questions, but the red
And boiling river should have solved the first.
Lethe you'll see, when the repented dead,
Cleansed of the guilt with which they once were cursed,
May bathe themselves, but far beyond this pit."
And then he said: "It's time to leave the wood
Behind. You must keep close now. Look to it.
Untouched by falling fires, the only good
Paths are the margins. Any flame that nears
Dies in the rising mist of all these tears."

CANTO 15

A hard edge bears us on, and vapour makes
A shield above out of the stream below
Which, with its banks, is free from fire. It takes
A dam to stem the sea. This, Flemings know,
Between Wissant and Bruges, where they fear
The flood's rush; and the Paduans, beside
The Brenta, when the Chiarentana's near
To full from melting snow. Both high and wide
Those bastions are built. These, not so much:
10 But still in the same fashion. We had got
So far out of the wood that we'd lost touch
With what it looked like—had I turned, I'd not
Have seen it—when we met a troop of shades
Walking beside the bank. As when the sun
Has set, but light is still there, though it fades,
And under the new moon men look at one
Another, so these looked at us, with tight
Eyebrows, as might a tailor in old age
Search for his needle's eye. Held to the sight
20 Of this squad as I trod my narrow stage,
I had my hem gripped. "Marvellous!" a man cried,
And when he reached for me, I fixed my eyes
On his baked face, nor did those scarified
Features prevent that I should recognise

The man I named. "Master Brunetto. You?
You're here?" And he to me: "My son, don't be
Displeased if for a while I leave this crew
To their march while I turn and you keep me,
Your Brunetto Latini, close to hand."

30 And I: "I wish for that with all my heart,
And I will sit with you, should you demand,
If he allows who's led me from the start."
"My son," he said, "if any of this lot
Stops for an instant, for a hundred years
He lies unshielded from the fire. So not
A thought of pausing, lest it end in tears.
Go on, and I'll be clinging to your skirt.
I'll catch up later with my squad, who go
Forever mourning their eternal hurt."

40 I dared not, from the bank, step down as low
As where he walked, but kept my head inclined
Like one who walks with reverence. Then he said:
"What chance decrees or destiny designs
That you should be down here when not yet dead,
And who is he that guides your steps?" "Up there
Where life is bright," I said, "and my midway
In years not yet reached, yet I knew despair,
Lost in a valley. Only yesterday
At dawn I turned my back on it. But I

50 Would have returned, had he failed to appear
To lead me home by this road." He said: "By
Your star, if always by your star you steer,
You can't fail to make glorious harbour. Had
I sensed this rightly in your life so fair,
And not too soon died, seeing Heaven glad
To help you would have made me take more care
To aid your work. But that mean and malign
People who from Fiesole of old
Came down and still retain a certain sign

60 Of rocks and mountains—walls of Florence hold

The stones of that first hill—will make of you,
For your good works, their enemy. No chance
They won't do that, for never will it do
If sweet figs, in the bitter circumstance
Of sorbs, should come to fruit. The world's fame long
Has called them blind, half mad with envious greed,
And proud. So from this customary wrong
Get yourself clean. Your Fortune holds such seed
Of honour that both tribes will crave your flesh,
70 But as the saying goes, the goat and grass
Will be apart. Let those hill beasts make fresh
Food from themselves: if when they bare their arse
Above the dunghill any plant spring, let
Them leave it lie, for it might hold again
The holy seed of Romans, those who yet
Continued to grace Florence even when
It turned into a writing vipers' nest."
"If all my prayers," I answered, "were fulfilled,
You'd not yet have been banished from the rest
80 Of humankind. For in my mind, instilled
Immovably—and now it floods my heart—
Is the image, kind and fatherly, of you,
When many times you taught me by what art
A man becomes immortal: and what's due
To you from me in gratitude, my tongue
Must, while I live, declare. What you tell me
I'll note down, as I did when I was young,
And you spoke. And inside this scroll will be
What Farinata said, so both texts can
90 Be brought to one who, should I reach her, will
Know what they mean. But this much of my plan
I would make plain, to keep my conscience still.
What Fortune wishes, I am ready for.
Your forecast is not one I haven't heard.
Let Fortune turn its wheel at will, and more:
Let the hick hack with his mattock." This last word

Brought my Guide's head back, turning to the right,
To look at me and say: "He listens well
Who takes notes." None the less I took delight
100　In gossip with Brunetto, bade him tell
Which of his squadron had most fame and rank.
And he to me: "Of some it's well to know,
Of others we do best to leave a blank,
For lack of time to say now, as we go,
So much. But, in a word; clerics they were,
And great, famed scholars; all of them defiled,
When living, by the one same sin. The slur
On that crowd touched the one you, as a child,
Learned Latin grammar from, famed Priscian,
110　And Francesco d'Accorso, who taught law.
And if you like scum you might see the man
Sent to Vicenza by the Pope, before
Florence should see his sin-worn nerves collapse:
Andrea de' Mozzi. Bishop, in your youth.
There's so much more to say. Not now, perhaps.
I can't go further speaking the sad truth,
For see, a new cloud rises from the sand:
People I mustn't meet will soon arrive.
My book, called *Treasure*, is at your command:
120　Read it. I ask no more. There, I'm alive."
He turned then, and he ran like one of those
Who in Verona's field race for the prize
Of green cloth. Like the first, the last man knows
He, too, will be marked out before all eyes.
But this one ran as if the race were his
To win, not lose. As his life was, and is.

CANTO 16

Already at the point where the long roar
Of water falling into the next loop
Was like the hum of beehives, I now saw
Three shades split at the run from their host group
And come towards us, each one shouting: "Stop!
You there whose clothing had its origin
In our degraded city!" Ah, the crop
Of wounds they bore, both old and new, burned in
By flames! Just to recall them grieves me still.
My Teacher listened to their cries, then turned
To me and said: "Let's wait: to them we will
Do well to show respect. Though all is burned—
First on the surface, later through and through—
In this place by its nature, yet I'd say
Haste is less suitable to them than you."
We stopped, and at their former quick pace they
Came on, and when they reached us, then all three
Made of themselves a wheel, in the same way
That wrestlers do, nude, oiled, and keen to see
Advantage for their grip, their dance a sign
Of thrusts and blows to come. And, wheeling so,
Each kept his face directed towards mine
Wherever in the circle he might go,
So that his neck moved always with his feet.

10

20

"If by the sadness of this sandy waste,"
Said one, "and by our aspect, seared by heat
To hairless blackness, we ourselves are placed,
Along with our petitions, in contempt,
May our fame sway you to incline your mind
30 To tell us who you are, that walk exempt
Through Hell. He that you see me tread behind
Was one, though he goes naked now and peeled,
Much grander than you think: grandson of good
Gualdrada, she who first raised high the shield
Of Conti Guidi. Be it understood
That he was Guido Guerra: both with blade
And wise words he did great things while he breathed.
The one who stirs the sand behind me made
Tegghiaio Aldobrandi a name wreathed
40 In laurels, and he would have done that more
Had what he said been heeded. As for me,
Put here with them to this cross, I, before,
Was Jacopo Rusticucci. Let it be
Made clear that nothing brought me half as much
Grief as my savage wife." If there had been,
Down there among them, shelter from the touch
Of fire, I would have thrown myself between
Their bodies, and I think my Teacher might
Have stood for it, but fear soon left for dead
50 My goodwill: baked and burned as black as night—
Too ardent an embrace. So I just said:
"No, not contempt, but grief, fixed by your state
So deep into my mind it will be long
Before it leaves. I first felt its full weight
When my lord told me to expect a throng
Of men like you would be here. I am of
Your city, and your deeds and honoured names
Always I've heard and spoken of with love.
Leaving the gall, as I will leave these flames,
60 I go to the sweet fruits my truthful Guide

Has promised. But I first must go below
To the centre." "That the soul may steer your stride
And fame shine after you," said Jacopo,
"Tell us if courtesy and valour yet
Abide in Florence, or are they quite gone?
For Guglielmo Borsiere, whom we met
Quite recently—look there, where he goes on
In fellowship with us to share the pain—
Afflicts us with his words." And then I cried:
70 "Florence! New men and lust for a quick gain
Drive you to mad excess and vaulting pride!
Already you're in tears!" With straining face
Lifted towards my object of disdain
I yelled all this, and those three, who could trace
The course of my gaze, had their answer. Each
Looked at the others as men often stare
Who hear the truth. "If, any time, to teach
The facts leaves you so little cost to bear,"
They all replied, "then truly you are blessed,
80 Speaking as you desire. Therefore if you
Fly free from these dark realms of the possessed
And see the beauty of the stars anew,
Speak well of us." The wheel was broken, then,
And legs in sand were nimble wings in air
So fast they flew. You couldn't say "Amen"
And they were gone. My Guide thought we'd been there
For long enough. I followed him. We went
Only a little way before the sound
Of water would have drowned out what we meant
90 If we had tried to speak. As at one bound
That river called the Acquacheta, where
It flows high up, as first to hold its course,
Eastward from Monte Veso where you bear
Left on the Apennines, before, full force,
It roars over the cliff into the air
At San Benedetto dell'Alpe, down to burst

And find its lower bed at Forlì, fleeced
With foam again, and, having done its worst,
Changes its name, might well have leapt at least
100 A thousand times, there, down the cliff-like bank,
Dark water boomed, so, as the time increased
That we spent near it, our stunned ears grew blank.
The cord I wore with which I once had planned
To snare the leopard with the painted pelt,
I loosed completely at my Guide's command,
And passed him what had been my hidden belt
Now coiled and knotted. He swung to the right
And flung it. Far out from the edge it went
And down into the deep pit of the night.
110 For the strange signal, something must be meant
To answer strangely, or the master's eye
Would not so closely follow it. Men ought
To treat with caution those that clarify
The deed by seeing deep into the thought
That lies behind it. He to me: "Soon, now,
What I seek and you dream of will be brought
To light. It will come up. You'll soon see how."
About a truth that sounds just like a lie
A man should keep his mouth shut, if he can,
120 Since it will surely shame him by and by,
Though he be not at fault. But not this man,
Not here. I must speak. By the melodies
Of this my Comedy—may they not fail
Of lasting favour—reader, on my knees
I swear I saw swim upward through the stale
And murky air a figure, fit to stun
A stout heart, as that rising one returns
Who went down diving to get something done
About the anchor caught in the reef's ferns
130 Or something else the sea hides. Coming near,
He stretches, draws his feet in. He is here.

CANTO 17

"Behold the beast with pointed tail, the one
That breasts the mountains as he breaks through walls
And weapons! He's the beast whose poison none
Escapes. He breathes, and soon the whole world falls
Into a fever." Thus my Leader spoke
To me, while signalling the beast to come
Ashore beside where the stone causeway broke
Off short, and that foul image of the sum
Of all things fraudulent slid in to land
10 His head and chest, but left his tail out there
Free of the bank. His face bore not one brand
Beyond the stamp of justice: a fine air
Of grace he radiated. All the rest
Was serpentine: two paws, wrapped thick with hair
From wrist to armpit, and the back and breast
And both flanks decorated with rich knots
And peacock targets. Not Tartar or Turk
Ever made stuffs with colours in such lots
Within the weave or added on as work,
20 Nor did Arachne, spider woman, lay
Webs on her loom like these. As sometimes boats
Lie at the shore, part dry, part in the play
Of water, or the patient beaver floats
Its tail out from the bank to lure its prey

In Germany, where gluttons rule the roost,
So this vile brute lay on the rim that rings
The waste of sand with stone. Its tail was loosed
To roam the void, thus raising its twin stings,
The lethal scorpion-fork that armed its tip.
30 My Leader said: "Now we must seek the ledge
That leads to where that monster keeps its grip
On something solid." Thus along the edge
Down to the right, we went ten paces, well
Away from sand and flames. We reached his head
And I saw people, where the sandbank fell
Away, who sat beyond. My Master said:
"That you may keep full knowledge of this zone,
See how they are, but let your talk be quick.
Meanwhile with this one I will speak alone:
40 We need his shoulders." So I had to pick
My way all by myself along the rim
Of Level Seven to the place where those
Sad people sat. Pain filled them to the brim
And burst forth from their eyes, which could not close.
On either side their hands beat in defence
Now from the flames, now from the burning sand,
As dogs in summer fight the insolence
Of fleas and gnats and gadflies with a grand
And useless dart of snout or sweep of paw.
50 I looked at faces. Not a face I knew
As fire fell on them all: but then I saw
That each neck wore a pouch of certain hue
And coat of arms. They fixed their eyes on these
Once noble signs, and when I looked about
Among them, I saw various liveries:
Blue lion on purse yellow, I picked out,
And then, on purse blood-red, a goose bright white,
Whiter than butter. And a light blue sow
Expectant on white wallet hove in sight,
60 Whose owner said: "Why are you here and how,

In this death pit? Get out, and, since you live,
Know well that Vitaliano, from my town,
Will sit here on my left. They won't forgive,
Those Florentines, that I dared to come down
From Padua. Often they pound my ears:
'Let Buiamonte come, the sovereign knight
Whose pouch bears three goats!' " Thus our years
Of noble deeds end with a fool's delight
In lending money. As he made a face
70 With twisted mouth and tongue stuck out to lick
His nose like a lost ox, I, lest disgrace
Should fall on me (I was already sick—
I should have kept it short), left this sad troop
To view my back, and went to find my Guide
Already mounted on the huge beast's croup.
"Be strong and bold. From here on down, we ride
On flying stairs. Get up in front of me,"
He said, "so I can guard you from the tail."
As one so near malaria's ecstasy
80 Of shivering that his every fingernail
Turns blue, and at the merest sight of shade
He trembles head to foot, such I became
At these words, but a servant can be made
More staunch by a good master, for the shame.
And so, on those great shoulders, I got set,
Wishing to say, except no voice was there
To match the thought: "Now hold me! Don't forget!"
But he that in another time took care
Of me, and in another danger, on
90 The spot embraced me. Ready for the air,
I heard his voice behind me: "Geryon!
Let's move. And make your circles slow and wide
As we go down. Remember your new load."
And as a small boat inch by inch will glide
Backwards from where it was, so was the mode
Of Geryon's departure. Feeling free

At last, he gently turned, until his tail
Was where his breast had been. Then, finally,
He stretched the tail out. On a giant scale
100   It was an eel, and so it moved. His paws
Pulled in the air. I think no greater fear
Had Phaethon when his hands betrayed his cause
And dropped the reins, and so let the sun sear
The sky where we now see the Milky Way,
Nor Icarus, when he first felt his wings
Work loose because, too near the light of day,
The wax turned soft—the man who built the things,
His father, shouting "Wrong turn!"—than I knew,
When everywhere I looked was only air,
110   And all except the beast was lost to view.
Slowly he swims, as if with time to spare,
Slowly he wheels, and gradually descends,
But I think only of the wind I face—
And that wind from down there where the flight ends.
Now, on our right, the torrent shook the base
Of reason with its sobbing throb, whereat
I craned my neck and looked down. Then my fear
Increased of getting down from where I sat.
For I saw flames, and heard sad cries come near,
120   So that I shrank back trembling. Then I saw—
As not before—our circular descent
Against the background of a single law
Expressed in all the forms of discontent.
And as the falcon too long on the wing
Without a sight of lure or victim makes
The falconer cry: "Come on home, poor thing,"
And wearily starts down, and finds it takes
A hundred turns to get back to the spot
It left so swiftly, and lands in a sulk
130   And angry near its master, and yet not
All that near, Geryon, in his great bulk,

At last had set us down on the deep floor
Close to the jagged rock's base. Then, set free
Of my weight, with no orders any more
From my Guide, like an arrow finally
Let loose to fly, he vanished instantly.

CANTO 18

Now, Malebolge is a place in Hell
All iron-coloured stone, just like the wall
That goes around it, and a wide, deep well
Gapes in the middle of its foul field. All
The workings of that pit I shall expound
In due course. But for now, let's say the belt
Between it and the high rock bank is round,
With ten concentric valleys, each a welt
Sunk in the earth. As where moat after moat,
10 Guarding the castle, makes ring after ring
And scored ground shows a plan that we can note,
The general layout here was the same thing,
And as such forts have bridges from their gates
To the outer bank, so from the rock's base run
Ridges from dyke to dyke to where awaits
The pit that cuts them short, providing one
Point of collection. Dropped by Geryon
From his back, there we were. My Leader held
Tight to the left, and I, behind, came on.
20 On our right hand, new kinds of anguish welled,
New torments, new tormentors: with this tide
The first ditch brimmed. The sinners on its floor
Were naked. They came facing us, this side
Of centre. On the other side, they bore
In our direction, but with longer stride,

Just as in Rome, the year of Jubilee,
The crowds of pilgrims on the bridge were split
So those on one side, as they crossed, could see
The Castle and were always facing it
30 As they approached St. Peter's, while those on
The other walked towards the hill. But here
Along the sad rock they were set upon
On both sides by horned demons. From the rear
Each victim felt a huge whip at the task
Of cruel encouragement, and flicked his heels
At the first stroke. Nobody had to ask
For a second or a third, though such appeals
Would have been granted. As I went, my gaze
Was met by one of them. Quickly I said:
40 "I saw enough of him, once." To appraise
Him further, I slowed down, and he who led
Allowed me to turn back a bit. And that
Afflicted soul believed he could conceal
Himself by lowering his face: but at
The vain attempt I said: "You just reveal
Yourself by doing that, for I still know,
Unless my eyes deceive me, the true face
Of Venedico Caccianemico.
But what brings you to this sour, pickled place,
50 So like the ditch where dead outlaws are thrown
Near your Bologna?" And he answered: "I
Say this with bad grace, but your speech so plain
Recalls the old world, so I must comply.
The Marquis d'Este got his chance to gain
Ghisolabella only with my aid.
Yes, I played pander with the helpless bait
Of my own sister. Thus the deal was made,
However now my countrymen relate
The vile tale. And I'm not the only soul
60 Once of Bologna now lamenting here:
This place is full of them. Not in the whole
City between two rivers are such sheer

Numbers of tongues that speak our dialect.
And if you want the proof, recall to mind
Our avaricious spirits, and reflect."
And even as he spoke, hard from behind
A demon hit him with a whip, and cried:
"Go, pimp! There are no women here to trade!"
I joined my Escort, and, with him to guide,
70 Soon came to where a ridge formed an arcade
Out from the bank. We climbed up there with ease,
Turned right along the crags, and left that gang
To their perpetual circularities.
When we were at the dizzy overhang
Above the trench for those beneath the lash,
My Leader said: "Stop here. Take in the sight
Of yet another form of ill-born trash:
Faces you've not yet seen in the right light
Because they walked with us, and not towards."
80 From the ancient bridge we watched them as they came
Towards us on the other side, the hordes
Lashed onward like the first lot, just the same.
My Poet said, unprompted: "It's him! Look!
That great one, who weeps not, for all his pain,
Is Jason. Who by craft and courage took
The Golden Fleece from Colchis, the rich gain
Its men all lost. Lemnos he left behind,
Whose women, bold and callous, gave their men
To death, and where he played upon the mind
90 Of Hypsipyle with soft words and then
Again with trinkets, she who had beguiled
The other women when they wished to slay
Her father—and she, now, was left, stark wild
With grief and pregnant, as he sailed away.
This torment fits his guilt. Medea, too,
Is here avenged, for he gulled her as well.
And with him go all those deceivers who
Do likewise, and let this be all we tell
Of this first valley and those in its jaws."

100 Now we were where the narrow pathway cuts
Across the second dyke and thus ensures
Support for the stone arch the dyke abuts.
Here we heard people moaning in the next
Crevasse. With snouts they snorted, while they slapped
Themselves with open hands. Their cruelly vexed
Exhaling grew a mouldy crust that wrapped
The banks, repellent to the eyes and nose,
The depth so hollow that it can't be seen
Save when the arch's crown is climbed, which lies
110 The furthest out above that sad ravine.
We went up there, and in the ditch below
Were people plunged in the cloacal slime
Of human privies, far too thick to flow,
And as I scanned the filth, taking due time,
I saw one with his head so fouled by shit
I couldn't tell if it was shaved or not.
Layman or cleric? He cried: "Why is it
I catch your greedy eye more than this lot
Stuck in their slop?" My turn: "Because I know
120 That head. If I'm right, I've seen you before,
With clean hair. If you are Alessio
Interminei, that's why I eyed you more
Than all the rest." Then he beat on his crown
And cried: "See how my flatteries have cloyed,
That while I lived could never drag me down."
And then my Guide: "Lean out into the void
A touch more, and you'll get a better view
Of that foul rag-bag female horror's face.
Squatting or standing, either of the two,
130 She always scratches some disgusting place
With filthy nails. Behold Thaïs, the whore,
Whose client asked if he was dear to her.
She flattered him ('I couldn't love you more')
And made a clown out of a customer."
We've seen that flattery is filthy stuff.
Let's say for now that we have seen enough.

CANTO 19

Now, Simon Magus and his acolytes;
You wretches who for silver and for gold
Made strumpets of the things of God (by rights
The Brides of Righteousness); all you that sold
The priceless, now the trumpet sounds for you,
For you here, in the third pouch. We were now
At the next tomb, on that high part of the new
Rock ridge that hung above the ditch. But how,
Wisdom Supreme, how great the art you show
In perfect Heaven and on evil Earth,
How justly portioned out your power! So
I saw along the sides and in the girth
Of that grim ditch's floor a livid stone
With holes in it, the holes all the one size
And each one round. One size and shape alone
Had all the fonts, it seemed to my fond eyes,
In my lovely church St. John, and one of those
I broke when helping someone out who would
Have drowned, and this I swear to, to foreclose
All further rumours that I meant no good.
From each hole's mouth a sinner's feet stuck out
And legs up to the calf: the rest inside.
All had both soles on fire. Joints thrashed about
With such force that a willow lashing tied

Around them would have snapped: a rope, the same.
As flame on oily things moves over just
The surface, so it was here with this flame,
Playing from heels to toes. "Master, I must
Know this," I said. "That one who's writhing there
30 More even than his fellows, who is he,
Licked by a redder fire?" "If you should care,"
He answered, "to be lifted up by me
And carried down by that more stony bank,
You'll hear from him of who he is and what
He did." And I: "All that to you whom I most thank
Is pleasing, suits me well. For I do not—
You know, my lord—depart from what you will.
Also you know what I don't say." Then we
Were on the fourth dyke, turned left, went downhill
40 To the pitted, narrow floor, and he set me
Down from his hip when finally we faced
The hole of him who with his shanks wept most.
"Whoever you may be who are so placed,"
I said, "sad soul, heels over head, a post
Well planted, speak now if you can." Just as
The friar that shrives the sneaking killer, who,
The job done, calls him back and thereby has
Further delay before death, I stood, too,
And listened, as he cried: "Already here,
50 Boniface? Is it you that's standing there
So early? Three years more, or pretty near,
The writing said you'd take to get here. Where
Was truth in that? So soon, you're satisfied
With all you did not fear to take by guile
From Our Lady Beautiful and then bestride
Her prostrate holiness? So short a while
Your stolen splendour fed your hungry pride?"
Like those who stand as if they might be mocked
By some reply they don't quite comprehend
60 And can't reply themselves, they are so shocked,

So I became, and Virgil said: "Quick! Mend
His error. Say: 'Be sure I am not he.
He isn't here.' " As I was asked, I spoke,
At which the shade's feet in their agony
Twisted together, and he sighed, and broke
Into a sob, and said: "What do you seek
With me, then? If to know my name concerns
You so much that you came down here to speak
With me direct, behold: here writhes and burns
70 A pope: the mighty mantle I once wore
As Nicholas III, although in truth
The she-bear sign was what I wore before—
A son of the Orsini. Our clan's youth
Was my chief cause. The whelps brought out my worst.
For them I stacked my wealth. Here, I am stacked.
Below my head are others who went first
In simony, and, where the rock is cracked,
Are, through those fissures, now dragged down, squashed flat.
And down there I will go too, in my turn,
80 When he, for whom I so mistook you that
I asked a hasty question, comes to burn
At long last. Longer still, though, is the time
Already that I've been here upside down
With roasted feet than he, for his great crime,
Will spend with red feet, planted. Our same crown
Will fall to Clement, of yet fouler deeds.
He'll be, that lawless shepherd from the west,
As bad as both of us. Just as one reads
In the Maccabees, of Jason and his best
90 Bid for the priesthood, which the king forgave,
Prepare for the new Jason, favoured by
The King of France to buy and sell the bread
Of life." I can't be positive that I
Was not too bold, when everything I said
In answer was as strict as this: "How much
Did Our Lord ask, pray tell, in treasure when

He gave the keys to Peter? Was there such
A thing as price? No, all that he asked then
Was 'Follow me.' Nor did Matthias pay
100   The others when he took the vacant place
Of Judas, self-condemned. So here you stay,
Well punished, pondering the long disgrace
Of what you charged for boldness in that plot
Against Charles of Anjou. And I should heap
Yet harsher words upon you, were it not
That reverence for the keys you got to keep
In the glad life forbade me. Lust for gain
Like yours saddens the world, tramples the good,
Exalts the wicked. You ruled in the brain,
110   Bad shepherds, of the one who understood
The Apocalypse, I mean the Evangelist
Who wrote of her that sits on water, seen
Committing fornication with a list
Of kings, that harlot who had been
Born with the seven heads, her strength obtained
From ten horns for so long as her bridegroom
Thought pleasure was a virtue. You thieves reigned,
Making a God of gold and silver. Room
Does not exist between the idolaters
120   And you, except they worship one, and you
A hundred. Constantine! You set the spurs
To evil, not by cleaving to your new
Religion, but by how, when you moved east,
You gave Sylvester, just to stay behind,
The Western Empire's wealth." He never ceased
While I sang him this song—whether his mind
Was chewed by anger or remorse—to kick
Out hard with both feet. I believe indeed
It pleased my Guide, who clearly could not pick
130   One fault of fact as I spoke. I could read
The pleasure in his eye. Then he took me
In both arms—I was lifted to his breast—

And up we went the way we came, and he
Tired not of holding me. Back to the crest
Of that arch from the fourth to the fifth dyke
He carried me clasped close. And then he set
Me gently down, for what that ridge was like:
Rugged and steep, rough as few goats have met—
And there beyond, another valley yet.

CANTO 20

It's Book One, Canto Twenty. I must make
New matter and new verses from the pain
Of those in these depths, where the floor's a lake
Of anguished tears I stare at tight with strain,
Seeing them come along the valley's curve,
These silent people weeping, at the pace
Of worldly litanies. I needed nerve
Even to notice, there below each face,
The twist between the upper chest and chin.
10 The head faced the behind, and thus they came
Reversed, so as to see in front. If in
Some case of palsy it has been the same,
A man turned right around, I have not seen
Such things, nor do I think they can be true.
So God grant, reader, you yourself should glean
Fruit from your reading, and think how I knew
To keep dry cheeks when I saw from close by
The human form so twisted that its eyes
Could bathe with tears its rearward cleft. And I,
20 I wept indeed, held up in my surprise
By one rock of the ridge. My Escort said:
"You're witless as the rest? Here pity dwells,
But only when it's absolutely dead.
Who is more guilty than he who by spells
And mysteries makes it seem as if divine

Judgement were subject to his will? Raise, raise
Your head. The earth, like a collapsing mine,
Once opened up beneath this one, in days
Of old. The Thebans saw it, shouting: 'Where
30 Do you rush off to, Amphiaraus,
Why do you quit the fight and take the air?'
A question he did not stay to discuss,
But plunged straight down till he was in the care
Of Minos, who looks after everyone.
See how his shoulders make a breast, he that
Would see so far ahead, and now is spun—
If he would reach what he is looking at—
Around to see behind while he goes back
Towards his front. And see the soothsayer
40 Tiresias, who gave two snakes a crack
With his staff, for their coupling. But they were
Revenged when all his features changed from male
To female. He, transformed in every part,
Must strike again those twined snakes without fail
Before he could resume his manly art.
And backed up to his paunch is Aruns. 'Hail
Caesar!' the entrails said: which came to be.
In the hills of Luni, where the ground is tilled
By those who come up from Carrara, he
50 Once had a cave, as if it had been drilled
Through the white marble, and from there his view
Of sea and stars was boundless. And look there
At her whose breasts have been concealed from you
By her long hair thrown back, and her short hair
Is also at the back. She is Manto,
Tiresias's daughter. Many a land
She searched through. Finally she chose to go
Where I was born, and settle. Understand,
On this you should know some of what I know.
60 After her father died, Thebes had the brand
Of slave. She roamed the world for many years.
High up in Italy, in the foothills

Of the Alps that fence the Tyrol when it nears
The German lands, there Lake Benaco spills
A thousand springs—there could be more by far—
Of gathered rain that bathe the Apennines
From Garda south to Val Camonica,
And in the centre a sweet spot combines—
Or would combine, if they just went that way—
70   The blessings from all pastors out of Trent
And Brescia and Verona. To dismay
The Brescians and any army sent
From Bergamo, a strong and handsome fort,
Peschiera, at the low part of the shore,
Lies waiting, and there all that can't stay caught
In the bosom of Benaco forth must pour
And then become a river, flowing down
Through green fields. Now its name is Mincio,
And on it runs as far down as the town
80   Called Governolo, and so to the Po:
And finally it finds a level, slows,
And spreads to make a marsh—in summer more
A bog that sometimes violates the nose.
Passing that way, the deadly virgin saw
Land in the fen, untilled, unpeopled. Keen
To shun all human concourse, there she stayed
With her assistants, which could only mean
She'd found the place to ply her arts. She laid
Her bones there. Afterwards, from all around,
90   The people gathered, for that spot was strong,
The bog on every side, and on that ground
And those dead bones that searched the world so long
They built the city, and from her who first
Picked out its place, they gave the place a name:
They called it Mantua, to slake all thirst
For augury. It rests upon her fame.
There used to be more people there, before
That prize dupe Casalodi let his clan
Be tricked away by Pinamonte. More,

Much more of how my city's life began
There is to tell you, but for now, that much
Will serve to arm you against false reports."
And I said: "Master, this account holds such
Assurance for me and so meets my thoughts,
All others would be embers. But now teach
Of these that pass. Of which ones have I read?
Such is the satisfaction I beseech."
Then he: "The one whose beard contrives to spread
Across his swarthy shoulders from his cheeks,
Was augur for a Greece devoid of males
Even in cradles. Therefore his name speaks,
Along with that of Calchas, for the sails
Launched by the cable cut in Aulis. Yes,
Eurypylus, the very one. I sing
Of him in my high tragedy. But less
Of that now, for you know it, the whole thing.
That other one, so skimpy in the loins,
Was Michael Scot, named for his land of birth:
He knew the game of disappearing coins.
Guido Bonatti, whose star charts were worth
Their weight in gold, which his Duke gladly paid.
Asdente, toothless soothsayer. Said sooth
He'd sooner now have foregone, like his teeth,
And made more shoes, his trade, and only truth.
And see those wretched women stream beneath
Who gave up needle, shuttle, distaff, thread,
And turned to telling fortunes, brewing spells
With herbs and dolls. But come, for Cain's white head
Of thorns now proves what no black art foretells—
With both the hemispheres confined, the waves
Below Seville shine silver, and last night
The moon was round. It's certain your mind saves
The memory, which sometimes eased your plight
Deep in the wood." And so, with much to say
Of lawful forecasts, we went on our way.

CANTO 21

From bridge to bridge, talking of other things
Of which my Comedy declines to sing,
We came to a high point: of all the rings
Of Malebolge, this was the next ring,
The next incision and the next vain tears,
And it looked strangely dark. The arsenal
Of Venice boils a pitch when winter nears,
Viscous, to caulk cracked ships and seal the hull.
In winter they can't sail. Instead, by one
10 A new ship's built, another plugs the ribs
Of his that often sails, and something's done
To this prow with a hammer, and that jib's
Patched up, and ropes are twisted, and a stern
Has some new post set upright while they stitch
A mainsail's edge: just so, not from a churn
Of fire but by divine art, a thick pitch
Was boiling down there which stuck to the bank
On every side. I saw it, but in it
Saw only how the bubbles rose and sank,
20 Swollen by boiling, settling in the pit.
While fixedly I gazed down there, my Guide
Said "Watch out! Watch out!" drawing me to him
From where I stood. Then I turned to one side
Like someone keen to see what is so grim

He must escape it, and is unmanned quite
By sudden fear, and, even while he still
Keeps looking, does not think to stay his flight
Because that urge does not wait for his will,
And I saw, running up the ridge behind,
A black devil. How savage was that face!
How fierce his actions seemed to my stunned mind:
The open wings, the light tread, and in place
Around his shoulders, that were sharp and high,
A sinner sat, held firmly by the feet.
From our bridge the black goblin gave the cry:
"You, Evil-Claws, here is your chance to meet
A grand old man of Lucca's ruling thieves.
You stick him under. I'll go back for more.
That city teems with them, and each believes
In barratry as if graft were the law,
Except, of course, Bonturo, still deemed clean
Up there where cash may conjure Yes from No:
They call him straight, that bunch. What can they mean?"
The imp flung down his load and turned to go.
Having addressed an audience unseen,
He left the ridge of flint in greater haste
Than any mastiff sent after a thief.
The load went under, by the pitch embraced,
Then popped up doubled up, but no relief
Was offered by the imps we couldn't see
Below the bridge. "The Holy Face," they cried,
"Of your cathedral isn't here to be
Your comfort, and the swimming in this tide
Is not your river Serchio. Unless
You want our hooks, stay down there in the pitch."
A hundred probing gaffs helped to express
Their theme. "Dance under cover in the ditch,
And if you have to steal, steal out of sight."
Just so, cooks make their scullions shove the meat
Down in the pot so it can't come to light.

My Master then to me: "To keep discreet
Your presence here, crouch down behind a rock
For shelter, and from outrage offered me
By anyone, you should not suffer shock.
I've seen these things. It's not a novelty."
He went on past the bridgehead, and when he
Came on to the sixth bank he soon had need
To show a firm front. With the spitting hate
And uproar of a pack of dogs that speed
70   From out of nowhere so the beggar's state
Of trance is not enough and he must plead,
These rushed out from beneath the bridge and drew
Their hooks on him. But he cried: "Let there be
No foolery from any one of you!
Before you catch me with a fork, let's see
Just one of you come forward that will hear
From me: and then decide what's to be done
About me and those hooks." Though they were near
They stopped, and cried: "Let Bobtail be the one."
80   So while the rest stood still, one moved. "What good,"
We heard him say, "will this do him?" My Guide:
"You think, Bobtail, somehow I safely could
Have come this far through everything your side
Could throw against me and not have the aid
Of God's Will and propitious fate? Now let
Us pass, for the decision has been made
Above, that I show one you haven't met
The savage path." Less insolent, the imp
Let fall his fork to clatter at his hooves
90   And told the rest of them, his voice gone limp:
"He can't be touched." My Guide: "I think that proves—
You that sit crouching in the rocks somewhere—
If you come back to me, you will be safe."
At which I rose, and, with no time to spare
I joined him, as I watched the devils chafe
At being still, a state they cannot bear.

They came on, at a clip that made me fear
They might not keep their promise. Thus, one time,
I saw troops less than eager to appear
Among their enemies. They feared a crime
As they, out of Caprona, moved unarmed,
Protected only by a guarantee.
Similarly afraid of being harmed
I pressed close to my Guide. All I could see
Was how they looked, which wasn't good, while they
Levelled their prongs, one saying "Shall I touch
Him on the rump?" I heard another say
"Sure, let him have it." But this seemed too much
For my Guide's interlocutor, who swept
Sharply around and said "Hold, Ragtag, hold!"
Then he to us: "To keep the path you've kept
By this ridge is impossible. The old
Sixth archway fell, and lies in bits below.
But if it is your pleasure to go on,
Go on along the rocky dyke: not so
Far off from here there is another ridge
Which grants a passage. Trust me. The time nears:
Five hours from now, minus one day, the bridge
Has lain there broken for twelve hundred years
And sixty-six more, when the world entire
Was shaken by one passion on one hill.
Some of this company goes to enquire
At my behest, if there be those who will
Be out to take the air. Go with them. None
Among them will molest you. Forward now,
Scumbag and Scallywag. Go, get it done.
And you, Dirtbag. And you can show them how
To do it, Tanglebeard. Let you go too,
Dogbreath and Blatherskite, and you, Pigface
With useful tusks, and Hairball, let's have you,
And Guttersnipe, and Snotnose. Search the place:
Check on the boiling tar, and let these through

Safely as far as the next ridge that goes
Intact across the ditches all the way."
I said: "My Master, what I see, who knows?
If you know how to get there, let us, pray,
Go there alone. An escort we don't need
And if we did, as cautious as you are,
Would you pick troops of this peculiar breed?
140 See how they grind their teeth and threaten far
More mischief for us yet with how they knit
Their brows." And he to me: "It is the lot
Of those down there, how they can worsen it,
That makes them fierce: so you need fear them not.
Just let them grind, and dodge the chips they spit."
Before they marched away on their new route,
Around the dyke there on the left they wheeled,
Poking their tongues out in a long salute—
A tribute to their captain in the field.
150 He turned, bent down, and as he watched them pass
He hailed them with the trumpet of his arse.

CANTO 22

I have seen horsemen ride, before today:
They moved camp, they rode out to the attack,
They mustered up, and sometimes rode away
Flat out in flight and they did not come back.
So, Aretines, I've seen scouts on your land,
And raiding parties ride, and seen the clash
Of tournaments and running jousts, a band
Of trumpets here, bells there, and then the smash
Of drums, and signals from the castle walls,
Flags that I knew, flags that were new to me—
But never horsemen moving to the calls
Of such a strange horn, no, nor infantry,
Nor ship that sailed by landmark or by star.
With these ten demons, savage entourage
Indeed, we went: but you know how things are—
Pray with the saints, drink with the sots. At large
My gaze roamed on the layout of the moat,
Each detail of the pitch, and all who burned.
Like dolphins when they signal men afloat
To save the ship by how their backs are turned
Above the wave tops, and the men take note,
So, now and then, a sinner would arch high
His spine to ease the pain, then hide again,
As quick as lightning. And as frogs will lie

Still in the ditch of water's edge or fen,
With just their muzzles out, the bulk of their
Fat bodies out of sight, not just their feet,
Just so the sinners, noses in the air,
Were otherwise unseen, but full retreat
Came only when foul Tanglebeard trod near,
And down they went beneath the boiling black.
I saw—and still my heart skips from the fear—
As when the frogs all dive yet one holds back,
One lingering soul, and Dogbreath, from close to,
Hooked him by his tarred hair and pulled him out
Just like an otter. I already knew
The names of all the imps, from the first shout
When they were chosen, and from what they'd called
Each other since. "Dogbreath, make sure you get
Your prongs right in there. Get some skin!" they bawled
In unison, those damned beasts, and worse yet.
"Master," I said, "please tell me, if you can,
Who this poor wretch is, helpless in the hands
Of enemies." My Leader asked the man,
Who said this: "In that loveliest of lands
The Kingdom of Navarre, there I was born.
My mother put me out to serve a lord,
For she had borne me to a wastrel, sworn
Foe to himself, who reaped his just reward:
Insolvency. The household of good King
Thibault was home to me, and there I gave
Myself to barratry. The reckoning
I pay in the thick heat of this black grave."
And then Pigface, his mouth armed like a boar's
With twin tusks, stuck one into him and ripped.
One mouse and many cats, their wicked paws—
For Tanglebeard now held him firmly gripped
And said: "Stand back and let me have him." Then:
"Ask him," this to my Guide, "if you would learn
More from him, before he gets shredded when

Another of my soldiers takes his turn."
Therefore my Leader said: "Tell us of those
Others beneath the pitch. Are any there
Italian?" He: "Just now, from one that knows
Them well, I parted. Now I'd like to share
That black redoubt with him again, no threat
From claw and hook." And Slimeball said: "That's it!
We've had enough!" and gaffed his arm to get
A muscle free to take like a titbit,

70 As Guttersnipe aimed low between the legs,
Whereat their captain with an ugly look
Wheeled on them all, so even they, the dregs,
Looked almost as if they'd been brought to book,
At which my Master quickly asked the man
Who still gazed at his wound: "But who is he,
The one you parted from—as you began
To say—so as to land unluckily
On this shore?" And he answered: "It was Fra
Gomita, from Gallura, of all fraud,

80 In each department, the undoubted star:
Within his grasp, the worst foes of his lord
Were so adroitly managed even they
Spoke well of him. He said: 'I took the cash
And they went quietly.' In every way,
In all affairs, no fuss, and nothing flash.
No petty crook, he was a sovereign cheat.
Don Michael Zanche keeps him company.
The Don's from Logodoro, so they meet
On common ground to talk incessantly

90 About Sardinia. I could say more
But look at that one grind his teeth! I fear
He wants to scratch my scurf and make it sore."
Their general turned to Slimeball, standing near
With rolling eyes and poised all set to strike.
"Get out of here," he ordered, "dirty bird!"
"If," said the frightened spirit, "you would like

To see or hear of those from Tuscany
Or Lombardy, I'll bring some here: but get
These Evil-Claws to stand back, lest they be
100 A source of fear to those who come. Now let
Me stand alone and whistle from this spot,
And I, just one, will summon seven. So
Our custom goes when one among our lot
Gets out." And Dirtbag's cruel face answered no,
With lifted snout and shaking head. Aloud
He said: "This is a trick of his, to throw
Himself down." At which he so well endowed
With stratagems said: "Yes, I am indeed
A trickster, making trouble for my friends."
110 But Dirtbag, though the rest paid the man heed,
Could not hold back, and threatened: "This truce ends
If you go down. I will come after you
Not galloping, but beating with my wings
Across the pitch. Now what we ought to do
Is get down off this peak and settle things
Against the dyke. We'll see if, on your own,
You more than match us." Reader, listen now
To news of a new sport. He stood alone
With all the demons watching to see how
120 He might jump, and the foremost was the one
Who'd been the least persuaded. From their dyke
They watched him. But as he had always done,
Man of Navarre, he chose his time to strike.
Planting his feet, he made a sudden leap
And left the marshal standing. They were all
Consumed with self-reproach, but none could keep
His anguish hidden less than he whose call
To let the quarry jump had wrecked the game.
So he went first, and cried "You're caught!" to no
130 Avail, for wings, though quick, are not the same
As terror. Down the prey went, and just so
The hunter went up with his lifted breast,

As instantly the wild duck goes below
And the falcon, vexed at having done its best
Without result, climbs back where it began,
With broken spirits. Guttersnipe, annoyed
At being tricked but keen to hunt a man—
The disappointment left him overjoyed—
Flew after him, and when he disappeared,
140　Turned on Dogbreath, right there above the ditch,
And clawed him, but hawk's claws are to be feared,
And this hawk was full grown. Into the pitch
They fell together. Bubbling heat soon seared
Them free from one another, but they stayed
Stuck in the glue that had weighed down their wings,
Till Tanglebeard, sad as the others, made
Four of them fly, across the taint that clings,
To the far bank, and each with practised haste,
Armed with his fork, as if this were a drill,
150　Came in to land and was correctly placed
On this side or on that. Then, to fulfil
The task, they pushed their gaffs out to the pair
Baked in their crust. We left them cooking there.

CANTO 23

Wordless, alone, without an escort, we
Went on. One walked behind the one ahead
As minor friars do. Insistently
My thoughts were driven by these scenes of dread
To Aesop's fable of the frog that tricked
The mouse into the stream and dived to drown
The mouse but when the mouse splashed the kite picked
The frog for its next meal and hurried down,
And both tales, for what happened at the start
And end, were just the same, the one aligned
With the other, and fear doubled in my heart
Just as the stories echoed in my mind.
It is by us, I thought, that they are fooled:
By injury and insult they are vexed.
Add anger to ill will and they are ruled
By double passion to make us their next
Objective, as if they, more savage still
Than any dog, snapped at the leveret.
Already my hair bristled at the thrill
Of fear, and so I stood with my stare set
Intently back, and said "Master, unless
You quickly hide us both, I am afraid
The Evil-Claws will catch us. I confess
I hear them make again the noise they made

When they thrived on a fugitive's distress."
And he: "Were I a mirror, I could not
Receive your outer image sooner than
Your inward now. Your thoughts make common lot
With mine in guise and action, so one plan
30 I make of both. If that slope on the right
Leads down into the next ditch after this,
We'll slip the hunt that haunts you in your fright."
His plan acquired an urgent emphasis
While he was still explaining it, for here
They came, with outstretched wings. They were intent
On taking us, and they were very near.
My Master took one look at them and bent
To pick me up, just as a mother would
Who wakes to hear the noise and see the fire
40 And picks the child up, thinking of its good
Above hers, as she flees, with no attire,
Even a shift, because time equals hope.
Down from the stone high ridge, flat on his back,
He let himself slide on the rocky slope
This side of the next ditch. At such a crack
Never ran water coursing through a sluice
To turn a mill wheel nearest to the blades
As my Guide did when he went fast and loose
Down that steep bank, and through the dry cascades
50 He bore me on his breast more as a child
Than a companion. Hardly had his feet
Touched down on the deep bedrock when that wild
Platoon was on the height above, to meet
Their fate made manifest, for the same high
Authority which gives them wings to guard
The fifth ditch has decreed they shall not fly
Beyond it. They knew that, but took it hard.
We found a painted people, there below,
Who circulated looking tired and sad.
60 They seemed defeated and their steps were slow.

In cloaks with cowl drawn forward they were clad
To hide their weeping eyes: cloaks of the kind
That Cluny monks wear, but these shone with gold,
As if to dazzle they had been designed.
Within, though, they were lead in every fold,
So heavy that those Frederick liked to see
Wrapped melting around traitors were mere straw.
A tiresome mantle for eternity!
We turned, still going left just as before,
70 Along with them, as they, preoccupied
With weeping, went, but, weary with their load,
They had to go so slowly, every stride
Of ours along that populated road
Brought us new company. Therefore I said
To my wise Leader: "Can't we, as we go,
Find someone among all these walking dead
Whose deeds we've heard of or whose name we know?"
And one caught by my Tuscan accent called
Out after us: "Slow down and get some rest!
80 You that so hasten through this air appalled
With dusk, perhaps you'll get what you request
From me." At which my Leader said "Let's wait,
And go on at his pace." I stopped, and saw
A couple who seemed in the mental state
To join us quickly, but their bodies bore
That load, and it was crowded on the way.
When they came up, each of them gazed awhile
Sideways at me and silent, and then they
Spoke to each other: "This one has the style
90 Of the alive. The workings of his throat—
A sure sign. And if both of them are dead,
By what rare privilege are they free to walk
Thus unencumbered by the cloak of lead?"
And then to me: "Tuscan, we know your talk.
You that have come to where the hypocrites
Assemble their sad faces, tired and worn

From faking a sincerity that fits
Their story, tell us yours. Where were you born?"
And I to them: "Where the fair Arno flows,
100 In that great city I was born and raised.
My soul is still contained in what it knows:
This body, mine from birth. Be not amazed,
But tell me who you are, for whom such pain
Distils itself and dribbles down each cheek.
What penalties drench you in golden rain?"
"So heavy you can hear each balance creak,
These yellow cloaks are lead," one answered me,
"One Guelph, one Ghibelline, we are the two
Jovial Friars of Bergamo. You see
110 The saviours of your city facing you—
I, Catalano: Loderingo he—
Both chosen by your council to bring peace
Where once one man alone fulfilled that role,
And the Gardingo district won't soon cease
To say how well we did it, on the whole."
Thinking of what they stole and where once stood
The Uberti palace, "Friars, your mad pride . . ."
I said, but said no more of what I would,
For then I saw one lying crucified
120 By three stakes in the ground. He saw me there,
And writhed all over, blowing on his beard
With sighs, and Catalano saw me stare,
And said: "That one who lies there, three times speared,
Is Caiaphas, who told the Pharisees
One man should do a people's suffering.
Stretched naked on the crowded pathway, he's
Well placed to feel the weight of everything
That comes along, as you can see. The same
For Annas—in this ditch put to the rack—
130 His mother's father, and for every name
On that black list to which the Jews trace back
Their troubles. Yes, I mean the Sanhedrin."

Then I saw Virgil standing there nonplussed
Above the one stretched vilely crosswise in
Eternal exile. "What you have discussed,"
He told the Friar, "for me is far from clear.
But if you are allowed, and if you please,
You'll tell us whether some way out of here
Lies near us on the right, so we may seize
140 Our chance to leave without a plea for aid
From black angels, that they may come to lift
Us up and fly us out." The Friar made
The following reply: "You were adrift
In all your estimates. Help is nearby,
Much closer than you hope. From the great wall
A ridge runs inward cutting through the sky
Of every valley so it links them all,
Except that, at this one, it lies a wreck.
You climb the ruins piled against the side,
150 A staircase starting level with this deck."
My Leader stood with bent head, mortified.
"The one that hooks the sinners over there
Sold us a bill of goods," he said, whereat
The Friar grinned. "Yes, wasn't that unfair?
I think I once heard, in Bologna, that
The Devil sometimes has resort to vice.
He has been known to say what isn't true.
I've heard he isn't really very nice."
My Leader strode on. As his anger grew,
160 His stride grew greater. Led by his sweet heels,
I left the souls who weigh the way guilt feels.

CANTO 24

In that part of the young year when the sun
Enters Aquarius to comb the hair
It shakes loose, and the long nights have begun
To turn south; when the frost is lying there,
A copy of its sister, the pure snow—
Except the pen's point soon grows blunt, the white
Is warmed away, and he, the shepherd, so
Annoyed when he woke up to the chill sight
Of snowy fields and thought he could not go
10 For fodder, slapped his thigh, and back inside
His house went to and fro to curse his fate
Like some poor wretch with doubt in every stride
Of what to do next, but the altered state
Strikes him when he goes out again, the rime
Has melted, the whole world has changed its face
And hope returned in such a little time,
He grasps his staff and out into the place
That shines no longer white he drives his sheep
To pasture. Thus my Master hurt my heart
20 Because his brow was clenched and furrowed deep,
But then the poultice came to soothe the smart,
For when we reached the ruined bridge, right then
He turned to me with that sweet smile I'd seen
When first I saw the mountain's foot, and when

He'd made a plan and picked the ruins clean
With his glance, he spread wide his arms for me
And held me, and as one who works and weighs
And reckons and provides beforehand, he,
While lifting me to one rock, bent his gaze
30 Upon another's suitability
To make its top a step. "Take that one there.
But first," he said, "see if it takes your weight."
A mantle here was not the thing to wear.
Though he was light and I was pushed, a great
Effort was needed going crag to crag,
And if the slope had been long on that dyke
As on the other, he'd have seen me flag.
For him, I don't know what that climb was like.
Since all of Malebolge dips towards
40 The inmost pit, the lie of every trench
Makes one side low. Where the last stone affords
A broken-off arrival point, this bench
I sat on with lungs bursting through my chest
From pain, and thought: No further. "Now you must,"
My Guide said, "quell the slothful urge to rest.
A swansdown seat and a soft blanket just
Keep you from fame, without which no one who
Consumes his life leaves more trace in the world
Than smoke in air and foam on water do.
50 Therefore arise, with your soul's flag unfurled
Above your fear, for so your soul prevails
In every battle if the body's weight
Can't sink it, and your enterprise entails
A longer stair yet, to a higher state.
Just to have left these spirits here is not
Sufficient. If you understand me now,
Do what you must, get more than you have got."
I rose then, trying hard as I knew how
To prove my breath was easy, and said "Go,
60 For I am strong and brave." We took our way

Up through the jagged narrows, twisted, slow,
Of this ridge steeper than the last. To stay
Alert, or seem to, I talked as we went,
At which a voice from the next ditch was heard,
Unable to say clearly what it meant.
But I, up on the transverse arch's crown
Already, knew that anger moved his speech.
Over the dark I bent my keen gaze down.
The dark went down too far for eyes to reach
70 The bottom. So I questioned: "What if we
Go on to the next bank and down its wall?
Because from here my hearing's doomed to be
One long misunderstanding, and for all
I see when I look down, there's nothing there."
"My one reply," my Guide said, "is to do
What you suggest. The answer to a fair
Request should be the silent deed." We two
Descended at the bridge's end, which meets
The eighth bank, and from there the ditch was clear
80 To my view, and the memory defeats
My words, and chills my blood with coiling fear.
I saw a writhing mass of every kind
Of serpent, and each kind was very strange.
Lucan in Libya could never find
Their equal in those hot sands to arrange
His catalogue of snakes to seize the mind,
Including those with one head at each end.
No, desert lands have no plagues on this scale
For poisoned multiplicity. Nor send
90 To Ethiopia to see the like, nor sail
The Red Sea, searching all its regions. These,
For cruelty and squalor, were as bad
As snakes can get. And through this heaving sleaze,
Ran people naked, terrified, who had
No hope of hiding place or to be made
Invisible by heliotrope. Their hands

Were tied behind with snakes, which slickly laid
Their heads and tails between the thighs, leg bands
Knotted in front. And look, a serpent sprang
100 On one who shared our bank, and hit the point
Where neck meets shoulder, and the serpent's fang
Started a fire, precisely at the joint,
Which spread as fast as you write *I* or *O*
With just one stroke, until he sank to ash,
And on the ground the dust reversed its flow,
Gathered itself together in a flash:
He was himself again. So they concur,
All the great sages, that the Phoenix dies,
And straight away is born again, in her
110 Five hundredth year, and in that time denies
Herself all herbs and grain. All she will eat
Is tears of frankincense and balsam, and
Spikenards and myrrh supply her winding sheet.
And just as one who can no longer stand—
But falls not knowing if the devil's force
Has dragged him down, or else some vital block
That binds a man, has been the secret source
Of weakness—when he rises, stares in shock
Around him, rattled by his pain, and sighs,
120 Such was this sinner when he rose again.
How stern the power of God, that can devise
Such and so many blows for vengeance! Then
My Leader asked him who he was. I quote:
"From Tuscany I came down like the rain
Not long ago into this feral throat.
A mule I was, a brute I would remain:
A man's life didn't please me in the least.
I started as a bastard, led the Blacks
In my town. Vanni Fucci, called the Beast,
130 Is my name. If you go back on my tracks,
You'll reach my den, Pistoia." Then I said
To my Guide, "Tell him not to slip away,

And ask him what crime weighed so on his head
To thrust him down this far, for the display
I saw was of a man of rage and blood."
The sinner heard, and did not feign, but set
His mind and look on me, his face a flood
Of shame. He said "I feel more anguish yet
That you have caught me in the misery
140 You see me in, than I felt then, when I
Was taken from the other life. For me
To leave your question without due reply
Is not allowed. Down this far I am brought
Because once, in the Sacristy of Fine
Adornments, when I stole, I had the thought
Of pinning that crime blasphemously mine
On someone innocent. Such was my sport.
So now you know. But lest my pain has been
Too sweet a sight, if ever you get out
150 Of these dark regions, add to what you've seen
The sound of what I say. Be in no doubt—
I speak to you, the White Guelph Florentine—
These things will happen. First, Pistoia will
Thin out the Blacks. Then Florence will revive
Her people and her ways. Mars will fulfil
His role for her, and find a Black to strive—
From Val di Magra he will ride to kill—
Against Pistoia's Whites. Nicknamed the Mist,
He'll bring sad clouds with him, a bitter storm
160 Of battle in Piceno's field. The list
Of horrors will grow long, and the fierce form
Of flame in a black sky touch every White.
I tell you this to haunt you in the night."

The thief raised both his hands when he said this,
Two fingers up from each, the figs: and cried
"You get it, God? You know what you can kiss?"
From then on, all the snakes were on my side,
For one looped round his neck, as if to say
"You've said enough." Another, as before,
Bound up his arms and in its usual way
Attached itself in front so he no more
Could make a move that brought them into play.
10 Pistoia, ah, Pistoia! Why not vow
To burn yourself to ashes and live on
No wicked moment more than you do now,
You that are worse than your bad seed long gone,
Colleagues of Cataline? Through all of Hell,
Its darkest circles, I saw not one shade
So arrogant, not even he that fell
At Thebes, Capaneus. So this one made
His exit, speaking not another word.
A raging centaur came past on parade.
20 His shout was of the pitch that peaks and breaks:
"Where is he, then, the crook?" I have not heard
Even Maremma has so many snakes
As he had on his croup as high as where
The horse form sleeps and human form awakes.
Behind his shoulders, high up near the hair,

A dragon spread its wings and set on fire—
Sending its breath down while it stayed up there—
Whomever it might meet. My Master said
"That's Cacus, who beneath the Aventine
30 Made many times a bloodbath for the dead,
And from his brothers takes a different line,
Another road, because he stole by fraud
A nearby herd and lured it to his cave.
The herd belonged to Hercules, his lord,
Who heard the cattle lowing, and so gave
Cacus, to end his mean streak at a stroke,
A lesson with his club. A hundred blows.
Not ten were felt." But while my Leader spoke,
The centaur had gone by and there arose
40 Three shades beneath us that we didn't see
Till they said "Who are you?" At which we ceased
To speak, our thoughts on them entirely.
I didn't know them, but by chance—increased
By time—one had to name another. "Where,"
One of them asked, "has Cianfa stopped?" That said,
To keep my Guide's attention focused there,
I held my finger upright so it led,
Touching, from chin to nose. If you are slow
To credit, reader, what I tell you now,
50 No wonder. I, who saw it to be so,
Scarcely believe it still. But this is how
It happened. While I kept the three in view,
A serpent with six legs ran up in front
Of one of them and stuck to him like glue
All over, so he bore this sudden brunt.
His paunch was seized on by the middle feet,
His arms by the front ones, while through his face
Fangs piercing either cheek were keen to meet.
His thighs were where the hind feet found their place,
60 And in between his thighs the tail was poked
And stretched up over his behind. No tree

Was ever yet with ivy tighter cloaked
Than this shade with the beast's disgustingly
Adapting limbs that hid the limbs they choked.
And then, as if they both were hot wax, they
Stuck to each other in a dreadful blend:
Their colours mingled and went either way
So both were one, with neither start nor end,
And how they looked before, you couldn't say
70 From seeing what they had become. Just so,
Across the paper, close before the flame,
We see a kind of coloured darkness go,
Not black yet, but the white dies just the same.
The other two looked on, and each cried "My,
Agnello, how you've changed! You are not two,
You are not one!" For once they didn't lie:
Two heads were one, one face shared, in plain view,
Only what two had not lost, and one pair
Of arms was made from four arms, and two thighs,
80 One belly and one chest were strangely there—
Shapes never seen before. When what had been
Was blotted out, all former features gone,
The gross deformity that seemed to mean
Two things but nothing clear, slowly moved on—
Still neither here nor there, but in between.
As does the lizard in the worst dog days
Seem lightning when it streaks from hedge to hedge
To someone trudging under the sun's blaze,
So suddenly appeared from our view's edge
90 A small and fiery vivid serpent, black
As peppercorn. Its path seemed set to strike
The bellies of the other two. Its track
Soon fixed on one, and by its navel—like
Our own part for receiving nourishment
When in the womb—it stuck to him, and then
Fell down before him and stretched out. Intent
On what had struck him, he, the stricken, when

He stared, said nothing. Silent, he stood still
And yawned, as if by sleep or fever sapped
Of understanding, energy and will.
He and the serpent eyed each other, wrapped
In one another's gaze and also in
The smoke that from the beast's mouth in a jet
Came pouring out to mingle with its twin
That poured from the man's mouth, so their smoke met.
Let Lucan now be silent when he prates
About Sabellus and Nasidius,
Snake-bitten soldiers. Better that he waits
To hear of this. The same for Ovid, who
Tells us how Cadmus turned into a snake
And Arethusa, fleeing nymph, changed too,
Into a fountain. True it is I take
No umbrage: Ovid doesn't once transmute
Two natures face to face as they exchange
Their substance. By an impulse more acute
These two were moved, the one to rearrange
Its tail into a fork, the wounded one
To blend its feet, the thighs together pressed
So close that soon the joinery was done
With no mark left by which you could have guessed
At separateness. And then the serpent's tail,
Divided as it was now, took the shape
Of human legs. Its skin turned soft and frail
While the other's hardened. Armpits were agape
To take in shrinking arms. The beast's front paws
That had been short, grew long to match the pace
Of shrinkage, and the hind paws, with their claws,
Twisted together, made the part men place
Away from view. His part, unbound by laws,
Put forth a pair of feet. While smoke involved
Them both with novel colours and supplied
More hair here, and yet there the hair dissolved,
One rose, one fell, but neither turned aside

The baleful gaze beneath which each had gained
The other's looks. He that was now upright
Lifted his face towards his temples, strained
The skin till it expelled, from being tight,
The excess matter that would form the ears
From both cheeks, and then, from the stuff still left,
There grew, as if the seconds now were years,
A nose, and from the mouth, that lipless cleft,
Lips of due size appeared. He that lay flat
Advanced his snout, and then the ears slid back
Into his head like snail's horns, and then that
Which spoke for him, his tongue, began to crack
And split in two. The other thing's tongue, split
Already, unified. Smoke ceased to flow.
The shade turned brute fled hissing in a fit
Along the ditch, the talking one not slow
To follow, nor to aim the human spit
That snakes don't like. But then he turned his new
Shoulders on that one and said to the third,
The one unchanged: "I would have Buoso do
What I have done, and do it word for word:
Run on all fours along this very road."
The dross of Level Eight I had now seen,
The dregs, the ship's least valuable load,
Had seen it change and interchange, and mean
One thing and then another. Should my pen
Fail in its task, let newness be my plea:
And if my eyes were getting tired by then,
My wits confused, still it was clear to me
That though they fled in secret, these two were
Puccio the Cripple, sole one of the three
Companions privileged never to incur
The agony of being thus reborn,
And he who brought to you the sword and spur,
Gaville, trading his wrath for your scorn—
Francesco Cavalcanti, name to mourn.

CANTO 26

Florence, rejoice! For you are grown so great
Your wings beat proudly over land and sea,
And even Hell proclaims your rich estate,
Speaking your name abroad, your destiny.
Among your citizens, I'd just found five
To shame me that I shared their place of birth.
Their skill at theft when they were still alive
Brought you no honour. What their schemes were worth
You'll find, if near the dawn our dreams come true,

10   When Prato rises up against your greed,
A craving felt by other places too:
The sooner done the better, and indeed
Done years ago it had been overdue—
It must be done, or it will weigh the more
On me as I grow older. We moved, then,
And on the stairs the rocks had made before
For our descent, my Leader climbed again
And drew me up. We went the winding way
Among the rocks and splinters, and the foot

20   Made no advance without the hand in play.
I grieved then and I grieve now when I put
My mind to what I saw, and I rein in
My powers more than usual, lest they run
Where virtue guides them not, and I begin

To curse the gift my lucky star, or one
Yet higher, gave me. Count the fireflies
The peasant sees when he rests on the hill—
In the season when the one who lights our eyes,
And all the world, least hides its face, and will
30 Soon sink to give the fly's place to the gnat—
The lights he sees along the valley floor
Might well be glowing in the vineyards that
He gathered grapes in, or the fields that wore
Him out from tilling them that day. The same
Number of lights were strewn in the eighth ditch
Gleaming, so I could see them when I came
Within sight of its base. The night looked rich:
A lake of lights, and each light was a flame.
Elias, whom the bears avenged when he
40 Was baited by small boys, once watched it flare—
Elijah's chariot, majestically
Drawn skyward when its horses pawed the air.
No matter how he fixed it with his eyes
He made out nothing but the flame alone:
He saw a little shining cloud arise,
The glow surrounding where the fire had flown.
Just so each flame here moves along the throat
Of this ditch and none shows it is a theft
Of some vile sinner's form we may not note.
50 I stood there on the bridge above the cleft
Grasping a rock as I stretched out to see.
For sure I would have fallen had I not
Held on—and then my Leader, seeing me
Look so intent, said "All these flames are what
False counsellors must wear and be burned by."
"Master," I said, "I'm sure now, having heard
You speak, of what I guessed. Already I
Wanted to ask, before you said a word,
About that fire, divided at its peak
60 As if it were the pyre of those two sons

Of Oedipus who killed each other. Speak
Of who is in there. Are there two? Which ones?"
He answered. "Two are punished there inside.
Ulysses is in there, and Diomed.
In vengeance now together they are tied
As once in wrath. They groan for pain and dread
Within the flame, and for the clever plan
Of the gift horse that opened up the gate
For the noble seed from which great Rome began
70 To first burst forth, and in that fiery state
They rue their craft by which Deidamia
Gave them Achilles, and they feel the heat
For what they stole from Troy and took so far
The stricken city sought its own defeat:
Pallas Athena's image. There they are.
The thieves of the Palladium. In there."
"If they can speak," I told my Guide, "I pray,
If they can speak inside these lights they share,
This light, I pray that you might let me stay—
80 May it avail a thousand times, this prayer—
Until that flame with double horn comes near.
You see I bend towards it with desire."
And he: "Your prayer deserves praise, never fear:
And therefore I will grant what you require.
But guard your tongue. I'll be the one to speak.
I understood what you would like to know,
And they might scorn your language: they were Greek."
After the flame had reached the time and place
My Guide thought fitting, thus he spoke to it:
90 "You that are two within one fiery space,
If while I lived you ever thought me fit
To be respected when I wrote of you—
If I was worthy of you, whether much
Or little, when I did my best to do
You justice with my heightened lines—let such
Devotion from me sway you to stand still

While one of you tells where, when he was lost,
He went to die." Hearing my Master's will,
The larger of the flaming horns was tossed
100 And murmured as if by the wind misled.
Its point waved to and fro as if it were
A tongue that spoke, a voice thrown out, that said:
"When I left Circe, having lived with her
More than a year in Italy, before
Aeneas got there, no love for my son,
No duty to my father, and what's more
No love I owed Penelope—the one
Who would have been most glad—could overcome
In me the passion that I had, to gain
110 Experience of the world, and know the sum
Of virtue, pleasure, wisdom, vice and pain.
Once more I set out on the open sea,
With just one ship, crewed by my loyal men,
The stalwart who had not deserted me.
As far as Spain I saw both shores, and then
Morocco, and Sardinia, and those
Numberless islands that the sea surrounds.
But men grow old and slow as the time goes,
And so did we, and so we reached the bounds
120 Of voyaging, that narrow outlet marked
By Hercules so nobody should sail
Beyond, and anybody thus embarked
Knows, by those pillars, he is sure to fail.
Seville on my right hand, I left behind
Ceuta on my left. 'Brothers,' I said,
'Dangers uncounted and of every kind
Fit to make other sailors die of dread
You have come through, and you have reached the west,
And now our senses fade, their vigil ends:
130 They ask to do the easy thing, and rest.
But in the brief time that remains, my friends,
Would you deny yourselves experience

Of that unpeopled world we'll find if we
Follow the sun out into the immense
Unknown? Remember now your pedigree.
You were not born to live as brutes. Virtue
And knowledge are your guiding lights.' I gave
With these words such an impulse to my crew
For enterprise that I could not, to save
140 My life, have held them back. We flew
On oars like wings, our stern, in that mad flight,
Towards the morning. Always left we bore.
Stars of the other pole we saw at night,
And ours so low that from the ocean floor
It never once arose. Five times the light
Had kindled and then quenched beneath the moon
Since first we ventured on our lofty task,
When we could see a mountain, though not soon
Could see it clearly: distance was a mask
150 That made it dim. But it was high, for sure:
Higher than anything I'd ever seen,
It climbed into the sky. Who could be more
Elated than we were, had not we been
Plunged straight away into deep sorrow, for
The new land gave rise to a storm that struck
Our ship's forepart. Three times the waters led
Us in a circle. Fourth time, out of luck.
Stern high, bow low, we went in. Overhead
Somebody closed the sea, and we were dead."

CANTO 27

The flame already was erect and still,
Saying no more as it prepared to go—
According to my gentle Poet's will—
When, with a sound that it was hard to know
The meaning of, arrived another flame
Behind it, and that strange noise drew our gaze
Towards the new fire's point from which it came,
A blurred voice at the apex of the blaze.
Just as that bull designed in Sicily,
10   To roast the tyrant's victims, bellowed first
With the voice of him by whom it came to be—
He shaped it with his file, wishing the worst
For all that it would kill: his fate was just—
Just as that bull, although it was of brass,
Cried with its victims' voices so it must
Have seemed thrust through with pain, no words could pass
Straight from this fire, no matter how unstrung.
But after they had come up through the flame,
All the vibrations that had moved the tongue
20   Were given to the point, to sound the same.
"You there to whom I speak," we heard him say,
"Who just spoke Lombard, saying 'Let it wait,
The rest of it: time to be on your way,'
Though I have come, perhaps, a little late,

Please don't be irked to stay and talk awhile:
You see it doesn't bother me, and I
Am burning. If just now into this vile
Blind world you fell from Italy on high,
The sweet land where I got the guilt I bring
Down here, then tell me of the Romagnoles:
Do they have peace, or war? For I still cling
To memories of land that climbs and rolls,
The mountains looming over everything
Between Urbino and the final height
That sets the Tiber free." I was still bent
To listen when my Leader, with a light
Touch to my side, said "You know what he meant,
So speak to him. He comes from Italy."
I knew my answer, which without delay
I gave. "O soul kept here in secrecy,
You know there's not, nor ever was, a day
When your Romagna's tyrants, in their hearts,
Were not at war. But I saw none who were
Overtly so when I left. In those parts
Ravenna stands as usual. Over her
The Eagle of Polenta broods: its wings
Keep Cervia covered. Forlì, that once bore
A long siege and reduced the French to strings
Of blood and guts, now finds itself once more
Beneath the Green Claws. Both the young and old
Mastiffs that ruled in Rimini and made
A shambles of Montagna, take and hold
And tear up with their fangs all those they flayed:
Two Malatestas of Verrucchio,
Dogs on the loose. Faenza, Imola,
Bow down to one who, as the seasons go,
Changes his party, and his markings are
White lair, young lion. By the Savio
Bathed on its flank, Cesena, in between
Mountains and plain, to tyranny one day

And liberty the next will always lean.
But who you are I now beg you to say,
So your name in the world may keep its place.
Be not more slow to send your words my way
Than I to you, for courtesy and grace."
True to its usual manner the flame roared
Awhile, then moved its sharp point here and there
And gave breath: "If I thought now to afford
An answer to one bound to breathe the air
70   Again in the fair world, this flame would stand
With no more movement, but since none return
Alive from these depths, if I understand
Correctly what I hear, how could I earn
More infamy that I have now? A man
Of war I was at first, and then, to make
Amends, or so I thought, I had a plan
To be a friar of Francis, and to take
The cord. Indeed it would have all come true
But Boniface, the Great Priest—give him Hell!—
80   Pulled me back in. The things I used to do
I did again, the old sins. It were well
That you should know the how and why. When I
Still wore my mother's gift of flesh and bone,
My deeds were not the lion's. I was sly,
A fox. All wiles and ways to slink alone
Unseen, I knew, and practised hidden arts
So everywhere on Earth they were renowned.
Then, when I came to where our youth departs
And men should strike their sails and make a round
90   Heap of the ropes, that which before had been
So pleasing grieved me. With repentance, then
Confession, I turned friar. I was clean.
Ah, misery! For then the worst of men,
The Prince of the new Pharisees—at war
Right there in holy Rome, and not with Jews
Or Saracens, but Christians who before

Had neither conquered Acre nor would choose
To fight the Saladin against the law
Forbidding mercenaries—in despite
100 Of his own holy order's sacred chair,
And my cord of devotion, best worn tight
To make the wearers thin from what they wear,
As Constantine brought back Sylvester from
Soracte with a cure for leprosy,
So this man came to me for a nostrum
To cure the fever of his pride. To me,
Guido da Montefeltro! While he sought
My counsel, I was silent, for his speech
Seemed profligate with drink, or so I thought.
110 He spoke again: 'Trust me, and let me reach
Your heart. Henceforth your sins are all absolved
Forever. All you have to do is teach
My troops what stratagems might be involved
In flattening Palestrina, the stronghold
Of the Colonna. That the power is mine
To lock and unlock Heaven, you've been told
And know well. Know, too, that my sign
Of office, the two keys that Celestine
Did not hold dear, I do.' And thus his weight
120 Of argument, despite what it might mean,
Drove me to where my silence seemed the state
Of most offence. And so 'Father,' I said,
'You cleanse me of the sin which I must now
Embrace, and in the scant observance bred
From lavish promise you will soon endow
Your lofty seat with triumph.' Thus, as soon
As I was dead, and Francis came, a black
Cherub told him: 'You can't grant him the boon
Of taking him with you. He must come back
130 With me among my minions, for he gave
Fraudulent counsel, and from that day on
I had him by the hair until the grave.

For no crime not repented of is gone,
Nor can repentance and the will to do
An evil coexist. They contradict
Each other.' I, poor broken wretch, was too
Shocked not to tremble when he laid his strict
Arrest on me and said: 'Well, now you know:
I'm a logician.' Down to Minos borne,
140   Eight times I saw him flex his tail to throw
A coil around his rough back: a tail torn
By his own teeth, such was his rage. And he:
'This wicked one is for the fire of thieves.'
And therefore I am lost here, as you see,
And clothed like this I go as one who grieves
In burning bitterness." And speechlessly
The mourning fire departed, pointed tip
Twisting and tossing. We, I and my Guide,
Moved on with constantly adjusted grip
150   Over the ridge to where, on its far side,
The arch begins that spans the ditch where they
Who gain by sowing discord come to pay.

Even with fluent words and with the tale
Told often, who could tell of all the blood
And wounds that I now saw? All tongues would fail
For certain. Overwhelmed with such a flood
Of fact, our speech and memory can stand
Only so much. If all those stricken folk
In Southern Italy, that fateful land,
Who once bewailed their blood shed by the stroke
Of Trojan sword, could only be one band
Again—but they knew also the long war
With Carthage, when the golden Roman rings
Were piled in heaps by Hannibal: a store
That Livy notes, true always in these things—
And if to all of these were added more,
The ones who suffered grievous blows when they
Resisted Robert Guiscard, and all those
Whose bones at Ceperano to this day
Still lie in heaps, and everybody knows
The Southerners broke faith; and it was hard
By Tagliacozzo that Alado won
Purely by strategy, his troops unscarred,
But on his victims fearful work was done;
And if some were to show limbs that were cut,
And others were to show the limbs they lost,

10

20

It would be horrible and endless, but
Nothing beside the mess that had been tossed
To fester in the ninth ditch. Not a cask,
Through loss of end-board or of stave, could gape
Like one I saw who, from below the mask
30   Of pain that was his face but held its shape,
Was torn wide open right down to the crack
That farts. Between his legs his entrails hung:
Intestines on display, and the foul sack
That turns the food we swallow into dung.
While I was all eyes, he looked back at me
And with his hand he further spread his breast,
Saying: "Behold, I split myself. You see
Mahomet mangled. And there go the rest
Before me. First Ali, my son-in-law,
40   His face from chin to forehead sliced in two,
Then everyone who in the life before
Sowed scandal, schism, and therefore must do
Time twice. Thus we who split things are now split.
There is a devil in behind us here
Who cruelly cares for us and sees to it
That all who make the circuit and are near
To healing as they come around again
With closing wounds on this sad thoroughfare,
Will meet the cleaving sword's edge there and then
50   In front of him. But who are you up there
Who lingers on the ridge? Do you delay
In fear of penalties for what you are
Accused of?" "Neither has he reached the day
Of death," my Master said, "nor yet by far
Does guilt bring him to torment. But to give
Him full experience, he must be brought
Down here by me, I who no longer live,
But know the way through Hell from its forecourt
Through circle after circle to the end.
60   And as you hear me speak, this is as true."

More than a hundred heard this from my friend
And stopped to look at me, their wonder too
Intense for pain to be remembered. "Soon,
Perhaps, you'll see the sun again. Tell Fra
Dolcino, then, that down here, where the moon
Gives all the light, he surely won't be far
Behind me if he doesn't stock supplies
Of food against the fall of mountain snow
That just might give Novara the surprise
70 Victory it shouldn't have." All set to go,
With one foot raised, Mahomet said all that,
Then set it on the ground and left. Then one
With pierced throat, nose cut off exactly at
The eyebrow's bottom line, and one ear done
Away with, stopped with all the rest to gaze
In wonder, and before them all he cleared
His windpipe, which outside wore a red glaze,
And said: "In one piece you have here appeared,
For guilt does not condemn you that I met—
80 Unless too close a likeness tricks my brain—
Above in Italy. Please, don't forget—
If ever you return to the sweet plain
That from Vercelli slopes to Macabò—
Piero da Medicina. Make it known
To Fano's two chief men—make sure they know,
Guido and Angiolello—they'll be thrown
Out of their ship and drowned. This comes to pass
Near La Cattolica, through treachery
Of a foul tyrant. No crime of this class
90 Was ever seen by Neptune in the sea
From Cyprus to Majorca, whether done
By pirates or by Greeks. That traitor who
Sees with one eye, the Young Mastiff that none
Can challenge now in Rimini—and you
Already know that someone here would like
Not to have seen that city—will contrive

To bring them to a meeting, and then strike
In such a way that they will not arrive,
Nor need to pray against Focara's gale,
100 That deadly wind they'll never have to face."
And I: "Point out to me and tell his tale,
The one for whom the mere sight of that place,
Rimini, was so bitter. Give me this,
If you would have me carry back your news
Into the world." Not minded to dismiss
A threat to all that he had left to lose,
He reached out sideways to another's jaw
And forced it open, crying "Here he stands
And does not speak. Expelled from Rome by law
110 He fled to Caesar in the Gallic lands,
And told him that delay, for one prepared,
Meant loss, and he should cross the Rubicon:
And by that bad advice, war was declared
And glory won, but unity was gone."
The tribune Curio! And how aghast
He seemed, his tongue slit in his throat, the man
Who spoke so boldly, back there in the past.
But now, with both hands missing, one began
To lift his torn stumps through the murky air
120 So blood besmirched his face that said "You will
Remember Mosca also, who was there
In Florence to say something fit to kill
The members of two families, one his own:
'A deed that's done is over.' So I said,
And should be here for saying that alone,
For still today the Tuscans count the dead."
I added "Death to all your stock," at which
With sorrow heaped on sorrow, off he went
Crazy with grief. But I stayed in the ditch
130 To watch the ruined people, how they spent
Their time, and then I witnessed such a sight
As I would fear to tell of, had I not

More facts held in reserve than now I write
In my account of it; but I have got
My conscience here to bolster me, the good
Companion that can render a man bold
Under the breastplate of his pure manhood.
I saw, and seem to see still—all I've told
Is true, and this is too—a headless thing
140　That walked with all the rest of the sad band.
It held its severed head by the bunched string
Of its own hair, and swung it with its hand
As if it were a lantern. The head stared
At us, and "Woe is me" was what it said.
A light unto itself, the two were paired—
The shining lantern and the bright-eyed head—
Finding a path as only He would know
Who governs. When it reached us at the bridge
Where we stood high so it was just below,
150　It exercised its awful privilege
And raised its head high with its arm, and so
Its words were nearer to us. These were they:
"See now my grievous punishment, you there
Who breathe, and look, as you go on your way,
Upon the dead: see if just one despair
Can match mine. And, so you may tell one day
My news, know now the man that I once was:
Bertran de Born, noble and troubadour.
Henry, young king of England, just because
160　Of my bad counsel, made unlawful war
Against his father. When Ahithophel
Wickedly goaded Absalom to fight
Against King David, he did no more well.
Because I parted two that had the right
To crowns, I carry now my brain through Hell,
But sundered from the corpse that was its root—
For such a crime, the punishment to suit."

CANTO 29

Strange wounds for many people had so made
My eyes drunk, that they would have stayed and wept,
But Virgil said: "How is your gaze repaid
By lingering down there where they are kept,
So many kinds of miserable, maimed shade?
You haven't done this in the other rings.
You want to count them? Then consider this;
That valley, its floor crawling with those things,
Runs twenty-two miles round. And did you miss
10 The moon? Already it's beneath our feet.
The time permitted to us now is short,
And there is more to look at than will meet
Your eyes here." I said: "Had you given thought
To why I looked, you might have granted me
A longer stay." While I made that reply
My Leader had moved on unheedingly.
"I think," I added, "in that cave, where I
Stared so intently just now, there might be
A shade, my kin, who now weeps for the pain
20 Which is guilt's price down there." My Master said
"From now on you should let your thoughts remain
Untroubled by his fate. Let them be led
By other things. Let that one stay down there.
Below the bridge, he pointed up at you

And fiercely shook his finger with an air
Of threat. I heard a name I thought you knew:
Geri del Bello, yes? But you were so
Wrapped up in him whose head was his to hold
As once he held Hautefort, that there was no
30 Chance you would see, even if you were told,
The other one until he went." "My Guide,"
I said, "My father's cousin is not yet
Avenged for the foul blow by which he died.
The partners in his shame seem to forget
They owe him this, and so he was outraged
And therefore, as I judge, without a word
To me, he moved on, and the war he waged
Within himself so silently has stirred
In me much more compassion than before."
40 Did grace desired mean honour's claims deferred?
We talked of this until the nearest bluff
Which shows the next ditch from the ridge. With more
Light on the subject we'd have seen enough
To know what it was like down to its floor.
But as things were, when we arrived above
That final cloister so that we could see
Its sad lay brothers, then I had to glove
My stunned ears with my hands for sympathy,
Because the shafts of sorrow they let loose
50 Were barbed with pity and the grief was strange
That thus assailed us. It was not diffuse:
It was as if some cruel force might arrange
That all the ills of all the hospitals
Of all of Val di Chiana from July
Until September, and Maremma's halls
Of fever, and all those marked soon to die
In sick Sardinia, should pack the walls
Of one crypt. So it was here, and the stink
Came out of it as if from limbs that rot.
60 Down from the last ridge, down to the last brink

Still keeping left we climbed, until I got
A clear view downward all the way to where
Justice Infallible, the Sovereign Lord's
Handmaiden, marks the names and keeps in care
The counterfeiters, and where she awards
Their punishment. No, no more sorry sight
Was offered by Aegina's populace
When all of it was stricken by the blight,
The air so pestilential in that place
70 All animals down to the merest worm
Fell dead, and Jupiter transformed the ants
To men, so that the plague should have its term
And the ancient tribes might have a second chance,
Or so the poets say. But this was worse,
This sight, along the valley, of the shades
Who lay in heaps, and every heap diverse.
One lay face down, one made his shoulder blades
The bed-frame for another, and one moved
On hands and knees along that dreadful road.
80 Speechless and step by step we went. They proved,
The sick, they had no strength to bear the load
If they should try to raise themselves. We saw,
We heard. I saw two sitting propped
Against each other like pans set next door
To one another so the cold is stopped
From getting in between, and these two wore
Thick scabs from head to foot. No curry comb
Was ever plied by stable boy urged on
By master eager to ride out from home,
90 Or boy awake too long with patience gone,
As were the raking nails of these two souls
Against their own skins and the endless rage
Of that itch no emollient controls,
And bit by bit, but always at the stage
Of just beginning, their nails scraped them free
Of scabs, just as the knife strips off the scales

Of bream, or fish with larger finery.
But cleaning fish succeeds. This always fails.
My Leader said to one of these two "You
Whose fingers take your armour off one link
Of chain mail at a time, and sometimes do
The work of pincers, tell us what you think:
Are there Italians here? Your nails may toil
Forever at the task that they have now."
"Italians both, we who make you recoil
At our disfigurement. But tell us how
You're here to ask this," said one as he wept,
And then my Leader: "I am one who goes
From level down to level and have kept
This living man with me, and he well knows
My mission is to show him Hell." Then they
No longer could support themselves, and each
Turned trembling toward me. Further away
Others turned also, who had heard this speech.
My Master drew close, saying "Tell them what
You want." And since he wanted that, I said:
"So that the minds of living men may not
Forget your name, so it may not be dead
To that sweet world, and live for many years,
Say who you are and from what people. May
Your loathsome sentence not arouse false fears
That you will suffer further if you say
These things to me." And one replied: "Know me
For Griffolino of Arezzo. I
Was burned by Albert of Siena. He
Called me magician. But that wasn't why
I came here. It is true I said to him
That I could rise up through the air and fly,
And he, inquisitive if somewhat dim,
Told me to show him how, and just because
I didn't make him Daedalus, he had
Me burned by the Inquisitor, who was

His natural father. But to this last sad
Ditch of the ten, I was condemned and sent
For something worse. Minos, who doesn't err,
Got me for alchemy. That's how it went.
I'm here now because that's the way things were."
I to my Poet: "When was there so light
A people as the Sienese? By far
140 The French are less so." Then the leprous fright
Who had been silent, spoke. "Perhaps some are,
But Stricca wasn't. He knew how to spend
In moderation so well he took weeks
To bring his patrimony to an end.
Then there was Niccolò. The whole world speaks
Of how he made the clove into the taste
No one could eat without. He knew the seed,
The root, the garden. He knew how to waste
A fortune. And we also should pay heed
150 To those twelve of the Spendthrift Club, the gang
Who dressed in gold and silver, man and horse.
Their money talked and those who loaned it sang
In vain. To help that bunch in their wise course
Was Caccia of Asciano, who burned through
A vineyard and a forest, and that great
Official whose sound judgement we bowed to—
The dolt we called the Blunderer. But wait:
You should know now who seconds you in your
Appraisal of the Sienese. Look hard
160 At me, for you have seen this face before.
Look past the blisters, give me your regard,
And see Capocchio, in Siena cooked,
Without the cloves, for alchemy. I made
Fake metals, but you know how good they looked,
If you are who I think you are. My trade
Was falsifying nature. I did well
In life. But everything is real in Hell."

CANTO 30

When Semele was loved by Jupiter
And Juno raged because of it, and shook
The house of Thebes to make it kneel to her
Time after time, Athamas could not brook
Her anger, and went mad, and when he saw
His wife go by weighed down on either side
With their two children he cried "Tooth and claw!
Let's spread the nets and capture all the pride:
The lioness and both the cubs, as they
Go by." And he himself had claws that grasped
One child, Learchus, whirling him away
To dash him on a rock. She, while she clasped
The other child, escaped, but just to drown:
And then, when Fortune laid the Trojans low
From their great loftiness, and brought them down
From where they once dared all, and spurned them so
That king and kingdom both lay in the dust,
Sad Hecuba, forlorn, enslaved, when she
Saw Polyxena dead, and knew that must
Be Polydorus on the beach, though he
Was hard to recognise, quite lost her mind
For grief, and, like a dog, she barked. But no
Fury that fell on Thebes or Troy could find
A place—no matter whom it struck and though

It tore up beasts and limbs of men—next to
The cruelty that now I saw. Two pale
And naked shades ran as a hog might do
Loosed biting from the sty, one to assail
Capocchio. Sharp fangs sunk in his neck's nape,
30 It dragged him and his scabs along the ditch
Whose hard floor made his itchy belly scrape.
Then Griffolino, left to look and twitch
Beside me, said: "That goblin in a rage
Is Gianni Schicchi, and he deals with all
That way, himself the great fraud of his age."
And I to him: "So it may not befall
The other one should fix its teeth in you
Before it makes off, tell me who it is."
And he to me: "The shade of Myrrha, who
40 Was by her father, as if she was his
By law, made concubine. She joined the sin,
Pretending she was someone else; as that
One there, who goes off, took the whole world in—
To get the horse that everyone aimed at,
The Lady of the Stud, he took the name
And style of Buoso di Donati, made
The will, and then, to prove his wily fame,
Faked Buoso's death in bed. Such was the trade
Of Gianni Schicchi, and his lasting shame.
50 A mimic. May his lustre never fade."
And when those two on whom I'd kept my eyes
In all their fury had at last moved on,
I turned to all those ill-born others. Prize
Exhibit among those was one upon
Whom fingers might have played. He was a lute,
Or would have been, if cut short at the groin
From that part where a man is forked. Acute
Dropsy—by which the members cease to join
In just proportion, humours are disposed
60 The wrong way, and the belly answers not

The face—decreed his lips were never closed,
Much like the rabid one whose thirst runs hot
So one lip curls down always to the chin,
The other upward. "You that walk here free
From any kind of punishment for sin
Through this grim world, how such a thing could be
Who knows? But look, give heed now to the grief
Of Master Adam. While alive, I had
All that I wished, but now know no relief
70   From thirst for just one drop of water. Mad,
The mere thought makes me of the little streams
That from green hills of Casentino flow
Down to the Arno, channels like sweet dreams
Run cool and wet before me, and are no
Frivolity, for just their image seems
To parch me worse than all the ills that waste
My features. The unbending justice which
Examines me and makes me breathe in haste
Starts up there where I sinned, not in this ditch:
80   There in Romena, where I falsified
The coins stamped with the Baptist, and for that
I left my body up there when I died,
All burned. But even if I could be at
My dearest Fonte Branda, I would give
That chance for only one glimpse of the three
Brothers who got me into it. Two live:
There's Alessandro and that other one. For me
The one who counts is Guido, and he's here
Already, if those angry shades who run
90   Around this ring speak truth. Why would he fear
Me, though? My limbs imprison me. Just one
Inch in a hundred years: if I were just
That light, I would have set out on the road
To find him among all these misshapes. Trust
My promise, though I'd have to haul my load
Eleven miles around and more than half

A mile across. But through them, here I am.
I made the golden coin a golden calf.
Our florin, pride of Florence, was a sham,
100   Minted by me. Three carats of hardware
To drain its worth." And I to him: "Those two
Poor wretches lying near your border there
Who give off smoke the same way wet hands do
In winter, who are they?" And he: "You care?
I found them when I rained into this trough.
They didn't move then, and they haven't since,
Nor will they stir, unless my guess is off,
For all eternity. You think she'd wince
At least, that lying wife of Potiphar
110   Who did for Joseph. Sinòn is the Greek
Who fooled the Trojans. And now here they are,
A pair of fatal fabulists. That reek
Comes from their burning fever." Then Sinòn,
Who took it ill, perhaps, that he had come
To be so scorned, punched his accuser on
His paunch of leather, which boomed like a drum,
And Master Adam struck him in the face
With his huge arm—his punch seemed no less hard—
Saying: "Although my limbs keep me in place
120   By their great weight, still I am not debarred
In such a case, from having one arm loose."
Sinòn replied: "When you went to the fire,
You hadn't, but you had it free for use
When striking false coin. All you could require
Of strength you had then, so that's no excuse."
The dropsied one said: "In this you speak true,
But nothing that you said was true in Troy,
Where simple truth was all they asked of you,
A guest they had made welcome, and with joy."
130   "If I spoke falsely," said Sinòn, "the fault
Was mine just once. You with your lying coins
Struck many times. You kept up an assault

That earns you, more than anyone who joins
Us here, a place of honour." Thus addressed,
He of the paunch replied: "The horse, the horse!
Remember, perjurer, the way you pressed
Your wooden gift on them, and let remorse
Plague you that all the world has come to know."
"And you be plagued," the Greek said, "with the thirst
That cracks your tongue, and with that liquid so
Corrupt it swells your guts into the first
Thing that you see, a hedge before your eyes."
The counterfeiter then: "Thus your mouth gapes
To set you wrong, and never otherwise.
I thirst, yes, and foul humour cruelly shapes
My belly so that it attains this size,
But you have burning fever, your head aches,
And you would need small urging to lick dry
The mirror of Narcissus. All it takes
Is just to say it's made of water." I
Was all absorbed in listening, but then
My Master said: "You keep this up much more
And I will lose my patience with you." When
I heard him speak it shook me to the core,
He was so angry, and with so much shame
I turned towards him that it haunts me still
In memory. My thoughts were just the same
As in one of those dreams when something ill
Is being done to you, and in the dream
You wish it were a dream, so that you long
For that which is as if it weren't, and seem
To see yourself afraid, and are not wrong.
Just so, I felt I'd lost the power to speak
From wanting to excuse myself, and yet
Excused myself until my voice grew weak
Repeating all I hoped he would forget.
"Much greater faults than yours are washed away
By much less shame," my Master said. "Unload

Your heart of all grief. I am here today
170 And always, at your side on the long road,
To tell you, if by chance you're led astray
By people in a quarrel, that the wish
To listen while they fight is devilish."

The self-same tongue that first had stung me so
It dyed my cheeks with shame by what it said,
Had offered me the medicine. As we know,
Achilles' spear, that was his father's, wed
Those same two properties. It first brought woe,
And then brought solace. Thus we turned away
From that sad valley, and went up the bank
Enclosing it, with no word left to say.
Here it was less than night—sight wasn't blank
10 Ahead—though it was also less than day,
So I could not see far. But I could hear
A horn's blast, so loud that it would have made
A thunderclap sound faint. It rang so clear
That straight from me to it the path was laid
For my gaze to rebound. Not when Charlemagne
Lost to the Saracens in one sad rout
His sacred army, did Roland in pain
Raise up his horn in such an awful shout—
His ivory horn, lamenting for the slain,
20 That his king heard three miles away. Not long
Was my head turned that way before I thought
To see tall towers in a looming throng.
"Master," I said therefore, "tell me what sort
Of city stands out there." And he to me:

"Because you gaze through shadows far too deep
Your fancy strays, and when you're there you'll see
How distance tricks the senses. Therefore keep
Your steps ahead. More speed." And kindly he
Said as he took my hand: "Before we go
30   Much further, so the fact may seem less strange:
Those things ahead aren't towers. You should know
They're giants, and around the pit they range,
Sunk, from the navel down, in its rock rim."
As when the mist thins, and sight bit by bit
Gives shape again to what has been made dim
By air the cloud loads, so I conquered it,
That thick and foggy atmosphere, and neared
The brink, but as I did so, error fled
And was replaced by everything I feared,
40   The hints and outlines of a sight to dread.
For just as on the circle of its walls
Montereggione has towers for a crown,
So, on this pit's embankment, it befalls
That giants tower, although from halfway down
They are unseen. But what is seen bulks large
And horrible as when they first attacked
Olympus, and Jove had to stem their charge,
And still shouts thundering vengeance for that act.
Now I began to pick one out: the face,
50   The shoulders and the chest, and a good part
Of the belly, and, by both sides held in place,
The arms. Yes, Nature, when she quit the art
Of making creatures of this kind, did right
To keep from Mars the warriors he would
Have wished for. Though she still smiles on the might
Of elephants and whales, we think that good,
If we look carefully. She's just and wise,
For only when ill will and massive strength
Are joined with mental power does it arise
60   That the invincible is born. The length

And bulk of the great man-high bronze pine cone
In Rome before St. Peter's: thus his head.
And he was huge not in his head alone:
His bones were in proportion. As I said,
The bank, his apron, hid him from the waist
On down, but up above he was on show
To such an altitude you could have placed
Three Frieslanders, whose startling height we know,
One on the next and they would vainly hope
To reach his hair. From that notch where a man
Buckles his cloak you could have hung a rope
Straight down for seven strides. The mouth began
To cry: "Palabra wort kotoba word parole!"
Such senseless sounds had no sweet psalms to fit.
My Master cut him off: "You stupid soul,
Keep to your horn. With that you may emit
Your rage, or any passion. At your neck
You'll find the strap that holds it tied. It lies
Across your pompous chest, you poor sad wreck."
To me: "He stands accused by how he cries,
And so condemns himself with scrambled speech:
Nimrod. The wicked tower was his design
We call Babel, by which all countries each
Have different tongues, and even yours is mine
Only in part. Let's leave him there. Why talk
When every tongue to him is random sound
As his to all the others? Come, let's walk."
And so we set off, turning left, and found,
A bow-shot further on, another one,
Far bigger and more savage. He'd been bound
By expert hands. Whose? Still, the job was done:
His left arm caught in front, his right behind
By one chain wound around the half that showed
In five coils. "This proud one was of a mind
To scale the heavens by a giants' road—
Made from piled mountains that they went to find—

And challenge Jove. And this is his reward."
So said my Leader. "He made his assault
When gods feared giants. Order was restored.
Ephialtes, this is, come to a halt.
The arms that once moved mountains move no more."
And I to him: "Please may I see the vast
Briareus with my own eyes? You swore
In your book he had fifty heads. At last
I'll see him for myself." "The one for you,"
My Master said, "is near and speaks unchained:
Antaeus. He will lead us down into
The depths of guilt. There's little to be gained
From him you want to see, who's far ahead,
Bound up like this one and built much the same,
Except his face is fiercer." So he said.
Ephialtes then shook his hulking frame
More violently than ever earthquake shook
A tower, and more than ever I feared death.
The terror of the sight was all it took,
Even without that chain, to take my breath.
So we went on and came to Antaeus,
Whose top half, from the rock up, stood the full
Five ells, or seven strides, and all this plus
The head. "You that once stood where Hannibal
And all his army lost to Scipio
In Libya, and turned their backs and ran—
That fateful valley—you that could not know
All that would happen there of Heaven's plan,
But took for prey a thousand lions, you—
Through whom, had you been with your brothers when
They fought the gods, the dreams could have come true
Of those sons of the earth, who might have then
Had powers of conquest—now have this to do:
Take us below and set us down—nor should
You show disdain at this—down where the cold
Locks up Cocytus. It will do no good

To take us on to Tityus, that bold
Titan Apollo burned, nor to Typhon,
Buried in Etna. This man here can give
The thing you crave. Come, then, and take us on.
Forget that curling lip. By him you live:
He can restore your waning fame up there.
He is alive, and plans to stay that way
For a long time, unless Grace calls him where
It wants him sooner." This I heard him say.
The giant then reached out the hands in haste
Whose mighty grip was felt by Hercules
And took my Guide. Feeling himself embraced,
Virgil looked down and said: "Come closer, please:
It's your turn." And he held me round the waist
To make one bundle of us both. Just as
Bologna's tower, the Garisenda, seen
From underneath, persuades you that it has
An even greater angle to its lean
When clouds go over in the contrary
Direction to the way it hangs, so seemed
Antaeus when I watched him bend. For me
It was a moment when I might have deemed
A different road the better bet. But he
Set us down lightly there where Lucifer
I knew must be with Judas, in the deep,
Engulfed. Somewhere down here was where they were.
Our bending giant had a gate to keep.
He couldn't stay like that, but like a mast
He straightened up—and we were there at last.

CANTO 32

Had I the bitter, grating rhymes to fit
This grim hole on which all the other rocks
Bear down, I'd do a better job of it
When pressing out my thought's sap. But what blocks
The flow is just that: my soft, childish tongue.
It is with fear that I begin to speak,
Because a language we employ when young
To call our mother "mummy" is too weak
To use, even in sport, when touching on
10 The lowest level of the universe.
But may the Muses who helped Amphion
To build the walls of Thebes now reimburse
My service to them and give me the tools
To match the brute facts with the tale I tell.
Ah, traitors! Beyond all the separate schools
Of misbegotten sinners in this well
So hard to speak of, you had best have been
Brought here as sheep and goats! Down in the dark
Cistern below the giants' feet we'd seen
20 Only the wall above us, high and stark,
When I heard said to me: "Watch where you tread.
The wretched weary brothers locked below
Can't move, and you might tread on someone's head."
At which I turned, and saw that it was so:

Before me and beneath my feet, a lake
Was made by ice to look much more like glass
Than water. Northern rivers, though you take
The Danube or the Don, could not surpass
This hardness even under their cold sky
30   Of winter, when their veils grow thick to freeze
Their flow. A mountain would have had to fly
And fall on this from any height you please—
Mount Tambernic, or Pietrapana, I
Leave you to choose—for it to show a crack,
Or creak at the thin edge. And as the frog
That sits, with muzzle out and body slack
Below the water, will croak through the fog
Of reverie that wraps the peasant maid
Who gleans her flax, so, livid up to where
40   Shame flushes in the face, each suffering shade
Lay in the ice, and all with their teeth bare
And set to make the sound of the stork's bill.
Each keeps his face bent down, but testifies,
With how his mouth looks, to the killing chill,
Confessing his heart's misery with his eyes.
I looked around awhile: then, at my feet,
I saw two pressed together so the hair
Of their heads mingled. I said: "You that meet
With such strain chest to chest while lying there,
50   Who are you?" They bent back their necks, those two,
And when their faces were raised up, I saw
Their eyes, which had held tears as sad eyes do,
But all within the lids, now shed far more,
That spilled over the brim, and the frost tied
Their tears between them, and the two were locked
As hard as beam and beam lie side by side,
Squeezed by the clamp's jaws. Whereupon, each shocked
The other. Butting heads, like goats they vied,
Such fury ruled them. And one who had lost
60   Both ears from cold, his face still turned down, spoke:

"Why do you gaze so long into the frost
And see yourself with us, like frozen smoke?
If you would know who these two were, the stream
So sweetly named Bisenzio flows through
Their father's valley, which it was the scheme
Of each to own, and that's what led them to
Their crime against each other. From one womb
They came, and all of Caina you may search
And find no shade more suited to a tomb
70 Of crystal ice. Their fate was to besmirch
Their father's name, Alberto. Even he
Whose breast and shadow, pierced with just one blow
From Arthur, gaped so deep that men could see
Right through him, I mean Mordred, isn't so
Deserving of the place that these hold, nor
Focaccia of Pistoia, who began
The feud of Blacks and Whites, nor him before
My eyes here, this infuriating man
Who constantly obstructs me with his head
80 So that I can't see past. He was Sassol
Mascheroni, who thought he merited
His nephew's wealth, and killed him. If the roll
Of Florentines includes you, then his fame
Is known to you. But now, that you spare me
The task of talking further, know my name
Is Camicion de' Pazzi. I will be
Exonerated by a greater shame,
Carlino's, when a castle of the Whites
Is given up by him." And after that
90 I saw a thousand faces from dogfights
All snarling with the cold, so, looking at
A frozen pond, I shudder still today.
And when we neared the central point where all
Of gravity converges, on my way
In fear along the strange floor of that hall,
I shivered in the long chill. Then—by fate

Or chance, I can't be sure which—as I stepped
Among the heads, I trod on one full weight,
Square in its face. It shouted as it wept:
"Why do you trample me? Unless you come
Because you think revenge for your defeat
At Montaperti has not reached a sum
Sufficient, why choose my poor cheeks to beat?
Because my face is cold, you think it numb?"
And I: "My Master, wait now for me here,
Before you make me hasten as you wish.
But first, through this man, I have doubts to clear."
My Master stopped, and to the feverish
Blasphemer I said: "You that so revile
Another, who are you?" "And who are you,"
The answer came, "that walks the dreadful mile
Through Antenora—named for that man who
Betrayed Troy to the Greeks—and kicks my face
Harder than if he lived?" "I live indeed,"
I said, "And if in fame you seek a place
So that your name is seen by all who read,
My noting it may be worth much to you."
And he to me: "I crave the opposite.
Get out of here, if that's all you can do,
And give me no more grief. You lack the wit
To flatter at this depth." And then I took
Him by the hair and said: "Your name, right now,
Or I will make your scalp an open book."
And then he said: "Even if you knew how
To strip me bald, my name you'll not be told,
Nor would I tell you even if you fell
Upon my helpless head a thousandfold."
I had his hair already in my fist,
Twisted, one tuft torn out, and set for more.
He barked but held his head down as my wrist
Quivered to tear again. "But why so sore,
Bocca?" cried someone else. "You're not content

100

110

120

130

With jawbone music? Now you have to bark?
What devil drives you to this new lament?"
"Well, now that I'm no longer in the dark,"
I said, "foul traitor, I can take, in spite
Of you, a true report." "Say what you like,
Just go," he said. "But back there in the light
Be sure, of him just now so keen to strike,
You tell the tale. For down here he laments
The silver the French gave him when he waved
Them into Italy. Speak in this sense:
Just say 'I saw him of Duero, saved
To cool with all the other traitors.' Should
They ask you who was here, beside you lies,
From Beccheria, he that planned no good
Against the Guelphs in Florence, and his prize
Was getting his throat slit. Sent by the Pope,
And then sent here. And then there's that two-faced
Gianni de' Soldanier, at last, we hope,
Pleased that he knows exactly how he's placed,
Who should have hung from both ends of a rope.
And further on is Ganelon, the cause
Of Roland's death, traitor to Charlemagne,
And Tebaldello who flung wide the doors
Of slumbering Faenza so that pain
Could enter in." But we had left him there
Already, when I saw two in one hole,
Fast frozen so that one head seemed to wear
The other for a hood, and the damned soul
Above was fastened on the one below
As hungry men chew bread, but at the spot
Where brain and neck's nape meet. Exactly so,
Tydeus of the Seven Kings, who got
His mortal wound from Menalippus, chewed
The temples of his killer, from sheer rage.
This one assaulted, as if they were food,
The skull and other parts. "You there, that wage

A war of hatred against him you eat
170 And prove it with the signs of a mad beast,
Why do you do this?" I asked. "Let us meet
In this agreement. If there is at least
Some reason for your manner of complaint
Against him, I, if only I knew you
And what his sin was, could remove the taint
From your name in the world above. It's true
The tongue I talk with has to stay intact.
So far it has. So far it hasn't cracked."

CANTO 33

Lifting his mouth from that most savage kind
Of meal, the sinner wiped it on the hair
Of just the head he'd wasted from behind,
And thus began: "You ask me to declare
A desperate grief which, merely in my mind,
Torments my heart before I talk. And yet
If what I say could be the seed that bore
The fruit of infamy for him I get
My only food from, I will speak, and more:
I'll speak and weep together. I can't guess
Who you might be, and by what means you came
Down here, but when I hear your bold address
I sense a Florentine. So know my name:
Count Ugolino. The Archbishop here,
Ruggieri, is my neighbour. Let me tell
You why. How by his wiles he drew me near
To him, and won my trust so that I fell
Beneath his thrall, was captured, and was slain:
I needn't say all that. But what you don't
Know yet—just how my death in pain
Was cruel beyond imagining—you won't
Be spared from hearing, and then you may see
How wrong he was. A mere slit in the wall
Of that loft they named Hunger after me—

And in which others yet, beyond recall
Will be shut up—had shown me through its chink
Already several moons, when a bad dream
Shredded the veil of all I liked to think
The future held. This man was made to seem
30 A lord and master hunting wolf and whelps
On that high hill for which the Pisans can't
See Lucca. With hounds lean, trained, their cruel yelps
Echoing eagerly, he'd sent—I shan't
Pretend I didn't see the wolves were meant
For people—his prey racing out ahead,
And soon, from fear and effort, the legs went
In father and in son, and then they bled
From flanks pulled open, slain where they fell spent,
Ripped up by sharp fangs. The Gualandi died,
40 Along with the Sismondi. Pieces torn
From the Lanfranchi were strewn far and wide.
It was a shambles. Then, before the dawn,
When I awoke, I heard my children cry
While still asleep—but I forgot to warn
You of this news, that they were there—and I
Could hear them beg for bread. You're cruel indeed
If you do not grieve, now you have in view
What my sad heart foresaw: and if you need
Worse things to make you weep, then when do you
50 Weep ever? But by now they were awake.
Our meagre daily ration was now due.
Each boy was still afraid from the heartache
Felt in his dream, and then I heard, below,
That foul keep's front door being shut with nails.
At which, without a word, lest they should know
From my voice how a heart feels when it fails,
I looked into the faces of my sons.
I didn't weep, for I had turned to stone
Within. They wept, and of my little ones,
60 Anselm, the smallest, said, all on his own,

'Father, why do you look like that? What's wrong?'
And still I shed no tears, nor all that day
Gave answer. And the next night was so long,
And still I didn't, till the first small ray
Of light from the next sun had reached the world,
And as that beam invaded our sad cell
I saw, lit clearly where its flag unfurled,
Four faces, and I knew then, all too well,
Those faces looked like mine. I bit my hands
70 For grief, but why they thought it must have been
For hunger, any starved man understands.
They rose as one. You must know what I mean
When I say that all four said the same thing:
Their voices added up to this. 'Far less
Pain there will be for us if you should feed
On us, Father. For you gave us the dress
Of mortal flesh. Now it is what you need,
So take it back.' And, not to make them more
Unhappy, I was silent. For two days
80 We all were. And how was it you forbore
To open up, hard Earth? Did you want praise
For steadfastness? And then the fourth day dawned,
And Gaddo threw himself down at my feet.
'Father,' he cried, 'how is it you have scorned
To help me? Is there anything to eat?'
He died then, and, as you see me, I saw
My other three, in two days, dying one
By one, and though I heard them breathe no more
I held them close, and stroked them, while the sun
90 Came back twice. I kept calling them by name,
And felt for them, for I was blind by then.
And then the strength of hunger overcame
Even my grief." That said, he seized again
Just as before, but with his eyes aslant,
That wretched skull, and how his teeth were strong
You'd have to measure by the way dogs plant

Their fangs in bones. Ah, Pisa! Though the song
Of our word "yes" joins all of Italy
Including you, you still shame all the rest.
100 Your neighbours for some reason leave you free
Of punishment. Here's how it would be best:
Capraia and Gorgona, out to sea,
Shift in and bar the Arno's mouth, to drown
Your every soul. Count Ugolino had
The name of selling out and bringing down
Your strongholds, and that fault, I grant, was bad:
But torturing his children, that was worse—
And that was you. Youth made them innocent.
Besides the two I just named in my verse,
110 Brigata, Uguccione also went
Through agony because of you we call
The new Thebes for your barbarous cruelties.
And further on, another tribe were all
Swathed roughly in thick ice but did not freeze
Face downward. They froze face up. Weeping there
Allows no weeping. Pain, trapped in the eyes,
Turns inward to increase itself, for where
The first tears coalesce, they crystallize
Into a visor: underneath the brow
120 Each cup was full. And though my frozen face
Felt nothing, like a callus, still somehow
I felt the wind, and more than just a trace.
"Master," I said, "What causes this? I thought
All heat down here was quenched." And he to me:
"Your eyes will soon be able to report
Directly, for the cause you'll plainly see
That drives the blast." And from his frozen crust
One of the wretches cried: "O souls so cruel
You roam free in the last pit of despair,
130 Lift off my brittle veils and break the rule,
That I might just a little give release
To the sadness that swells my heart, before

My tears freeze up again. So they will cease
Where they began." And I to him: "You wish
My help? Then tell me who you are, and should
I fail you, may I go down like a fish
To the bottom of the ice." He understood,
And spoke. "I am the evil garden's fruit,
Fra Alberigo, he who called down doom
On his own brother, and his son to boot.
I asked for fruit there in the dining room.
That was the sign. Now, here, in this cold tomb,
It's date for fig: which means that my return
On outlay is far more than I foresaw."
I said: "You mean you're dead? I live and learn."
"My body's life up there is a closed door
To me," he said. "This zone that gathers in
The treacherous to guests—and so is named
For Ptolemy, exemplar of that sin—
Is ranked so high that some who have been shamed
Come sooner to their fate than Atropos
Determines death. That you might lift the glaze
Of grief from my eyes with less sense of loss,
Know that a soul like mine, when it betrays,
Loses its body to a devil who
Controls it henceforth till its time comes round:
And then, this tank is where the soul comes to,
Falling headlong. The body might be found
Above of this shade spending winter here
Behind me. You must know. You just came down.
Ser Branca d'Oria. And many a year
Has passed since he fell to his cold renown,
Locked in the ice." "You're fooling me, I fear,"
I said, "For Branca d'Oria never died.
He eats and drinks, wears clothes, lies down in sleep."
And he: "Up in the ditch of the black tide,
Where Evil-Claws tend sticky pitch and keep
Watch on the bubbles, they had not yet seen

140

150

160

A sign of Michael Zanche when this shade
170 Gave up its body to an imp. He'd been
In league with a near kinsman. They both made—
With Branca's father-in-law caught in between—
The mischief, and that other, there, acquired
A devil for his body so his soul
Could come to us. Now do what I desired.
Reach out your hand and make my poor eyes whole.
Open them up." And I did not, and felt
That it was courtesy to scorn the hopes
Of that man. Let his eyes wait till they melt.
180 Ah, Genoese, you that know all the ropes
Of deep corruption yet know not the first
Thing of good custom, how are you not flung
Out of this world? For right there with the worst
Romagna has to offer I was faced
With one of you who for his deeds is cursed:
In soul, to lie there in the frozen lake—
In body, through the world to walk awake.

CANTO 34

"*Vexilla Regis*," said my Leader in
His tongue, *"perveneunt inferni."* I
Thus knew the banners of the Prince of Sin
Were near upon us. Virgil: "Therefore try
To look ahead. See if you can discern
The Evil One." As when thick fog or night
Comes to our hemisphere and we see turn
A windmill in the distance, such a sight
I seemed to see, a structure of that kind.
Then, for the wind, and lacking barricades
Against its brute force, I drew back behind
My Guide. I was already where the shades—
It is with fear I set this down in rhymes—
Were wholly covered, and showed through the ice
Like straws in glass, and there, a thousand times
In different ways, they all paid the same price.
Some lay down either way, some were erect,
With either head or feet up. Some were bows
Bent face to feet. Deep down, I could detect,
Were more, and off to either side, who knows?
When we'd gone far enough that my Guide thought
It good to show me him who once was fair,
The brightest of the Seraphim who fought
Michael in Heaven, Virgil moved aside

From just in front of me and made me halt.
"Behold Dis, and the sad place," said my Guide,
"Where your resolve must be without a fault."
Reader, don't ask how chill and faint I turned:
I couldn't write it. All the words would fail.
30   I didn't die, but couldn't live. I learned
What living death and death-in-life entail.
But you must ponder, if you have the wit,
What I, denied both life and death, became.
The evil Emperor stood forth in his pit
From his mid-chest on up, and just the same
Or worse as my arm to a giant's arm,
A giant's arm to his compares, so think
How huge his whole capacity for harm
Must be. His mighty strength gives you the link
40   Between his two lives. If his beauty was
A match for all the foulness he has now,
We see that all our sorrow came because
He set his face against his Maker. How
Miraculous it seemed, what I now saw.
He had three faces: the front one was red,
And on each side of that he had one more,
Each ending at mid-shoulder. Overhead
All three joined at the crown. The right-hand face
Was whitish yellow, and the left-hand one
50   Recalled in looks the people of that place
The Nile comes down from, stared at by the sun.
Between each face two giant wings emerged
Of size to suit so big a head, and sails
At sea I never saw like these. Quite purged
Of feathers, like a bat's, they beat like flails
To generate the three winds by which all
Cocytus is kept frozen. With six eyes
He wept, and three chins let the foul tears fall,
And bloody foam. Each mouth was of a size
60   To take a sinner, torn up by the teeth

As with a harrow, and worse were the claws
That stripped their backs to show the bones beneath.
"The soul up there most punished, and for cause,
Is Judas," said my Guide. "With just his legs
He signals pain. His head is not on show.
We do not see or hear the way he begs
For that same mercy he did not bestow.
And of the other two with heads outside
That triple throat, the noble one that hangs
70 From the black face is Brutus, once the pride
Of Rome. But now his words, pierced by those fangs,
Are lost. And there's his fellow regicide,
Cassius. So they expiate their crime.
But night ascends again. We ought to move,
For we have seen all, and we're short of time.
This journey took time even to approve."
Just as he wished, I clasped him round the neck.
He watched his chance of time and place and when
Those wings were spread he left the icy deck
80 And caught hold of the furry flank, and then,
From tuft to tuft between the matted hair
And frozen crusts, went down. When we had found
The thigh's turn, at the swelling haunch, just there,
My Leader strained to bring his head around
To where his legs had been, and caught the fur
Like someone climbing up. I thought for one
Bad moment we'd be back to where we were,
In Hell. "Hold on," he panted as if done,
"From so much evil we need stairs like these
90 To get away." And he passed through the cleft
Of a great rock, just squeezing by degrees,
And sat me on the edge, where I was left
To wait until his cautious step reached out.
I raised my eyes to Satan. There he was,
As he had been, but he was turned about,
Legs upward. If I was perplexed, I pause

To let the dull decide, who do not guess
The point that I had passed. (The central knot
Of this world: there, I've said it.) Saying less,
My Master, thus: "Get up, for we have got
A long, hard road to go, and yet the first
Hour after sunrise is exhausted." This
Place was a dungeon carved when crushed cliffs burst.
No palace hall, it had floors you could miss
Your footing on if light were not the worst,
And yet it swayed me to analysis.
"Master, before I extricate myself
From this abyss," I said as I arose,
"I have perplexities still on the shelf.
Clear them a little. Here's one case to close:
Where is the ice? And how did he get fixed
Heels over head? How is it sunlight flies
Without a pause, as if the two were mixed,
Unhindered between sunset and sunrise?"
And he to me: "You think you linger yet
On the far side of the centre, where I took
Hold of the pelt of him you can't forget,
That evil worm who pierces with his nook
The middle of the world. But just so long
As I descended, you were on that side,
And when I turned, you passed where all weights throng
Together, drawn from all parts by the tide
Of heaviness, and now you are below
The hemisphere opposed to that which swathes
The great dry land, whose zenith, as we know,
Shines on Jerusalem, and therefore bathes
The hill where that Man who was born to live
Without a single sin was brought to die
For all of you. There's none he can't forgive
Except us who were born too soon. But try
To think of where you are now as a sphere:
A little sphere you stand on, the reverse

Face of Judecca. When it's morning here
It's evening there, and him that we so curse,
Whose hair we made a ladder of, is still
Fixed as he was. On this side he fell down
From Heaven, and the land which used to fill
This space, before the sea came in to drown
The whole lot, chose the sea to make a veil
For fear of him, and came up to our sky:
Perhaps to flee from him, all here turned tail
And rushed up, leaving emptiness. That's why
This Hell-hole parallels on such a scale
A mountain you will soon see." Down there is
A place set at the far end of the tomb
From where Beelzebub presides in his
Grim glory, a place known from the long boom,
Not for the sight, of that stream which descends
Through rock worn hollow by its winding course
And gentle slope. And here the journey ends
Through Hell, where that sad flood is a spent force—
Which later on, as Lethe, makes amends.
My Guide and I were on the hidden road
That leads back out to where the world is bright.
No need for rest. We bore an easy load:
The task of getting back to the sweet light.
And up we went, he first, I second, to
The point where I could see an opening.
And it was there I saw, when I looked through,
A sight more wonderful than anything—
Some of the loveliness revealed to men
By Heaven. We could see the stars again.

BOOK

II

———

PURGATORY

CANTO 1

More favourable waters now invite
A raising of the sails on the small craft
Of my poetic gift, so she runs light,
Leaving the heavy sea retreating aft
That crushed her prow, but now lies in her wake.
For I will sing now of that second realm
Where souls are purged and so made fit to take
The path to Heaven. As I hold the helm,
O holy Muses, here let poetry
Arise again from death, for I am yours.
Bring forth Calliope to be with me
And join, with her sweet voice that Heaven adores,
My song, as once her lilting measures turned
Those mournful girls to magpies when they dared
To taunt her, as from Ovid we have learned.
Poor daughters of Pierus, they despaired
Of pardon, with their earthbound effort spurned—
They sang for Titans, but she made them cry.
The sweet clear tint of sapphire in the east
Gathered to make serene the sweep of sky
From zenith to horizon. It released
The gladness in my glance again, for I
Had weathered the dead air that never ceased
To weigh down on my heart, and hurt my eyes.

The comely planet that prompts us to love,
Veiling the school of pretty fish that lies
Each springtime in her train, was there above,
And she made all the east laugh. To the right
I turned, and on the other pole I set
My mind, and saw four stars that were a sight,
Seen by the first men, that has never yet
Been seen again. The sky seemed to rejoice
In these four flames. North, you're a widow, since
You are denied that sight! I made the choice
To take my gaze back from those merry glints
And turned a little to the other pole.
The Wain was gone already, and I saw
Beside me an old man alone, his whole
Aspect deserving of a reverence more
Profound than any owed by any son
To any father. His long hair and beard
Were streaked with white; the hair, two streams from one,
Fell on his breast; and on his face appeared
The light of those four holy stars to make
It seem as if he faced the sun. "And who
Are you," he said, giving his locks a shake,
Those signs of honour, "You that have come through
And fled the eternal prison, even though
The blind stream was against you? Who's your guide?
Who was the lamp that lit your path to go
Free from the deep night that from side to side
Blots out Hell's valley with perpetual dark?
How are the laws of the abyss defied?
Has Heaven decreed that those who bear the mark
Of doom, the damned, should come to my cliffs now?"
My Leader then with speech and hand and sign
Directed me to reverence, knees and brow,
And then he said: "The idea wasn't mine
To come here, but a lady came to me
From Heaven, and according to her prayers

I gave this living man my company
To help him through the darkness to the stairs.
But since you wish to have it made more plain
How things in actual fact stand with us two,
I can't deny you. This man, in such pain,
Had still not seen his last hour. It was due:
Folly had brought him near, and almost all
His time was gone. I was, as I said, sent
To save him in the last part of his fall,
70 And had no way except the way we went
To get him out. I showed him first the race
Of guilty shades, and now propose to show
The spirits to him of a different place—
Spirits that in your tutelage, Cato,
May purge themselves. But it would take a book
To tell you how I brought him through to here.
Enough to say that what it really took
Was virtue from above, which still keeps near
To help me give him you, so he may look
80 And listen. May it please you now to bless
His coming. He seeks liberty from vice,
A freedom dear to him, to you no less:
He knows who gives his life as sacrifice
For such a prize. You know it too, for you
In Utica, faced with the cruel defeat
Of your great cause, did what you had to do
And were not bitter, and your flesh will meet
Its true fate on that Day of Judgement when
It will come back in splendour, as you shed
90 It long ago out there with honour. Men
Don't break eternal laws. This man's not dead,
And Minos doesn't bind me. I am of
That circle where your Marcia's chaste eyes
Now lie, she who still prays with looks of love
That you should hold her, Holy Breast, and prize
Her for your own, as you did up above

When she came back to you. Incline, therefore,
To us, for her sake. Grant us right of way
Through all your seven kingdoms. I'll be sure
To tell her of your kindness on the day
That I return to Limbo, if you deem
It fitting to be spoken of down there."
"My Marcia so put the very gleam
In my eyes when I once breathed the world's air
That I did any kindness that she sought.
But now she dwells beyond the Acheron:
She can no longer move me in my thought.
That law was made the moment I was gone
From there. But if this heavenly woman guides
And moves you, as you say she does, there's no
Need of fair words. On high the power resides:
Enough to ask me for her sake. So go,
And bind him with a straight smooth rush to mark
His humble advent, and his face wipe free
Of any dirt. The eyes may not be dark
With fog for anyone called in to see
The first of all the ministers who keep
Watch on the road to Paradise. Around
This little island's edge, when from the deep
The waves come in and fall, there can be found
The rushes that you need. In the soft mud
They grow like nothing else that puts out leaves
Or hardens, though the waves fall with a thud.
But don't come back this way. This way deceives
By looking easy, but leads back to Hell.
The sun's up. Take the better road it shows
For going up the mountain. Now farewell."
He vanished, and without a word I rose
And drew close to my Guide, and fixed my eyes
On him. "Follow my step," he said. "Let's turn
Around. This plain slopes down to where it lies
Bounded by water." Dawn began to burn

The morning breeze away, and far away
It lit the trembling sea. We moved across
The lonely plain, as one who goes astray
And, looking for his path, still feels the loss
Until it's found again. Then, when we came
Into a shaded place where drops of dew,
Safe from the sun, stayed more or less the same,
140   My Master laid both hands spread in full view
On the wet grass. Knowing his purpose, I
Offered my tear-stained cheeks, and he revived
All of the colour underneath the dry
Tears that I cried in Hell. Then we arrived
On a deserted shore that never sees
A man who sails its waters and yet knows
How to return. My Guide, as it might please
Another, girded me. The plant he chose—
Ah, miracle!—so lowly, though thus torn
150   From where it grew, was instantly reborn.

CANTO 2

The horizon whose meridian at its height
Covers Jerusalem had by now been
Reached by the sun, and, step for step, the night
That circles opposite in the unseen
Was climbing from the Ganges with the scales
That it lets fall when dark outlasts the day,
As if the power of its fingers fails
In winter, and it can't take what they weigh.
So, where I was, the white and rosy pink
10 Cheeks of the fair Aurora, as her age
Increased, were turning orange. Made to think,
We tarried by the sea's edge at that stage,
As those who seek the road at heart may go
Onward but in their bodies pause. Look there!
Just as, when morning nears, we see the glow
Of Mars, rose-red in the thick misty air
Above the ocean floor and lying low
To decorate the west, so there appeared
To me a light that came across the sea
20 So fast no flight could match it as it neared.
I took my eyes off it to ask my Guide
"What is it?" I looked back to see it loom:
Its size and brightness had both multiplied.
On either side it put forth a white plume.

Two plumes, but were they plumes? And bit by bit
Below them came a third white plume. And still
My Master said no word concerning it,
And what its three white plumes might be, until
The first two unmistakably were wings,
30 And then, the pilot clear to him at last,
He said: "Bend, bend your knees, for this boat brings
The Angel of the Lord! Clasp your hands fast.
From here on you will see such ministers.
See how all human tools are scorned by him.
For him no oars or sails. No, nothing stirs
Or swells except his wings to make him skim
From shore to distant shore. See how he holds
Them raised toward the sky. The air is swept
With everlasting pinions: pleats and folds
40 Of feathers that will be forever kept
Pristine, and never change as even fine
Plumage will always do on Earth." And as
He came close it was clear he was divine,
For he grew brighter than men's vision has
The strength to bear, and down I cast my eyes,
And with his fleeting boat he touched the shore,
A boat so quick and light it almost flies
Above the water, which gives way no more
Beneath it than as if it had no weight.
50 The steersman on the poop-deck stood still now:
Stood so his blessedness that was so great
Seemed written on him, and that boat, from bow
To stern, had, sitting in it as it slid
Ashore, more than a thousand spirits. "When
Israel," they sang in Latin—this they did
With one voice—"out of Egypt came . . ." Right then
They sang it all as written. Then he made
The sign above them of the Holy Cross.
They flung themselves, as if they had obeyed
60 His order, on the beach. With little loss

Of time—as fast as he'd arrived, in fact—
He left. The crowd remaining there seemed new
To this place. They were caught up in the act
Of testing something. As new people do,
They gazed about. And on all sides the sun
Volleyed the day, and Capricorn was chased
With keen-tipped arrows from the zenith. One
And all the new arrivals rose and faced
Towards me, saying: "If you know the way
70 To reach the mountain, tell us." Virgil, thus:
"You think we know this place? We came today,
Just before you. It's all as strange to us
As it must be to you. The way we came
Was different, and so bitter, hard and rough
That now the climb before us will seem tame."
The souls, who had already seen enough
Of how I breathed to know I was alive,
Turned pale with wonder, and as if to see
The bearer of an olive branch arrive
80 And hear his news they all had rushed headlong
Uncaring who got crushed, so one and all
Of these most favoured souls gazed at my face
Transfixed, as if forgetting their first call—
To go and become beautiful. With grace
One came to me, and with such warmth that I
Met his embrace with mine, I was so moved.
Ah, shades! Your looks seem solid, but they lie!
Three times I held him and three times it proved
That I in vain had clasped my hands behind
90 His back and brought them back to meet my breast.
My face displayed the wonder in my mind,
I think, because the shade made manifest
His pleasure in a smile, and then withdrew
As I, to follow him, stepped forward. He
Gently suggested that I stand. I knew
Then who he was, and bade him talk to me

A little while. He said: "As I loved you
When I was mortal, so I love you still
Now I am free, and therefore I remain.
100 But you, why do you want to climb the hill?"
I said: "Casella, only to regain
The place I came from do I take this road.
But now you're here, how much time have you lost?"
And he to me: "He stays true to his code.
He takes up who he wants—there was no cost
To me—and when he wants. If many times
He has denied me passage, these are just
Decisions on his part, and never crimes.
A righteous will frames his will. What he must,
110 He does. Nevertheless, for three months now
Without fuss he has taken all who would
Embark, and I, well, I had come at last
Down to the Tiber's mouth, and there I stood
Where water that was fresh turned salt, and he
Gathered me in. For he has set his wing,
Through all this year of Papal Jubilee,
On visiting that river mouth, to bring
Those crowded souls away who do not sink
Down to the Acheron." And I: "If no
120 New law forbids you now to even think
About the thing you once could not forgo,
If you can still remember and still do
What you once did, make music for a song—
And the very first to set my words was you,
Your songs of love lulled me when I would long
For anything—so may it please you here:
Refresh my soul with music for a while,
For with my body it grew tired from fear
And effort on the road from mile to mile
130 With nothing lovely to placate the ear."
"Oh love, that speaks," he then began to sing,
"Speaks in my mind . . ." he went on, and so sweet

Were words and notes together, like one thing,
That still today the song stirs to repeat
Its clear lilt in my memory, lingering,
Always the same and never changing. I,
My Master and those people there with us,
Seemed as content as if, while time went by,
Nothing remained to think of or discuss,
140 When suddenly the old one cried "What's this,
You laggard spirits? What's this negligence?
Why the delay? All this is artifice!
Run to the mountain, for your slough prevents
God's being clear to you. It must be stripped
From you. Yes, you are here to be made clean."
As doves, collecting when their food is tipped
Where they can get their beaks to it, are seen
To pick up wheat or tares, with little sound
And nothing of their usual show of pride,
150 But they will leave their food there on the ground
If something comes to scare them, for beside
Their new concern, their first concern turns pale,
Just so I saw that troop of fledglings go
Towards the slope, and heard their last notes fail.
They left their song, but did not seem to know
Where to go next, yet had no time to waste—
And we went too, and went with no less haste.

CANTO 3

While they were scattering in their sudden flight
Throughout the plain, I turned my gaze to meet
The mountain, where by reason at its height
We are examined. Think of the defeat
I would have met without my true friend near.
So near I drew, for how would I have fared?
Who else would take me up that hill from here?
And yet he seemed somehow not to be spared
From self-reproach. Ah, pure and dignified
Of conscience, how a tiny fault can sting!
When his feet slowed down from the hasty stride
That drains the dignity from anything,
My mind, till then restrained, was newly keen,
And with that wider range I set my face
Towards the hill that from the sea is seen
To rise high in the search for Heaven's grace.
Behind me and above, the sun flamed red.
Before me, the ground shone around the shape
I made when sunlight stopped at me instead.
I turned to one side with my mouth agape
In fear that I been abandoned when
I saw that only I thus turned the ground
To darkness, but my Comfort asked me then:
"Why so distrustful? Have you not yet found

10

20

That I am always with you, I, your guide?
Now it is evening where my body lies
With which I cast a shadow. I abide
In Naples, sent there as a treasured prize
From Brindisi to mark the fond esteem
30 Of great Augustus. If no shadow now
Is thrown before me, may its absence seem
No more a marvel to your mind than how
The heavens do not block each other's rays.
The Force that makes our bodies fit to bear
Torments of heat and cold has secret ways
Of which we cannot hope to be aware,
And he's a fool who thinks our reason can
Trace all the paths one substance takes in three
Persons, for they are infinite. Mere Man!
40 The *quia*, the mere fact, is bound to be
What you must be content with, for if you
Had ever been enabled to see All,
Then Mary would have had no need to do
The thing she did, and give birth. You'll recall
How you have often seen men's vain desire
That their desire to see things whole—a grief
Eternal—should have leeway to retire.
Not only Plato yearned for that relief
But Aristotle too, and many more."
50 And here he bent his brow down, and he fell
To silence, looking troubled and unsure.
Meanwhile, the mountain. We saw all too well
The way its foot was a sheer cliff so steep
The nimblest legs could not have been of use.
From Lerici to Turbia, you'd keep
Your feet more easily where, broken loose,
The rock lies wildly strewn, but still presents
A staircase easier than this. "Who knows
Which side to scale the slope on makes more sense,"
60 My Master said, his steps stayed, "so that those

Who have no wings may climb?" And while his face
Was held down, and he pondered the best way,
I gazed up round the rock, and in one place,
There on the left, appeared a whole array
Of souls, who moved towards us, and yet so
Slowly they seemed not to approach. "See there,
Master," I said, "these ones might let us know
The answer for which you seek everywhere
Within yourself, if you just lift your gaze."
70   He did, and with an air of one set free
From some weight on his mind, said "Our best way's
That way, for they come slowly. You must be,
Dear son, firm in your hope." Those people still
Were at the distance—after we had gone
A thousand paces—that a slinger will
Attain with a good hand, when, hard upon
The high bank's solid wall they pressed against,
They stood close-packed and still, as men will pause
To look when not yet from their doubt dispensed.
80   "You that have ended well, souls that with cause
May call themselves elect," declared my Guide,
"By that peace which I do believe awaits
You all, tell me the slope that meets the stride
With favour, for a waste of time frustrates
The wise the most." As sheep depart the fold
By one and two and three and all the rest
Stand timid, and down to the ground they hold
Their eyes and muzzles, and the first is pressed
From back there by the others if it slows,
90   Since they all do what it does, and do that
Simply and quietly, and not one knows
Quite why, if one stops, all stop, these were at
That same point. Those who led the lucky flock
Came forward, modest, dignified. But when
They saw that on my right I made a block
For light, so that my dark shape walked again

Between me and the cliff, they stopped in shock,
And back a pace they drew, so all who came
Behind, not knowing why they should have done
100 What everyone in front did, did the same.
"Before you ask, let me tell everyone
This is a human body that you see,
By which the sunlight on the ground is split.
Don't marvel, but believe, that he can't be
Without the aid of Heaven's power to pit
Himself against the wall he comes to climb."
Thus Virgil, and a spokesman for that group
Of worthies said: "For just a little time
Turn back, and then go on before our troop."
110 (The hand, reversed, at this point made a sign.)
"Whoever you might be, turn, as you go,
Your face, and think if ever you saw mine
Out there." I turned to him. I tried to know.
I looked. He was fine-featured and fair-haired,
A noble presence, but a blow had cut
One of his eyebrows through. When I had spared
No humble words to tactfully rebut
Any suggestion I had known him, "Look!"
He said, and bared, high on his breast,
120 A gaping wound. "Behold my open book!
Yes, I am Manfred, torn up from my rest
And thrown out of the Church's lands. Grandson
To Empress Constance. Thus I beg of you,
Visit my lovely daughter when you've done
Your time here and go back. Mother of two
Kingdoms, of Sicily and Aragon,
If she has heard another tale, she ought
To hear the truth. When life could not go on,
My body cleft by two strokes, I then thought
130 To yield myself to Him who freely gives
His pardon. Yes, my sins were horrible.
But the healing goodness that forever lives

Has arms so wide they take in all who will
Turn to it. If Cosenza's bishop, sent
By Clement to hunt me, had rightly read
That page of God that says he whose intent
Is to approach Me shall be housed and fed
And not cast out, then still my body's bones
Would now, at Benevento's bridgehead, lie
140 Under the shelter of those heavy stones
Stacked in a cairn. They would be warm and dry.
But now the wind is at them, and the rain
Soaks them, beyond the Kingdom, by the stream
That marks the border: bones brought in disdain,
With tapers quenched. But though the pastors deem
A man heretical, he can't be lost
To that point where eternal love can't save
His soul, if hope keeps love free from the frost,
And evergreen. It's true that if the grave
150 Opens for one denied the sacraments
By Holy Church, he must stand on the sill—
No matter how intensely he repents—
For thirty times the time he set his will
Presumptuously high, if holy prayers
Don't shrink his sentence. So now, if you can,
Bring gladness to me in my present cares,
By telling the good Constance of the man
Whose soul you saw here, sadly made to wait—
For prayer from elsewhere can unlatch the gate."

CANTO 4

Let pain or pleasure touch a faculty
Of ours, and soon our soul will concentrate
Entirely on that. It seems to be
Alert to that one power: all others wait.
And this exclusiveness is contrary
To any notion that one soul has been
Brought high above our several souls (for such
Was Plato's error). That a thing we've seen
Or heard can occupy the soul so much,
10   Time passes and one doesn't know it—for
The faculty attuned to it is one,
And that which holds the whole soul is one more,
The first one bound, the second free to run—
Of this I had experience. This soul,
Manfred, I'd heard and marvelled at, and while
I'd been absorbed, the sun had climbed a whole
Fifty degrees, and, in my usual style,
I hadn't seen it do so. Then we came
To where the spirits all together cried
20   "Here's what you want!" An opening the same
In shape, but many times as wide,
The peasant fills with forkfuls of thick thorn
To keep thieves from the grapes when they grow dark.
Our own gap in a hedge we now found torn

Before us in the rock. That was our mark,
Now that the group had left us. You can go
Up to San Leo or down all the way
To Noli or climb where the rock is so
Steep at Bismantova the locals say
The town's a summit, and all that on foot:
But here you had to fly—with the quick wings,
I mean, of great desire, with plumage put
To the high task of following what brings
Us hope, the guidance that for me made light.
We climbed inside the rock. The surface on
Each side pressed close to us. The walls were tight.
The floor was rough, for hands and feet. Upon
All fours, almost, we reached the upper edge
Of the high bank, on the open hillside. "So,
Master," I said, "Which way?" There on the ledge
He said "Not one step back. The way to go
Is up, and close behind me, till some wise
Guide comes for us." The summit was so high
It went beyond the limits of my eyes.
The slope went up more steeply through the sky
Than a right angle bisected. I was spent
When I spoke thus: "Sweet father, look back here.
Unless you stop, I'm left alone." He bent
Back down, and said "My son, a place is near
Where you may rest awhile. Just drag yourself
As far as there." He pointed to the rim,
Above, of what soon proved to be a shelf
That ran around the hill. Inspired by him,
I forced myself to clamber the last few
Hard yards behind him till the ground turned flat.
We sat there facing east, from which we two
Had come, as Revelation does, so that
Was probably a help. The shore below
Was where I bent my eyes first. Then I raised
Them to the sun, and marvelled we were so

Struck by it from the north. It should have blazed,
In summer, south. The Poet noted well
How stunned I was the chariot of light
Went by in the wrong place. "If it befell,"
He said, "that, parties to this brilliant sight,
Along with the sun's mirror, were the twins
Castor and Pollux, then that glowing wheel
The Zodiac, whose timeless flight begins
And ends in north and south, you'd now see steal
70   Still closer to the Bears, unless it quit
Its usual path. If you would ponder how
This thing might be, put all your mind to it:
Picture Jerusalem and this hill. Now
Think of them placed on Earth so that they share
Just one horizon, but their hemispheres
Are each their own. Then, in the air,
You'll see how Phaethon's highway here appears—
The road he failed on and so sealed his fate—
On this side of the mountain, and Zion
80   On that. Just think about it. Concentrate."
"Truly," I said, "Master, my doubts are gone.
I can see clearly now—as never yet,
For lack of wit—that the mid-circle of
Celestial motion, which is always set
Between the sun and winter up above—
The Equator, to use the special name
One science gives it—lies, and you said why,
As north from here as Hebrews saw the same
Straight line move south towards a different day,
90   On hotter land. But if it pleases you,
I'd like to know how far we have to go.
This mountain needs more than my eyes can do
To reach its peak." And he: "The start below
On this hill's always hard, but as you climb
Higher, it takes less effort. Therefore, when
It seems so pleasant, in the course of time,

That going up is far less taxing, then—
When the ascent is like a drift downstream
By boat—then you will find the high trail's end.
100 There you may rest your weariness. I deem
This to be truth. This answer I defend,
And say no more." As soon as he had said
These words, a voice nearby: "Perhaps before
You get that far you'll need a seat." Eyes led
By that sound, we both turned, and there we saw
A great stone we had neither of us seen
Till then. We went there. There were people there
In the shade, resting, as men whose rest has been
Sought out through indolence. One, with an air
110 Of weariness, his arms around his knees,
Sat with his face between them. "My dear lord,"
I said, "Behold, for here are mysteries:
The laziness of this one could afford
Comparison with Sloth, as if she were
His energetic sister." The soul turned,
Slowly took note of us, and deigned to stir
His face above his thigh, so I discerned
An inch of space between them. "You're so strong?"
He said. "Go up." I knew who it must be,
120 And my fatigued breath, still short from the long
Ascent, only for moments hindered me
From going to him. He scarce raised his head
When I reached him. "Have you made out the way
The chariot is driven," the soul said,
"By the sun past your left shoulder?" His display
Of lazy movement and his few words moved
My lips to smile a little. I began:
"Belacqua, since your future is approved
I do not grieve for you. But if you can
130 Summon the urge, pray tell me why you sit
Just here. Is there an escort you await?
Or are you back to form? Can that be it?

Slow off the mark and always running late?"
And he: "My brother, tell me what's the use
Of going up. God's angel at the gate
Would never let me through on an excuse
To meet the torments. First the heavens must
Revolve around me, while I wait outside,
As long as when I lived—and it is just,
140 Because it was so late I rightly sighed—
Unless a helpful prayer should first arise
From some indulgent heart that lives in grace.
A sinner's pleading scarcely signifies
In Heaven." Now the Poet took his place
Before me, saying "Come on, use your eyes:
The sun strikes the meridian, and night
Treads on Morocco's shore and its last light."

CANTO 5

I had already parted from those shades
And followed in my Leader's steps, when one
Behind me cried "But look how the light fades!"
He pointed at my walking shadow. "None
Of all the rays shine to his left below.
He seems to bear himself like one alive."
I turned to see who should be speaking so
And saw them watching, buzzing like a hive,
Amazed at me and at my broken light.
"Why," said my Guide, "so tangled in the mind?
How can you be concerned by what they might
Be murmuring there? Stay with me close behind
And let them talk. Stand like a tower, staunch,
Unshaken at its top by gusts of wind,
For always when a man has thoughts that launch
Themselves one from the next, his mark is pinned
Further away, as one thought drains the force
Out of the other." So what could I say
Except "I come"? I said it with remorse
And felt my face gain colour in a way
That sometimes makes a man fit to receive
A pardon. Meanwhile people walked across
The slope ahead, and sang, as if to grieve,
The *Miserere* line by line. But loss

Was not their fate, for Mercy, I believe,
Was theirs already, although in the psalm
They went on pleading for it. When they saw
The way I blocked the sun, they changed their calm
Cantata to an "Oh!" long-drawn and raw,
30 And one of them, the messenger, ran out
To meet us, asking "What should you disclose?"
My Guide: "You can go back and be about
Your business straight away of telling those
Who sent you that this man is made of flesh,
And if his shadow stopped them, that should be
Sufficient answer: they need none afresh.
Just do him honour and collect the fee."
I never saw at nightfall the clear sky
Cloven by kindled vapour in a streak
40 Of light, nor ever saw the lightning fly
Through sunset clouds in August—here I speak
Of things on Earth—to match for sudden speed
The way those two returned above, and when
They reached the rest, they turned, thus to proceed
With them towards us, as a troop of men
Turned into horses given rein might run.
"These souls are many and they come to press
Petitions on us," said the Poet. "None
Should stop you. Move on. Make your pace no less,
50 And listen as you go." "O soul that goes
With, for your bliss, the self-same limbs that you
Were born with," they cried as they came, "Suppose
You slowed your steps a little. If you knew
Any of us before—look hard—you could
Take news of us back yonder. Why go on?
Why don't you stop? Hear what we say. You should.
For all of us by violence died, far gone
In sin until the last hour, when the blaze
Of Heaven's light brought understanding. We,
60 Repenting and forgiving, from life's ways

Emerged into God's peace. The urge to see
Our benefactor fills our yearning heart."
And I: "I search your faces thoroughly,
But don't see one I know. All that apart,
If there is anything, souls born for bliss,
That I can do to please you, by the peace
Which I go seeking from that world to this
With such a guide to follow, I'll not cease
Striving to get it done." And one began:
70 "In your good offices it needs no oath
If there be power enough for the will's plan:
Therefore, before the rest I'm nothing loth
To speak. If ever you should see the land
Lying between Romagna and that held
By Charles—by which I mean, you understand,
All Naples—then I pray you be impelled
By courtesy to beg them in Fano
Good prayers be made for me, so that I may
Purge my grave sins, for I am Jacopo,
80 Who came from there, but I was far away
Near Padua when all my deep wounds poured
My life's blood, and the sons of Antenor,
Heirs to the Trojan traitor, could afford
No safety to me. He of Este bore
The burden of the crime, if not the sword.
He hated me beyond the bounds of law,
Yet if towards La Mira I had turned
My flight, after his horsemen tracked me down
At Oriaco, then I might have spurned
90 My fate, and taken refuge in that town
And still be up there, breathing. But I ran
Into the marsh. Trapped by the reeds and mud
I fell full length, the measure of a man,
And saw the spreading pool of my own blood."
Another spoke: "As I pray your desire
Be satisfied, that draws you to the high

And fruitful hill, just so may I require
Your gracious pity's helping hand. For I
Was born in Montefeltro: Guido's son,
Buonconte. Not my wife, Giovanna, no,
Nor anybody else, not even one,
Has care for me. And so alone I go,
Even among all these with downcast brow."
And I to him: "What force, what chance, took you
So far from Campaldino no one now
Knows where your body's buried? It was true
We beat your Ghibellines, but you, somehow,
Were not among the dead." And he: "A creek
Below the Casentino's foot they call
The Archiano. It comes down from the peak
Above the Hermitage. For all its fall
The Apennines surround it. To the place
Where that small stream gives up its early name,
With wounded throat and flying foot, a trace
Of dark blood all across the plain, I came.
Then I lost sight and speech. I had the grace
To end by naming Mary as I fell,
And just my flesh remained. But now I would
Say what is true. Make it the truth you tell
Among the living. God in his great good
Sent down His Angel, and the one from Hell
Cried 'You from Heaven, why do you rob me?
You take from me this man's eternal part
For just one little tear. It's larceny.
But with his mortal flesh I'll make a start
On dealing in another way!' You know
How humid vapour, gathering in the air,
Returns as rainfall when its upward flow
Climbs to the colder realm which holds it there
Until it liquefies, then lets it go?
The Prince of Ill-Will has a mind to care
Only for evil, and he moves the cloud

And wind by his peculiar natural force.
So Campaldino's valley, where a shroud
Of mist, when that sad day had run its course,
Covered the mountains rising from the plain
From Pratomagno to the peaks. The sky
Turned dense, the saturated air made rain:
More water than the earth could nullify
140 Flooded the ditches, and the rivulets
Collected in the streams that fed the great
River that finds the sea. No one forgets
The Arno rules us in a princely state
Even when it's at peace, but now its source,
The Archiano, rampaged at such a pace
Nothing before it could resist its force.
The torrent found my frozen corpse. Its face
Swallowed me up and swept me on, until
The Arno took apart upon my breast
150 The cross I made when pain had worked its will
And overwhelmed me. All along its banks
And bed the river rolled me. Then it decked
Me with its spoils, and so I owe it thanks
For giving me a grave none can detect."
The third soul spoke: "When you return into
The world, and rest has eased the price you paid
For this long road, think how I said to you:
Siena made me. What Siena made
Was broken by Maremma. And think who
160 Said this. I am La Pia, murdered on
The orders of my husband; locked away
And dealt with so that he might, with me gone,
Marry again. He's still up there today.
He knows about it, he who with his jewel
Pledged love, and faith, and wed me, and was cruel."

CANTO 6

The game of chance breaks up, the loser stays
Behind and grieves. He thinks about his throws
Over and over. In his mind, he plays
Again, sad lesson learned. The winner goes,
And all the rest go with him, one in front;
Another grabs him from behind; one more
Is by his side, a lapdog at the hunt,
Whining "Remember me?" He can't ignore
Them all, but he does not stop moving while
10   He listens first to this one and then that,
And gives each one his hand and a small smile
So they will fall back satisfied, and at
The right point he is set free from the throng:
He saves himself. So, in that crowd, was I:
I turned my face to them, first here, then there,
And by my promises got free. To die
By violence had been the fate to share
Between these: I could see the Aretine,
A judge, that fierce Ghino di Tacco killed
20   In open court; the next had fled the scene
From Campaldino and his lungs had filled
With water; and there begged with outstretched hands
Federico, a Novello, beaten dead
In battle; that slain youth from Pisan lands

Whose father, good Marzucco, was, instead
Of plotting his revenge, moved to forgive
The murderers. Count Orso I saw, too,
Whose cousin worked it so he should not live;
And that soul severed, if the tale is true,
30 By spite and envy from its body, not
By that crime he was hanged for: yes, Pierre
De la Brosse. May she not say she forgot
That story when she's here, and find it fair,
The Lady of Brabant, that no worse lot
Than being sent to this flock is her fate.
As soon as I was free of them, whose one
And only prayer, while they were forced to wait,
Was for the prayers of others, thus to run
Sooner to holiness, I said: "To me
40 It seems, my Light, you took pains to deny
Through Palinurus, a divine decree
Is ever bent by prayer, and that was why
He never reached the kingdom of the dead,
Yet these here pray for prayer alone. Will they,
Too, pray in vain, or are those words you said
Something I didn't take in the right way?"
"My writing's plain," he told me, "and the hope
Of these souls is well founded. You just think
With sound mind now as we ascend: the slope
50 Ends at the height of justice. Will it sink
Simply because the fire of love supplies
In one quick flash what each soul here is owed
In satisfaction? What I wrote implies
A prayer was bound to fail that had no road
To God. But such a question is too deep
For you to take a stand on, without first
Hearing from her who in the full great sweep
Of light from mind to faith is so well versed.
I speak of Beatrice. Did I puzzle you?
60 Above us, on the mountain's lofty peak,

Her smile and ecstasy will fill your view."
"My lord," I said as soon as I could speak,
"Can we go faster? I'm less weary now,
And see, the mountain casts a shadow." "We'll
Go on with this day's march," he said "as much
As light permits. And yet, be sure what's real
Is far from what you think. Before you touch
The peak above, you'll see that one return
Who now lies hidden in behind the hill
70 So you don't break his beam. But look and learn:
See there a soul who sits alone, and will—
He looks towards us—point the quickest route."
We came to him. Ah, Lombard shade, how high
And mighty was your poise, how absolute
The dignity behind the steely eye
Of your regard! He said no word to us.
He would have let us pass. He only gazed,
A crouching lion. Nothing to discuss.
But Virgil went right up to him and raised
80 The question of the best ascent. He gave
No answer, but inquired of our birthplace
And our condition. "Mantua . . ." my grave
But gentle Guide began. The shade, a case
Till then of total self-involvement, leapt
Towards him, saying "Mantua! Behold
Sordello of your city!" And each swept
The other close as eager arms could fold.
Slave Italy! Hostel of grief! Lost ship
Without a pilot in a storm! No more
90 Princess of peoples but a swarming tip!
A brothel! Think of what you were before
And could have been again! This noble soul
Was so keen, just for his dear city's name,
To greet its citizen, and now your whole
Country is never free from sword and flame,
And all the living are shut in with wall

And moat, and each enclosure does the same—
Chews at the others. Wretched one, search all
Your seashores, then look deep within
Your breast, and see if any part rejoice
In peace. What boots it that Justinian
Gave you the reins of law to guide your choice?
The saddle's empty, the horse riderless,
Left to itself. If there had never been
A law, there had been less shame to confess,
But you know what restraint was meant to mean,
So your excess is strictly recklessness.
You clergy, who were pledged to be devout,
And should, if you paid God's instructions heed,
Let Caesar ride the horse, the truth is out:
From lack of guidance by his spurs, the steed
Turned vicious, for its bridle, in your hand,
Can only lead astray. Ah, Emperor!
Albert of Saxony, who saw our land
Not even once, and who abandoned her
To be what she's become, savage and wild!
You that should now bestride her saddle-bow,
Let starry judgement fall on man and child:
Let your successor fear forthcoming woe!
You and your father Rudolph, both held back
By greed, have let your Empire's garden go
To pieces, desolation, ruin, rack.
Come see the Montagues and Capulets
Monaldi, Filippeschi, families ranged
Against each other, those that grace forgets,
Wretched, in dread, because you were estranged,
Having no care. Come, cruel one, come and see
Your nobles in distress and soothe their pain.
You'll see the level of security
In Santafiora, where Siena's gain
Means loss of land for all those Ghibellines.
Come see your Rome, that, widowed and alone,

Weeps night and day. "Caesar, my lord," it keens,
"Why aren't you here with me?" Come see your own,
Your people, how they love each other. Or,
If our plight fails to move your pity, come
For shame of your repute. If it be law
For me, supreme Jehovah—you, the sum
Of all good, who were crucified on Earth
140   For us—to question you, are your just eyes
Turned elsewhere, or do you arrange the birth
In the chasm of your counsel for some guise
Of good we are unable to perceive?
For all our cities here in Italy
Are full of tyrants. Even clowns believe
That playing partisan means they must be
Marcellus, dreaming he made Caesar grieve
By talk against the Empire. You may well,
My Florence, take your ease at this
150   Digression, which has little truth to tell
About you, for your people never miss
A trick in their resource. Others, at heart,
Have justice, but that arrow leaves the bow
Too slowly, for the thought must play its part
Of what the heart means: but your people know
Law only at the tongue's tip. Others avoid
The weight of office, but your people cry,
Unasked, their eagerness to be employed.
"I'll bear the burden!" A good reason why
160   You should be happy, for your cause is good:
So rich, and so at peace, and oh so wise.
I speak a truth borne out by facts. Nor could
Athens and Sparta, chosen to devise
The ancient laws and thus be civil, give
One hint beside you of the proper way,
My Florence, that a city ought to live.
You make provisions so fine every day
The threads you spin in one month do not last

To the middle of the next. Can you recall
170 How often you've changed, in your chequered past,
Your laws, your money, offices, and all
Your customs? And thrown out your active men
Or brought them back, according to which crew
Is in control of cleaning up the den?
And if you see yourself unblinking, you
See a sick woman who turns seeking rest
On a bed of down, but is no less distressed.

After these greetings, proud yet high of heart,
Had been repeated three times and once more,
Sordello drew back. When they stood apart
He said "But who are you?" Virgil: "Before
Souls worthy of the climb to God came here
To this hill, my dead bones were buried by
Augustus. I am Virgil. For that mere
Defect—lack of the faith that I could not
Have had, because a child was not yet born—
10 I lost Heaven." So spoke Virgil of his lot.
As one who marvels at the sudden dawn
Before him of a thing he both believes
And disbelieves, and says 'It is . . . and yet
It isn't . . .' and then finally retrieves
His power to move, Sordello with bent head
Again went humbly to my lord, embraced
Him low down as the lowly do, and said
"O Glory of the Latins, you that graced
Our tongue and proved its power to the Earth,
20 What deed of mine or blessing shows me you?
Honour eternal for my place of birth!
If I deserve your words, tell me what's true:
You came from Hell? Which cloister?" Virgil then:
"Through all that kingdom's circles of regret

I have come here. But it was only when
The power of Heaven helped, that I could set
My aim this high. It's not that I did wrong,
But I did nothing, and so lost the sight
Of that high Holy Sun for which you long,
30 And I knew of too late. Out of the light,
Below, there is a place where sadness lies
In darkness, not in torment; where laments
Are never cries of pain but only sighs.
There I abide with little innocents,
Seized by death's fangs before they reached the prize
Of baptism, and so they were not free
Of human guilt; and also I abide
With all those souls who aren't clad by the three
Virtues called holy, but set sin aside
40 Through following the other four. Yet we
Would hear from you—if you know and may say—
Directions by which we might quickly climb
To where true Purgatory begins. Which way?"
Sordello said "But now you're pressed for time.
For us here, no unchanging place is set.
I may go up and round. I'll go as far
With you as I'm allowed, but not quite yet.
See how the day declines. From where you are,
To go by night up higher can't be done.
50 It's time to find a refuge. See these shades
Here on the right, apart from everyone?
If you consent, before the last light fades,
I'll bring you to them. They'll be overjoyed
To meet you." Virgil answered: "How is that?
Does that mean someone who climbed in the void
Of night would miss what he was aiming at
Because of some external force, or would
He just lack strength?" "You should not cross this line
After the sun is gone." So said the good
60 Sordello, and with his finger made the sign

There on the ground. "Though be it understood,
There's nothing else to hinder your ascent
Except the dark that tangles up your will
With helplessness. You even might have meant
To go back down, yet wander round the hill
For all the time the sun is locked out by
The dark horizon." And my lord, as though
In thought, said "Lead us there, where we may lie
At ease as you have said." And it was so:
70 We'd gone a little way, when I saw how
The mountain's face was scooped out, just as though
A valley pierced a mountain here and now.
"We'll go there," said the shade, "where that slope makes
A shelter, and await the sun's return."
A level, winding path with sudden breaks
Of steepness, brought us where, we would soon learn,
The dell's wall at half height looked down upon
A garden. Gold, fine silver, cochineal,
White lead, and indigo spread so it shone
80 Both bright and clear, and emerald with the seal
Of its hard skin split, all these were outsoared
In colour by the grass and flowers there
Foregathered on the valley floor, greensward
Ablaze with pigments. Nor did the soft air
Fall short of this parade of nature's tints:
A thousand perfumes, each sweet on its own,
Made one, a blend that I have not known since—
Nor, to men living, was it ever known.
From where I was I saw, on that bright green
90 Among the flowers, spirits that sang the last
Hymn of the day, by which, of course, I mean
Salve Regina. Beyond the valley's rim
They were unseen. "Soon now the sun will sink,
And find its nest," the Mantuan began
Who had directed us. "Yet do not think
Before it does, to ask me if I can

Lead you among them there. But from this bank
You'll see each face and movement better than
If you were down there with them. Highest rank,
And therefore highest seat, goes to that one
Who has the look of letting duty lapse.
See how his lips are still, while there are none
But him who do not sing. And he, perhaps—
Rudolph the Emperor—he might have healed
The wounds that have slain Italy. Too late
For someone else to save her. Her fate's sealed.
That other one, who seems to comfort him,
Rules where the waters spring that the Moldau
Brings to the Elbe, fills it to the brim,
And the Elbe takes them to the sea. Where now
Reigns Wenceslas, there once reigned Ottokar,
His father, who in swaddling bands was worth
More than his bearded wanton son by far.
And he whose nose is of small height and girth,
So cheek by jowl with him of the fair face,
The first is Philip, third king of that name,
Who led the fleur-de-lis to great disgrace,
And died of shame and heartbreak. A sad fame
To have. No wonder here he beats his breast.
And see the other one, who lays his cheek
Upon his hand and sighs, more than the rest:
Henry the Fat, King of Navarre. We seek
In those two the twin fathers of the pest
Of France, Philip IV, hard to forgive;
He sent the papacy to Avignon.
The foul and vicious way he chose to live
They both know, and the grief is never gone,
But like a lance it pierces them. And he
So strong and handsome, wore a belt of strands
One each for all the virtues, proud to be
Peter of Aragon. Beside him stands
Charles of Anjou (that long-nosed one, you see?):

100

110

120

130

A vicious streak, but still the first great Guelph.
And if the youth who sits behind him had
Reigned longer after than the man himself,
His virtue, all the good and nothing bad,
Might well have passed from one cup to the next.
But Peter died before his father. Nor
Were all those other heirs of his less vexed:
140 James, who had ruled in Sicily before
He did in Aragon, and Frederick, who
Took Sicily, each has his realm, but not
A better heritage. Those times are few
That human worth hangs on to what it's got
While rising through the branches. This holds true
Because who gives it wills it must be sought
From Him. I speak of that one with the nose
Not less than Peter. To them both, that thought
Applies. Apulia is in the throes
150 Of pain. So is Proenza. There was need,
From Charles to Charles, of a maintained process.
The plant was so much stronger than the seed,
The second to the first was that much less
In force than Peter to the second. See
Henry of England sitting there alone
Who ruled his life with pure simplicity,
He fathered one who did well on his own:
Edward, that brave boy. He that sits most low
Among them, on the ground, and with raised eyes,
160 Is Marquis William Longsword, whom we know
Lived in a cage, held as a human prize
By Alessandria, and died, and so
Let loose the war, and Monferrato weeps
And Canavese: war that never sleeps.

CANTO 8

Now was the hour that longing turns around,
For sailors, towards what they left behind;
The hour that melts their hearts when, outward bound
For just one day, the last light brings to mind
That they have said goodbye to dearest friends;
The hour that pierces the new pilgrim deep
With love, if he should hear what the bell sends
From far away, the sound of chimes that weep
In mourning for the dying day. It ends
10 In sadness, and I started not to hear
Sordello, as a soul had caught my eye
Who'd risen and made signs to catch my ear.
He lifted his joined palms, stared at the sky
Eastward, and seemed to say "Nothing I care
For anything but that." A Latin phrase,
Te lucis ante, floated on the air:
The prayer at nightfall. Such sweet interplay
Of notes came from his lips, and so devout,
That I was taken from myself, and then
20 They all joined in, and sang the hymn throughout,
Sweetly and piously, and once again
They eyed the starry wheels of the divine.
Now look with sharpened eye towards what's true,
Reader, for surely here the veil's so fine
That going in is scarcely hard to do.

I saw that noble host, without a sign
Or word, pallid and humbled, look on high
As if in expectation, and I saw
Appear above and come down from the sky
30 Two angels, and the flaming swords they bore
Were broken short, without points. Garments green
As leaves born just a breath ago they wore,
Trailing behind them. These clothes could be seen
To fluctuate, made airy by their wings.
One stopped and took his stand a little bit
Above us, and the other varied things
By landing on the far bank, thus to fit
The company between them. Their blond hair
Was plain to see. Their faces, though, left me
40 Bedazzled, since no faculty can bear
Excess. "Both angels are the progeny
Of Mary's bosom," said Sordello. "They
Keep watch here on the valley, for the snakes
Will shortly come." Not knowing quite which way
To turn, I turned around, chilled with the shakes,
And sought the trusty shoulder. "Now let's go,"
Sordello said, "down there into the dell
And hear what those shades have to say. I know
To see you walk alive will please them well."
50 Only three paces downward, I believe,
Brought me below, and I saw one who stared
At me as if, albeit looks deceive,
He might have known me. Now the light so fared
That the air already darkened, yet night's gain
Was not our loss. What was shut off before
Between his eyes and mine was now made plain.
We stepped towards each other then, and more
Delighted I could not have been. What pain,
Noble Judge Nino, had you, being dead,
60 Been guilty too! But you were here. Between
Us two were no fine greetings left unsaid,

And then he asked: "And how long has it been
Since you sailed on the distant seas that led
To this high mountain road?" "The way I came,"
I said, "was through the sad realm, and it was
This morning, from the first life. All the same,
I hope to gain the second life, because
This leads to that." Judge Nino, having heard
These thoughts, drew, like Sordello, a step back,
70 As men, bewildered by a sudden word,
Who strive to find the clarity they lack.
One turned to Virgil, and the other turned
To someone seated there, and "Conrad, rise!"
He cried, "Come see what we have learned
God's grace has willed! Stand up and feast your eyes!"
To me, then: "By those special thanks you owe
To Him who keeps the purpose of his will
So secret no one can completely know
Its nature, there's a task you should fulfil:
80 When you return across the wide waves, show
Giovanna, my dead daughter, where to plead
My case, for heed is paid to innocence
In Heaven. Her poor mother now, indeed,
No longer brings, I fear, to my defence,
Much love for me. She gave up the white veil
Of widowhood, which she must now regret
In misery. She shows us it must fail,
The force of love, and women will forget
In time, unless the flames by sight and touch
90 Are kept alert. The viper of Milan
Which leads their troops afield won't do as much
To make so fair a tomb as I began
To do with my device, which was the proud
Cock of Gallura. Were we man to man
As one Visconti to another, bowed
Would that one be, and she would love me yet."
He spoke like that, and as he did, his face

With that invariable will was set
Which burns first in the heart, and earns its place
100 Through piety. Meanwhile, my greedy glance
Kept going to the sky just where the wheel
Of stars slows, as spokes near the axle dance
A stately measure. Virgil: "Son, why steal
So many looks up there?" I seized the chance
To have my question answered. "What are those
Three torches I see flaming at the pole?"
And he: "These three shine here at the day's close
Where those four shone this morning, but their role
Is different. Supernatural virtues these
110 Betoken, while the others on the whole
Stand for the best of earthly qualities."
While Virgil spoke, Sordello reached for him
And held him, saying "Look! Our enemy!"
Pointing a path into the air grown dim.
And where the dell had no wall, we could see
A snake, such as, perhaps, gave Eve the food,
The bitter fruit. Through flowers and grass it slid,
The vile streak, and it had the attitude—
Turning it head as often as it did
120 And licking its own back—of some smug beast
That preens itself. I didn't see just how—
So can't say here, though I can hint, at least—
The holy falcons set out, but they now
Both plainly flew across the lesser light.
The serpent heard their green wings cleave the air
And turned and fled back to its nest, the night.
The angels then regained their posts, a pair
Of hunting birds abreast. Meanwhile, the shade
Close to the judge since he was called, did not
130 One single moment shift his gaze. It stayed
On me. "So may it prove that you have got
In your free will enough wax for the fuel
The lantern needs to light you to the peak,

The enamelled summit," he began, "the rule
Is, if you bring the news with you, then speak
To me of Valdimagra or the land
Nearby, for there I once was very great—
I, Conrad Malaspina. Understand:
Not the old Conrad who built our estate
140 Beside the sea, but nephew to him, and
That loving care I lavished on my kin
Is here refined to proper love, of God."
"I never came to where your lands begin,"
I said, "The earth you owned I never trod,
But who in Europe knows not the renown
Of you and yours? Your honoured family name
Exalts your lords and holdings with a crown.
Those who were never there revere your fame.
But now you're here, and I can swear to you—
150 As one who hopes indeed to go above—
Your honoured line, whatever it might do,
Will never throw away the praise and love
Brought by its liberal purse and skilful sword.
Nature and practice will take turns to bring
Such privilege when they're in close accord,
The guilty head in Rome can't change a thing.
Although he turn the world awry, your line
Goes straight, alone, and scorns the evil path."
And he: "True, true. That very thought is mine,
160 And seven years will bring an aftermath.
Scarcely so often will the sun return
To rest in that bed which the Ram bestrides
With all of its four feet, before you learn
Such kind opinions can be nailed inside
Your brain by sharper nails than men can talk,
Driven by power far beyond men's pride.
Unless God's wishes can be held in balk,
You will be there to see a sweet release
From agony. My family will make peace."

CANTO 9

In Italy the dawn, once mistress of
Worn-out Tithonus, whitened with its light
The window of the east, and from her love
Drew free. The gems on her sweet brow were bright,
Set in the form of that cold little beast
The scorpion, that stings men with its tail.
And here, the night, in step with that increased
Illumination, set out on its trail
Into the dark. Two climbing steps it made,
10 And almost on the third had closed its wings,
So it was nine at night. In me had stayed
Something of Adam's human weight, that brings
The need for sleep. Exhausted, I stretched out
Where five of us were seated on the grass,
And there I dreamed, and that dream was about
The hour near morning when the swallows pass
Their time in plaintive song—the memory,
Perhaps, of Philomela's ancient woe—
And when our minds, from mortal weight set free,
20 And mortal thought, in that state seem to know
The future like the past, so what we see
Looks like a vision of the not yet so.
I seemed to see an eagle gliding high
And poised, with feathers gold, and open wings

To plummet in a moment from the sky.
And I was at the place that Ovid sings—
My Virgil sang it too—where Ganymede,
Lost to his hunting friends, was taken up
By Jove—who took an eagle's shape and speed—
30   And rode the clouds, with all the gods to sup
And sit in council. For myself, I thought
Perhaps it strikes here only, and disdains
To use its mighty claws for the transport
Of anyone from elsewhere. For my pains
I was rewarded when I saw the bird
First wheel awhile before it fell my way
As frightful as the lightning. In a word,
Upon the instant I became its prey,
And up I went to meet the fire between
40   Earth and the moon, and there, it seemed, we burned
Together, and the flames that I had seen
Only in sleep so scorched me that they turned
Me out of bed, awake as I had been
Before I slept. Just as Achilles sprang
Awake after his mother, as he slept,
Transferred him—and of all this, Statius sang—
From Chiron's care to Skyros while she kept
Him in her arms, until, from there, the Greeks
Won him away, so I was startled too.
50   Sleep fled, and I felt, in my ice-cold cheeks,
The colour fade, which it is bound to do
In any face that feels fear. There alone
Beside me was my Comfort, and the sun,
Already two hours high, was on its own
Beyond its star companions. Night was done.
My gaze turned to the sea. "Now have no fear,"
My Leader said, "Take heart, for it bodes well
For us. Renew your strength, for you are near
To Purgatory, and there is how you tell:
60   That rampart rings it in. So now we're here.

And there's the entrance, where the mound looks split.
Not long ago, at dawn before the day
When your soul, on the flowers by which is lit
The place below, still slept, there came your way
A lady who said 'I am Lucy. Let
Me take this man that sleeps, so I can speed
Him on his road.' Sordello lingered yet,
With all the noble souls, and her first deed
Was taking you, and when the daylight shone
70 She took you up. I followed, till she put
You down, here, but her eyes first fixed upon
This opened entrance. Then she turned her foot
And she and sleep together were soon gone."
As those in doubt, when reassured, may find,
Through truth, that fear is turned to confidence,
So I was changed. My Guide saw how my mind
Was free from care, my face no longer tense.
He climbed the mound. I tagged along behind.
Towards the summit. Reader, you see how
80 I rise to a high theme. Don't wonder, then,
If I should elevate my manner now
With stronger rhymes and figures from my pen
As intricate as fancy may allow.
We drew near, and came to a point from which,
Where first I thought I saw only a gap
As if a dam were broken by a ditch,
I saw a gate, and that gate was the cap
For three steps leading up to it, each rich
With colour, and a porter, who said naught
90 As yet, and as I stared at him intent
Where he sat on the topmost step, I caught
The full force of his face, the way it sent
More light to me than I could bear the thought
Of feeling further on my eyes. A sword
Was naked in his hand, fit to reflect
The rays on us so I could not afford

One long look, but was driven to collect
The merest glimpses of its untoward
Brilliance. "From where you are, say what you seek,
And on whose warrant. See that your long climb
Be not to your harm. Name your sponsor. Speak.
Or do I look as if I'm made of time?"
"A woman from the sky, who is astute
In all these things," my Master answered, "said
To us just now 'You must be resolute:
Go that way. It's the gate. Just go ahead.' "
"And may she guide your footsteps on the route
To good," the courteous warder added. "So,
Come forward to our stairs." And we approached.
The first step was white marble with the glow
Of clarity, and smooth: no blur encroached.
I saw in it the face that best I know.
The second, darkest purple, burnt and rough:
A stone split lengthways and across. The third,
That weighed down from the top, looked near enough
To porphyry, yet flamed and swam and stirred
Like red blood spurting from a vein. On this
God's angel rested both his feet, then sat
Upon the threshold, which analysis
By eye alone said must have been a flat
Wide slice of adamant, without a flaw.
Up these three steps (Step One meant the first stage
Of penitence: contrition. By that law,
Step Two betokened the next shining page,
Confession; and Step Three, a true remorse—
The end point of regret's hard pilgrimage)
My Leader drew me with the holy force
Of his goodwill. "Now bid him that the bolt
Should be withdrawn, which is his given task:
But do it humbly." Those feet without fault
I threw myself in front of, there to ask
Devoutly that he open up, but first

I smote my breast three times. Then seven Ps
He traced across my brow with that sunburst
He called a sword, while I was on my knees.
"You're in," he said. "Try not to think the worst:
These wounds wash off." Cold ash, or earth dug dry,
Would match his raiment, out of which he drew
Two keys—one gold, one silver—to apply
140 (First one, the white, and then the yellow) to
The door so I could be content. "When one
Of these keys fails to open up the lock,"
He told us both, "the vital thing's not done:
The passage stays shut, solid as a rock.
One cost more, but the other one demands
More skill and wisdom if it is to move
The lock's wards, for it's he who understands
Who solves the knot. Mere doctrine may not prove
Sufficient. They were Peter's, and he bade
150 Me err through opening, not keeping closed—
So long as longing souls continue glad
To throw themselves, the way that they're supposed
To do, at my feet." Then he pushed the door
Of the hallowed gateway open. "Enter. But
You have to look," he said, "always before—
Look back and you will find the door swung shut,
With you outside again." Each single hinge
Belonging to that heaving, booming mass
Of metal door creaked fit to bring a cringe
160 Of shame to Rome's great rock that cried "Alas!"
The Tarpeian, that treasure house, roared less,
Nor showed itself more stubborn when the good
Metellus lost it by the ruthlessness
Of Caesar, and its groaning gate withstood
A legion, then gave way to the excess
Of force, and then that strong box was laid bare.
But this held treasure of a different kind.
"*Te deum.*" The sweet notes hung in the air.

"*Te deum laudamus.*" They touched my mind,
170 Those voices, and perhaps they started there.
I heard the same thing that we sometimes find
When human song and organ sound are joined,
And now the words are blurred, and now new-coined.

CANTO 10

When we were in the threshold of the gate
So rarely used because of misused love—
The fault that makes the crooked way look straight—
I heard it boom shut. Would I be excused,
I thought, if I should turn my eyes to it?
We climbed though a rock's cleft which turned one way
And then the other in a manner fit
For waves, that flood and flee but never stay.
"Here it would suit to use a little art
10 And alternate the side we fasten to,
Since each moves close before it draws apart."
So said my Guide about what we should do.
It made our steps so small the waning moon
Was back in bed and sinking into sleep
Before we left the needle's eye. But soon
Upon that, in the open, where the steep
Mountain draws back, we found our freedom. I
Was weary and we both lacked certainty
As to the way. We stopped, to get the lie
20 Of the land, on a place that looked to be
As flat and lonely as a desert track
Edged by the void, walled by the mountain's face.
In width it was a man laid on his back
Three times across. When I searched into space

As far as my keen eye could make its flight,
The terrace seemed to me to be the same:
Now on the left hand and now on the right,
No variation worthy of the name.
Our feet had not yet moved when I perceived
30 The curving wall, impossible to climb,
Was made of a white marble unrelieved
Except by carvings, calling up the time
Of Polycletus, though they would have shamed
Nature as well as him. The angel who
Came down to tell mankind—which had been blamed
For Adam—that there would be peace anew
And Heaven open now, had not been named
As Gabriel, but you could tell that there
He was, and carved so truly for his grace
40 Of attitude, he seemed to speak. One's ear
Heard *"Ave"* as he praised the lifted face
Of her who turned the key to love supreme,
And in her bearing were the words "Behold
The handmaid of the Lord," and did not seem
To be, but were, clear as a stamp may mould
A seal in wax. "Let not your eye grow fond
Of these alone." He had me on that side
Of him that keeps the heart. I looked beyond
The news for Mary, and then took a stride
50 Past Virgil and drew near to make the bond
By eye with what was there. Carved in the same
White marble wall, the cart and oxen drew
The Sacred Ark. Sad Oza won his fame
By touching it, and men learned not to do
What God had not said. But there was no name:
Not his, nor anyone's. There was no need
For that. Before the Ark appeared a crowd
Of seven choirs. Two senses disagreed:
"They're silent," said one, and "They sing aloud,"
60 The other said, prevailing. Similarly

The nose and eye disputed at the smoke
Of incense, for its lavish pungency
Was there and not there, and I smelt it soak
The air yet couldn't see it. And now he,
The humble psalmist, more and less than king,
Before the blessed vessel, danced his dance,
Swathed merely in a cloth. To hear them sing
And watch the monarch pirouette and prance,
Michal, Saul's daughter, and the king's first wife,
70 Was figured at a window straight above,
And clearly she was sad about her life
And scornful at his show of higher love.
Past her I moved to where another tale
Gleamed white, the glorious deed of that great prince
Of Rome whose gift for justice without fail
Moved Gregory to intercede, and since
That day he has a place in Paradise,
And not in Limbo: Trajan. And a poor
Widow was at his bridle, and the price
80 She paid in grief was seen there to be sore:
Her posture and her tears. The place around
The Emperor was trampled by a throng
Of knights—and once again I heard the sound.
The eagles on the gold flags all along
The grand procession felt the wind and flew.
Among all this the widow seemed to say
"Avenge me, Lord, for my dead son. For who
But you can ease my grief?" And he: "Today?
When I return." And she: "My Lord, when you
90 Return?" Her grief was urgent. "You might not."
And he: "Then he who takes my place will do
What you request." And she: "What have you got
Of goodness if another does the good
That you forget?" And he, at last: "You're right.
Take comfort, for I must do what I should
Before I go. Compassion for your plight

Asks me to stay, and justice orders me."
Nothing was ever novel in His sight,
And yet He said these wise things visibly—
100 I mean that you could see the sound—and that
Was new to us, because unknown on Earth.
While I took such delight in gazing at
These images of such exceeding worth
In this depiction of humilities
Distinguishing the great, and in the skill
Shown by the Craftsman of that sacred frieze,
My Poet said: "Forget about the hill
For now, and look on this side. See them walk
Towards us, many of them, but with slow
110 Steps. They will tell us, if we make them talk,
The best way to the next stairs. They must know."
My eyes, content by now with rich new things,
Were quick to turn to him. But, reader, don't
Imagine I would have you fold your wings
And fall from good resolve so that you won't
Know how God wants you to repay your debt:
Don't linger on its form but think of what
Comes next, and that, as bad as things can get,
Beyond the great Last Judgement it's not got,
120 And can't. "Master," I said, "these that we watch
Approaching us don't seem like people, and
I don't know what they are, such a hotchpotch
My vision has become." "Please understand,"
He said, "the grievous nature of their test
Has bent them double, so that even my
Eyesight is barely adequate at best
As to their nature, but you may descry—
If you try hard to pick apart what shows
Beneath their folded form—how each is served
130 With castigation as he slowly goes,
Crushed by the stone that keeps him tightly curved."
Christians vainglorious! Tired wretches who,

Made sick by the mind's vision, come to trust
A backward step, is it not clear to you
That we are caterpillars born, and must
Become the angelic butterfly that sails
Defenceless up to judgement? Why does your
Poor mind float so high that it strains and fails,
Since you are half-formed insects and no more,
140 Nothing but worms? As when a corbel props
A roof or ceiling, there is sometimes seen
A figure, breast on knees, whose strangeness stops
The heart of him who sees it, so I'd been
Impressed by these, each one bent more or less
As his sore back had more or less to bear,
And one that looked resigned to his distress
Seemed also, by his weeping, to despair,
Saying "I'm finished" with his will still there.

CANTO 11

"Our Father," sang the shades in unison,
"Who are in Heaven, where you reign unbound
Except by the great love you place upon
Your first works, the high circles spread around
Your throne like ripples, hallowed be your name
And power by every creature, as is fit
That they give thanks for what remains the same
For ever, your sweet love, the warmth of it.
Your Kingdom, may its peace reach down to us.
If it does not, we may not, left alone,
Reach it, no matter how industrious
We are. And as your angels all disown
Their will, and sing hosannas, so let men
Yield their will too. Give us that daily bread
Today, without which he goes back again,
Through bitter desert, who most looked ahead,
And laboured for release and to advance.
As we forgive all those who do us wrong,
Forgive us by your heart, without a glance
Towards our just deserts. And now our song
Is not for us: but don't put to the proof
Men's doubtful strength against the enemy
Of old. Teach them instead to stand aloof
From him who stirs its evil wrath. Though we

No longer need this, Lord, we ask it for
Those who remain behind us. So we sing
Our *Paternoster* for ourselves and more."
And thus beseeching fair wind and strong wing
Not just on their behalf but ours, they went—
30 Beneath their burden, as we sometimes dream
When we sleep badly, each a testament
To different weight of grief—done with their theme,
Their weary way around the terrace, all
Their effort dedicated to the purge
Of the world's fog. We'd do well to recall
Their soft words, meant to help us, that emerge
Always for love, and ask what should be done
And said by us for them, granted our will
Is good. Thus we might profit many a one,
40 Washing the stains away they carry still,
So they may go, at last made pure and light,
To see the starry wheels. Then Virgil: "Pray,
In order that you soon attain the height
By spread wings lifting you when you will weigh
No more than your desire, which way to take
Is best for a short route to find the stair?
And if there's more than one stair, for his sake
Who has come with me, and has clothes to wear
Of flesh like Adam's so one goes to sleep
50 Watching him climb, although it's only fair
To say he tries hard, which is the least steep?"
It wasn't clear who spoke up in reply
To what my Guide said, but this was the speech:
"Come with us to the right, where he can try
A passage where a living man may reach
The next stage up. Were I not hindered by
This stone which keeps my neck bowed and ashamed
And makes me hold my face down, I would look
At him who still lives yet has not been named
60 To see if I know him, and if he took

Pity on me for this, my load of pride,
To thank him. I was born in Italy,
A Tuscan. Family, on my father's side,
Aldobrandesco. I should say that he
Was actually Guglielmo. I don't know
If his name might have been once known to you?
My forebears' blood and great deeds made me so
Superb that I forgot how all men grew
To the common taste of milk. As you might know,
70   I scorned them all, and took my arrogance
So far I died from it. The Sienese
Will tell you how. They came to watch me dance
At home in Campagnatico, but fleas
Need time to kill a dog, and in the square
I rode and slew them by the bunch until
One of them got behind me. That day there,
My castle's children all remember still.
I am Umberto. Pride, ah, would it were
On me alone that it had wrought its ill:
80   Gladly I would have been sole sufferer.
But all my kinsmen it has ravelled in
The same calamity. I bear the load.
You saw humility. Here see the sin
Of lacking it. And so I walk this road
Till God is satisfied. I never did
Any of this among the living. Now
I do it with the dead." I heard, and hid
My face, and one of them, I don't know how—
He had not spoken—twisted underneath
90   His weight, saw me, and watched me all the while
He laboured, and he called through gritted teeth,
As I went with them, bending in their style,
Which strains the spine in every little part.
"Aren't you," I said, "the pride of Gubbio,
That Oderisi, lauded for the art
That Paris calls Illumination?" "So,"

He said, "they call me, brother. But the palm
Goes to Bologna, where young Franco's brush
Embellishes the pages with a calm
100   Intensity of form that makes me blush.
To him the honour, of which part is mine,
But no more. While I lived, though, I might well
Have taken on this point a different line,
Unbalanced by my impulse to excel.
But here, for pride like that, we pay the price,
And I would not be here yet, had I failed,
With power to sin, my boastful vice to quell.
I turned to God. Ah, how we are assailed
By empty glory in our skill! How brief
110   The green life of the leaves, unless an age
Of dead wood comes, to put it in relief!
But after Cimabue was the rage,
Make way for Giotto, hard upon his heels,
To dim his fame. And so it is with verse:
One Guido stands up as the other kneels.
It doesn't mean that Guinizelli's worse,
It only means that Cavalcanti's new,
And takes the title, Glory of Our Tongue—
And chances are the poet who will do
120   The same to him's already born, and young
And strong, and fit to chase him from the nest,
And once again sing what was never sung
Before, with turning head and puffed-up chest.
The world's noise is the breath of a light breeze
Which goes this way and that and changes name
Only because it changes quarter. Please,
Convince me how you might have the more fame
If you die old than if you died before
You gave up talking baby-talk, and when
130   A thousand years have passed, which is no more
Than one blink to the universe, what then?
The slowest wheeling stars move one degree

From west to east in every hundred years—
The merest moment of eternity—
And fame we measure by our falling tears,
That flow for just a while, and then run dry.
Of him ahead of me who struggles on,
All Tuscany resounded, and now try
To hear a whisper of him. His fame's gone.
140 Yes, even in Siena, where he reigned
When Florence's high riders were destroyed.
So full of pride they were, and it was drained,
And now they are like cheap whores, to avoid.
Your fame, it is the colour of the grass
Which comes and goes because what withers it
Is what induces its green tips to pass
Up through the earth." And I: "I must admit
Your speech makes my heart tremble, and abates
My own swelled head. But who is he of whom
150 You spoke just now?" "One of the one-time greats,
It's Provenzan Salvani," he said. "Room
Has here been found for him because he thought
In his presumption to have in his hands
All of Siena, so in pride he fought
And not against pride, until all those lands
Were his, and he has gone thus, without rest,
Since he met death. Such is the coin he pays
In quittance who, back there, would be the best."
And I: "I'm told the spirit that delays
160 Too long in life before repenting must
Remain outside that door and not ascend
Thus far unless good prayers are paid in trust
For long enough to match, from end to end,
His lifetime, so how comes it he is here?"
"When he was in his prime," the answer came,
"He chose—and his own shame he did not fear—
Siena's marketplace to be the frame
In which he stood, a living portrait of

Humility, as ransom for a friend
170 Rotting in Charles's gaol. This act of love
Was visible as suffering, to rend
The heart. His every vein and sinew shook.
I say no more, and know that what I say
Is dark, but soon your townsmen, who once took
Your part, will send you on a lonely way.
It was his self-abasement brought you through.
The bitter begging-bowl awaits you too."

CANTO 12

I and that burdened soul, as far as my
Sweet teacher let me, side by side went on
As though we were yoked oxen, brought low by
A load that curved us, all defences gone.
But then my Guide said "Now you must leave these
Behind, and move, for here it would be well,
With sail and oar and all your faculties,
To drive your own boat." Quickly, truth to tell,
I straightened up my body, though my mind
10   Stayed bowed and shrunken. Scared of come-what-might,
I set out eagerly to stay behind
My Guide, both proving that our steps were light,
And he: "Turn down your eyes. It will be well
For you to make your path a pleasure by
Seeing the flags you tread, the tales they tell."
As pavement tombs, to call up those who die,
Bear carved designs of what they were before,
For which so often tears are shed by those
Who have the gift of pity, as their store
20   Of memory is stirred, so there arose
From this unyielding and yet living floor,
The same sense of fine craftsmanship, but all
Of more verisimilitude, the whole
Breadth of the roadway from the mountain wall

Out to the edge. More noble in his soul
Than any creature, there see Satan fall
Like lightning from the sky on the one side.
Briareus, on the other, by the spear
Of Heaven pierced, lay heavy, petrified
30   By chill death. And Apollo, he was here,
With Mars and Pallas, all of them still armed,
About their father Jupiter. They gazed
On scattered giant limbs. Nimrod, alarmed
At his own cleverness, as if amazed
By his great babbling tower, stared at the charmed
People of Shinar, likewise proud of it.
Niobe! I saw you with crying eyes
Traced on the road, with company to fit
Your pride—alas, too late to make you wise—
40   Those fourteen helpless children slain. And you,
King Saul, you lay there dead on your own sword
In Gilboa, where never rain or dew
Would come again—abandoned by the Lord
For pride. And sad Arachne, you there too:
I saw you in the wrecked web of your thread,
Already half a spider, wretched, changed
From challenging Minerva. Every shred
Was there, and your new long legs were arranged
To show their bent joints high above your head.
50   Next, Rehoboam, King of Israel, whose
Depiction here seemed not to threaten, since
It fled by chariot as if to lose
Pursuers, but they weren't there. So that prince
Proved how his father, Solomon, was sage,
By being foolish with his rates of tax,
Goading the usual rumble to a rage.
And that hard pavement showed, as if in wax,
How Alcmaeon once proved that sad pearl string
Was costly to his mother; how his sons
60   Fell on Sennacherib to kill that king

In his own temple. And you'd swear blood runs
Just here, where Tomyris tells Cyrus "Now
The blood you thirsted for is yours to drink,"
She's talking to his severed head. Somehow,
Above the vat, his eyes appear to blink.
And here was Holofernes being slain,
And all his army of Assyrians
Fleeing in desperate rout across the plain,
Bereft of their proud leader and his plans:
70 I heard the slaughter, saw the cries of pain.
And Troy I saw in ashes. Ilion!
Pride brought your topless towers low, and vile
You were before you caught fire and were gone,
And these designs showed that in stunning style.
What master of the brush or chisel could
Have traced the shapes, incised the outlines there
Which even experts would have thought too good
For words? It seemed as if the living breathed the air,
And all the dead were dead. One who had seen
80 These actual things could not have seen them more
Clearly than I who saw all that had been,
As I went stooping. More now than before,
Chest out, head high and eyes front, sons of Eve!
Never look down to see your evil trail.
More of the mountain than I could believe,
We had encircled. That the sun could sail
So far so fast I'd likewise failed to guess,
Having been too absorbed, when he who gazed
Always ahead said: "Heads up! We have less
90 Time than you think for ambling round amazed.
Here comes an angel, as the time of day
Is marked by the sixth handmaid of the car
That hauls the sun. In flames she breaks away.
Make sure your look and general bearing are
Reverent to meet the herald. Let him be
Pleased to direct us. Days like this can dawn

Just once." Used to his well-worn homily
That I should not waste time, I was not torn
As to his meaning. The fair creature stepped
100   Towards us. He was clad in white. His face
Trembled, a star at sunrise. His wings swept
Wide with his open arms. "This is the place,"
He said, "that has the steps. From here, ascent
Is easy. Yet few come to meet this call.
You race of men, from birth you all were meant
To fly: how is it you consent to fall
Back down again just for a little bit
Of breeze, a puff of glory?" Then he led
The two of us to where the rock was split.
110   He struck my forehead with his wings, and said
My journey would be safe, he'd vouch for it.
As on the right hand when you climb the hill
To San Miniato there are stairs to break
That long hard pathway steep enough to kill—
Stairs put there by a city that could make
The right decisions, guard its measures, still
Keep records—so the bank that came down there,
Steep from the upper circle, could be climbed
With ease, but still the hefty rock, laid bare
120   On each side, pressed in close. And then there chimed,
As we stepped in between, voices in tones
So sweet—"Blessed are the poor in spirit"—no
Mere words could match. But how these broken stones
Were different from the doors I'd come to know
In Hell, for here the entrance teemed with songs
And there with lamentations! Now as we
Mounted the sacred stairs—and here one longs
For one plain phrase that fits—I seemed to be
Far lighter than I was before. "What weight,"
130   I asked my Master, "has been shorn from me
That I so blithely go up through the gate,
Almost without an effort?" "When that mark

Of *P* repeated on your brow sixfold—
Which once was seven—has all grown less dark
And disappeared, divine goodwill will hold
Your feet in such a mastery that they
Will find not only ease but sheer delight
In being urged on upward." Just the way
Those do when something unknown to their sight
Is on their head but they can guess by signs
From others that it's there, and with one hand
They search for it and find it, on those lines,
With my right hand's spread fingertips I scanned,
And did indeed find, just six times, the trace
Of that rune the keyholder with his brand
Had touched there to my brow, that tender place.
My Leader watched me with a smiling face.

Now we were on the top step of the stair,
A cutback in the mountain greeted us
A second time: there was a terrace there,
Ringing the hill with lesser radius,
And thus a sharper curve. No shade, all bare,
No carving. Just the blank road and the bank,
The livid stone. "If we should wait to ask,"
The Poet said, "our choice may, to be frank,
Be left too long." And so he made his task
To stare into the sun, and of his right
Side make a pivot, and bring round his left.
"You that I trust on this new road, sweet light,"
He said, "to show us through the warp and weft
Of this place we need guidance in, you give
Warmth to the world to match the light you cast.
Unless Grace argues otherwise, we live
According to your beams from first to last."
Already, there, we'd gone what we would call
A mile here—made quick by our eager will—
When we heard spirits flying that were all
Voices. Unseen they flew to us, to fill
The air around us with their biddings to
Love's table. And the first voice that flew past
Shouted "They have no wine!" and as it flew

Beyond us cried the same thing, and at last
Was almost out of earshot when the next
Went by us crying "I'm Orestes!" Nor
Did that one stay. "Father," I said, perplexed,
"What are these voices?" But there was one more.
30 It said "Love those from whom you've suffered wrong!"
My Guide: "The sin of envy meets its scourge
In this round, and of that scourge every thong
Flaying that disposition must emerge
From love. And thus the curb that speaks against
The sin must sing the virtue. You will hear
That sound, if I judge right, when we've commenced
Our entry to the Pass of Pardon. Near
Us now, if you look straight ahead, you'll see
People before us, spaced along the cliff."
40 With wider eyes I looked in front of me,
And there sat shades in cloaks that looked as if
They shared the colour of the stone, and when
We went a little further I heard cries
Of "Mary, pray for us," of "Michael," then
Of "Peter" and "All Saints." Still my mind tries
In vain to think of just one man alive
On Earth today so hard he'd not have been
Transfixed by pity. Nor did I arrive
So near them that their movement could be seen
50 Without the eyes that saw them being wrung
By great grief. A coarse haircloth seemed to wrap
Their figures, and one from the other hung
On proffered shoulders, side by side, no gap,
All propped up by the bank. Just so the blind
And destitute turn up to beg at church
As if they sought indulgence, and you find
Them leaning on each other and you search
Your pockets, moved to pity not just by
Their words but by their looks which plead no less.
60 And as the blind take, from the sun on high,

Small profit, so the light brings no largesse
To these shades in this place I speak of here.
All had their eyelids stitched with iron wire
Like untamed falcons. And it did appear
To me that my effrontery was dire,
Seeing these others while I was unseen.
I turned to my wise Comfort. Well he knew
What my embarrassed silence had to mean,
And said "Speak to the point, but speak up, do."
70 As we walked on the terrace past this scene,
Virgil was with me at the edge where one
Might fall, for that side had no parapet,
And on my other side I saw tears run,
Bathing the cheeks of those shades I see yet:
Devout shades, but their eyes were ghastly seams
Remorse, from envy, forced their weeping through.
To them I said "The one aim of your dreams,
To see the light on high, will come to you,
You may be sure, and grace will then soon clear
80 The scum your conscience builds, so that the flow
Of memory may run without a smear.
In view of that, pray tell me if you know—
And if you do, I'll hold the kindness dear—
If anyone Italian is among
Your number. If I'm told, it may be well
For him." And then I heard someone give tongue.
"Brother, there is a truth you need to tell:
All here are of one city. If there were
Any that lived in Italy, then say
90 They lived as pilgrims." This polite demur
Came from, I thought, a little up the way,
So that I raised my voice. Among the press
I saw a shade marked by expectancy—
And if you wonder how I came to guess,
It raised its chin the way the blind do. "Be
Frank with me, spirit," I said. "You that bow

To mount up high, if it was you I heard
Just then, your name and city tell me now."
"Siena," she replied, "and, in a word,
I cleanse myself here of my life of sin
Like all the others, weeping to Him, that
He give himself to us. Wisdom was in
My name but not in me. My name fell flat,
Sapia, for I rejoiced in others' hurt
Far more than at my own good luck, and lest
You think that I deceive you, I assert
The truth: that when the arc had passed the crest
Of my years, I was mad already. My
Townsmen were in Val d'Elsa, but the foe
Joined battle with them. And that day, on high,
The thing was willed that I had prayed for. So
My nephew and his Ghibelline pigsty
Of suckers-up were hounded down the track
Of bitter flight, and, as I watched the chase,
Gladness beyond bounds seized me. I threw back
My head and aimed at Heaven my bold face,
Crying to God 'I fear you now no more!'
Just like the blackbird when the sun returned.
Near death, I sought God's peace, and I'd be sore
Pressed for a lessening—or so I've heard
It said—of all my debts by penitence
Had Peter the Comb-Seller, holy man
And hermit, not wrapped me in his immense
Mantle of charity. Yes, he began
To put my name in his petitions. Mine!
But who are you that, as he goes, enquires
About us, and, I think I can divine,
Speaks with the breath, whose eyes are free of wires?"
"I, too," I said, "will lose my eyesight here,
But only for a little. My own sins
In envious looks were small. A greater fear
Suspends my soul until it slowly spins:

I mean the grief below. Brought on by pride.
That load is with me as this climb begins."
And she: "You're here with us. Who was the guide
That brought you up, if you think to retrace
Your steps?" And I: "He that is with me, who
Does not speak. And I live. Now, by the grace
To which you've been elected, spirit, you
140 Have not yet asked, as others in your place
Have done, if, yonder, I can speak and move
On your behalf." "Ah," she replied, "so strange
Is this to hear, that it's enough to prove
God loves you. Somehow, then, you might arrange
To help me with your prayers. You I implore,
By what you crave most, if you ever tread
The soil of Tuscany, that you restore
My name among my kin. You'll find them spread
Among that vain race who wait for their dream
150 In Talamone. Yes, our own seaport
One day, but now a long and fevered scheme
For losing money, of the self-same sort
As our eternal quest to find the stream
That flows beneath our land. Siena! Sail
On wings of fantasy! How can you fail?"

CANTO 14

"Who's this, that makes the circuit of our hill
Before death comes to him to grant his flight,
Who shuts his eyes and opens them at will?"
"I don't know, though I do know to this height
He doesn't come alone. But you ask first,
Since you are nearest. Make your greeting kind,
That he may speak." In that way they rehearsed:
Two spirits propped together, of a mind
To talk with us. "Embodied soul," one said,
10   "Who heads for Heaven, tap your sympathy:
Tell us your name and provenance. We're led
To marvel not just at the novelty
Of your arrival here, but at the grace
You're given." I: "Through central Tuscany
A stream winds, whose beginnings we can trace
To Falterona, for a hundred miles
And more, and on its banks this shape was born.
My name? A man must make a name who styles
Himself by name, and blowing my own horn
20   Would make no sense, as yet." And then the shade
Who'd spoken first said "If I have the wit
To catch your meaning, by those words you made
Allusion to the Arno." "Think of it,"
The other chipped in. "Why did he conceal

The river's name? Such secrecies are fit
For those to whom a horror is too real."
The shade who'd been addressed said, "I don't know,
But it is fitting such a valley's name
Should perish, since for all its rancid flow
30   From far up in those mountains with the fame
Of having given birth to a large part
Even of Sicily—a source that teems
With many waters—with a racing start
Of far more than its share of brooks and streams,
From that source, all the way downhill to where
It gives back to the sea all that the sky
Draws from it so that rivers may be there,
For all the way that river meets the eye
Virtue is held an enemy by all:
40   A snake to flee from. This could be because
Of mischief in the ground, or you might call
The gift a custom, passed on without pause
Through generations, so that those who dwell
In that sad valley are now so debased
In nature, it might seem they might as well
Be Circe's pigs, pastured on their own waste.
At first, through Casentino, among hogs
Who filthily eat acorns and prefer
That diet to man's food, through ponds and bogs
50   It makes its feeble way, and then the spur
Of land that bends it brings it to the dogs
That snarl out of Arezzo more than they
Have any right to for their actual power.
From there, in scorn, it turns its snout away
And goes on falling, swelling by the hour.
The more it does, the more does the accursed
And ill-starred ditch find dogs transmogrified
To wolves, at Florence, which should be the worst,
But there is more, because, from either side
60   Hemmed in, it falls through gorges, down to meet

The Pisan foxes: lithe and full of guile,
They know no trap their cunning can't defeat.
Nor will I, even for a little while,
Stop talking just because this mortal hears:
He ought to bear in mind that what I say
I am inspired to lay forth for your ears
By truth, and I see there will come a day
When your grandson, who hunts the wolves and sends
Them frantic in their fear, will sell their meat
70 Still living, and for many their life ends
In slaughter, like old cattle. It's complete:
A double robbery. They lose their lives
And he his honour. From the wretched wood
He comes forth bloody, having cut with knives
The trees that will not once more come to good
Inside a hundred years." As when bad news,
No matter where it comes from, pales the face
Of him who hears, I saw the other lose
Composure as these words sank into place.
80 The speech of one, the other's look, made me
Eager to know their names, and so with much
Entreaty, I put questions, whereat he
Who spoke to me before said "You, by such
Demands, would have me do for you what you
Do not for me. But seeing that God wills
His grace to shine through you, this I will do
Without a grudge, a servant who fulfils
Your wish. Know, then, I am the Ghibelline
Guido del Duca. So did envy flame
90 In my blood, that no sooner had I seen
A happy man, but colour overcame
My features. I was livid. Here I reap
The straw I sowed. Ah, humans, why this urge
To set your hearts on what no one can keep
Except alone, so you can never merge
In partnership? But my companion here

Is Rinier, great Guelph, pride of the stem
Of Calboli, for none since has come near
Inheriting his worth. But all of them—
Not just his line alone—all have been shorn
In the Romagna, of their virtues, real
Or just for show, possessed or merely worn,
For in that land the ground by now, you feel,
Is so full of envenomed shoots, the plough
Would never get them out. But Lizio,
The good and courteous, where is he now?
Pier Traversaro and the kind Guido
Da Prata? And so many others. How
Is it that they are gone? The Romagnoles
Have turned to bastards. Tuscan, don't be stunned
That I should weep for all those noble souls,
The ladies and the knights, the endless fund
Of stories about deeds and sports to which
Love moved us, and good manners. And now think
How hearts are grown malicious and are rich
In nothing but the depths to which they sink.
Ah, Bertinoro! My sweet nest! Where I
Spent years of safety high above lush fields!
How is it you don't will yourself to die,
When all your finest families and their shields
Are fled from the corruption? Better far
Bagnacavallo, where they breed no more.
Both Conio and Castrocaro are
Worse off because the counts spawn as before.
Again, so many others . . . But enough.
Tuscan, go on your way, for now my choice
Is not to talk but weep, so much the stuff
Of our discussion wrings my heart." His voice
Fell silent. Since we knew they heard us leave,
That they were mute made us more confident
Our way was right and it would not deceive.
And then again, as on alone we went,

Another voice, as if a lightning bolt
Should cleave the air, flew into us, and said
The words of Cain acknowledging his fault.
"Whoever finds me, slays me," and it fled
As thunder, at the sudden cloudburst, dies.
And when our ears had just a moment's rest,
Another roared as if to split the skies
140 Like one more thunderclap that closely pressed
Upon the first. "I am Aglauros, turned
To stone because my sister had the love
Of Mercury. I envied, and I earned
A place here." On our way to high above,
I took a step aside, instead of straight
Ahead, so as to have my Guide's support.
The air by now was in a quiet state
All round, and he: "That stretch, one would have thought,
Was hard enough to hold a man in bounds,
150 But not you. No, you took the bait. The hook
Of your old enemy, his sights and sounds,
Got into you. He reads you like a book,
And then no curb applies or prize appeals.
The heavens call you, whirl about you, show
Their endless beauty. You—and the mind reels
At all the petty stuff you crave to know—
See only the sad business of the Earth.
He smites you, He who knows what that is worth."

CANTO 15

Evening in Italy, and here, midnight.
The same amount the sun, that always plays
Between its tropics like a child, gains height
From dawn to the third hour, was, in the day's
Last quarter, left to run, down where you are,
And here the beams struck us full in the face,
For we had gone around the hill so far
We headed straight into the west. The place
And time weighed down my brow more than before

10 By far, the splendour of it. But the cause
Being unknown, I was left dazed, and wore
My hand above my eyebrows without pause,
To temper the excess of light with shade.
As from the water or the mirror rise
All rays at the same angle that is made
When they go down, and so come to our eyes
With undeflected force and do not fade—
As science and experiment have proved—
Just so it seemed to me that I was hit

20 By such a light that my poor eyesight moved
Away at high speed. "Tell me, what is it
That I can't shield my eyes from, gentle Guide,
And seems to come near?" "Do not be amazed,"
He said, "If Heaven's household, glorified,

Still dazzles you and leaves you walking dazed.
This is a messenger, who has been sent
To call you to the climb, and very soon
The sight of these will hold no element
Of hardship, but indeed will be a boon:
30   Delight as great as you are fit to feel."
The blessèd angel, when we reached him, said
With glad voice: "Enter here." This soft appeal
Was further eased when we began to tread
A stairway less steep than the others. We
Were soon through, and were mounting, when we heard
"The merciful are blessed." The melody
Was sung behind us, and then, word for word,
"Rejoice, for you have won." My Guide and I
Ascended by ourselves, and as we walked
40   I thought to profit from his words. "So why
Did that one from Romagna, when he talked
Of 'owners,' 'partners' and what each can buy,
Think I would understand?" And he: "He knows
The cost of his worst fault, and so it's not
A wonder he reproaches it, to close
The gap between himself and what he got
From envy: great regret. And as for you,
It is because your wishes are still set
On having more by sharing less, that through
50   Your heart the sin of envy even yet
Can blow its bellows and you sigh: but should
The love of higher things bend up your need
Away from one man's sense of what is good,
That fear would leave your breast. For it is greed,
And there on high, the more who love the phrase
'It's ours' more than 'It's mine,' the more of worth
Each one possesses, and the more the blaze
Of charity in that court." I then: "Dearth
Of knowledge deepens. If I'd held my peace
60   Before, I would have less perplexity.

How can it be that each one may increase
His share the more the more there are to be
Given the share?" And he: "Let wonder cease:
Because your mind's still set on earthly things
You gather shadows from the light. Above,
The good is endless, beyond words. It wings
With all speed in the same way towards love
As sunbeams do to something bright. It gives
Itself the more the more of love it finds.
As charity extends, the more it lives,   70
And all the souls in love up there it binds
Together with more love. Love propagates,
Returning from a mirror. If my speech
Leaves you still hungry, then a feast awaits.
You will see Beatrice, and how she, from each
And every craving that you have, will make
You free. Seek only to expunge the five
Wounds you have left, though doing that will take
A painful healing. Grit your teeth and strive:
Two gone, and five to go." And when I was   80
About to say "All right. Bring on the day,"
I saw we'd reached the right road, and because
My eye was keen, not one word could I say.
Visions of ecstasy held me enthralled.
A populated temple. At the door,
A woman, sweet-faced like a mother, called:
"My son, how can you do this to us? For
Your father and I seek you, and are sad."
She said that, then she vanished. There came next
A further woman. On her cheek she had   90
The running waters of somebody vexed
With rancour at another. Fighting mad,
She said: "If you are Lord of Athens, whose
Name brought the gods to battle, and from which
All knowledge shines, then vengeance you should use
On those bold arms that fancied themselves rich

And well enough born to reach out and hold
Our daughter. Pisistratus! Justice calls!"
Her lord, it seemed to me, without being cold,
100 Was gentle, gracious, tranquil. "If it falls
To us to choose, what shall we do to one
That seeks our harm, if we should so condemn
Someone who loves us? Come, can this be done?"
But I saw others, and the case with them
Was otherwise. In wrath they slew a youth
With stones, and they were shouting "Kill! Kill! Kill!"
And down he sank to earth, because, in truth,
Already death weighed down on him, but still
His eyes were gates to Heaven even in
110 His agony, bidding the Lord bestow
A pardon on his killers in their sin,
And by his look you knew it would be so,
For it unlocked compassion. When my soul
From just itself came back to what was real
Outside of it, existence as a whole,
I saw that these dreams had been sent to deal
With things in my mind. And my Guide, aware
That I was fighting my way free from sleep,
Said "What's wrong? Have you come back? Are you there?
120 For half a league or more I watched you keep
Upright with difficulty, your eyes veiled,
Your feet adrift as if fatigue or wine
Or both befuddled you." And thus assailed,
I said "Kind father, such fault was not mine.
Listen, and I will tell you why I failed
To keep my feet. I saw something. But what?"
And he: "Had you a hundred marks upon
Your forehead, still your faintest thoughts would not
Be hidden from me. What you saw, now gone,
130 Was shown to you so you would not neglect,
From lethargy, to open up your heart
Before those peaceful waters that collect

First in the fountain where they have their start
And then pour forth eternally. Nor did
I ask what ailed you as one asks who sees,
Unseeing, someone lifeless, lying rid
Of all signs, but I asked it to appease
My urge to give your feet force, in their bid
To climb. So must the slow be spurred. They waste
Their waking hour when it comes back." We went
On through the evening, and the way we faced,
Ahead, our concentrated gaze we sent,
Against the bright late rays, when, plume by plume,
Black smoke approached, and I mean black as night.
No getting out of it: there wasn't room,
And soon it took from us our whole eyesight
And all our pure air, so we might as well,
Even up here, have been back there in Hell.

CANTO 16

Neither in Hell's gloom nor in cloudy night
Bereft of stars and planets, had I yet
Known in my life a veil that blocked my sight
So thick, of stuff so harsh, as that one set
To my eyes by the smoke that wrapped us there,
Choking the eyelids shut. Therefore my wise
And faithful escort moved in close, and where
His shoulder was, I felt, and in the guise
Of someone blind who stays behind his guide
10 To skirt what, knocked against, might hurt or kill,
So I edged through the foul and bitter tide.
He kept on saying—I can hear it still—
"Don't get cut off from me." On every side
Were voices, and they seemed to pray for peace
And mercy to God's Lamb, that took away
Our sins. And always those hymns without cease
Had the same words, beginning *"Agnus Dei,"*
And just one measure, their accord complete.
I asked, "Are all these spirits that I hear?"
20 And he: "They are. The prayers that they repeat
Mean that they strive to bring the moment near
When they will lay the knot of anger loose."
"Who are you that come here to cleave our smoke
And speak as if you tell time by the use

Of words that once were Roman?" one voice spoke.
My Master: "Answer, and make sure you ask
Is this the way up." And I: "You that make
The cleansing of yourself your present task
So you may shine in fairness when you take
30   The road back to the one that made you, you
Will hear a marvel if you stay near me."
"I will, as far as I'm permitted to,"
He said, "And if the smoke won't let us see,
Hearing will keep us joined." And then I said
"Wrapped in the flesh that death undoes, I find
My way up, and I came here through the dread
Reaches of Hell, and since God has a mind
To take me into grace, and I am led
Alive, like no one else after St. Paul,
40   To see His court, don't hide from me, but tell
Me who you were, and if the entrance hall
To the next stage is on this road. Then well
May your words be our escort." "I knew all
The world," he said. "I, Marco. Lombard, I:
Lover of qualities for which they now
Can't bend the bow to let the arrow fly,
Let alone hit them. Straight ahead is how
You go. I pray that when you reach the sky
You'll pray for me." And I to him: "I pledge
50   My faith to you to do what you now seek,
But still a doubt within keeps me on edge
To breaking point. What I have heard you speak
Doubles the doubt I brought here from Guido,
And so confirms the world must be indeed
Barren of virtue, as you've let me know:
With evil decked, and evil in the seed.
But now I pray you say why this is so.
Tell me the cause, that I may tell the world.
Some say the fault is in our stars, and some
60   It's in ourselves." And here a sigh unfurled,

Saying "Alas" for grief. "Brother, you come
Indeed from the blind realm, for you, that live,
Refer all causes to the sky alone,
As if it, only, had the power to give
Movement to things. Were it to wholly own
That property, however, all free will
Would leave you, and there'd be no justice in
Joy for good deeds or grief for doing ill.
The star-field helps your impulses begin.
70 I don't say all of them, but if I did,
On good and bad and on free choice it shines:
Choice which, if it survives that first armed bid
To shape it, will be raised on the right lines
And conquer all. It's to a greater force
And better nature you, since freedom's yours,
Are subject. Therein lies the one true source
Of your mind, which the mere stars lack the laws
To rule. Thus, if the present world should veer,
The cause is in you, and it must be sought
80 In you. To prove this to you, I am here,
Your faithful scout. Just like a child in sport,
With tears and smiles, our little simple soul
Emerges from His hand. He looks at it
With fondness, though as yet it lacks the whole
Of knowledge, and so far is scarcely fit
To be considered as itself. It moves
Because its Maker moves it, when it turns
To what attracts it, and at first it proves
Each trifling good by taste, and what it learns,
90 Being beguiled, is to run after more,
If guide and curb don't turn its love aside.
For law to be a brake on this, therefore,
There was a need, a law to override
The impulse of delight: need for a king
Fit to make out the tower's tip at least
Of the true city. Law: well, there's a thing.

The law exists, but by default has ceased
To be enforced. No emperor, and the Pope
Knows the law's letter but ignores its heart.
100 Our shepherd, going on before, can cope
With worldly things, but the unearthly part
Escapes him. He has half the pastoral scope.
He chews the cud, but has not the split hoof,
And therefore is unclean: we may not eat.
Just watch the people, if you want the proof:
They see him snatching at the easy meat
They too are greedy for, and do the same,
Asking no more. Thus you can see it plain:
Ill guidance is the cause of the ill fame
110 The world has earned, this wicked world of pain—
Bad leadership, not nature gone to rot
In you. For Rome, which made the just world, could
Boast two bright suns once, as it now cannot.
Each clarified one path: not bad and good,
But world and God. And now what have we got?
One quells the other. Sword and shepherd's crook
Are joined, and all for ill, since, joined, the one
Has no fear of the other. Take a look—
If you should doubt this tale of mischief done
120 By false ambition—at an ear of corn,
For plant is known by seed. There on the land
Between the Adige and Po, were born,
And grew for generations, a great band
Of all the brave and courteous, and then
The Emperor Frederick met his nemesis,
The papacy, and now only those men
Can cross it safely who would rather miss,
For shame, all converse with the virtuous,
Or even a mere meeting. Growing old
130 Down there are three men we might well discuss
As paragons the ancient times may hold
Up to the new as figures of reproof.

Currado and Gherardo were dead straight,
And Guido da Castel was not aloof
From all the horsemen who passed by his gate—
Such that the French would call him, in their style,
The guileless Lombard. So we may deduce
The Church of Rome, divided all this while
Into two powers, falls without excuse
140 Into the mire, itself and its great task
Both utterly befouled." "You put the case
With skill, my Marco," said I. "I need ask
No more why Levi's sons and all that race
Who served the tabernacle were debarred
From worldly goods. But tell me who he is,
Gherardo, who yet breathes to give a hard
Lesson in virtue from an age once his
To this age of barbarity in which
We now must live." He said: "Either your speech
150 Deceives me, or it tests me. Phrase and pitch
Are Tuscan, yet somehow I have to teach
You everything about Gherardo. Him
I know by no last name, because it's been
Dragged in the dirt, its lustre dusted dim,
By his loose daughter Gaia. This I've seen,
A true sign of today. Now may the Lord
Be with you, for no further can I walk
With you. There is a risk I can't afford,
Much as I have enjoyed our little talk.
160 You see there, where the smoke is turning white?
It will turn brighter yet, and you will see
An angel, for he is that source of light.
But I must leave you before he sees me."
He turned back, cutting short our colloquy.

Remember, reader, if you've ever been
Caught in the mountain mist so nothing could
(Except as moles see, through the skin) be seen,
How, when the day showed signs of coming good,
The dense white vapours started to unclasp
And through them the sun's feeble disc appeared?
Remember that, and your mind soon may grasp
How I, at first, and as its setting neared,
Now saw the sun again. And so I came,
My step matched to my Guide's in that pale glow,
Forth from the fog to see the beams whose flame
Was close to dying on the beach below.
Imagination! With your power to steal
Our thoughts, at times, away from actual things—
So that, although a thousand trumpets peal
Around us, still we pay no heed—who stings
You into life when our dulled senses feel
Nothing to offer you? The light that moves
Your workings takes its form in Heaven, by
Itself or by God's will, which, if that proves
To be the maker, sends it down the sky
To you. Of Philomela's sister, when
Pursued for her foul deed she changed her shape
Into a nightingale, the imprint then

10

20

Entered my thoughts. My mind tried to escape—
Ah, Procne, how your crime dismayed all men!—
Into itself, so nothing from outside
Could be received. But then came raining down,
Through my high fantasy, the crucified
30 Figure of Haman; scornful his fierce frown,
Dying in anger, and around him were
Ahasuerus in his greatness, and
Esther his queen—it was because of her
That Haman's plot against Jews in that land
Was foiled—and there her cousin Mordecai,
Of such integrity in word and deed;
And as the image on my inner eye
Paled by itself, a bubble in sore need
Of the water that it formed in, there arose
40 The vision of a girl in bitter tears,
And she said "Queen, how was it that you chose,
From anger, to cut short your natural years?
You died for me, for your Lavinia,
To keep me. But you should have loved me less,
And now I am the one who mourns, for far
More than the ruin of my Turnus. Yes,
The wreck I weep for endlessly is yours."
As sudden new light causes sleep to break,
Which, being broken, fitfully restores
50 Itself before it fades and we're awake,
So my imagination fell away
As soon as a bright light shone in my face,
Brighter by far than in our usual day.
I turned to get my bearings in this place
When, through the dazzle, I heard some voice say:
"Here is the place to climb." So I was drawn
Away from all thoughts else, and my desire
To see that speaker had so white a dawn
It needs no rest, for it will never tire
60 Until we meet at last. But as the sun

Weighs down our vision with excess of fire
And veils its outline with its power to stun,
Just so my power at this point came up short.
"A spirit hidden in its sacred light,"
My Leader said, as if spurred by my thought,
"Is guiding us unsought from height to height,
As we ourselves might give ourselves support,
No questions asked: for he who waits to ask
Is of a mind to face refusal. Now
Let's time our steps in answer to the task
Of going where he points, and so somehow
Ascend before it darkens. After that
We can't go on until the sky turns fair."
Into the stairway which we now were at
We turned our steps together, and right there,
On the first step, I thought I felt a wing
Beside me fan my face, and clearly heard
"*Beati pacifici.*" The key thing
It said next I remember word for word:
"They have no sin of anger." Lingering,
The last light rays were shining far aloft,
So high up on the hill that the sky's sides
Were spattered with the points, still sparse and soft,
Of the first stars. Night comes while day abides.
"My strength," I said within myself, "Why do
You drain away?" For in my legs I felt
The force suspended. Here the stairs came to
Their end, and I could sense my impulse melt
Like a ship approaching shore, as in the new
Circle I listened for a while to see
If anything was happening, then said
"Kind father, what offence is it, tell me,
That is purged here? Our feet may have been led
To stillness, but let not your speech be still."
And he: "The love of good is here restored,
That fell short of its duty. With a will

The oar is plied anew that had grown bored
And trifled with the water. To fulfil
Your hope more quickly of an easy mind,
100 Turn it to me, and you will benefit
From this delay. My son, as you will find
Deep in your knowledge and informing it,
Neither Creator, no, nor any kind
Of creature was there ever without Love,
If of the mind, or natural. It may not,
The natural, err, and ranks above
The other in that aspect. Minds have got
Two ways to err in love: the wrong object,
Or else the vigour with which love's pursued—
110 There might be excess, there might be defect.
Directed at the primal good, imbued
With no more than a rational respect
Toward the second thing, the world, it won't
Cause sinful pleasure; but when evil turns
Its head, or when its inner counsels don't
Govern the rate at which its longing burns
For serving its own good—perhaps too much,
Perhaps too little—then the creature spurns
Its own creator, and the two lose touch
120 Except as adversaries. From that fact
You'll understand that love must be the source
In you of every virtue and vile act
Deserving punishment. Since love, of course,
Can never turn against the one who feels
The love, but has his welfare most at heart,
All beings are protected by strong seals
Against self-loathing. No one is apart
From the First One, none self-sustaining. No
Creature can be cut off by hating Him.
130 Only a neighbour's evil is loved so,
And this love, in your human life and limb,
The common clay in which you come and go,

Springs up in three ways. There is he that hopes
To rise beside his neighbour's sharp descent
And looks with favour when the downward slopes
Demote another's greatness, as was meant
To be, he thinks: and he thinks that from Pride.
There's he that fears his power might be lost
And all his honour and high state denied
140 Because another has them, at his cost,
Or so he feels, although they rank the same.
Sorely aggrieved, he longs to see reversed
The other's rise to equal power and fame,
And it's by Envy that he has been cursed.
The third man feels disgraced by some insult
And hungers for revenge, and plots and plans,
And makes another's harm into a cult
Which hangs around the house like pots and pans,
And this is Anger. These are the three kinds
150 Of love gone wrong they weep for back in those
Three circles you've just come through. In their minds
They had the vice, and they do not suppose
To be excused, although the sin remained
Just a propensity, mere sinfulness.
But now there is still more to be explained:
Those who pursue the good, but strive with less
Than their full measure to attain it. All,
Although confused, find good to apprehend
In which the mind can rest. This they may call
160 An object of desire, a fruitful end
They try to reach, but should they try and fail
Sufficiently to see, or gain, the goal,
This terrace here, and all it must entail
Of penitence, awaits each slothful soul
With torments for its fault. And then, beyond
This terrace rise a further three, to hold
Those who were far from feeble but too fond
Of all the pinchbeck that they thought was gold,

The pleasures of the world, which give no joy,
170 Which don't ring true, but click like counterfeit—
The earthbound goods fit only to destroy
Good's essence, and to draw love by deceit.
Love lost like that is wept for up above
In those three circles, but the three distinct
Divisions of that all too faithful love
I won't describe now. How they're interlinked
Will be apparent to your intellect
When you, through toil, have learned what to expect."

CANTO 18

When my exalted Teacher reached the end
Of his discourse, he looked me in the face
Intently, with a gaze that did not bend,
To see if I was satisfied. The place
Of my last thirst, in fact, was full again
With yet another, but I held my peace,
Saying within myself "It could be, when
I ask him all these questions without cease,
It troubles him." And then I said aloud:
10 "Master, my vision, quickened by your light,
Sees all your words with clarity endowed.
I pray therefore, dear father, that you might
Explain love to me: love to which, you say,
Good actions are reduced, and equally
Their opposites." And he: "Direct the way
To me, the eyesight, keen as it may be,
Of all your understanding. Plain as day
The error will strike you about the blind
Who would be guides. Created to be quick
20 In love, it's quickly moved, the mind,
Towards all pleasures. By the merest flick
Of pleasure it is whipped to action. Your
Perception takes in from the world outside,
A sense impression, which it holds before

Your mind, and spreads about both long and wide
So that the mind turns to it. If, so turned,
The mind inclines that way, then we must call
That inclination love. It is not learned,
It's instinct, to be reinforced by all
30 The pleasures you might have. For just as fire
Moves upward, as a form that's born to climb
To where it most thrives, so, into desire,
The mind thus seized must enter at the time
Of being taken—for desire moves as
The spirit moves it—and may never rest
Until the thing it loves it truly has
In its possession, and so finds the crest
Of joy. Now you may see how truth's concealed
For those who say that all love merits praise
40 Just for itself. Its matter stands revealed
As good, they think: but here their judgement plays
A trick, because the wax might well be good—
That is, the instinct—and the stamp be bad,
Which is the thing loved." "My wits have understood
Your words. Some of the questions that I had
About love's nature are now answered, yet
Perplexity increases, for if love
Is offered us as something we might get
From outside, and the soul's not thinking of
50 Which foot should fall, but sets foot as it must,
There is no merit in which way it goes,
Crooked or straight." Thus I to him. He: "Just
As far as reason sees can I disclose
The truth to you. Beyond, there you must wait
For Beatrice, who deals in faith. In men,
As in all things, there lies within, innate,
An essence, the substantial form. Again
This form—for man, it bears the name of soul—
Is both united with and yet distinct
60 From matter, which it keeps within, a whole

Specific virtue which is tightly linked
To its own action and is not perceived
Or demonstrated save by its effect,
As is the first life in a plant green-leaved.
It follows that the human intellect
Can't have the first idea of how we know
About our first ideas and how they came
To us, or how desire finds objects so
Alluring. They're inside you, just the same
70 As the honey-making urge is in the bees:
Nor does the primal, central will admit
Earning of praise or moral penalties.
So that your wishes may conform to it—
The balance, that is, to your natural urge—
There is, innate in you, to hold the fort,
A faculty of counsel, thus to merge
The two against a yielding. This we ought
To call the principle in which is found
The merit of your reason, by how well
80 It gathers in our loves from sky to ground
And winnows out the guilt from grain that fell
Too smoothly to the sickle. Those who went
In reason to the roots, the ancient Greeks,
Unearthed the freedom, realised what it meant,
And gave us the great texts in which it speaks:
They gave us *Ethics*, clear proofs that though each
And every love you burn with must arise
Out of necessity, the power to reach
And guide it is in you. This is the prize
90 Whose endless value Beatrice will teach
You of, the noble faculty, free will:
Have it in mind, because the chances are
She'll speak of it to you, there on the hill."
The moon was late, and we had come this far
Without it. It was almost midnight. There
It was, to make the stars look scarcer. Like

A fiery bucket it moved through the air,
Its course on those tracks that the sun will strike
When, seen from Rome, it plunges down between
Sardinia and Corsica. That shade
By whose great books Pietola has been
Honoured above all Mantua, had laid
His head down. I had heard him well. Yes, I,
Replete with his informed and clear discourse,
Rambled in drowsiness, but by and by
Half sleep was torn awake with sudden force.
Some people had come round behind our backs,
And as Ismenus and Asopus saw
The troops of tumult and the mock attacks
Along the bank at night when Thebes would roar
And prance for Bacchus, so I saw them come
Around that circle, but with something more
To celebrate, for I could tell the drum
That drove them was no pagan pulse of blood
But goodwill and just love. And soon they were
Upon us, all these runners, like a flood,
And two in front cried out in tears: "Praise her!
Praise Mary hastening to the hill!" And this:
"Caesar made speed to Spain!" And in the rear
The rest cried: "Go! Go! It would come amiss
To lose time for too little love! We cheer
For zeal in grand deeds that bring back to life
The green of God's grace!" Then my Leader said
"You people in whom fervour runs so rife
To wake, maybe, what you have left half dead,
Through lack of will, delay and negligence,
This man who stands here—it's the truth I speak—
Before the morning sunshine should commence
Again, would go up. Give us what we seek.
Show us the gap." At which one of that band
Said "Follow us and you will find the break.
We need to move, you have to understand:

We may not rest. Excuse us if you take
Our penance for rebuff. I, at one time,
Was abbot of San Zeno, in the days
When Barbarossa ruled Verona. I'm
Aware Milan still loathes him, but he stays
Revered where I lived, and there is one there now,
Alberto, who has one foot in the grave
140 And must soon shed tears on account of how
His monastery is run. No throne will save
That lord of grief from using power there
In those cloisters, and because he set his son—
Warped in the body, worse in mind—to wear
The abbot's cowl, a basely born wanton
In place of the true shepherd." I don't know
If he said more or else fell silent, as
Already he had run to pass us so,
But thus I heard and in my mind it has
150 Remained. And he that was my help said "Turn
Around here. See the two that bare in wrath
Their teeth while they tell lessons all should learn
About historic instances of sloth."
They came behind the rest, and as they came
They said "The sea was opened, but they failed
To get back to the Jordan all the same."
They must have meant the Hebrews. And "They sailed
As far as Sicily but had no thirst
For more horizons, and Aeneas left
160 Without them. Thus they lived on, and were cursed
With lack of glory, of all fame bereft."
Then, when these shades were gone so far from us
We couldn't see them, a new thought was born
Within me that I needed to discuss,
And then another, and my mind was torn
In all directions like a tumbling stream:
My eyes closed, and my thoughts turned to a dream.

CANTO 19

In that hour when the whole heat of the day
Is overcome by Earth's cold and the cold
Of Saturn, and no longer keeps at bay
The cold moon, while what geomancers hold
To be their "Greater Future"—that small spray
Of six stars—rises in the east before
The dawn, using a path that won't remain
Long dark for it, and light will close the door,
There came to me a woman, racked with pain,
10   Into my dream, and she was crossed of eye
And crooked on her feet, with broken hands,
And sallow, and she stammered fit to die.
I stared at her, and as the sun commands
Warmth into limbs benumbed by the chill night,
My look untied her tongue, and in a while
She straightened up. Wan features were made bright
With colour, as love finds the proper style.
Her speech set free, she then began to sing,
And hard it would have been to turn my mind
20   Away from that song, such a charming thing
It was. "I am the siren, of my kind
The sweetest, and the sailors I can fetch
In from the sea, and them to me I bind
As prisoners of delight. For quite a stretch

Ulysses, eager voyager, was held
Fast by my song. Whoever dwells with me,
So thoroughly are all his longings quelled
He rarely leaves." The pretty melody
Was over, but her lips were not yet closed
30 When there beside me a new face appeared,
A woman holy, vibrant yet composed.
Briefly she spoke, in sharp tones to be feared
For anger. "Virgil, Virgil, who is this?"
His gaze paid homage to that honest one.
With altogether different emphasis
He seized the other, and the thing was done:
Tearing her clothes in front, he laid her bare,
Showing her belly, and the stink of her
Awoke me, and I heard my Guide declare:
40 "Three times I called you, and yet still you were
Enchanted. Rise now and get out of there.
We have to find the gap where you go in."
I rose, and high day had already lit
The circles, from low down, where they begin,
All the way up the holy mountain. It
Was full of light. Propelled by the new sun,
We went on. As I followed him, my brow—
I knew by how it felt—I bore like one
Whose thoughts weigh down on him, to make him bow
50 Like the half-arch of a bridge, and then I heard
"Come, here's the passage," in a voice more sweet
And gracious to the ear than any word
In this our mortal world we ever meet.
The speaker had the spread wings of a swan.
He showed us upwards in between the walls
Of flint-stone, and we felt, as we moved on,
The fanning of his feathers, with soft calls
Of *qui lugent*, which means all those who mourn
Are to be blessed, for consolation will
60 Possess their souls. "By what doubt are you torn?"

My Guide asked when our new place on the hill
Was higher than the angel's. "Why do you
Stare at the ground?" And I to him: "I go
Compelled by much misgiving from a new
Vision, which to itself has bent me so
I can't stop thinking of it." "But it's true,"
He said, "that ancient witch is mourned nowhere
Except in circles yet to come. You saw
How men are free of her. Enough said. Spare
70 Your feet your waverings, and fix before
Your eyes the real enchantment, the spun flare
The Eternal King, to mark the joy in store,
Has lit with the great wheels, their starry trace."
Just like the falcon, which, when it is hailed,
Looks first down to its feet, then turns to face
The call, and stretches, by desire assailed
For food, so I was, in that cloven place,
And went up through the rock to where one takes
The circuit. I came out in the fifth round.
80 People were there who wept as the heart breaks:
They helplessly lay face down on the ground.
"My soul cleaves to the dust," they said with sighs
So deep the words were hard to pick apart.
"Elect of God," my Poet asked, "whose prize
Is here to have the anguish in your heart
Made less acute by justice and by hope,
Which is the best way up?" "If you're exempt
From lying here on this round of the slope,"
The answer came, "the route for your attempt"—
90 These words came from a little way ahead—
"Is quickest if your right hand stays outside."
After I found that face by what it said,
I turned with a mute question to my Guide,
And gladly he assented with a sign.
Free now to act, I drew above that soul
Whose words had made me note him. These were mine.

"Spirit whose weeping ripens to a whole
Without which nobody returns to God,
For my sake stay awhile your chief concern.

100   Who were you all? Why do you, in this odd
Manner, show us your backs? This I would learn,
And whether you, when I go back alive
Into the world, would want from me a boon."
And he to me: "Just how it should arrive
That Heaven turns our backs to it, you soon
Will know. Know now that Peter was
First in my chair. I was Pope Adrian,
Count of Lavagna, titled so because
That fair stream serves our land. I was the man

110   Who proved in five weeks what the mantle weighs
On him who keeps it from the mud. No load
Comes close to it. Alas, there were delays
Before my feet were set on the right road,
But when I was made Shepherd there in Rome
I saw how life was just a pack of lies,
I saw the heart could never be at home,
I saw it was impossible to rise
In that life, so that this life, with no end,
Kindled my love. I, wretched till that hour,

120   Separate from God, believed that my best friend
Was avarice. You see me in the power
Of its fit penitence. What avarice
Can do is here declared, so as to purge
Converted souls. No pain is worse than this
In all the mountain. Just as that foul urge
Kept our eyes low, misled by worldly things,
So justice here has sunk them to the earth.
Just as that rage reduced to flickerings
Our love of good, and labour died at birth,

130   So justice here takes care to hold us fast,
Bound hand and foot, and keeps us for as long
As it should please the Lord. From first to last

We lie still and outstretched. We were that wrong."
I'd knelt, and was about to speak, but when
He heard one word, he guessed my reverence.
"What cause," he said, "has set you kneeling, then?"
And I: "Your dignity commands my sense
Of fitness." He to me: "Brother, set straight
Your legs, and rise. I am, make no mistake,
140 A fellow servant of one Potentate,
Along with you and others. For the sake
Of those words in the Gospel which make clear
All earthly marriages are here annulled,
Be sure of what I mean. I have not, here,
My earthly rank, so try not to be gulled.
Now go your way. I would not have you pause
Longer than this. Your presence interferes
With how I weep according to the laws
Of that full ripening you say my tears
150 Will bring me to. Alagia, my niece,
Lives yonder. By her nature she has all
The virtues. May our house leave them in peace,
And not corrupt her with its tempting call,
For she is all my treasure left unspent
As I lie here in this, my long lament."

CANTO 20

Against a better will, mere will fights ill:
Therefore, to please him—this did not please me—
I drew the sponge that I had wished to fill
Out of the water, curiosity
Unsatisfied. I moved on round the hill—
My Leader, too, moved—keeping to that part
Left free from bodies close beside the rock,
As battlements provide, by builder's art,
A walkway for the guards. Too great a stock,
10   The other edge contained, of people who
Poured from their eyes the evil, drop by drop,
That fills the world. Old wolf, a curse on you!
You with your hunger that will never stop
For more prey than all other beasts! When, when,
O heavens—by whose wheeling, it's believed,
Conditions shift and change for living men—
When will he come by whom we are reprieved,
And put the wolf to flight? And on we went
With short, slow steps, and on those weeping shades,
20   Their lamentations, I remained intent,
Until by chance I heard, through his cascades
Of tears, one up ahead of us call "Ah,
Sweet Mary!" like a woman giving birth.
"That meagre hostelry below the star

Where you lay down your burden of great worth
Tells us how poor you were!" And then I heard:
"Fabricius, Consul who did not betray
Rome for a bribe, but chose to keep your word,
Virtue in poverty must far outweigh
30 Riches in wickedness!" These last words stirred
Such pleasure in me that I pressed ahead,
To know that soul from which they seemed to come,
And he went on to tell of how it's said
St. Nicholas bestowed a generous sum
As dowry on three girls who faced disgrace
From destitution. "Soul who speaks so well
Of such good, who were you? Why, in this place,
Do you alone renew the tales you tell
Of well-earned praise? Be sure your words will be
40 Repaid if I get back to life, and walk
The last part of the road that's left to me."
And he: "Not for that boon of which you talk,
Comfort from yonder, but because I see
Such grace in you before death, I will speak.
Of that most evil tree I was the root,
The tree that overshadows with its bleak
Wide canopy all Christendom. Good fruit
Is rarely gathered there. But if Douai,
Lille, Ghent and Bruges had sufficient force
50 They'd take revenge for that fact, which is why,
From Him who judges all things in due course,
I beg an intervention. I was called
Hugh Capet, yonder. All the Kings of France
Called Philip or else Louis now installed
On that throne have my loins for provenance.
I was a Paris butcher's son. The old
Kings faded, all but one of them, who was,
At my insistence, chosen to uphold
A cloistered life, and that became his cause:
60 A grey-clad monk. At which I could enfold

The reins, in my safe hands, of government
And kingdom, much new power and many friends:
Such an abundance that my son's head rose
Into the vacant crown. From there extends
The line of their bones, and we all know those
Are consecrated. Just as long as that
Great dowry of Provence had not deprived
My line of shame, it more or less stood pat:
Of small account, at least it still contrived
70   To do no harm. But then with force and fraud
Began its rapine. Three French petty states
England gave up, persuaded by the sword.
Charles of Anjou, so history relates,
Was gentle when he killed young Conradin,
And sent Thomas Aquinas to his rest
With thoughtful tact. I see the times begin
When Charles of Valois, at the Pope's behest,
Comes out of France to Florence. He wants fame
For self and people. He arrives unarmed
80   Save for the Judas lance, the shaft of blame,
And drives it home so that the city's harmed,
Its paunch bursts, and he picks up from the game
Not land, but sin and shame. And every White
Is driven out when he lets in the Blacks:
The more he calls that victory his by right,
The more the guilt he has, the grace he lacks.
The second Charles of Anjou, from his ship
Was taken prisoner. Now I see him trade
His daughter, as the pirates crack a whip
90   For other women slaves, who must parade,
And when the bidding flags they force the price.
O Avarice, what can you do to us
To match what you have done? How can you twice
Draw to yourself my grasping bloodline thus,
So we devour each other? But there's worse,
Worse than before, or after. Philip brings

The fleur-de-lis to settle like a curse
On where Charles Valois gets away from things,
And makes him captive—thus, a second time,
Mocking the Lord. Once more the vinegar!
Again the gall! And dying for no crime
Between two living thieves! And this, by far,
Is not enough for our new Pilate, no.
Outside the law he sails in all his greed
To rob the Templars. Lord, when can I show
The joy of seeing you bring what we need,
Your vengeance, which, while it stays hidden so,
Makes your wrath sweet? We know that we await
A reckoning for sinners. When I cried
The bride's name of the Holy Ghost so great,
And brought you, for more comment, to my side,
Such was, for us, as long as day lasts here,
The object of our prayer exemplified,
But we invoke the worst when night draws near.
In darkness we call up Pygmalion:
Gold-fever made a traitor and a thief
And worse. By his untamed hand, death was done
To his own sister Dido's husband. Grief
For her, but gain for him. Did anyone
Know misery like the greedy-guts in chief,
King Midas, who was granted his fond prayer
To have the world turn golden at his touch,
And now forever all men fight for air
Laughing at him? And all here, just as much,
Remember foolish Achan, how he stole
The spoils at Jericho and earned a hail
Of stones from Joshua, and now the whole
Anguish he feels again. And we assail
Sapphira and her husband with our scorn,
They who took money that the people willed
To the apostles. And the horse-kick borne
By Heliodorus after he had filled

His pockets from the temple, we salute.
The name of Polymestor, King of Thrace—
Who murdered Polydorus and, to boot,
Filched all his wealth—we grant a lasting place
In infamy. And the last one on the list?
'Crassus, you drank gold. Did you like the taste?'
For that Triumvir had a grasping fist
140 And died of it, and in his mouth the waste
Of his great love was poured, but he had missed
The moment when he might have lived the proof
That avarice is loss. Some of us speak
Forth boldly here, and others, more aloof,
Speak low. The ardour, strong or weak,
Compels our voice with force the more or less,
And thus, although I seemed alone just now,
We all talk day by day of what we bless,
The good. But I was loudest. That was how
150 You picked me out." We had already left
Hugh Capet, and were out to cover ground
As fast as we could go, when the whole heft
Of that great mountain shook and moved around
Like something getting set to fall. A chill
Seized me as if I'd been sent to my death.
Did Delos, the floating island—by Jove's will
Set fast so that Latona might give breath
To Heaven's twin eyes—ever shake this hard
Before Apollo and Diana stood
160 On earth made firm? My Master was my guard:
He drew close, to convince me this was good,
As on all sides arose a mighty shout:
"Fear not, I am your guide!" was one thing heard,
Also a cry of *Gloria* rang out,
And *in excelsis Deo* chased that word
Into the ear, although those close about
I heard the best, and was not always sure,
Such was the noise. Unmoving, in suspense,

We stood surrounded by that sweet uproar,
170 As once the shepherds were deprived of sense
By what the cry they heard said was in store
For them, and all mankind: something immense.
But then it ended, and the trembling ceased,
And we could take once more our sacred path,
The shades that lay there, having thus released
Their outburst, melted in the aftermath,
Their usual weeping. Never did ignorance
Goad me to know—if rightly I recall—
As it did then, in that twin circumstance
180 Of song and earthquake. But since that was all
There was to see and hear, and time was short,
I dared not ask, and could not, on my own,
Work out the implications. Lost in thought,
Too shy to ask a question, left alone
Behind my Guide, I went on past that long
Line of the ones who weep at their own song.

CANTO 21

The natural thirst that's never quenched if not
By the same sweet water that Samaria's
Most humble woman begged might be her lot
Tormented me, and haste urged me, and as
I hurried on that crowded way behind
My Leader, a compassion for the just
Vengeance that made them weep welled in my mind,
And lo, as Luke recalls in words we trust
As from a witness, when Christ reappeared
Out of the tomb's mouth and was seen by two
There in his way, just so, to us, there neared
A shade behind our backs while all we knew
Was that which lay before us, and we saw
Nothing of him until he spoke. "God yield
You peace, my brothers." Virgil's gesture bore
Acknowledgement for what had been appealed,
But then he spoke. "Alas, God never will
For me. But may the faithful court on high
That keeps me exiled hopelessly until
The end of time, bring you in peace where I
Can never go, the assembly of the blessed."
"And how," the shade asked, as we speedily
Went on, "if you're unworthy of this test,
Have you been brought so far on stairs that He

Built for one purpose?" And my Teacher said
"Look on the marks borne by this man, and see
An angel traced them so he might be sped
To where the righteous reign. But since the fate
Lachesis, spinning that thread day and night
30 Which is our life, has not yet the full rate
Of flax from Clotho, who selects the right
Amount for all alive, and loads and packs
The distaff, so his soul—your sister, and
Mine too—could not alone make tracks
This high, because by nature it is banned
From seeing in our way, through intellect:
And thus was I drawn from Hell's yawning jaws
To guide him, and will guide him, I expect,
As far as reason reaches with its laws.
40 But can you tell us why the mountain shook
So violently just then, and why we seemed
To hear one giant shout, which surely took
All of the souls sent here to be redeemed
Down to its wave-washed base?" Thus questioning,
He put the thread's end through the needle's eye
Of my desire so neatly that the thing
I wished to know made me less thirsty by
The measure that my hope was raised. Whereat
The other said "The mountain's holy laws
50 Do not brook the disorderly, or that
Which injures custom. This place, for that cause,
Is free from change. Only when Heaven calls
Itself unto itself, are changes made,
But only then, and therefore no rain falls
Or hail or snow or dew, and there is laid
No carpet of hoar frost, not anywhere
Beyond the three-step staircase you have seen.
There are no clouds here, whether dense or rare,
Nor lightning flash, nor has there ever been
60 Iris the rainbow, who, down there below,

Will bridge the sky to echo the sunshine.
Nor does the wind's friend, the dry vapour, go
Higher than that third step which draws the line
Where Peter's vicar sets his feet. Although
The mountain, lower down, might sometimes shake
A little or a lot, it will not be,
Up here where we are, subject to a quake
From wind the earth hides. If, to me,
The reason is a mystery, still I'm sure
70 It trembles when one soul feels purified
So it may finally arise and soar
On its ascending path, the upward glide,
And then we hear the shout you heard before.
Pureness of soul is by the will alone
Proved true, and then the soul, set free at last
To change its place, by no will of its own
Is taken by surprise. The will holds fast
The soul, and for the soul it will prevail.
Until that time, the soul might will indeed,
80 But set beside desire its will is frail:
Desire for sin, and then the equal need
For penitence, that mirror-image urge
Inspired by Holy Justice. I have lain
Five hundred years and more in pain to purge
My sin, and only now feel my will gain
Its freedom for the flight to re-emerge
On a better threshold. That was why you felt
The earth quake, and you heard the spirits shout
Their praises to the Lord. May they be dealt
90 The same great benefit, all the devout
Throughout the mountain, and soon make the climb."
He spoke thus. Since the draught is more enjoyed
The more the thirst, I lack the words and rhyme
To say how much I gained from that filled void.
Then my wise Leader said "Now is the time
When I see how you're tangled in the net

And how you are let loose. I see why, here,
It trembles, and why you rejoice. Now set
My mind at rest and let the truth appear,
And tell me who you were. Then you can let
Me gather from your words why you have spent
So many centuries here, lying down."
"When goodly Titus," that soul said, "was lent
Help from the holder of the Highest Crown
To raze Jerusalem, a gesture meant
As vengeance for the blood the gashes spilled
To pay off Judas, then I bore the name
That lasts best, and is most with honour filled,
The name of poet. Yes, I had that fame
But not the faith. Still, it was sweet, my song:
I, from Toulouse, was drawn to Rome. My brows
Were decked with myrtle. Still, after so long,
Men yonder speak my name, which yet endows
My themes with dignity. It's Statius.
I sang of Thebes at first, Achilles next.
That second subject I could not discuss
Fully, for lack of time. In each context
The spark that lit my fire came from the blaze
That lit a thousand fires—I mean, of course,
The *Aeneid*. In my poetry, it plays
The roles of nurse and mother, spring and source:
Without it I'd have weighed a drachma. Less.
To have lived when Virgil lived! Here in this place
I would have spent a year more in duress
Before my banishment gave way to grace,
Just for the chance of treading the same ground."
At these words Virgil fixed me with a look
That said, in silence, "Silence." But he found
The will cannot do all things by the book,
For tears and laughter are close followers
Of passions, since they tend to spring from them,
And with a truthful passion it occurs

Most often that we're likely to condemn
Their insolence. But still, I only smiled
Like someone hinting. The shade held his peace
And searched into my eyes as if beguiled
By something puzzling that might find release
Just where expression most resides. "Your glance
Showed mirth just then. That it may end in good,
140 Your labour, please explain that merry dance."
Now I am held two ways. There's one that would
Have me keep silent, and the other seeks
The opposite. My sigh is understood
By my Guide. "Fear not. Now be one who speaks,
And tell him what he so much craves to learn."
And I: "You wonder, old soul, at my smile,
But I would have a greater wonder burn
Its way into your mind. For all this while,
Plainly before you as he guides my eyes
150 On high, it has been Virgil standing here—
Virgil from whom you took the gift as prize
To sing of men and make the gods appear,
And if another cause you did surmise
For my smile, know it has to be untrue:
Put it aside. The reason was your voice,
The praise it spoke of him. I smiled for you,
Because my secret pleasure left no choice."
He bent down to embrace my Teacher's feet,
But Virgil said "Brother, it's just no use.
160 You are a shade and it's a shade you meet."
And Statius, rising, said "My one excuse
Is my great love for you, its burning heat.
I clean forgot, because I felt so much,
That shades are here to see, but not to touch."

CANTO 22

Our guiding angel who had led us here
To the sixth circle, we had left behind.
One of my scars he'd made to disappear
From my face, and, as matter for the mind,
He had declared to us that those who thirst
Sufficiently for righteousness are blessed,
His message terminating with the first
Word of the verse, pronounced without the rest:
Just *sitiunt*, "they thirst." And I went on
Lighter than in the other stairwells. I
Followed the swift souls up where they had gone
Without much work. I hardly had to try.
And Virgil said "Love, lit by one virtue,
Always ignites another, though its flame
Appear only without. And thus it's true
That from the moment Juvenal in fame
Came down to Limbo and made known to me
Your fondness, Statius, my own goodwill
Towards you had a reciprocity
As great as ever possibly could fill
The heart of one for one unknown. So now
These stairs, to me, will seem short. But pray tell—
And as a friend forgive my nerve for how
I wax familiar—just how it befell

10

20

Your breast was occupied with avarice
As well as all the wisdom your zeal brought?"
In the beginning Statius smiled at this,
And then replied: "In truth, one would have thought—
Though your each word makes my heart more content
30 As token of your love—things sometimes seem
To give false matter for bewilderment
Because their cause is hidden. Thus I deem
Your question to me makes plain your belief
That I was grasping in the other life,
Doubtless because that sad flaw was the chief
Mark of my circle here. Yes, it was rife.
Know, then, my vice was just the opposite.
I was a prodigal, and this excess
Thousands of moons have punished. Done with it,
40 I can say now that I first found redress
For my bad habits when I read those lines
Where you, deploring human nature, cried
'Thrice-cursed gold-hunger, to what dark designs
Do you not drive men to be satisfied?'
Had I not read that, I'd be rolling weights
And jousting dismally. I learned our hands
Can spread like wings, and spending dissipates,
And I repented, as of the demands
Of other sins. Many will rise again
50 With cropped hair, who have lost through ignorance
Their due repentance. They shall live, as men,
Their last hour playing games with their last chance.
Know, too, that each sin's counter-sin is here,
Keeping the vigil with its opposite,
Consumed by its own juice. Though I appear
To be among the avaricious, it
Is not for that I weep like them. I fear
It's for the contrary that I grieve so."
"Now when you sing," the poet said who wrote
60 The *Bucolics*, "about Jocasta's woe

Caused by two warring sons, there's not a note
Lent to you there by history's muse, Clio,
That indicates the one faith was yet yours
Without which mere good deeds are not enough.
If that be so, what brought you to the shores
Of light—what sacred sun or earthly stuff
That makes a candle—so that you could raise
Your sails and steer behind the fisherman?"
And the other: "It was you that turned my gaze
70 Towards Parnassus so that I began
To drink in its cool caves. Yes, it was you,
First after God, that set my mind alight.
You were the guide whose lamp shows the way through
To those behind him as he goes by night:
Not for himself, but to make others wise,
He shines. 'The age,' you said, 'turns new again.
Justice returns, the first days take fresh guise,
And out of Heaven a new race of men
Descends.' A poet and a Christian, I,
80 Because of you. But to be clear just how,
I'll set my hand to stir a deeper dye
And colour in my outline for you now.
The waiting world was pregnant everywhere
With the true faith, sown by the messengers
From the eternal realm. Your words were there—
The ones I spoke—and so in tune with theirs
I formed the habit of frequenting these
New preachers. In my eyes they came to seem
So holy that Domitian's cruelties
90 Against them saw me trying to redeem
Their tears with mine. While I was there beyond,
I helped them. Their straight ways made me deplore
All other sects. So moved, I pledged my bond.
I'd been baptized, in secret, well before
I brought the Greeks to threaten, in my lines,
The Theban rivers. But, for fear, I hid,

A closet Christian making pagan signs,
And this lukewarmness about what I did
Earned me four hundred long years without cease
100 Of touring the fourth circle. Tell me, then—
You that first raised the curtain to release
My vision of the good—of those four men,
I named, Caecilius and Varius,
Terence and Plautus. Are they damned to Hell?
If so, in which part? This we must discuss
While we ascend this hill." "Those four, as well
As Persius and I," my Leader said,
"Are with the Greek most favoured by the milk
Of the Muses, in the first ring of the dead
110 Blind prison, where the elders of our ilk,
The ones that raised us, proudly we invoke:
Them and their singing mountain. In that place
With us—and I can't name them at a stroke,
They are too many—you can see the face
Of Antiphon, and know Euripides,
Simonides and Agathon, each Greek
Whose brow wore laurels once. To please
You more, I'll mention those of whom you speak:
Ismene and Antigone. Thetis . . ."
120 The list was long, but finally the two
Poets were silent. Well content with this
Exchange, from having talked as poets do,
They took the chance to look around them, freed
From climbing and the walls. The hours that drew
The sun, one handmaid always in the lead
Each hour, were four down, and the fifth was in
The harness, burning horn upright. "I think,"
My Leader said, "the best way to begin
Is with our right side outward to the brink,
130 And then bear left as usual round the wall."
Just so our habit served there as a rule,
And off we went with scarce a doubt at all,

Because that soul from the elected school
Agreed with us. Those two walked on ahead,
Talking of poetry and how it's made.
I walked behind and drank in what they said,
But soon their pleasant talk about our trade
Was interrupted by a tree that stood
Square in the way, and it was full of fruit,
140 And all the fruit smelled sweet as it looked good.
And as a fir, scanned upward from the root,
Tapers from branch to branch toward the tip,
So this tree tapered downward, so that none,
I think, should climb it. Some high lip
Of the cliff that walled our pathway spilled and spun
A fall of clearest water, which dispersed
Among the leaves above. The two approached
The tree, and from among its boughs there burst
A warning voice, as if they had encroached:
150 "You may not eat this food!" Then it went on:
"Mary dwelt more upon the marriage feast—
Its honour and completeness—than upon
Her own mouth, which up here has never ceased
To intercede for you. In times long gone,
A thirsty Roman woman was content
With water. Nor did Daniel eat his fill,
But spurned the king's feast always, and this meant
He gained in wisdom by his frugal will.
As beautiful as gold was the First Age:
160 Hunger made acorns tasty, thirst made sweet
Nectar of every brook, so you can gauge
How satisfied the Baptist was to eat
The locust and sip honey. Every page
About this in the Gospel shows, therefore,
His greatness and his glory. Less is more."

CANTO 23

While through the tree's green leaves I strained my eyes
As one who watches hawks and sees them waste
His life, my more-than-father was more wise:
"Come, son, for only so much time is placed
At our disposal. We must use it well."
I turned my face—and turned, at the same speed,
My steps—after the sages and the spell
Of what they said and, having that to heed,
The going cost me nothing. Then "O Lord,
10 Open my lips" we heard in Latin, wept
And sung in tones that brought, with one accord,
Delight and grief. And I said as we stepped
"Sweet father, what is this I hear?" And he:
"Perhaps shades, who, while going, loose the knot
Of debt." As when, absorbed in reverie,
A group on foot will not ease by a jot
Their speed when overtaking strangers (see
Them turn their heads and look, but keep their pace),
Just so a crowd of souls came from behind
20 Quicker than us, yet silent, with the face
Of piety, although they seemed to find,
In us, the cause of wonder. Each was dark
And hollow in the eyes, and pale of cheek:
So wasted that the withered skin took stark

Shape from the bone. What once had bloomed was bleak.
I don't believe even Erysichthon,
Punished by Ceres with a raging lust
To eat and eat till all the food was gone,
Looked quite so haggard when he realised just
One source of meat was left to fall upon.
He waited, starving, till he was the crust
That he could not resist. "Now see," I said
Within myself, "There is Jerusalem
Revenged, which went for months on end unfed,
And one called Mary set a mark for them
By eating her own child." Their eye-pits were
Like settings on a ring without the gem,
And he who thinks those sockets can confer
The letter M on faces would have found
OMO, to mean a man, stamped loud and clear
On each of theirs, the deep signs of a sound.
And who could know, who had not been up here,
How just a hint of water and mere scent
Of fruit, by the sheer craving they instilled,
Could bring about such grave disfigurement?
Keen curiosity was unfulfilled
Regarding what had starved them. Why were they
So lean? And I did not yet know the cause
Of their sad scurf. But one shade stared my way
From deep inside his head without a pause,
And then cried: "I'm in luck! What can I say?"
By looks alone I never would have known
Who this one was, but in his voice was plain
What in his face was shrivelled to the bone.
That spark revived the knowledge in my brain
Of his changed features, and I recognised
Forese, fellow sonneteer and friend.
He said "Try not to be too long surprised
By this tight scab that works to make an end
Of my skin's colour, or by how my flesh

Is lacking, but just tell me about you.
And if the news is true, it will be fresh.
And these who go with you, who are these two?
Speak now." And I: "Your face, for which I wept
When it was dead, now gives me no less grief,
Seeing how very little has been kept
Of what I knew, that there seems no relief
From the distortion. Tell me, in God's name,
What is it wastes you? Do not make me speak
70 While I so marvel, for the tongue falls lame
Whose mind is elsewhere." And he: "From the peak
We call God's will eternal, virtue falls
As water to the tree we left back there
Whose fragrance is so sweet it cruelly galls
The famished body that you see I wear.
All those who gave way to their appetite
Beyond all reason, and so now must weep
As they go singing, here hope that they might,
Through thirst and hunger, once more get and keep
80 Their holiness. The sweet scent of the fruit
And of the spray spread over the green leaves
Can only make the craving more acute
To eat and drink. And anyone who grieves
Will do so often as he goes around
This level, with its other trees of pain—
Or let's say solace, for it will be found
How that desire will lead us to the main
Tree of them all, the one that made Christ cry
The name of God, when from his every vein
90 The blood that freed us poured. He cried 'Eli!' "
And I to him: "Forese, not five years
Have passed since you exchanged your life on Earth
For something better, and you're here, in tears.
If your sin's power died before the birth
Of penitence—the good grief that weds men
Again to God—I thought to find you in

The first part of this hill, there where, again,
Time is made good by time, and they can win,
Those waiting, recompense for tardiness."
Then he to me: "It is my Nella brings
Me here so soon to drink—and, drinking, bless—
Sweet wormwood of the torments. She does things—
She prays, she sighs, she weeps floods—that have set
Me free from those first circles, from the slope
Where all must wait. As deep as love can get
Was my love for my widow, now my hope,
And she is loved by God now all the more
For being, in her good deeds, so alone—
For, in Sardinia, there's a running sore,
Barbagia, whose women are less prone
To rank immodesty than in the pit
I left her in, our Florence, yours and mine.
Brother, what words of mine would you think fit?
A time that soon must come I can divine,
When from the pulpit it shall be declared
That brazen women of our native town
Must not go walking with their nipples bared.
Did ever law need to be handed down
That barbarous women, even Saracens,
Should cover themselves up? Some code of fear
On which a simple sense of shame depends?
But had our shameless creatures an idea
Of how swift Heaven has prepared their fate,
Their mouths already would be open wide,
All set to howl, for if I estimate
The prospects rightly, they will meet a tide
Of sorrow before he who now is lulled
To sleep with song can show a hairy jowl.
But, brother, you by whom the sun is dulled,
At you we gaze. Your news, please, fair or foul.
Not only I, but all of us, ask this."
And I to him: "Recall what you once were

With me, and I with you. I'd be remiss
To overlook the way we used to stir
A mess of bad taste. It was my Guide turned
Me from that life. The other day, it was,
When that one's sister (where the high sun burned
I pointed) here shone full. It is because
Of him that I came through the deep dark night
140 Of all the truly dead with my real form
That follows him. He drew me to the light,
And his attentions, generous and warm,
Have brought me up this hill that sets you right,
You that the world made crooked. On this climb
Around the mountain, he will be with me,
He promises, always until the time
That I see Beatrice. There I'm bound to be
Without him. It is Virgil who thus speaks
To me (I pointed), and this other one
150 Is he for whom the slopes and troughs and peaks
Of this your kingdom shook as they've just done—
Because the mountain knew, deep in its heart,
Another soul was ready to depart."

CANTO 24

The going did not slow the talk, the talk
Slowed not the going. Saying what we said,
We went on with a rapid, buoyant walk
Like ships in a fair wind. They looked twice dead,
The shades that drew amazement at me through
Their deep eye-ports, aware I was alive.
I went on with my talk, referring to
The shade of Statius. "He will arrive
On high," I said, "more slowly than he could,
Perhaps, because of Virgil. But now tell
Me of Piccarda. Also if I should
Take note of any among these, so well
Equipped to gaze at me." "More fair than good,
More good than fair? My sister is on high,
Triumphant in Olympus, glory-crowned."
He said first that, then this: "Here we must try
To name names when we can, our faces ground
To dust with fasting, drained completely dry.
That one is Bonagiunta, who made rhymes
In Lucca, and beyond him, one who held
The whole Church in his arms in recent times,
Martin of Tours, a great heart too impelled
By greed, and so his face, more than the rest,
Is seamed, and he must fast to purge the eels

Of Lake Bolsena that he thought the best,
And drowned in wine and roasted. The mind reels."
And many others he named one by one,
And none of them seemed displeased to be named:
Not one dark look while this was being done,
30 For if I, in the world, could make them famed
For being saved, then harm there would be none.
Ubaldin della Pila I saw chew
On emptiness because he'd lingered so,
And Bonifazio, archbishop, who
Pastured his flocks high up, and, as we know,
Set his expenses higher. I saw, too,
Forlì's fine man Marchese, who had space
Down there to drink with far more thirst than here,
And yet he never drank his fill. The place
40 Was full of them, yet, as one does with sheer
Numbers, I noticed some above the crowd,
And so returned to Bonagiunta. He
Seemed most to want to know me, and, aloud,
But only just, he muttered this for me:
"*Gentucca*," meaning "little folk." The word
Barely emerged from where he felt the pain
Of justice most, his throat. But, having heard,
I spoke, believing he might brave the strain.
"Spirit that seems so eager to be freed
50 To tell me something," I said, "have a care
To say it plainly and thus meet the need
Of both yourself and me." "Back there,"
He said, "a woman's born who will indeed
Bear glowing fruit, though she does not yet wear
The wimple of the wed. And she will make
My city please you. Armed with this forecast
You go your way again, and if you take
A wrong turn from my muttering, at last
The facts will make all clear. But now reveal
60 If you I see before me really made
The new rhyme, lyrical as well as real—

The craft of language at its highest grade—
Beginning with 'You ladies who know love'?"
And I to him: "Yes, I am one that when
Inspired by love, notes what is spoken of
Within, and makes it sing to other men."
"Brother," he said, "now I can see the knot
That held back Jacopo and all the school
Of Sicily; Guittone and his lot
70 Of Tuscans who wrote verse to the old rule;
And kept me, too, short of the Sweet New Style
I hear now. I see well how love dictates
The movement of your pen, which, all the while
The heart speaks, follows close, and never waits.
It's certain this was far from true for us,
And anyone who sets out to detect
A difference, will find no more to discuss
Between our style and yours but that aspect:
The things we hinted at, you said outright."
80 And he was silent, as if satisfied
With his analysis. As cranes in flight
Along the Nile in winter make a wide
Array sometimes, and sometimes pull in tight
To get more speed by going one behind
The other, so these people faced around
And quickened step as if all of one mind,
By leanness and the wish to cover ground
Made light of foot. Like one who cannot find
More breath to run and lets his fellows pass
90 And walks until his chest no longer heaves,
Forese waved away that holy class
And stayed with me, and as to one who leaves
Too soon to suit us, spoke. "How long before
I see you here again?" And I: "How long
Am I to live? I don't know. Yet this shore
I'd sooner see again than know the wrong
Of where I have been put to live, which more
And more divests itself of good from day

To day, with ruin waiting down the trail."

"And I," he said, "can see now who will pay
For that disaster. Dragged by a beast's tail
Towards the valley out of which no way
Leads back again, my brother Corso's drawn
Faster with every foul step of the beast
Until he is dashed down and left there, torn
Revoltingly to pieces, a crows' feast.
These wheels"—he pointed upwards—"will not turn
Too often before what I have to tell
Will be more plain than I can say. You'll learn:
But now I have to leave you. A short spell
Of time is precious here. I lose too much
By lingering." And as a horseman rides
Out at a gallop, proud of losing touch
With his brigade, and goes to where resides
The glory of the first encounter, just
That way he went from us with longer strides,
And back on earth we would have eaten dust,
I and the two great worldlings. We remained,
And when he was so far ahead my eyes
Lost sight of him no matter how they strained—
As my mind lost his words—to my surprise
The branches of another tree appeared
As we came round the bend, and it was full
Of fruit, and green, and I saw, as we neared,
People beneath it lift, as if to pull
Fruit free, their hands towards the foliage,
Crying I know not what, as children do
Who, thoughtless, beg, and get into a rage
Of begging when the thing they beckon to
Unbidden, is held up to make them keen.
Then off they went as if they realised
How futile all their clamouring had been,
And to the tree that held the things they prized
We came, the mighty tree which can withstand
So many prayers and tears. "Do not come close.

Pass on, for far above, and not at hand,
There is the tree Eve ate of for her dose
Of knowledge, and this one is just a sprig
From that." Emerging from the leaves' green shrouds
140 The hidden voice went on. "Recall how, big
With food and wine, those creatures of the clouds,
The cursed centaurs, reeled under the blows
Of Theseus when they chased women. Keep
Also in mind the Hebrew soldiers: those
Who at the fountain drank themselves to sleep
So Gideon, when he took Midian,
Left them behind." So, passing on, we kept
To the wall side, regaled with tales of men
And gluttony, and what it earned. We stepped,
150 Spread out, a thousand steps along
The lonely road, each wrapped in silent thought,
Concerned with appetite, its right and wrong.
A sudden voice said "Give me your report
Of what you think of as you go, you three
All by yourselves." I started, as do scared
And timid beasts. I raised my head to see
Who this was. Never in a furnace flared
Metal or glass so glowing red as he.
The angel said "If up high you would climb
160 Here you must turn to find the peaceful sky."
His aspect stole my eyesight for a time
So that I trailed my teachers only by
My hearing. And just as the breeze of May,
Dawn's herald, when it stirs, gives out perfume
So full of grass and flowers, in that way
I felt a wind, fanned by each fluttering plume
Of his wing, strike my brow, and I could sense
The odour of ambrosia. "How blessed
They are who are lit up by such intense
170 Grace that the appetite within their breast
Stirs not the fumes of a too great desire,
But just the hunger justice might require."

The sun was in the Ram, and had declined
Two hours from noon, which left the Bull on high
In the meridian. By that same kind
Of movement, night had quit the tallest sky
Above Jerusalem, so you would find
The Scorpion up there if you could look,
And we were short of time for our ascent.
Pressed in advance for all the time it took,
We were as one that no impediment
10 Can stop, because necessity, his goad,
Pricks him continually, and our small crew
Met one by one the next stage on our road
By entering a gap so tight that you
Were forced to climb alone on its stone stairs.
And as the little stork might lift one wing
To quit the nest and thereby prove it dares
To fly but then pretends that no such thing
Had crossed its mind and drops the wing again,
Just so was I with my desire to ask
20 A question, and I almost spoke, but then
I didn't. My Guide, equal to the task,
For all our speed of foot, did not refrain.
"Your bow of speech," he said, "is tightly drawn
Right to the arrowhead and creaks with strain.

Please let it loose." With confidence reborn,
This time I got the words out. "How do they
Get thin when there's no need of nourishment?"
And he: "If only you recall the way
Meleager's life was lived and wholly spent
30 In one brand's burning, this point won't be hard
For you, and if you also think of how
Your image in the glass meets your regard
With every move you make—not soon, but now,
Exactly similar—yet isn't real,
You'll find it easier to realise
That souls can well reflect what bodies feel
And make it seem substantial to your eyes.
But just to set your puzzlement at rest
I call on Statius, and bid him heal
40 Your wounds." "If in your presence I attend,"
Said Statius, "to spirits seen as real—
Although the actual body is long gone—
In the eternal life, it is because
I can't refuse you." That said, he went on:
"My son, if, in your mind, you open doors
To take my words in, I can demonstrate
How this can be. The thirsty veins do not
Drink perfect blood, which, sharing the pure state
Of food kept from the table, takes in what
50 The heart confers, the power to generate
The future body's parts. Like blood that takes
The standard course through veins to fashion these,
The perfect heart's blood subsequently makes
Its way down to where words are bound to please
Less than a decent silence, and from there
It joins another's blood in the right place,
The natural vessel. In this way the pair
Of matched streams mingle as they share the space:
One passive, and the other, since it flows
60 From sheer perfection, active. The twinned stream

Begins to function as its thickness grows,
Coagulating, quickening its seam
Of virtue into potent readiness—
A soul, much as a plant's, but not the same,
Because the plant's soul sets out never less
Than all set to arrive, whereas the frame
Of this soul is sea fungus at the most.
It moves, it feels, it goes on to produce
Organs for faculties. It is the host
70 Of every little thing and each thing's use
That grows out of its seed. And now, my son,
The force unfolds and spreads out of the heart
Of the begetter, until all is one,
And nature has made shift for every part
And member. But you can't see how it's done
As yet—quite how from the dumb animal
A creature comes that speaks—and neither could
A wiser one than you. He saw it all,
Except one special part that would come good
80 And be the mind. No, Aristotle thought
The intellect was separate from the soul
And common to all men, and so he taught.
But open up your breast now to the whole
Truth of this tricky matter. It's like so:
No sooner does the structure of the brain
Get organised within the embryo
Than in comes the First Mover might and main,
Happy at nature's work of art, and gives
A potent inspiration to it, which
90 Incorporates all that already lives
In there, and so a single soul made rich
By these two elements begins to thrive,
And feel, and think. And lest these words of mine
Astonish you, of how men come alive,
Consider how the sun's heat turns to wine
When it combines with the substantial juice
That pours from the pulped grapes plucked from the vine.

Or think how, from the flesh, the soul pulls loose
When Lachesis runs out of flax. It takes
Along with it all the potentials for
The faculties: that is, whatever makes
The human or divine. The first no more
Are heard, the second (memory and thought
And will, the things that nothing can confer
Save the divine), freed from their last resort
In flesh, are more acute than they once were.
And so the soul falls, marvellously, towards
One of two shores (and all this will occur
Without a pause): the Tiber's, where it boards
The boat sent for the saved, or else the dark
Bank of the Acheron. And then it first
Becomes aware of how it will embark
And where it's bound. As soon as it's immersed
In space, its formative essential force
Sends out its rays, in just those shapes they took
For living members, taking the same course
That sunbeams take in rain-soaked air: we look
And see the colours. Thus the air around
Will set itself into the self-same form
The soul had when alive. There will be found
A stamp of the soul's power. Though not as warm,
The shape will, as the flame follows the fire,
Follow the spirit. Since it has by this
Its image from then on, so we require,
To fit it, the name "shade," for emphasis
On insubstantial visibility,
And from this air, organs for every sense
Are formed, even for sight. As we can see,
We speak, and smile, and weep, and heave intense
Sighs of the depth that might have met your ears
Here on this hill. As our desires impinge
On us, the shade takes form, and so appears—
At which you marvel." We were at the hinge
Of the last torment, taking a right turn,

And faced another care. Out from the bank
Flames shoot. To bend them, as they burn,
The path sends up a blast from its far flank
So that the fire is kept back. Thus we had,
One at a time, to take the open side.
For me this had two ways of being bad,
Since on the one hand there was this hot tide
Of fire to face, and on the other I
Feared falling. "Along here we must draw tight
On our eyes' reins, lest our steps go awry."
But then I heard, in that great burning light,
A song: *Summae Deus Clementiae*—
The hymn that tells us chastity is right—
Which made me keen to turn. Within
The flames were spirits walking, so I kept
Looking at them, my stunned glance hard to win
Away from them and back to where I stepped,
My gaze divided. Their hymn fully sung,
They cried what Mary said to Gabriel,
Thus: *"Virum non cognosco"* (in our tongue,
"No man was with me"), for the world knows well
That she was chaste. And then they all began
To sing the hymn again, and at the end,
This time, they cried "Diana hid from man
Deep in the woods, and would not keep for friend
The nymph Callisto, who with Jove had lain,
But banished her because she dared to drink
The poison Venus pours, the wine of pain."
And then they sang again—and will, I think,
First sing, then cry, then sing for all the time
They burn—of all the husbands and the wives
Who keep their marriage free of that sad crime
By being chaste, as wedlock wants our lives
To be. And with such precepts and such prayer
The last wound of them all we may repair.

CANTO 26

While one before the other thus we went
Along the edge, my Master often said
"Watch out, for what I warn is truly meant."
The sun now struck me, not from overhead,
But more on my right shoulder, for its beams
Changed all the west from azure into white,
But as pale fire, when cloaked with shadow, seems
More glowing, so my shadow made the light
More visible—for many shades a sign
To heed, and their first cause to speak of me,
Deducing that my flesh might still be mine.
"His body," said one, "does not seem to be
Unreal." And some approached me, just as near
As they could come without their breaking through
To where they would not burn: their only fear.
One spoke: "Pray answer, going as you do
Behind the others, not for tardiness
Perhaps, but more for reverence: say what's true.
Not only I, who burn with thirst, no less
From fire, long for an answer, but all these
Long for it as an Ethiopian
Dreams of cold water. Therefore tell me, please,
How comes it you're a wall that stops the sun
As if so far you have escaped death's net?"

So spoke one, and I would have said my name
Right then, had my attention not been set
On something else strange. Through the hall of flame,
And facing opposite to those we'd met,
Came people whose appearance held my gaze
30   Suspended. Then the shades on either side
Make haste to kiss each other, a mere graze,
Because they neither break nor slow their stride.
Just as the ants in their dark troop will touch
Muzzle to muzzle—as they ask the way,
Perhaps, or how the day goes—it was such
With these, who, ending their brief interplay,
Before they took their next step to move on,
Each tries his hardest to outshout the rest.
The ones who just arrived, to get them gone,
40   Cry "Sodom and Gomorrah!" and attest
To lusts in spite of nature, while the first
Group we encountered cries out "Pasiphae
Enters the cow to slake her raging thirst
With what the bull brings!" and so testify
To natural lusts ungoverned. Then, like cranes
That fly, some to the mountains in the north
And some south to the sand—for none remains
Of these when the frost comes, and those go forth
When too much sun shines—so the two crowds go
50   Their separate ways, and all return with tears
To their first chanting, and the cry they know
Befits their weakness. By their looks all ears,
Those came close who'd entreated me before.
Twice having seen their need, I said: "Souls who
Are bound to have, at the right time, your store
Of peace, my limbs are not left, either new
Or old, back there. They're here, both blood and joint.
It is to be no longer blind I climb.
A lady waits above fit to appoint
60   The grace for me by which I conquer time,

Bringing my mortal body through your world.
But so your greatest wish may soon be met
Where heaven's love most widely is unfurled
In highest light, say now—so I may yet
Put pen to parchment—who you are and what
That crowd is that goes back behind you there."
The mountain man's no more stunned by his lot
When, rough and rustic, with a speechless stare,
He comes into the city, than each shade
70 Was now, but when they were relieved of that
Amazement—which will always quickly fade
In lofty hearts—the one who, puzzled at
My shadow, first had spoken, spoke again:
"How you are blessed, you that, to better die,
Take on experience from us! Those men
Who go the other way from us and cry
So differently, were guilty of that lust
For which, in triumph, Caesar heard the call
'Regina!' from the crowd, and so they must
80 Go crying 'Sodom!' as you heard, for all
With self-reproach and shame thus reinforce
Their burning. Our sin, on the other hand,
Was double-sexed, but ran outside the course
Of human law, our hunger in command
As with the beasts. So, parting, we cry now
Her name, who made—we add, to our disgrace—
Herself a beast, inside the timber cow:
A beast within a beast. We're in this place
For deeds you now know, and our guilt as well.
90 If you would know our names, time would be short
To tell you, if I could. But I can tell
You this much: I can satisfy your thought
About who I might be, and who I was.
I'm Guido Guinizelli, and I make
Already my purgation here because
I sorrowed properly for my soul's sake

Before the end." As when Lycurgus grieved
For his child, and brought to the point of death
The woman whose neglect left him bereaved,
But her two sons staved off her dying breath
By rushing to embrace her, so, with some
Restraint, did I become, to hear him speak
His name, father of me and all that come
Along with me (and some make me look weak):
All those who speak the sweet and graceful rhymes
Of love, and deaf and dumb I went along
A long way, thoughtful, gazing many times
At him, the founder of our school of song,
But kept from coming near him by the fire.
My sight of him once fed, I offered him
My services for all he might require,
Assuring him that this was no mere whim.
And he to me: "You leave a trace so clear
In me, that Lethe can't destroy or dim
What you have told me. If you hold me dear,
However—if your words are true—you should
Also inform me why your look and speech
Show that. Make your affection understood."
And I to him: "Sir, your sweet lines that reach
From your time into ours and which will last
As long as people talk, have made their ink
Eternal treasure." "Brother, only cast
Your glance at him ahead, and you might think
Again," he said, while pointing. "He surpassed
Me as a master of the mother tongue.
He was the better craftsman in all forms
Of love verse and romantic tales. Among
Their writers he stood out. As for the swarms
Of idiots who hail the boring stuff
Of Giraut from Limoges, they think to heed
A widespread reputation is enough
To judge the truth, as if we might not need

To hear from art or reason. The same thing
Once happened with Guittone. One cracked voice
Croaked to the next that only he could sing.
But finally most made the proper choice,
The Sweet New Style. Now, if you have been graced
With so much favour that you have the right
To see the cloister where Christ is emplaced
140 As abbot of the brotherhood, you might
Say, just for me, a *Paternoster*, trimmed
Of its last words, for here the power to sin
Is gone from us, and so the need is dimmed
For that whole prayer." That others might move in,
Perhaps, and take his place, he disappeared
Into the fire as when a fish goes down
To the bottom through the water. Then I neared
The one who, for the sake of his renown,
Had earlier been pointed out. His name,
150 I told him, had a place of welcome set
In my enquiring soul, and so it came
To be that he spoke thus: *"We are well met.*
Your courtly question pleases me so much
I neither may nor could hold back the news
Of who I am from one with such a touch
For gentle manners. How can I refuse?"
Matching his mind to his expressive style,
In Provencal his eloquence was cast.
"I am Arnaut, who weeps and sings the while
160 *He walks. I see my follies of the past*
With grief, and yet I still see with a smile
The day I hope I will attain at last.
And now I beg of you, by that great good
Which guides you to the summit of the stairs,
That you will think of, and have understood
In time, my sins and penitential cares."
The furnace that refines them shone so bright,
When he stepped back he vanished in the light.

CANTO 27

As when it shoots its first rays where the One
Who made it shed His blood, and when, in Spain,
The Scales are overhead with night half done,
And noon burns on the Ganges' gathered rain,
So here, nigh on to sinking, stood the sun.
The day, therefore, was all set to depart,
When God's glad angel showed himself outside
The flames, and "Blessèd are the pure in heart,"
He sang, his voice far clearer than my Guide
Or I could boast. "There is no way ahead
Unless you brave the fire and feel its sting.
So enter, holy souls, and then be led
With open ears by what the voices sing,"
He said when we were near, while I became,
To hear him, like one laid low in his grave.
I stretched up my clasped hands, gazed at the flame,
Imagining how once, in a deep cave,
I had seen bodies burning. Then, to me,
My escorts turned, and Virgil said: "My son,
There may be torment here: death, there can't be.
Recall, recall! Even on Geryon
I kept you safe. So what shall I do here,
Nearer to God? You may well rest assured,
If you stayed in these flames year after year—

10

20

A thousand years—their fire could not afford
One singed hair to your head, so never fear:
And if, perhaps, you think that I deceive,
Go close, try with your hands and with the edge
Of what you wear, and then you will believe.
30 You'll put off every qualm and you will pledge
Your trust." Yet I continued to stand still,
Still hesitant, though I had no defence
Against my conscience. When he saw my will
To stay was so unbending and intense,
A little troubled he said "Now, son, look.
Dividing you from Beatrice is this wall."
And as we read in the time-honoured book
Of Pyramus and Thisbe, before all
The mulberry turned red he raised his eyes,
40 While dying, towards her, just so my streak
Of stubbornness dissolved, and to my wise
Leader I turned, for I had heard him speak
The name forever vivid in my mind,
At which he frowned, and said "Are we to stay
Always on this side?" But his smile was kind,
As if aimed at a child that we can sway
With just an apple. Then, with me behind,
He put himself into the wall of flame,
First having asked of Statius, who had
50 Been so long in between us as we came,
To follow on. And how I'd have been glad
To jump into a vat of boiling glass
Just to get cool, so did it burn beyond
All measure there where this had come to pass.
And my sweet father, in his voice so fond
To comfort me in my fear, said "I swear
I see her eyes already." Then a voice
To guide us sang before us, and on where
It seemed to come from we had little choice
60 Save fixing all our heed, and where the stair

Began, we came forth. There, within a light,
"Come forward all you that my father blessed,"
The voice sang, so that, startled by its might,
I couldn't look. And then it sang the rest:
"The sun gives way," it sang, "and soon the night
Will come. Don't stop. Before the west grows dark,
Step out." The way went straight up through the rock
At such a pitch I cut off the last spark
Of sunlight. The sun low, I was a block
70 To its weak rays, and we had barely gone
A few steps, when I and my sages saw,
By how my shadow failed to linger on,
The sun had set behind us, and before
The vast horizon had as yet assumed
One colour, and night ruled in all domains,
Each chose a step for bed. The mountain loomed,
And though we much desired to take the pains
Of climbing further, it denied our wish,
To do so, for its laws do not allow
80 Travel in darkness. Goats that were kittenish
And frisky on the heights are languid now,
Chewing the cud and silent in the shade,
Watched by the shepherd who leans on his staff
Yet, leaning, tends them lest a beast invade
His quiet flock and scatter them like chaff.
Just so were we three—though the goat was I
And they the shepherds—shut in on each side
By that high rock, and not much of the sky
Could I see, but in that gap gleamed a pride
90 Of stars, and they were bigger than I'd seen
Before, and brighter. There I lay to ruminate
And stargaze. Sleep, which frequently has been
First to announce what would eventuate
In my life, seized me. In the hour, I guess,
Before dawn, when sweet Venus in the east
First lights the mountain with her endlessness

Of loving fire insensibly increased,
I seemed to see, and see as if I dreamed,
A beautiful young lady gathering
100 Flowers in a meadow. As she went, she seemed,
While stooping for the pretty blooms, to sing:
"Whoever wants to ask my name should know
It's Leah, and I pluck, with hands so fair,
The makings of a garland as I go.
I like the look, but love the open air.
My sister Rachel, on the other hand,
Sits always at her glass, as keen to see
Her own bright eyes as I am for the land
Beneath my feet. But there you are, that's me:
110 I like to do, she likes to understand."
And now the radiant splendours before dawn—
Always more welcome to the pilgrim when
He lodges closer to where he was born—
Chased off the shadows on all sides, and then
My sleep as well, and so I rose, to find
My mentors up already. "That sweet fruit
Of Eden which you mortals have in mind
At all times, with your hunger so acute
You seek it out on every bough, today
120 Will give peace to your craving." Never was
There such a boon as I heard my Guide say.
Desire upon desire, without a pause,
Came over me to be above. I felt,
With every step, my feathers grow. Steps sped
Beneath us so the stairway seemed to melt,
And on the top step Virgil turned and said:
"You've seen the temporary fires up here,
And seen the fires of Hell that burn always,
And now, my son, the place is very near
130 Where I myself see nothing. Through the maze
I've brought you here with all my mind and art,
By which your nature has been purified.

It's ready now to play the major part.
From here on, you yourself must be your guide.
Steep ways and tight opposed you. You came through.
The sun shines on your brow. Now see the grass.
The trees and flowers here that spring anew
From this fresh ground are all yours as you pass.
Until those fair eyes come to welcome you
140   Which will rejoice as once they came to weep
To me for your plight, you may sit among
These glories or go walking. But don't keep
A vigil any longer for my tongue:
No word or any sign can you expect
From me. My work is done. Your will is whole
And free and upright, sure of its effect,
So don't deny its bidding. Of your soul
I make you captain. Most blessed among men,
Move on. You'll never hear from me again."

CANTO 28

Eager to search the dense, divine and green
Forest, to know it, both inside and out,
This place through which the new day could be seen
With splendour tempered, while from all about
Fragrance converged on me, I left the bank
Without the guidance of a word or sign
From Virgil, and with my own will to thank
I made my slow way in a level line
Across the ground. A sweet unchanging air
10 Fondled my brow, the soft force of a breeze
Bending the trembling boughs to that point where
The mountain's shadow first falls. At their ease
The boughs were swayed, and still remained upright
Enough for all the little birds to sing
Out of the tree-tops where they spent the night
And now turned their fine arts to welcoming
The morning hours, ecstatic in the leaves
Which gave an undertone to their sweet rhymes
As, near Ravenna, the Sirocco cleaves
20 The air—one of the winds, in ancient times,
Locked up by Aeolus—and the pine wood
Murmurs from branch to branch. Slow steps by then
Had brought me, from the place where I first stood
To enter, so far through the trees that when

I looked back I could not see whence I came,
But now my further progress was cut short
By a small stream whose tiny waves made game
To bend the grass that hedged its lively sport
Leftward. And all the waters that win fame
30 Here in the world for purity, would seem
Defiled compared to this. Though it flows dark
In the perpetual shade where not a gleam
Of moon or blaze of sun may light a spark
Below the surface, yet it can conceal
Nothing. My feet stopped there, while my sight passed
Over the stream, drawn forth by the appeal
Of freshly flowering branches in their vast
Variety. I saw that scene reveal—
As suddenly as when a thing for awe
40 Drives out our thoughts—a lady all alone
Who sang and picked the flowers that lay before
As she went on her way, her lilting tone
Matching the lightness of the petals. "Pray,
Fair lady, by love's fondling beams made warm,
If I am to believe what your looks say
Must be your heart's exalted inward form,
Come nearer to the stream, so that I may
Hear what you sing. For you make me recall
Proserpine, when she plucked flowers too,
50 And Pluto took her, scattering them all.
Her mother lost her and she lost the new
Glory that comes each year." With the slight fall
Of quick foot when the dancing woman turns
With feet together, neither one advanced
By more than just a touch—and one who learns
To do this tells you she has always danced
By her ease only—this one turned to me
On the red and yellow flowers like a veiled
Virgin with modest glance, and met my plea
60 With song, approaching so her sweet sound sailed

To reach me with its meaning. Then, when she
Was where the grassy edge was lapped and bathed
By the river's lovely waves, she had the grace
To lift her eyes to me, and they were swathed
In light, poured from her lids to flood her face
With such a brilliance that I don't believe
Venus herself gave out in her surprise
When Cupid let loose and could not retrieve
His accidental arrow as her eyes
70 Were on Adonis. While she stood upright
On the other bank, she smiled as she arranged
Her many colours, flowering at that height
With no seeds needed. We two were estranged
By just the distance that the stream was wide:
Three paces only. But the Hellespont—
Where Xerxes had to cross back with his pride
In ruins, and Leander, for his want
Of Hero, had to swim from side to side
From Sestos to Abydos—never got
80 More hatred than this pretty trickle earned
From me, who wished it gone, but it was not.
"You're new here. There are things you haven't learned,"
She said, "And it's perhaps because I smile
In this place set apart for humankind
To be its nest, you nurse your doubts awhile,
And there are clouds that linger in your mind.
But *Delectasti* is the psalm you should
Remember: 'Lord, your work has made me glad,
And I will triumph.' Those words, understood
90 Aright, for any qualms you ever had,
Will clear the mist with light. Now you are near
Before me, and are making your request,
So tell me if there's more that you would hear.
I'll set your curiosity at rest."
"This water, and the branches, how they sound,"
I said, "fly in the face of what I heard

From Statius, of how this higher ground
Can never change." And she: "Because the word
And fact seem different things, you marvel. How
100   This came to be, proceeding from its cause,
I can unravel for you here and now.
The Good Supreme, the grand sum of whose laws
Is His own pleasure, made man good, and made
Man love the good, and gave him this good place,
The Earthly Paradise. Man could have stayed
In peace here always. Such was not the case.
Through his own fault, his stay was only brief,
And honest laughter and sweet sport gave way
To tears, hard labour and abiding grief.
110   That the disturbances which, night and day,
The exhalations of the sea and land
Make there below—following where they may,
As students of those matters understand,
The ebb and flow of heat—should do no harm
To man, the mountain rose aloft thus far
To stand clear from the banished, and be calm.
But since the outer spheres, revolving, are
Moved by the Primum Mobile, that first
Rotation, unless interrupted, strikes
120   On this height—all impurities dispersed
From its surrounding air—and as it likes
It does. It makes the wood, for being dense,
Resound. The smitten plants have such
A potency, the air with their intense
Virtue is impregnated at a touch,
And so the wind must scatter it abroad,
And so the Northern Hemisphere, as both
Its fit self and its proper sky accord,
Brings forth, from diverse virtues, different growth.
130   This understood, small marvel would it seem
Down yonder, if some plant, no seed on show,
Should take root. In accordance with that theme,

This holy ground has every seed you know
Filling the soil, and fruits that are not picked
Back there. This water springs forth from no vein
Restored by vapour that the harshly strict
Cold has condensed (as earthly rivers gain
And lose their force), but from a constant, sure
Fountain it comes, and what pours forth like rain
140 By God's will must return to fill a store
Open on either side. Thus virtue flows
Down one side, so, when men are bathed with it,
Their very memory of sin all goes,
And, on the other side, the opposite
Occurs, and memories of their good deeds
Return. The stream, on this side, bears the name
Of Lethe; on that, Eunoe. It needs
First to be sipped at from both sides the same
To be effective, and there is no taste
150 Sweeter than this. And though your thirst may well
Be satisfied by this outline I've traced,
There's something more that I feel bound to tell
Just for your joy, and though these words may go
Beyond my brief, I think you'll find they meet
Your approbation. Those old names you know
Who once sang of a golden age replete
With happiness, perhaps exulted so
Because they dreamed of this place. On their peak,
Parnassus, their minds filled with this one. Spring
160 Eternal. Human innocence. All speak
Of just such fruit, nectar in everything.
Ovid himself said all this would come true."
She paused. Right then I turned around to my
Two poets, and I saw what they could do
Instead of speech. They smiled, and she was why.
Then once again the fair one caught my eye.

CANTO 29

When I turned back to her I heard the rest.
Though she had done with speaking, she sang on,
As if in love, "But how all those are blessed
Whose sins are pardoned!" and I was far gone
In thoughts of nymphs, alone in woodland shade,
Who wander, one alert to see the sun,
The other to avoid it. So she made
Her way upstream against the rippling run,
With little steps along the bank, and I
10 Kept level. In a hundred strides or less
The two banks made an equal bend, and by
My reckoning, which I'd call a good guess,
We now faced east again. We'd not gone far
That way, when suddenly she turned, and said:
"My brother, look and listen." Few things are
Sudden like lightning. This was. In my head,
As brightness swept the forest all around,
I told myself it must be lightning, yet,
Since lightning disappears as soon as found,
20 And this grew brighter still, I hedged my bet,
And asked myself "What's this?" And then a sound,
A melody, ran sweet through shining air,
And so my zeal for good caused me to blame
Eve's boldness, that a woman—when and where

All in the earth and sky obeyed the same
Divine will—should decline to further bear
(For she was only just formed, and alone)
The veil of ignorance, for, had she stayed
Submissive underneath it, I'd have known,
30 Like all men, this whole limitless parade
Of indescribable delights before,
And for far longer. While I went among
So many first fruits in the mighty store
Of bliss eternal—while my will was hung
Suspended in desire of all the more
Of joys and miracles—the air caught fire
Beneath the green boughs, and that lovely sound
Exploded into songs, choir upon choir.
Virgins most holy! Muses! Stony ground,
40 *Cold, hunger, vigils, I have borne for you, not true?*
But now my need drives me to ask reward.
Now let the whole of Helicon come through
With what it owes me, all it can afford.
Urania and her singers should step in
To help me versify things hard for thought,
Such as the following. I can begin
By saying that my puzzled eye was caught,
A little further on, by seven trees
Of gold, or what appeared to us as such,
50 A false impression reinforced to please
Our credulous perception by how much
Distance remained from us to them. But when
I'd come so near that these deceiving shapes
Remained ambiguous no longer, then
The faculty which no deceit escapes,
The power of reason, saw them as they were:
As candlesticks, and heard the voices sing
"Hosanna!" And up there without a blur
It flew alone, the lovely spreading thing.
60 More than the moon in the clear midnight sky

Of her mid-month, that fine array was bright.
I turned around with wonder in my eye
To Virgil, and his look had the same light
Of sheer amazement, and I lifted high
My face again to those things, which moved near
To us so slowly new brides would have been
More quick. The lady scorned me. "You appear
Amazed by just the living lights you've seen.
Where is your heed for what is not yet here
70 Yet comes behind them?" I saw people, then,
Who followed, clad in white: white so intense
As here there never was, and then again
The water shone so to my left, that hence,
As from a mirror, came my left side back
To my eyes when I gazed. When I was at
The part where just the streamlet kept my track
From meeting theirs, for a better view than that
I paused, and let the flames move on, to stain
Like streaming pennons all the air behind
80 With seven tinctures, as the sun and rain
Bring forth a bow in colours of rich kind,
And Delian Diana's girdle glows.
Beyond my sight the banners went back, and
As well as mortal eyes see or mind knows,
The outermost exemplars of that band
Of candelabra were ten paces set
Apart. Beneath the fair sky I describe,
Two dozen elders crowned with lilies met
My gaze two at a time. "Among the tribe
90 Of Adam's daughters," they sang, "you are blessed,
And blessed forever let your beauty be!"
The flowers and fresh leaves were left to rest
On the far bank by that light infantry
Of the elect. As brilliance follows soon
On brilliance there in heaven, came four more
Creatures on after, and these had the boon

Of green-leaf crowns, and each one of the four
Had six wings, all their plumage full of eyes,
And if the eyes of Argus were alive
They'd look like that. But lack of time denies
That I be lavish with my rhymes, and strive
In their depiction. Read Ezekiel,
Who saw them when they came in from the cold
With wind and cloud and fire, and just as well
As he described them then, his words of old
Applied here, save the figure of six wings
That Revelation gives them meets my count,
And not his four. (John had the truth of things
In this respect, and got the right amount.)
But anyway, between those four the space
Contained a fine two-wheeled triumphal car
Drawn by a griffin, which employed the place
On each side of the middle band—as far
On each side as the first of three—to spread
Its wings among the coloured streaks without
Cutting through any, and the wings instead
Rose so high that their tips left you in doubt
Where they might be. Where this bird could be said
To be bird, it was all gold, and where man,
Was white mingled with red. Not even Rome
Had honoured Scipio the African
Or great Augustus, when it cheered them home,
With so exultant a conveyance. Not
The sun itself could equal it: the sun
Whose carriage was destroyed when Phaethon got
His signals mixed, and Jove paid heed to one
Of Earth's devout prayers. He chose to be just
In secret counsel. And three ladies danced
A round at the right wheel. One, red as rust,
Was so red you'd have missed her had she pranced
Inside a fire. One more of emerald
Seemed made. The third looked like fresh-fallen snow.

The white one first, and then the red one, called
The time, and from that song's pulse, fast or slow,
They moved. And on the left, four others tripped
Their festival. They were in purple clad,
Their measure set by one who hopped and skipped
With three eyes in her head. The whole troop had,
Behind it, two old men in different dress,
From one another, but alike in grave
And lofty bearing, their shared seriousness.
One showed the spirit by which nature gave
The world Hippocrates, to help mankind
When ill. The other showed the opposite
Concern, for its sword, lifted, chilled my mind
Across the river's width, so brightly lit
And sharp it seemed, to castigate the soul.
Then came four humble holy ones. At last
An old man walked who slept, and yet his whole
Expression spoke for keenness. As they passed,
The final seven looked clad like the first,
Except this time no lily crowns were worn,
But roses and red flowers, an outburst
Of crimson round the brow I would have sworn,
From where I stood, was fire. And then a halt
Was called. A mighty thunderclap was heard.
The car had stopped, right there. The storm's assault
Appeared to mean permission was deferred
For that throng to go further. There it stood,
The pageant, flags in front. The force for good.

140

150

160

CANTO 30

Unlike the Bear that helps us navigate,
But still its seven stars must come and go
Or wear a misty veil, it was the state
Of this Wain, here above, to never know
Such flux. In their First Heaven they stood still,
The seven candelabra. Only sin
Could fluster them. They shone on, to fulfil
Their task. Between their light and the griffin
The truthful squad turned to the car as will

10   A man who seeks peace. Like a messenger
From Heaven, one sang out this line. "My spouse,
Now come with me from Lebanon." Nor were
The others slow to match him. As the house
Of all the blessed shall fill, at the last blast
Of trumpets, with souls leaping from the tomb,
Their voices once again what in the past
They were, and their song for the crack of doom
Will ring out Hallelujah! thus arose
There on the car, called by the elder's voice,

20   A hundred representatives of those
Who speak for life eternal. "Yours the choice
To come, and you are blessed," they cried, and threw
Flowers aloft and all around, and then
They quoted Virgil, all of whom they knew,

Transmitting God's word through the words of men:
"Give lilies with full hands." At break of day
I once saw all the eastern vista turn
Rose coloured, and the sky, clear every way
Elsewhere, was lovely, for the sun's full burn
30 Was softened as its face glowed in a shroud
Of vapours, and the naked eye could bear
The sight a long time. So, within a cloud
Of flowers rising here and falling there,
Flung from the angels' hands, a lady shone,
Her white veil girt with olive, mantle green,
Fretted with living fire. And then my soul,
Which had for years felt no cause for the awe
By which her living form once made my whole
Existence tremble, now, though barred from more
40 Knowledge by eye, still registered the force
Of hidden virtue and my erstwhile love.
Sight struck by virtue in its lofty course—
Pierced once again, now I was here above,
As once I was in boyhood—I turned left
With confidence, as any child will run
To mother when of fortitude bereft,
And said to Virgil "Not a drop, not one
Of blood remains in me that does not shake.
I know the sure signs of an ancient flame."
50 But Virgil, who'd done so much for my sake,
Virgil my father, Virgil, he that came
For me to give myself and him to take
Me onward to salvation, now was gone.
Nor did all Eden's sweetness, lost by Eve,
The ancient mother, take effect upon
My cheeks, dew-washed so all tear-stains should leave,
But here they were again. She said "Dante,
Weep not that Virgil leaves you, weep not yet.
For you must yet weep in another way,
60 For your sins." Just then, when I tried to get

A clear view of the figure that so spoke
My name—I note this, just to pay my debt
To sheer necessity—there, at a stroke,
I saw a lady at the car's left side,
A fleet commander gone from stern to prow
To see the other captains fight the tide
Of hardship and to urge them on, and now
The lady, who had just appeared to me
Veiled in the festival of angels, fixed
70 Her eyes on mine beyond the stream, and she,
Although her veil was still full, and was mixed
With olive leaves, which was Minerva's sign,
And therefore she could not be plainly seen,
Yet royally, like one with the design
Of holding back the heat her words might mean
While speaking, said this: "Look. Look at me well,
For I am Beatrice indeed. How do
You dare approach this mountain. Can you tell?
For man is happy here, yet here are you."
80 My glance fell to the clear fount, but I met
Myself, and brought it back up to the grass
Because shame weighed my brow. So children get
The collywobbles when their mothers pass
Judgement through pity. She was silent. Then
As one, the angels sang this. "Lord, in you
I had hope." But they all stopped singing when
They'd done the first nine verses, and come to
The bit about the feet and the large rooms.
Just as, along the back of Italy,
90 The snow piles up and solidly entombs
The tree trunks as the wind's intensity
Increases from the northeast, but will melt
When, out of Africa, the south wind blows,
And dribble like a candle that has felt
The fire, just so was I, as, first, I froze
And had no tears or sighs before they sang

In concert with the music of the spheres,
But when I heard that the deep, melting pang
Of their song fit for supernatural ears

100 Was all for me, then, more than if they'd said
"Lady, why shame him so?" the ice around
My heart turned breath and water, and it spread

With anguish through my mouth and eyes, unbound
From my tight breast. Still standing motionless
On the same side of the car, she then addressed

The good souls in their pitying distress.
"You watch the world a long day without rest
So neither night nor sleep can hide a thing

That goes on or is ready to begin.
110 Therefore my answer's made considering
Him weeping yonder more than you, so sin

And sorrow may be measured in like terms.
Not just by how the distant great wheels spin—
A movement which assigns and so confirms

An end to each seed as the stars dictate—
But by his lavish gift of the divine
Graces that rain from such a lofty state

Our sight can't reach the vapours that consign
The blessing, so in early life this man
120 Had every gift and talent in the book

For the fulfilment of a marvellous plan.
But often, when the soul has that good look
Of strength, the ground grows poisonous and wild

With matching vigour, as if bad seed took
A deeper root: bright prospects are defiled.
My countenance sustained him for a space.

I brought him with me, with my youthful eyes,
The right way. But I reached the entry place
Of proper youth, where adolescence dies,

130 At twenty-five, and there he turned his face
Away from me, his wishes otherwise.
My state was raised from beauty of the flesh

To that of soul, and virtue so increased
In me that I became less dear, less fresh,
Less welcome, and his questing steps soon ceased
To come my way, and went another way
Less true, after false images of good
Which keep no promises: nor did it pay,
Through dreams and all the other means I could,
140 To call him back, for he would not pay heed.
He fell so low, all means to save him fell
Short of the task. Deciding I would need
To show him the Lost People down in Hell,
I visited the threshold of the pit
And heaped with prayers the one that brought him here,
And every prayer in tears. No help for it:
God's high decrees would crack and hold no fear
If Lethe could be passed without a writ
Of penitence, and its dear sweet taste kept
150 Delicious in the mouth, with no tears wept."

"You that are on the sacred stream's far side,"
She said again, turning to me the tip
Of her speech whose mere edge had hurt my pride
Sharply enough, "speak now. Unlock your lip.
The accusation needs, if this be true,
Confession joined to it." My wits were so
Confused that what my voice set out to do
Began, but past my lips it could not go.
She let up just a little, then she said
"What are you thinking of? Pray answer me,
For those sad memories are not yet dead,
Slain in you by the stream." Uncertainty
Mixed with unbridled fear drove forth a "yes"
From my mouth that to hear you had to see.
Just as a crossbow, wound with too much stress
Breaks, when it shoots, both in the bow and cord,
And sends the shaft with less force to the mark,
So, broken by that heavy charge, I poured
Forth tears and sighs, and my trapped voice went dark,
At which she said "In the desires you had
For me which led you in the love of good
Beyond which nothing that can make us glad
Is to be longed for, what could have withstood
Your hopes of progress? What chain or cross-ditch?

10

20

And what attractions and advantages
Seemed prominent in other things, by which
They so diverted your allegiances?"
Heaving a bitter sigh, I strained my voice
To answer, and my lips just managed this:
30 "As soon as your face vanished, all my choice
Was for the present day and its false bliss."
And she: "Had you kept silent, or withdrawn
What you confessed, your fault would still be plain,
Known to the judge of everybody born.
But when a man's own cheek bathes in the rain
Of shame for his own sin, then in our court
The wheel turns back against the sword's edge. Yet,
In order that you bear the shameful thought
Of how you wandered, and thus duly get
40 More strength when you, in other times, are brought
Within the range of sirens, pray forget
The tears and listen. Hear of the straight way
My buried flesh would have consigned you to.
Never did art or nature, night or day,
Present such loveliness of form to you,
As that which harboured me, and it is gone—
Crumbled to dust, and if thus, by my death,
The highest beauty, as you've journeyed on,
Has failed you, then what was there, drawing breath,
50 That could have drawn you to it by desire?
Truly you should have, when the first shaft struck
Of lying things, trailed me as I went higher
Since I deceived no more. No girl with luck
Of looks, or other vanities of brief
And little worth, should ever have weighed down
Your wing to take more hits, and all the grief
That goes with them. New chicks have the renown
Of waiting as the shots fly, two, three, four.
The same is not true for the full-fledged bird,
60 Not when he sees the deadly net spread, or

The arrows climb." Just as, without a word,
A shamed child stands with eyes fixed on the ground,
Acknowledging its fault while listening
Repentant, I stood there and made no sound.
She said: "Since hearing sets you sorrowing.
Lift up your beard and get your grief by eye."
The wind from our land, or from where the king
Iarbas rules in Africa, may try
To rip the oak out but it's no tough thing
70 Compared to my resistance when I raised
My glance at her command, since by "your beard"
She meant a face still young and thus amazed
By its new hair, and venom to be feared
Was in her argument. And when my sight
Was lifted, it saw how those angels paused
In scattering their flowers with delight.
My eyes, whose lack of confidence she caused,
Saw Beatrice turn towards the beast whose one
Person is in two natures. Veiled beyond
80 The stream, to me she seemed to have outdone
Her former self, when still she knew the bond
Of life with mortals, and surpassed them all.
The stinging nettle of remorse was such
That out of everything I could recall
That which most bent me to its love was much
More hated now. Self-knowledge bit my heart,
And down I fell, and what I then became
She knows who caused it. When I was in part
Restored to sense, Matilda, that self-same
90 Lady I'd found alone, now watched me float
While she said "Hold me, hold me." In the stream
I was immersed as far up as my throat,
And she drew me behind her. Like a dream
Of lightness, lighter than the little boat
Whose name recalls the shuttle of the loom,
She passed across the water. We drew near

The blessèd further shore, where I heard bloom
"Purge me," a song so clearly sweet to hear,
I can't recall it, far less put in ink.
100 The lady spread her arms, then clasped my brow
And pushed me under, where I had to drink
The water. Then she pulled me out somehow
And led me, bathed, into the circling dance
Of those four fair ones, and each with her arm
Embraced me, and they sang "By law, not chance,
Here we are nymphs with forms of earthly charm,
But in the sky we're stars. When Beatrice
Descended to the world, we were ordained
Well in advance to be her handmaids. This
110 Is still our function. So far, you have gained
The sight of her but not yet seen her eyes.
Within their happy light three virtues shine.
Beside their radiant depth our dazzle dies,
Because their theological design
Sees more, and you will too, with all disguise
Laid open by your sharpened glance." They thus
Began to sing, and brought me to the breast
Of their great beast, when Beatrice turned to us
And they continued: "See you don't arrest
120 Your gaze. The holy emeralds are displayed
By us for you to see: gems by which love
Once loosed its darts." And then my eyes obeyed
A thousand wishes heated far above
All earthly fire, heat holding them to hers
While here she watched the griffin. Like the sun
Caught in a glass, that creature, whose form stirs
Two beings so completely into one,
Blazed in her eyes, now with the one, and now
The other, nature. Reader, do you ask
130 Whether I marvelled at the sight of how
The thing still in itself fulfilled the task
Of altering its image? While my soul,

Full of astonishment and happiness,
Tasted that food which satisfies the whole
Of its own need, but makes the need no less
For those that eat, the others then advanced
And by their bearing proved their higher state,
As their angelic roundelay they danced.
"Turn, Beatrice, turn your glance, and contemplate
140   Your faithful one, who, for one glimpse of you,
Has come so far, and by your grace confer
On us a favour you alone may do.
Unveil your mouth to him: as your eyes were
One beauty, here's another to reveal."
Splendour of living light eternal! What
Poet has ever grown pale when leaves steal
The sunlight on Parnassus, or has not
Known when to check the draught from its deep well,
That he would fail to seem as if he'd got
150   Brain fever from the doomed attempt to tell
Of you, as you appeared there, heaven-borne,
With heaven and its harmonies to frame
Your radiance in a perpetual dawn,
Forever changing, ceaselessly the same—
Looking like that? And first, you said my name.

CANTO 32

Drowned in their object after ten years' thirst
My eyes were so intent, all other sense
Was quelled in me, but while they were immersed
In that, they had only indifference
For all else. In that way, the holy smile
Had drawn them to it with the same old net,
But then the goddesses, in their own style,
Turned my attention left. "Too fixed, as yet,"
They said, referring to my gaze so keen
On revelation that it still was blind:
And blind I was, as if my eyes had been
Scorched by the sun. But when a lesser kind
Of object drew my sight—lesser, I mean,
Beside the greater from which I withdrew
Out of necessity—then what was seen
Through my dazed eye was soon adjusted to,
Being within my range, and so I saw
The glorious army, after a right wheel,
Returning with the sun and seven more
Flames in its face. As, rounding on its heel,
A squadron saves itself beneath its shields,
Turning its colours while the generals hold
Their main face full front as that squadron yields,
Just so the holy soldiers with their gold

10

20

And guiding banners came by in the van
And thus the pole brought round the car. Again
The ladies sought the wheels, where they began,
And so the holy griffin, now as then,
Shifted its blessed cargo, showing none
30 Of all its feathers shaken. Statius,
Matilda, the fair flower-gathering one,
And I, allowed the right wheel to lead us,
The inner wheel that made the smaller loop,
And as we travelled through the lofty wood
Left empty by her fault who was the dupe
Of that false serpent and thought his words good,
Angelic music timed our steps. The flight
Of just one arrow, three times multiplied,
We'd gone, perhaps, when Beatrice from her height
40 Came down, and from them all, from every side
I heard the murmur "Adam," and then they
Encircled a bare tree, its flowers stripped
Like all its foliage; and its display
Of branches, with no green stuff clad or tipped,
Spread wider as it climbed up and away,
Looking like piled-up hair which Indians
Would marvel at for height, they who grow tall
Trees in their woods. "You're blessed to have no plans,
Griffin, for plucking anything at all
50 With your beak from this tree with its sweet taste,
Lest your guts twist in torment." Thus they cried,
From that ring round the tree where they were placed,
And the animal twice-born said "There inside
The seed is kept safe of all righteousness."
He turned, then, to the shaft he'd pulled, and drew
The car close to the foot of that leafless,
Seemingly widowed, trunk, and tied it to
The tree with just one branch of that same tree.
As our plants, when the mighty light that falls
60 On them has joined the second sign of three

(The Carp, the Ram, the Bull) for what Earth calls
The spring, begin to swell in panoply,
Their colours all renewed, before the sun
Moves on to the next stars to yoke its steeds,
Just so I saw renewal had begun
For this bare tree, whose mere description needs
The tint of Christ's blood, less deep than the rose
But deeper than the violet. The hymn
The company sang then, nobody knows
70 Down here, nor did I have even a dim
Idea of what it meant when I was there—
I only knew that hearing what they sang
Right through was simply more than I could bear.
The eyes of Argos, without pity's pang,
By being told of Syrinx, went to sleep:
The eyes whose long watch over Io cost
So much. If by my writing I could keep
To that same standard, nothing need be lost:
As painters paint a model, I could tell
80 How slumber overcame me, but let that
Be done by one who wants to do it well.
I pass to when I woke up, startled at
A brightness breaking through the sleepy veil,
And heard the call: "What are you doing? Rise!"
As when their master, Jesus, made them scale
Tabor, the three apostles filled their eyes
With His transfiguration and a glance
At blossoms of the apple tree that makes
The angels crave its fruit and drives the dance
90 Of Heaven's perpetual marriage feast—it takes
Only a glimpse to leave the viewer stunned—
And Peter, John and James fell to the ground
In sleep, but Jesus, from his fund
Of rousing words found those to bring them round,
And they awoke to find their school was short
Of Moses and Elias, and the bright

Light of Christ's robe was no more what they'd thought
Had been a transcendental, blinding white,
So I came to, and there I saw again,
100   Standing above, she that before had been
My guide, Matilda. She had helped me when
I stepped along the river. "Have you seen
Beatrice? Where is she?" I said, all in doubt.
And she: "Look there beneath that new-grown green.
She's seated on the tree's root, hedged about
With just the seven virtues. All the rest
Followed the griffin upward, with a song
Sweeter and deeper yet." If she addressed
Me longer, I don't know—I could be wrong,
110   Perhaps she did—but now the one was here
Before me who had turned my cares to calm,
And there on the bare ground she sat, so near,
Left there to keep the chariot from harm
Where that two-natured beast put it to stand.
The seven nymphs were strung into a ring
That formed her cloister. Each held in one hand
A candelabrum never fluttering
In north wind or in south, as in our land
It would. "Here you will be a little while
120   A forester, and citizen always
Of that high Rome in which Christ has the style
Of Roman. The world falls on evil days,
But for the good in it, look closely now,
And what you see, write down when you return
Yonder." Thus Beatrice: and I, whose bow
At her command had nothing left to learn
Of the submissive, gave my eyes and mind
As she wished. Never fire came from dense cloud
Downward so swiftly from where lie confined
130   The vapours in the high air, than the proud
Eagle of Jove tore down through the fresh leaves
And flowers, and not just them. It stripped the bark.

It struck the car which, as a ship that heaves
Before the storm, reeled to the leeward mark.
Then to the windward, cast there by the waves.
And then I saw a fox jump at the car:
A starved fox, kept alive by robbing graves.
My lady mocked its foulness, and as far
As fleshless bones allowed, it turned and ran.
140 And then the eagle, from its former place,
Dived in again and rapidly began
To feather the car's insides from the base
On upwards with its plumage, and a cry
As from a grieving heart I heard descend
From heaven: "Little boat, you're weighed down by
Such ill." And I saw something rend
The earth between the wheels. A dragon reared
Upward and drove its tail through the car's floor,
And as a wasp takes back the sting it speared
150 Into the flesh, I saw the thing withdraw
Its evil tail, and wander off, and what
Was left was decked again, as fertile soil
With dog-grass, by the plumage, which was not
Perhaps intended solely to despoil,
But offered with a pure and gracious heart:
And both wheels and the shaft were cloaked with it
In less time than a sigh keeps lips apart,
And thus transformed, the frame grew heads to fit
Its holy structure. Three grew on the shaft,
160 One at each corner, and the three were horned
Like oxen, and the two fore and two aft
Had one horn from the forehead each. Be warned,
For such a monster never has been seen.
But here it was, a mountain fort. Secure,
An ungirt harlot with brows arched to mean
Sheer boldness sat there, all set to endure
As property, it seemed, to him that loomed
Behind her: for a giant leaned to kiss

Her lips, and she reached up, and they assumed
170 Their kissing pose again, and then did this
Again and then again. But then she turned
Her wanton eyes on me, and that great beast,
That savage lover, when he looked and learned
That she had done so, switched from his love feast
To beating her from head to foot, and then,
Still occupied with his colossal rage
And deep suspicion, let her go again
Enough to drag her, in his wild rampage,
Away until the wood obscured my view
180 Of harlot and strange brute, but still I could
Tell what these symbols were referring to:
For there depicted was the foul embrace
Of France and Holy Church, the latter gone
To lewd seed in the reign of Boniface,
And then, with Clement, gone to Avignon—
The car, that Christ the Griffin had left tied
To Empire's tree, beset from every side.

CANTO 33

"The heathen come to their inheritance,
O God," the ladies sang. Now three, now four,
Wept and responded, singing, in a trance
Of bitter grief, a sweet psalm to deplore
What they had seen, and Beatrice, sighing, heard
Their melody—and Mary at the cross
Looked no more sad—but when space for a word
From her was left in that long song of loss
From the other virgins, she rose on her feet
10 Glowing like fire: "A little while you will
Not see me, sisters, and then we will meet."
Echoing Christ in sight of his last hill,
She sent those seven forward, and she sent
Me with one gesture to a rearward place
With Statius and Matilda. So she went
Onward, and had not yet reached her tenth pace
When on my eyes her striking eyes were bent,
And with a tranquil air she said "Step out
More quickly, so that if I speak with you
20 You'll sooner know what I am on about."
And when I walked, as I was bound to do,
Abreast of her, she said "If you're in doubt
Why don't you question me? For I am here."
As one who finds his voice locked in his lips

Before someone that they too much revere,
So did I speak, tongue like a foot that trips.
"My lady, you must know, you know, my need
And what, and what will meet it." And she said
"From fear and shame forthwith I'd have you freed,
30   That you no longer seem to speak in dread
Of dreams. The carriage that the serpent wrecked
Was, and is not; but let who has the blame
Know that God's vengeance with its sure effect
In time will come, and things won't be the same
Always for that lone eagle without heir
That left its feathers so the car became
First beast, then slave, the rage and the despair.
I see and say it: that the time is nigh
When constellations free from all restraint
40   And contradiction will appear on high
To give these numbers—and they are not faint,
I see them vividly in my mind's eye—
Five hundred, ten and five. These figures mean
A duke, one sent from God, to slay that thief,
That woman, and the giant whose obscene
Embrace corrupts her in their pact of grief,
And my dark tale perhaps persuades you less
Because, like that of Themis and the Sphinx,
Its cryptograms have left you powerless
50   To follow, for the fogged mind never thinks
Until the facts come in, but so they will
As they did for the Naiads, with no loss
Of flocks and corn through that wolf sent to till
The fields of Thebes with fear, and plough the dross.
Face truth, wrapped in a puzzle. Note it well,
And teach the words I say to those who live
The life which is a race to death. You'll tell
Your tale in writing? Make sure that you give
Unhidden, all the details of the tree,
60   Which here has been twice robbed. Say what you've seen,

And say whoever commits larceny
Against it, or in any way has been
Violent towards it, promotes Blasphemy
Of Act against God, who for His sole use
First made it holy; and for just one taste,
The first soul, Adam, paid for his abuse
With life—almost a thousand years—laid waste,
And then four thousand more in death, until
The crime's avenger died—to expiate
70 That mortal hunger, though it lingers still.
Truly your wits are drowsy and sleep late
If they don't realise that for some due cause
The tree is tall and at the top grows great—
Reversed, that is. And if, without a pause,
The flow through your mind of vain thought and fad
Had been less like that local source of lime,
Our little river Elsa, and you had
Not dipped your poor brains in them every time
Like Pyramus in mulberry, there'd be none
80 Of your strange blindness to the moral right
Of this tree to require submission—one
Of scripture's four main meanings—and indict
The eating of its fruit. And this is done
By God to show how gaining righteousness—
And here the principle stands in plain sight
In all its ramified expansiveness—
Begins with the forbidden. But since you
Are turned, I see, in your poor brain, to stone,
And, being petrified, are darkened too,
90 So that my speech strikes light from every tone
To dazzle you, this also you should do:
Bear what I say away within your mind,
In pictures if not words, as they that bring
The staff back as a sure proof, when they wind
The palm around it, that this is a thing
That saw the Holy Land." And I: "Just as

The seal transforms the wax, so I am struck
By you; and what you said, my brain now has
Stamped into it; but still I'm out of luck,
Because your words are far above my head,
Longed-for but out of sight. The more I strive
The more I lose them. Why is this?" She said:
"Just so you'll know, your writing friends who thrive
On worldly knowledge can't, by what they preach,
Follow my words. Your path has been as far
From God's as any mortal thought can reach—
Paths far apart as Earth and Heaven are."
To this I said "I've no remembrance
That I from you was even once estranged.
My conscience is at ease." A smiling glance
From her cloaked this rebuke: "You haven't changed.
You can't recall because you can't recall
You drank today from Lethe, and if smoke
Means fire, then this forgetfulness is all
Your fault from that day your attention broke
Away from me and found some cause to fall
Elsewhere. But I will make my words as plain
From now on as your rude wits may require
To take them in without excessive pain."
More splendid and slow-stepping, the sun's fire
Held the meridian which shifts to match
The standpoint of the viewer. It was noon.
Just like a forward scout, should something catch
His eye, and he adjudge it not too soon
To turn and warn, the seven ladies paused
At the edge of a deep shade as might be cast
By mountains on cold streams and partly caused
By green leaves and black boughs. As they held fast,
I seemed to see, before them, from one source,
The Tigris and Euphrates spring, and yet
Like friends that part, each took a separate course,
Slowly but surely. "How, when they are met

Right at the start," I asked, "are these two streams
Parted like self from self? Light of the Race
Of Humans, Glory of Us All, this seems
Too strange for thought." And Beatrice turned her face,
Saying "Matilda is the one to ask."
And that fair lady said, as if she sought
To shake off blame, "But I fulfilled this task
140 Before. Of this I gave him full report,
And other things as well, and I am sure
That Lethe's waters still left what I taught
Intact." And Beatrice said "Perhaps there's more,
A greater care, which often robs the wits
Of memory, turning recollection dim.
But see Eunoe, where it flows, with its
Capacity to bring things back. Take him
To bathe in that, and do what you do best:
Revive his weakened faculty." And then
150 Matilda, at her mistress's behest—
With no excuses, but submission when
The moment came to be obedient
In will, having received the certain sign
Of someone else's will and what it meant—
With courtesy, her hand enfolding mine,
Said "Come with him" to Statius. And no,
I lack the space to write the smallest part,
Reader, of what I ought to sing. For so
Sweet was that draught that never would my heart
160 Have drunk its fill. But all the sheets prepared
For this, my second canticle, are filled,
And from the curb of art I am not spared
To take things further. Through the waters spilled
By that spring, I was remade. Forth I fared,
A new plant with new leaves in a new time.
The stars were there, and I was set to climb.

BOOK

III

———

HEAVEN

CANTO 1

He moves all things. His glory penetrates
The universe, and here it shines the more
And there the less, and of these various states
The one where I was gets more light. I saw,
There in the Empyrean, things which he
Who comes back down from it has not the strength
Or knowledge to record, for memory
Can't follow intellect through the same length
Of journey, as it goes deep to come near
10   What it desires. But all I could retain
As treasure in my mind will now appear
In this song. What's imprinted in my brain
Of the Holy Kingdom will be written here,
Apollo, with your help. For this last burst
Of my long labour, make of me the flask
Of your power, which you always, from the first,
Required, from all who took on such a task,
Before you granted the loved laurel. One
Peak of Parnassus has sufficed thus far—
20   The Muses my sole help to get things done—
But now I need you, too, for now we are
On the threshold of the last arena. Come
Into my breast and breathe there as when you
Flayed Marsyas the fool when he was dumb

Enough to challenge you. If you could do
Enough for me so I might, Power Divine,
Show forth the shadow of the paradise
I have in mind, you'll see me walk the line
To your elected tree, take the device
30   Of leaves my theme and you have helped me earn,
And put it on. So seldom has that crown
Been made for Caesar's or a poet's turn
At triumph, that the bough with the renown
Of Daphne surely gives Apollo joy
When anybody wants it. A great flame
Follows a little spark. Prayers may employ,
After my time, great words, because that same
Peak of Apollo, Cyrrha, meets the plea
Of poets' wishes. The spring equinox
40   Is just one of the entrances we see
The sun come in at, but this one unlocks
A better course. Four circles join with three
Slant crosses, and the stars and tempers match
To stamp the world's wax in the fruitful style
Of the world's lantern. It undid the latch
And entered very near that point, so while
The morning happened there and evening here,
That hemisphere was white and this was dark,
And Beatrice turned left, and looked. For fear
50   Of blindness, never eagle risked that stark
Exposure of the eye to the full sun
As she did then; and, as the second ray,
The one reflected, leaves the primary one
At that point where they meet and climbs away
Just as a turning pilgrim might have done,
So from her action mine was made, infused
From her eyes into mine by how I thought,
And, so unlike the way our eyes are used
In mortal life, my glance, when it was caught,
60   Was held, fixed on the sun. Much is allowed

In that place, to our powers, which here is not,
By virtue of the fact that there, unbowed,
Man lived before he fell, and then forgot
What once his senses knew. I had not gazed
Long at that light, yet had gazed long enough
To see the cataract of sparks that blazed
Like iron that the fire makes boiling stuff,
When suddenly it seemed the day was joined
By day, as if He who could will it so
70   Had gestured, and a second sun was coined
To deck the sky. While upward from below
The eyes of Beatrice were fixed solely on
The eternal wheels, I had raised mine to her
Now that from my high object they were gone,
And at her aspect things weren't what they were
Within me, as when Glaucus ate the herb
That had revived the fish, and he assumed
A sea god's form. To pass beyond the curb
Of mere humanity is a step doomed
80   Not to be put in words: let it suffice
That the example should be put to him
Graced with that history. Not in a trice
Was man first formed. Dust made his every limb,
But it was breath that made the living soul.
Love, it was your breath. Were I just that part
Of me that you made last, and not the whole,
Love, heaven-ruling, you would know. Your heart
Of light raised me. Now your eternal wheel—
Constructed and set spinning by desire—
90   Held me intent by what it made me feel,
Its harmony. Your voices form a choir
In tune, and spread among the spheres. The new
Great sound and the great light soon kindled such
Keenness of longing as I never knew
Before, to seek the cause. To reach and touch
And calm the turmoil in my mind, she who

Saw me as I did, spoke before I could
Start asking. "Your false fancies make you dense.
Thus blinded, you cannot see as you would
Without them. You are not on earth. Your sense
Misleads you. Lightning, flying from its sphere
Between the earth and moon, can't run as fast
As you regain your place, for you are near
To Heaven, which is your true land at last."
With these brief words she smiled at me, my doubt
Might well have been dispelled, but soon I was
In yet another question swathed about,
And said "I was content just then, because
Freed from a wonder, but I wonder now
That I, a solid body, may ascend
Through realms of fire and thin air. Tell me how."
She sighed with pity as if moved to bend
Her eyes on me just as a mother turns,
To her delirious child, a look that rues
The fate of all mankind, which never learns,
And said "All things that are, contain and use
Order among themselves. The universe,
Therefore, in structure, is to God alike
And in this primal part it must disburse—
While higher creatures watch it sort and strike—
That stamp of excellence, which never dies:
The very end for which the system's made.
And in this order, all things exercise
Their nature, to express their place and grade
Nearer the sun or else, contrariwise,
Far off from it. They move to different ports
Across the sea of being, each with its
Own instinct. Entities of different sorts
Are all borne on, and one of them transmits
Fire to the moon—pale fire for mortal things.
And this one binds and unifies the earth.
Not just for creatures with fur, scales or wings

And no brain, the bow shoots, but those whose birth
Blessed them with force and intellect. The light
Of providence that regulates all this
Soothes with its glow the first step to the height,
Inside which the quick spinning emphasis
Of the First Impulse reaches its great speed,
And that way now, appointed to that place
140 We're sent by the bowstring, as if its need
Is to attain the mark of joy and grace.
It's true that often, as a shape does not
Accord with art's intention, for a lack
Of workability in what it's got
For substance, so sometimes the track
Of creatures fit to follow a good course
Can find their upward impulse turned aside,
As we might see a fire endowed with force
To climb, fall from the clouds, a shot gone wide,
150 And back to earth. False pleasure takes the blame.
If I am right, I vow that your ascent
Unfailingly to Heaven has the same
Reason within it for astonishment
As when the average mountain spills a stream
Falling from head to foot. You'd have more cause
For wonder if, without a mote or beam
Of hindrance, you had stayed below, all laws
Defied, as if a living flame might seem
To stay still. You could truly marvel, then."
160 She turned her face up to the sky again.

CANTO 2

You sailors in your little boats that trail
My singing ship because so keen to hear,
By now it might be time for you to sail
Back till you see your shoreline reappear,
For here the sea is deep, and if you lose
My leading light just once, then steering clear
Might bring bewilderment. So you must choose—
Be warned, this sea was never sailed before.
Minerva breathes, Apollo steers, the nine
Muses will navigate me by the store
Of stars. You few that took this course of mine
In early times, to reach for angels' bread
By which men live but can't be satisfied
Down here, you might indeed have forged ahead
In your craft as the salt depths moved aside,
Ploughing the furrow till the waves again
Healed smooth. The glory-hungry Argonauts
Who crossed to Colchis were not so stunned when
They saw their Jason yoke the bulls. Your thoughts
Will make theirs seem unruffled. The innate
And everlasting thirst bore us away,
The thirst for Heaven in God's form. In spate
We sped, almost as fast as one might say
The star-wheel turned, while Beatrice gazed on high,

And I on her, and in the time a bolt
That strikes a target takes to load and fly,
I now saw I had hurtled to a halt
When something marvellous drew my eyes from her
To it. From her, my thoughts could not be hid.
30   She turned the fairest eyes that ever were
To me, and said this, glad at what she did:
"To God, who brings us here to the first star,
The moon, direct your thanks." It seemed to me
A cloud now covered us, if clouds there are
That can be dense yet still shine, solidly
Consistent, smooth, like star-struck diamonds.
And this eternal pearl now took us in,
As water will retain its seamless bonds
Pierced by a ray of light. How to begin?
40   If I were body (and down here we can't
Believe a body might be drawn into
A body, or we would be what we aren't)
This should accentuate our wish anew
Of climbing up to see that essence where
Our nature joins to God. There will be seen
All that we hold by faith. It will be there,
Not demonstrated, but, for what we mean
By knowing, known: known in itself. Which is
The primal truth that men believe. And I:
50   "My lady, how the credit is all His
That from the mortal world I reach the sky,
I say from my devoted, thankful heart.
But tell me why this body should be scarred
By dark marks, which from Earth are seen as part
Of Cain's crown, made from thorns long, sharp and hard?"
She smiled awhile, then said "If judgement errs
In mortals, when the key of sense won't fit
The lock, be not amazed if it occurs,
From now on, that your reason's winged remit
60   Falls short of what the senses apprehend.

Just keep the shafts of wonder out of it.
Let them fly past, there's nothing to defend.
All you need do is tell me what you think."
And I: "Presumably that which might seem
Up here to be divine means sunrays sink
Into the rare. But from the dense they gleam
Reflected." She: "Assuredly you'll find
That your belief is deep in error drowned.
If only you admit into your mind
70 The following objections, which are sound.
The eighth sphere shows us many different lights:
The fixed stars, which, if they are judged by size,
Or quality, appear as different sights.
If all those, like the moon, should harmonise
Their luminosity from dense or sparse
Collections of material, then each
Would have one virtue, in a single class
Distributed, as qualities might reach
From more to less through equal on the scale.
80 But that's absurd, for different virtues form
From principles, and your thought would entail
That only one of them provides the norm.
Again, if rarity should be the source
Of that obscurity you ask about,
The moon would either have, in parts, a course
Of emptiness right through it, or, without
Much difference from the way that lean and fat
Are portioned in a body, it would stack
The pages, in its volume, lying flat
90 One on the other: thin white and thick black.
But in the first case, at the sun's eclipse
We'd see the light shine through the moon, as through
Rare stuff. The second case lives on the lips
For little longer, since in this way, too,
Your view is false. If rarity falls short
Of going right through, there must be a mark
Where density ensures the ray is caught

And thrown back, giving light instead of dark,
Just as a colour is sent back through glass
With hidden lead behind. You might contend
Those rays show dimmer when they have to pass
Up from the depths than those which must descend
Less deeply to encounter a hard place—
Experiment, however, will remove
Such an objection, and from your false case
Release you: for experiment must prove
Always to be the spring that feeds the streams
Of your art. Take three mirrors. First you set
Two the same distance from you, so it seems
A window lies between them where is met
The third one by your eyes from where it stands
Yet further off. Then have, behind your back,
A lamp set up by which those two demands
For light are satisfied. See how the track
Rebounds of each beam. Though the one that comes
The furthest may look smaller, you will see
It shines with equal brightness. What benumbs
Your mind, now finally of error free,
Is that the truth has not yet taken hold.
Think of the snow when smitten with warm rays,
Bare of its former colour and its cold:
I want to fill your bare mind with a blaze
Of living light that sparkles in your eyes.
Within the heaven of divine peace spins
The Primum Mobile, whose virtue ties
Together all the being that begins
And ends within it. The next heaven, hung
With many lights, and called the Starry Sphere,
Assigns that being severally among
Different existences, so they appear
Many and various but are contained
Within its single virtue. Seven more
Heavens exist, and all of them ordained
To deal out separate qualities they share

Within, to suit their ends and good effect.
These organs and the universe proceed,
As you see, grade by grade, in due respect
Receiving from above all that they need
To operate below. Observe well how
I pass thus to the truth you seek, just so
You may know how to ford the river now
Alone. I give you grounds for where to go.
Now, then, your final step: the Holy Wheels.
Their motion, and their virtues, must derive—
As from the leaping sparks and ringing peals
Of constant hammering the smiths contrive
Their iron work—from Blessed Movers. These
Are the angelic orders, and the realm
Made fair by all those flaring entities
Is shaped by the profound mind at the helm,
And of that stamp becomes itself the seal:
And as the soul in your dust is diffused
Through different body parts each built to deal
With different faculties diversely used,
So the intelligence unfolds its hoard,
Throughout the star-field to be multiplied,
Which, wheeling always in its one accord,
From different virtues forms divine alloy
With any precious body it makes quick,
And with which, as in you, it will enjoy
Deep bonds, designed to strengthen as they stick.
So, by the joyous nature when it springs,
The mingled virtue shines through like the flash
In our eyes when we think of joyful things.
And therefore the whole range of flame to ash
Dividing light from light, comes otherwise
From how you thought. Not how dense or how rare,
But how glad are the angels, gives our eyes
Our vision of the dark and bright up there—
Proof that such excellence rules everywhere."

CANTO 3

The sun which first had warmed my breast with love,
By proof and refutation had shown me
The truth's fair face, and I raised—not above
The level needed if I wished to free
My mouth for speech—my head, just to confess
Myself corrected and assured. But then
A sight appeared that left me powerless,
Glued to it, so I couldn't think again
Of what I had confessed: the words had fled.
10   It was as if through smooth, transparent glass,
Or else through clear, still water whose creek-bed
Is not so deep our faces fail to pass
Back up to us so faintly that a pearl
Set on a pallid brow is not more slow
To reach us from the image of a girl,
That I saw many faces, poised as though
Eager to speak. I then made a mistake
Like that which joined the man and spring, and lit
Tinder between them that brought love awake,
20   Except my error was the opposite:
Narcissus was more credulous than me.
I saw these faces and I took them for
Reflections, so I turned my eyes to see
Where they might really stand, and what I saw

Was nothing, so once more it came to be
That I looked straight into the brilliant light
Of my sweet guide, her holy eyes aglow
With her smile. She said "Do not doubt it right
That I smile at your childishness, for so
30 Reluctant is it still to set its foot
On truth, that it feels bound to turn you back
To emptiness. But these are real, all put
In this place for a failure, for their lack
Of loyalty to vows. So speak with them,
Hear and believe. A true light gives them peace,
But, simply by that function, must condemn
The peaceful ones to keep turned without cease
Their steps towards it." I approached the shade
That most seemed keen to talk, and I said this,
40 Almost consumed by my will: "Spirit made
To know, in this eternal life of bliss,
The sweetness of its beams—a taste which must
Be tasted first before it is conceived—
It would be kind of you if you could just
Render my curiosity relieved
By telling me your name and of your fate."
And she, with smiling eyes of eagerness:
"Our charity shuts no doors, bars no gate,
Against right Will, for our will can't be less
50 Than His, who wills His whole court to be as
Himself. A virgin sister when I breathed,
I was—and you will find your memory has
A picture which, although now I am wreathed
With greater fairness, you will see is mine—
Piccarda Donati. I am put here
With all these other blessed ones, and in line
With their lot I, too, tarry in the sphere
Of smallest orbit and therefore least fast,
The slow sky of the moon. Our sentiments,
60 Which nothing sets ablaze save, first and last,

To please the Holy Ghost, find joy intense
In our conformity to His regime,
And this position which I occupy,
As low down on the scale as it might seem,
Is given us for failing to comply
Sufficiently in duty to our vows."
And then I said to her: "Your wondrous face
That I see now, diversity endows
With inner light of an amazing grace
70 Divine beyond my knowledge, changing you
From what you were, but now there's what you say
To help me recollect what I once knew.
Yet tell me: happy as you are to stay
In this sphere, do you not desire a post
Up higher, where you can see more, and feel
More loved yet?" With the others in that host
She smiled at this, and answered with such real
Gladness she seemed to burn in love's first fire.
"Brother, our charity is calmed by will,
80 Willing just what we have, with no desire
For more. If we wished to be higher still,
Then our desire would fail to jibe with His
Will that appoints us here. Such, you will find,
Cannot hold in these circles, if it is
Necessity, clear to the thinking mind,
To be in charity, and if you well
Study its nature. No indeed, the gist
Itself of this blessed state is: we compel
Ourselves at all times wholly to exist
90 Within the will divine, so that our wills
Are thus themselves made one. Therefore our rank
From height to height throughout the realm instils
Pleasure in all of it, and so we thank
The King who wills us to His will. For in
His will is our peace. His will is the sea
Towards which all things move just to begin—

The souls it makes and all the progeny
Of Nature. For it is creative twice,
In both these ways." She made it clear to me
That Heaven everywhere is paradise,
Although the Great Good's favour does not rain
In one mode. As, when one food might suffice
Yet craving for another may remain,
We thank our stars and yet we are bereft—
As when that happens, so did I, with speech
And gesture, strive to hear the weft
And warp—the shuttle driven through to reach
Its goal—of what the vow was she had left
Neglected. "Perfect life and its reward,"
She said, "place in high Heaven great St. Clare,
Whose rule in your world binds with one accord
Those novices in robe and veil who swear
That until death they'll always wake and sleep
With that Bridegroom who sanctions any vow
Made out of charity and aimed to keep
Him pleased. To follow her was why and how
I fled, a young girl, from the world, and wrapped
Her habit round me, dedicating all
My life to her chaste way. But I was trapped:
Men used to evil got in through the wall
Of good, and from the cloister I was torn—
And what my life was afterwards, God knows.
But see this other splendour here like dawn
Appearing to you on my right, who glows
With all the light of our sphere. She, too, was
A sister, and the same way lost her veil
And safety, but she never, just because
She'd seen the world triumph and custom fail,
Abjured the inward veil that soothed her heart.
This is the light of that great Constance, she
Who bore, when brought back from her life apart,
The third and last child with the pedigree

100

110

120

130

Of emperor, and the sire was that false start,
The second Swabian quick breeze to blow."
She spoke thus, then began to sing the hymn
Ave Maria, and, still singing so,
Went down like something heavy growing dim
Into the depths. My sight went after her,
As far as it could plunge. Then it returned,
140 When it had lost her, back where my eyes were
Faced with the greater mark. And there she burned:
All I could see was Beatrice, nor could move
My gaze away, although it hurt my eyes
So much at first I feared that it might prove
Too hard to go on looking, or devise
Questions whose shyness she would not despise.

CANTO 4

Between two tempting dishes each way set
Apart, and parallel in their appeal,
A man could, before either of them met
His lips, perish from hunger, his next meal
Untouched. A lamb between two wolves might stand
In equal fear of both and what they crave.
A hound between doves, on the other hand,
More like the man, could die, however brave,
Torn by irresolution. Thus if I
Kept silent, by two equal doubts compelled,
I neither blame nor praise myself thereby.
It was necessity. My tongue was held,
But my desire was painted on my face:
My question, too, and far more warmly than
In plain words. Beatrice took Daniel's place
When he guessed the bad dream and shrunk the span
Of Nebuchadnezzar's wrath, which made that king
Cruelly unjust, and she said "I see well
How one desire leads to another thing,
Drawing you on, so that, without a spell
For breath, your keenness binds itself and you.
You reason thus: 'If my right will prevails,
How is it something someone else might do
By violence can impede it so it fails

Even a little, the preferment due
To me by merit?' And you are perplexed
That souls seem to return, as Plato taught,
Into the stars. These questions, mixed and vexed,
Press on your will. First, I shall treat the thought
30 Containing the most poison, which is that
Stemming from Plato, who wants different skies
For each grade of beatitude, and at
The threshold must be those who might not rise
To be exalted. Let that thought be gone.
Not even the first Seraph at God's side,
Not Moses, Samuel, or whichever John
You choose, and no, not even heaven's pride,
Mary herself, are in a different seat
Than this First Circle where these souls appear.
40 All heaven is this place. For all you'll meet,
Eternity's the same length, to the year.
They all make heaven fair, and life is sweet
For each, but since the far is always near,
The difference of their bliss is measured by
Only their distance from the breath divine
And everlasting, in a single sky.
These ones have shown themselves, not by design
Of sphere allotted to them, but to prove
That they are least exalted, last in line
50 To go up nearer. Seeming still, they move.
Here I must speak directly to your sense,
For only how you see and feel can seize
That which your intellect finds too immense
At first encounter. It's by such degrees
Of teaching, that the Scriptures condescend
To your capacity. Thus the Supreme
Being is given hands and feet. The end
Is allegory, and a hidden theme
Is also served when Holy Church brings news
60 Of Michael decked out with a human face,

And Gabriel, and Raphael. The views
Put by Timaeus, pinning down the place
Of souls, are not reflected here, for what
He says he seems to think true: that the soul
Returns to its own star, from which it got—
When nature formed it as a separate whole—
Released. Perhaps, however, that was not
The true import of what his words express,
And there's a meaning we might not despise.
His arrow flies with some truth, more or less,
If he means that their influence, in guise
Of honour or of blame, rejoins these wheels.
This principle, ill understood, misled
Almost the whole world, which in part still feels,
Falsely, the names of stars meant what they said
In the first instance: Mars and Mercury
And Jupiter as gods to be revered.
The other doubt that shakes your reverie
Is not so poisonous. You won't be steered
Away from me and into heresy
By mischief of that kind. Our justice may
Appear unjust to mortals. That just proves
How faith, not wicked doubt, has final say
In the more mystifying ways God moves.
But since your understanding is well fit
To penetrate that truth, I shall content
Your need to know about the violence. It
May well be that there's no thought of consent
By the victim to the violator, yet
These souls were not excused on that account:
For will, if it wills not, is still not set
Aside completely, but like fire will mount
Straight up again although a thousand times
Blown reeling sideways, and it therefore bends
As much or little, in the face of crimes,
As it condones them. So it all depends
On what these did next. And they might have fled

Back to the holy places, if their will
Had been unbroken. Stretched on his hot bed,
100 Lawrence remained determined to fulfil
His destiny; and, unmoved, the right hand
Of Mucius stayed in the fire. The same
Determination, you must understand,
Would surely have brought these back whence they came,
As soon as they were free. The path they'd been
Abducted from was there still. Still, such force
Of will is rare. But if the things I mean
Form part, from now on, of your mind's resource,
Then your false reasoning is cancelled out
110 To trouble you no more, as it well might
Have done. But now, to turn your course about
If you were by yourself, another tight
And hard, exhausting place lies close ahead.
It's near enough to be plain to your sight.
It's set now in your mind, what I have said:
There can be no lies from a soul in bliss,
For it is near to primal truth always.
Piccarda might have seemed to counter this
When she said Constance, with her constant gaze
120 Forever on the veil, did not return
To where she might have worn it once again.
But, brother, many times, as you should learn,
It happens that, against the will of men,
Escape from danger means that something's done
Which shouldn't be. So Alcmaeon achieved
Revenge on her—although he was her son—
Who killed his father. He was twice bereaved,
But pitiless in piety at last.
Learn this, then, at this point. There is a blend
130 Of force and will where no offence is passed
Beyond excuse, though means lead to good end.
The absolute will knows no yielding law:
But, when conditional, will may give ground
Because it fears, if it resists, that more

Trouble will come. Piccarda, then, was sound:
She meant strict will by what she said before,
And I the other kind. Thus you have found
The truth two ways." Such was the rippling flow,
Setting one wish and then the next at rest,
140 Of the holy stream that holds all we can know
Of truth, and from the fountain forth is blessed.
"Beloved of the First Love, you that so
Divinely speak," I said, "you flood my soul
To make it always warm and more alive,
Not all of my affection, not the whole
Of what I say, no matter how I strive,
Will serve to match your grace to me with mine.
May He do that who sees, and can do, all.
I see well how, unless the truth divine
150 Enlightens it, our intellect must fall
Short of the truth, unsatisfied. That line
Once crossed beyond which human truth can range
To holy truth, the beast is in its lair.
Home gained, it rests, impervious to change:
And all of our desires were empty air
Without this. It means doubt is like a shoot
Springing from truth. It is a natural urge.
The questioning has nature at the root.
We're pushed from height to height till we emerge
160 Up at the summit. It's all nature's plan,
And so I am invited and made bold
To ask you of another truth less than
Clear to me, lady. Let me now be told
If ever it can happen that a man
May make it up to you by doing good
For vows he has not kept." She looked at me
With eyes so full of love my powers could
Do nothing to withstand the clarity
That sparkled there within. My vision shook.
170 I almost fainted, stunned by that one look.

CANTO 5

"If, in a flame of love beyond all seen
On Earth, I glow to you so that your eyes
Are conquered in their power, let that not mean
You marvel, for you have to realize
This comes when perfect vision apprehends
The good, and, knowing what it is, moves near.
I see now how the light that never ends
Shines in your mind: light which, seen to appear,
Alone and always kindles love. From this,
Come all things that beguile you: even though
From just a trace of it, and hit and miss
Your understanding of it, yet the glow
Shines through." So saying, Beatrice began
The canto, and, like one who would not break
Her speech, she said "God's greatest gift to man
In all the bounty He was moved to make
Throughout creation—the one gift the most
Close to his goodness and the one He calls
Most precious—is free will. Creatures that boast
Intelligence have this, but none that falls
Outside that category is endowed
With any. Now it will be clear to you,
In view of this, the worth of what is vowed,
If it be such that God does as you do:

That is, consent. For it is in the pact
Of God and man that the great treasure chest—
Free will, as I have said—by its own act
Becomes the sacrifice. What would be best
To offer for a vow that's unfulfilled?
30   Nothing. Nothing you give in recompense
Will serve, for what you will is now ill-willed:
Good works with stolen gains would make more sense.
By now you are assured on the chief point,
But Holy Church can sometimes waive its laws
In this regard: which might seem out of joint
With what I've said is true. So you must pause
For thought, sit at the table for a while.
The tough food you have swallowed won't stay down
Without help. Let your mind, in its best style,
40   Be open to my words and win renown
For holding on to them, since to have heard
Without retention can't deserve the name
Of knowledge: the mere thought would be absurd.
Two things in close accord but not the same
Supply the essence of that sacrifice.
One is material, the thing you give
Or else give up. That's the substantial price.
The other's formal. How you vow to live,
The pact itself. This last can't be annulled
50   Save by observing it. Regarding which
I spoke just now, with never a point dulled.
Just as the Hebrews had, without a hitch,
To make their offerings, though what those were
Could change, as you are no doubt well aware,
The formal part, to which I now refer,
I made clear when I told the tale back there
About the vow. That part indeed may be
Such that no fault, if matter is exchanged,
Need be incurred. But still, let no one free
60   His shoulders from a burden once arranged,

Unless, to back his choice, the silver key
Of priestly wisdom, and the golden one
That signifies priestly authority,
Have both been turned, to prove it may be done.
And every such exchange is reckoned vain
Unless the new load outweighs the one shed
By six to four at least, so that a gain
Of burden, not a loss, is there instead.
A vow, which tips all balances on Earth,
70 For value, can't be matched by anything
At all, no matter what that thing is worth.
Therefore let humans take great care to bring
Their full attention to a vow, and not
Be frivolous. Nor should they be perverse
Like Jephthah, who pledged wildly, and forgot
That keeping faith might make a bad thing worse.
He said that he would offer, to be burned,
The first thing that emerged from his front door.
It was his daughter, and too late he learned
80 That saying 'I did ill' would have earned more
Credit with God. And Agamemnon, too,
Showed the same folly when, to sail for Troy
On a fair wind, he offered payment down:
His daughter Iphigenia. The joy
Went out of her fair face. To grieve for her
Is wise for all who've heard about that rite,
And simple. How could such a thing occur?
Christians, let not your attitude be light
To undertakings. Feathers in every wind
90 Ought not to be your model, nor will all
Waters restore clean skin when you have sinned.
Remember how, to save you from a fall,
You have the Testaments, both New and Old,
To guide you, and the Pastor of the Church.
Give not the Jew that's with you in the fold
His opportunity. If you besmirch

Yourself with wicked greed at his cheap rates,
The pardoner is glad. You must be men,
Not stupid sheep. For ridicule awaits
100 The lamb that leaves its mother's milk, and then,
Foolish and wanton, fights itself to suit
Its brainless pleasure." Just so, Beatrice spoke
In these words that I write, and then turned, mute,
Yet more with longing than I can evoke,
To where the universe is brightest. Such
A falling wordless and a change of look
Silenced my eager mind, already much
Preoccupied with pages—a whole book—
Of extra questions. We sped like a shaft
110 That strikes the mark before the cord is still,
Into the second realm. As if she laughed
Aloud, I saw my lady's fair face fill
With joy when entering the radiance
Of that next heaven, and the planet turn
The brighter for it, and the star enhance
Its aspect with a smile, though it could burn
More brightly only in this circumstance.
Imagine, then, what I became, when by
My nature I am so transmutable!
120 As in a fish pool that's a calm, clear sky
To all those fish beneath, they form a school
Around what comes from outside, which they guess
To be new food, so now I saw at least
A thousand splendours make the distance less
Towards us, gathering around the feast.
From them I heard "How this one will augment
Our lives!" and as each eager soul came near
It seemed so full of happiness it sent
Bright flames out all around. If I stopped here,
130 Think, reader, how you'd crave a testament
More full. Then you will know how much desire
I had to hear from them about their state,

As soon as I could see them in their fire.
"You, born for good, for whom it is the fate,
Given by grace, to gaze on the great chairs
Of triumph in eternity although
Your war continues, each one of us bears
The light of charity that spreads its glow
Through all of Heaven. Thus, if you're inclined
140 To be enlightened about us, then at
Your pleasure ask away. Just speak your mind."
One of those pious spirits said all that,
Then Beatrice said this: "Speak, speak, you'll find
Them trustworthy as gods." I: "I see well
How you nest in your own light, which is drawn
From your eyes: for when you speak, I can tell
It must spring from your smile, an extra dawn
Adorning daylight. As for what you are,
However, I don't know, nor why you rank
150 In this sphere, that another's beams debar
From mortal sight, for Mercury is blank
Beside the blazing sun." Thus I enquired
Of that effulgence which addressed me first:
A light that then became, as if inspired,
Far brighter than before. Like the sunburst
That comes when, all dense vapours burned away,
The sun conceals itself with excess light,
Just so the holy form put on more day
As if the day it had was merely night,
160 And hid in its own joy. What can I say?
Such eloquence can spring from hidden things.
But what it said next, my next canto sings.

CANTO 6

"When Constantine, two centuries before
My time, removed the eagle from the west
And sent it east, then never anymore,
For all those years, did its first place of rest
Rule all the world. The bird of God defied
The wind that brought Aeneas first to Rome
Through marriage with Lavinia. Flung wide
To Europe's edge, it reigned in its new home,
Byzantium, two hundred years at least—
10 Close to the mountains where it first took flight
To travel with Aeneas from the east
Into the west. And there, in all its might,
Under the shadow of its sacred wings,
It held the world, and passed from hand to hand
That held it, till the one in charge of things
Was I, Justinian. In that far land
I reigned as Caesar. By the First Love's will—
Which I could feel within—I trimmed the laws
Of all their folderol and overkill.
20 Before I set my effort to that cause,
I still believed the heresy that Christ
Had just one nature, which was all divine
And never human. That idea of Christ
I was content with, and I called it mine

Until Pope Agapetus spoke to me
Describing the true faith, which I believed,
As you yourself can see transparently
That any contradiction is achieved
Only between the true and the untrue.
As soon as I walked with the Church, it pleased
God in his grace to spur me to the new
High task, and by it I was wholly seized,
And my dear Belisarius obeyed
My orders to take arms, and he was blessed
By God's right hand, and so much ground was made
In our name, that I took the sign to rest
From battle, and devote myself to peace.
Here ends, then, the brief answer to your first
Question, and yet its tenor begs increase
To my response, so you, so long immersed
In faction fights to counter or to claim
The holy standard, may see why they act
That way: how courage brought the banner fame
And reverence, all of which began, in fact,
When Pallas, fighting for Aeneas, gave
His life to found the city where it flew
And flies again, designed by God to wave
Above the Church if not the Empire. You
Well know the eagle stayed three hundred years
In Alba, till at last a fight took place
For its sole sake, when three from there crossed spears
With three from Rome. Both teams, matched face to face,
Had Trojan blood, but only one could win:
The one from Rome. Then, under seven kings,
The city saw its outward reach begin.
You know that too, and know of all the things
The eagle did. The rape of the Sabines,
Lucretia's suicide, the neighbours cowed
In all the realms. Oneness, it meant and means:
The banner borne against the Gauls (allowed

By Brennus to get close) and borne against
Pyrrhus and other princes and communes—
A list that lasts forever once commenced.
All those proud Arabs brought from the sand dunes
Of Africa to cross the Alpine peaks
By Hannibal—the crags you fall from, Po—
The eagle brought them down, as history speaks.
Under that flag, such youths as Scipio
And Pompey had their triumphs. To that hill
70   Fiesole, where you were born, it proved
Bitter. Then, near the time when Heaven's will
Decreed that all the world at once be moved
To match its state of peace, the holy sign
Was grasped by Caesar, at behest of Rome,
And so the earthly realms were brought in line
With Heaven. Where the wild Gauls had their home
Across the mountains, where the rivers run
In all the valleys of the Rhone from Var
To Rhine, the fighting tribes bowed, every one,
80   And then the banner, having come so far,
Turned back with him across the Rubicon—
A flight beyond what tongue or pen can tell—
And then it went where Pompey had moved on.
To Spain it wheeled the host, and then, as well,
Durazzo, and Pharsalia. Pompey gone
To Egypt, his last grief came to a head.
The head was his. Caesar, not knowing this,
Continued his pursuit, and so was led
To where Troy once had been. Nor did he miss
90   The sight of Hector's tomb. And then he came
To Egypt, whereupon the banner shook
With rage at Ptolemy, then fell in flame
On Mauretania, where Caesar took
The throne of Juba. Once more westward then
The banner flew, to Spain, where Caesar stilled
The trumpets of the last of Pompey's men.

It dipped in Rome when Caesar's blood was spilled.
With his successor the flag flew again,
And that inheritor ensured by deed
Brutus and Cassius would howl in hell,
And Cleopatra, too, that broken reed,
Still weeps. She fled before the flag as well,
And from the viper took, with dreadful speed,
Her death. On with Augustus, the flag's flight
Reached the Red Sea. With him it gave the world
Such peace the shrine of Janus was locked tight
While that great hand held high the cloth unfurled.
But everything the flag that moves my speech
Had done till that time and had yet to do—
Though all the mortal world its rule could reach—
Seems small and dim and its achievements few
Compared with what it did when held on high
By the third Caesar. To Tiberius
The glory went—when seen with a clear eye
And right mind, this truth is revealed to us—
Of bringing fit revenge on Adam's sin
By crucifying Christ. Pilate's assent
To that death proved divinity was in
The emperor's hand, and Living Justice meant
The eagle. (By this justice I, too, am
Inspired.) Now be amazed at what I say:
For, next, with Titus, it ran on to damn
And blast Jerusalem, all in the way
Of proper punishment for that first act
Of vengeance. After that, the Lombard tooth
Bit Holy Church. Charlemagne counter-attacked
Under the eagle's wings, and fought for truth
And saved her life. Now you can judge, in fact,
Those faction-men that I before accused
Of their offences, cause of all your ills:
For by the Guelphs, the fleur-de-lis is used
Against the eagle flag, which yet fulfils

The role of banner for the Ghibellines—
By which group is the banner more abused?
So let the latter faction, by all means,
But with another flag, keep up their arts,
For he who splits the banner so it leans
Two ways, splays its intentions in two parts:
Eternal justice, and the shifting aims
140 Of politics. This new Charles of Anjou,
The weak one, ought to moderate his claims,
And not imagine he can really do
Much to the talons that have dragged the skins
Off many bigger lions than him. The sons
Weep often for the way a fault begins
With their own fathers, and so folly runs
In families. Let young Charles not think the Lord
Will change his eagle-bearing coat of arms
For sprays of lilies, nor that a toy sword
150 And putty shield will work like lucky charms.
Now to your second question I afford
An answer. They adorn this little star,
Good spirits who did what they did to earn
An honoured form. And when it goes so far,
The will for fame, that it can even turn
Honour to glory's ends, then it must mount
More than the rays of true love, which lose force
Accordingly. But when we make the count
Of our reward and our desert, of course,
160 Part of our joy is in the way we find
It neither less nor more. With even hand
The Living Justice sweetens to the mind
His judgement just because we understand
That justice has been done, and true desire
Can never be warped to evil. Thus we see,
As different voices join in the sweet choir,
So different rankings make sweet harmony
Among these starry wheels. Within this pearl

There also shines the light of Romeo,
170 Who came to Provence as the merest churl
To serve Count Raymond Berenger, and so
Successful was his management, his liege
Tripled in wealth and saw four daughters wed,
Each as a queen. But envy soon laid siege
To Romeo's position. Things were said
By crafty tongues that flattered the Count's ear,
And foolishly he listened to their lies.
He asked his faithful servant to appear
With all the bills, to judge, with clouded eyes,
180 How every penny had been spent. The end
Had come for one who could have done no more
To make his lord rich, and thought him a friend.
Thus from the court he came to, young and poor,
The faithful Romeo left poor and old,
And if you knew the mighty heart he had,
Begging his bread by scraps, out in the cold,
You'd think him something more than merely sad—
And call his smug foes stupid to be glad."

CANTO 7

"Hosanna, holy God of hosts, who makes
Yet more resplendent with his brightness all
The happy fires that burn here for our sakes,
Lighting this realm in every hallowed hall!"
Singing these Latin-Hebrew notes, he spun,
That spirit upon whom a double light
Of earth and heaven joined to flame as one,
And I could see him sing, and heard the sight,
As he and all the rest moved in the dance,
And like the flight of quickest sparks were veiled
By sudden distance. I could not advance
Without doubt, for inside myself I quailed,
And told myself "Tell her, for she knows how
To slake my thirst with sweet drops." But that awe
Which at her name unmans me even now
So that mere fragments of it start a war
In my soul (be, eat, at, ice) made me bow
Like one who falls asleep. She didn't leave
Me long like that, but shone a smile on me
To make a man rejoice, instead of grieve,
If he were in the fire. "You doubt, I see,"
She said. "Your show of silence can't deceive
My judgement, which is not subject to fault.
The question of Jerusalem has set

You thinking how a vengeful armed assault
Upon just vengeance can itself have met
Standards of justice. Let me free your mind
Right now. And listen, for my words contain
Great doctrine. Adam never sought to find
30   The limit to his will. It knew no rein,
Not even for his good. So, never born,
He cursed himself, and all his heritage.
Always conceived in sin, mankind lay torn
With sickness and in error from one age
Into the next, until God's Word was pleased
To come down and unite what had been split:
Man's nature, that He'd made, and Him. He seized
The first, and, to the second, added it
By one sole act of his eternal Love,
40   And all within Himself. Now turn your sight
On what must follow. Rescued from above,
Man's nature, thus restored to share the light
With what had made it, once more good and pure,
By its own act was banned from Paradise
For having turned aside from the one sure
Way of the truth and its own life. The price
Was high. Compare the anguish of the cross
With what the human-natured Holy Word
Betrayed, and it was just, that painful loss.
50   But neither was there ever wrong incurred
To match the agony unleashed against
The human that the nature rested in.
From one act, diverse outcomes were dispensed:
The same death worked two different ways to win
Pleasure for God, and also for the Jews.
The earth quaked and the sky gaped. No more, then,
Should it seem harsh to you to hear the views
Of those who think just vengeance was done when
Just vengeance was avenged in a high court.
60   But now I see your mind is in a knot

Of tangled thought pulled tight through tangled thought
It longs to be released from. You say 'What
I hear I follow: why God willed this way
To our redemption leaves me in the dark.'
Though this rule never sees the light of day
In anyone whose mind has missed the mark
Of growing as a flame to adulthood,
Yet since so many take aim with such zeal
And with so little sense, perhaps I should
70   Inform you why that way seemed the most real
Of all the ways that might lead men to good.
Goodness divine, which spurns all envy hence,
Burning within, so sparkles, it displays
All the eternal beauties. That intense
Ignition point sends out a further blaze
Without end, since its imprint, once embossed,
Does not grow pale. That which comes down like rain,
Free straight away, with not a droplet lost—
Nothing expended that it can't regain—
80   Pays no heed to the power of changing things.
Conforming to that Goodness, it is more
Delightful to it, since the light that rings
The Holy Ardour puts its greatest store
Of brightness in what most resembles it.
Of all these gifts to man, if even one
Is lacking in full force, then it is fit
That he should fall from his place in the sun.
Nothing but sin can disenfranchise him,
And make him so unlike the Good Supreme
90   That, even lit by that light, he stays dim
And can't regain his place and thus redeem
His Dignity, unless he fills the void
Made by his fault, and pays the penalties
Fit for a pleasure sinfully enjoyed.
Your nature forfeited these dignities
When first it sinned, back there in the first man,

Who bore the seed of sin, and you were torn
From Paradise, and not since time began
Could what you lost within you be reborn
Except by crossing one of these two fords:
God in his clemency is moved to spare
The sinner, or the sinner's just rewards
For folly are offset through what he gives
By way of satisfaction. Fix your eyes
Within the unplumbed well where it most lives,
The Eternal Counsel. Closely scrutinise
My words. Within his limits, man could not
Ever give satisfaction, for so low
He could not humbly stoop—no matter what
Obedience he found it fit to show—
As he had thought, by disobedience,
To rise up, and this is the reason why
Man was debarred from any competence
To render satisfaction and go high
All by himself. And thus God was compelled,
By his own ways, to give full life again
To man through truth, or mercy, or the meld
Of both. But since to do good feels best when
The doer does it most from his good heart,
Goodness Divine, which shapes the world alone,
Was glad, in raising you for a new start,
To use both ways. Nor was there ever known—
Nor will be, in between the first of days
And last of nights—a process so sublime
And glorious in either of those ways,
Justice and mercy: not in all of time.
Giving Himself so man, if he would rise
Again, could do so, God was bounteous
Beyond what He would now seem in our eyes
If He had simply, and for His own use,
Granted a pardon. Other means fell short
Of justice. So the Son of God took on,

In all humility, a form of flesh.
But seeing all your doubts are not yet gone,
One point I'll touch again and treat afresh,
So you may see it clearly. You say: 'I
See water, I see fire, and air, and earth,
And all their blends, grow old and putrefy,
Not lasting long. Yet these things had their birth:
Creation, unless you told me a lie,
Should have preserved them.' Brother, here's what's true:
The angels, and this spotless country here
Where you are now, you might say came into
Existence wholly as they now appear—
Immediately entire. But those things you
Have named (the elements, and mixtures made
From them), all these receive their being from
Those powers which themselves are second grade,
Virtues created here, in this kingdom.
Their matter was created, and the power
Of all the stars that wheel around them. Each
And every soul of animal and flower
Starts as a set of elements that reach
A complex balance fit to be inspired
By shining movement from the holy lights.
But your soul's life is on the instant fired
By one abrupt breath from the height of heights:
The benefaction flows straight from its source
In Him, and so imbues the soul with love
Of Him: it wants to join Him with full force
For ever after, where He reigns above.
And from all this, it follows that you can
Argue your case for resurrection. Just
Recall how flesh was first formed into man.
For your first parents, too, rose from the dust
At one breath. Bodily decay began
Only with sin. Immortal life you lost,
But now you are redeemed. At what a cost!"

CANTO 8

Venus of Cyprus—the world once believed,
To its great peril—radiated love,
Mad love, in her third circle as she weaved
Her wiles around this star, the centre of
Her crazed affections. Ancient people thought
(An ancient error) that not only she
Should have the honour of their full support
Through sacrifice and song, but Dione
Her mother, and her little son, Cupid,
Who lay, they said, in Dido's bosom, where
He lit the fire for what that lady did
To lure Aeneas and to keep him there.
And from the goddess, with whom here I take
My start, the star-map makers took the name
Of Venus, she that finds two ways to make
Love to the sun, first with her morning flame
And then again at evening. I was not
Conscious of rising into it, but more
That I was simply there, a sense I got
Further assurance of, now that I saw
My lady grown more fair. And as within
A flame we see sparks, and within a voice
We hear another voice as both begin
To interweave, each making its own choice,

One holding close to the melodic line,
While the other comes and goes to harmonise,
So I saw lights within that light define
Their separate circles each in separate guise
Of speed, some swift, some slow, thus to accord
30 With their eternal vision, so I think—
And never, down from cold cloud, winds have poured,
Seen or unseen, quicker than eyes can blink,
As not to seem hamstrung to anyone
Who saw those lovely lights fly to our side,
Leaving the dance that they had first begun
Up there where the most powerful abide,
The Seraphim. And from those ranged in view
Before us, came "Hosanna," with a sound
That ever since I've longed to hear anew.
40 Then one drew near and said this: "You have found
All of us ready at your pleasure. You
May have your joy of us. We circle round
In one orbit, with one thirst, at one pace
Along with those high princes you addressed
As 'You that move the third exalted place
By understanding,' and at your behest,
And just to do you pleasure for your grace,
A little quiet may be no less sweet—
Since we are all so very full of love."
50 After my reverent eyes were raised to meet
My lady's, and returned from there above
With notice of approval, they again
Turned to that light which had pledged me so much,
And I said "Tell me who you are." And when
I spoke, I showed how deep had been the touch
Of that sweet vow to answer me. And then
I saw its size and incandescence grow,
Fuelled by the new joy added to its joys.
Thus changed, it said: "Not long the world below
60 Held me. For not a man's life, but a boy's,

I led. Had I lived longer, much that now
We know as evil never would have been.
My joy hides me from you, and this is how:
Its rays, cocooning me, keep me unseen,
A worm in its own silk. How you loved me
Had cause, for if I'd had more time to dwell
Down there, you would have had much more to see
Of my love than the leaves. I, Charles Martel,
Would have been there to offer you the fruits.
70 All of Provence I would have held as lord,
And everything of Naples to its roots
Down in Ausonia had been my ward,
And Hungary was set to be a crown
On my brow, shining, as the Danube flows
When it leaves Germany. And then look down
Beyond the end of where your own land goes,
To Sicily, which also had been mine,
Even that coast where the sirocco blows
In from the sea to scour the gulf's curved line,
80 And Etna's sulphur, not Typhon beneath,
Darkens the land which would have found its kings
Through me, to wear the future's royal wreath,
Passed down from the conjoining line that springs
From Rudolph and my father. But bad rule
By Charles the First made such a botch of things,
The French were slain because one man was cruel,
One of their own, and so Palermo cried
'Death, death to them,' and if they could not say
The shibboleth, then on the spot they died,
90 And finally the rest were sent away.
And if my brother Robert learned from this,
He'd shun already the catchpenny greed
Of Catalans, and put due emphasis
On how the nobles from that country need
More stipends all the time. He should make sure,
Or someone should, there is no further load

Put on his ship, for it can take no more.
His forebears were large-hearted, but the road
Of royal charity runs out in him.
100   He's mean, and should have chevaliers to serve
His cause whose first concern is not to skim
His income as if that's what they deserve."
And I: "Because, my lord, you see as well
As I do, the deep joy your words have filled
Me with—because you have a way to tell
Through that source by which all good is instilled
Into existence without end—so I
Am all the more glad, and I hold it dear,
That you see this in seeing God on high.
110   You've made me happy, and you've made things clear,
Because by speaking you've raised in my mind
The question how we come to get sweet seed
From bitter fruit." And he spoke in this kind:
"The human character does not just breed:
God gives it to us, working through the stars.
I'll show you how this is a truth you need
Before your eyes: your attitude debars
Real knowledge, and your back hides what is meant.
The Good that spins the kingdom of the skies
120   You climb, and makes the whole of it content,
Determines, in the world that lives and dies,
All that occurs, and works its will through these
Celestial bodies. All, all is foreseen
In the divine mind: the varieties
Of nature, yes, but also what they'll mean
Disposed across the universal frame,
Thus forming the well-being of the whole.
For anything the bow shoots, it's the same:
It falls contributing to that one goal
130   Of providence, an arrow to the mark.
If that were not so, this sky where you walk
Would generate confusion and go dark,

Make ruins and not art. Our senses balk
At such a prospect, for it would entail
Faults in the minds that move the starry wheels,
The First Intelligence would have to fail
In giving out the guarantees and seals
Of all perfections. Do you need this theme
Expounded further?" And I: "Not at all.
140   I see how nature, to complete its scheme
Can fail in nothing. It's impossible."
Whence he continued: "Think on this then. Would
A man be worse off if on Earth he were
No citizen?" And I: "That's understood.
No proof is needed." He: "Can that occur
(Citizenship) unless, in different ways
Men live below and do the things they do?
All this your Aristotle well portrays."
He argued thus, and then continued. "You
150   Must know, therefore, your actions all diverge
At root. For one man, Solon, legislates,
While Xerxes fights, having a different urge.
Melchizedek's a craftsman: he creates
In one way, but then Daedalus invents
The means to fly, and so his son is lost—
And circling nature, in the broader sense,
Employs one art. The mortal wax embossed
With her seal has no house that stands apart
From all the other houses. So it was
160   That Esau was not Jacob, and the heart
Of Romulus was no less great because
He was a peasant's son. Indeed Rome thought
Mars was his father. All that are begot,
If Providence did not act as it ought,
Would echo their begetters, like as not.
As the divine decides, so men are wrought
To be themselves. Now what was held concealed
Behind your back you see before you. But,

Just so my joy in you can stand revealed,
170 Take this corollary and wrap it shut
About you, one more cloak around your gown:
Always, should nature meet with fortune ill
Adapted to it, then, like seed flung down
Away from its own soil, it can't fulfil
Its usual expectations of success,
And if the world below could only set
Its mind on fundamental naturalness,
What men were meant to give you, you would get.
But you switch someone—cut out to profess
180 The art of wielding the long, war-like sword—
Towards religion; and you make a king
From someone whose proclivities accord
With preaching sermons; and that way you bring
Yourself to lose track, and lose everything."

CANTO 9

After your husband Charles enlightened me
In this way, fair Clemence, he then went on
To outline all the kinds of treachery
He knew his seed would meet when he was gone,
And then he said "But silence. Let the years
Revolve." So there is nothing I can say
Except that, from your wrongs, deserved sad tears
Must follow. But the soul had turned away
Already—lamp inside that holy light—
Towards the sun that fills it, to the Good
Sufficient to all things. Ah, souls of night,
Creatures beguiled and void of reverence, would
You turn away your hearts from such a source
Of virtue, and seek vanity instead?
You would, alas. But now, on the same course
Towards me—and again such light was shed
The form was cloaked—another spirit moved
In brightness, and by brightening yet more
In silence, its desire to please was proved.
And Beatrice, too, by resting as before
Her eyes on me, without a word expressed
Assent to my desire. Then I: "Pray bring,
Blessed spirit, means to set my mind at rest
With all speed. I need proof of just one thing:

That when I think, I have no need to speak,
Since you're a mirror that reflects my thought."
The light, in whose depths I could only seek
Vainly to know who shed it, as I sought,
Continued, from the depths whence it had sung:
30 "In Italy, depraved land, where the hills
Climb behind Venice up to meet, among
The crags, the Brenta's first pool where it spills
Out of the spring, and the Piave flows
To make its mark, there is a slope whence came
The firebrand Ezzelino. The world knows
He laid the district waste. That was his fame,
And I, Cunizza, was his sister. Here
I shine because this star's light ruled my life,
And set Sordello singing in my ear
40 When I already was Riccardo's wife.
He ruled Verona, but the troubadour
Took me away, and after him I fled
With Bonio, and there were several more
I loved, and then a couple more I wed.
But I forgive the cause of my warm ways—
This might seem strange to you and to your crowd—
Because it led me up into this blaze
Of love perfected. For the brilliant, proud
And precious jewel beside me, fame remained,
50 And will remain, from now, for five more turns
Of century like this one. It's ordained,
Thereby, that man, from this example, learns
How striving in the first life to do well
Can bring a second life the first one earns.
But nobody observes that principle
Among the ragtag bunch that teems between
The Tagliamento and the Adige:
Though punished often, they are never seen
To get the point. Yet there will come a day,
60 And soon, when Paduans, because they balk

At duty to the emperor, will sprawl,
Spreading their blood where men wade as they walk,
In the marshland of Vicenza. And the tall
Proud head of that Rizzardo who commands
Treviso doesn't know the web is spun
Already that will snare him. At the hands
70 Of Feltre's bishop, evil will be done.
That godless one will give up those who take
Refuge with him, and so they will be slain,
And Feltre will weep long for that man's sake,
So faithless, no one's ever known the pain
Of being locked up in the Citadel
Of Padua who more deserved that fate—
Not even in its tower, that slice of hell
They nickname 'Malta' for the stony weight
That comes down on its dungeon, a cold roof
To match the muddy floor. For great indeed
Would be the vat to hold the liquid proof
Of how those Ferrarese in their need
80 Were sold out, and whoever gets the task
Of weighing out that spilled blood cup by cup
Will soon grow tired and lean against the cask
He pours it into. But the priest goes up
In the Guelph party's eyes for this one gift
So courteously given, as befits
The custom of his country. Here we lift
Our thoughts aloft to where God's judgement sits,
There where the mirrors shine that you call Thrones,
And from them shines on me the right to think
90 And say such things." And then her singing tones
Fell silent, as she turned to form a link
Of that ring where she was before, or so
I guessed. The other radiant happiness,
Already known to me for its rich glow,
Became more precious yet, became priceless,
A perfect ruby struck with the sun's fire:

For up there, every joy becomes more bright
Like laughter here, but here, when thoughts retire
In sadness, shadows spread through the delight
And it goes dark. I said: "God sees it all,
And how you see is in Him, so no wish
Can hide from you. How, then, does it befall
That your voice is an insufficient dish
To satisfy my hungers, though it shares
With singing six-winged seraphim the role
Of pleasing Heaven? Without splitting hairs,
If I dwelt in the centre of your soul
As you in mine, you would not need to state
A question." He: "The giant valley where
The sea that girds the world spills through the gate
And spreads east through its misbehaving pair
Of shorelines so far that the day comes late
From east to west, the sea against the sun
Until Jerusalem's meridian
And Spain's horizon could be drawn as one
Right angle: there I lived my earthly span
In the area marked out, on the north strand,
Between the Ebro and the Magra, just
Across the water from the rocky land
Where Bugia lies, so each day the sun must—
In Africa and where I live—both rise
And fall at roughly the same time. And my
Marseilles, when Caesar took it as a prize,
Once made the harbour thick with blood. And by
People who knew my name there, I was called
Folco. This heaven here is stamped with love
As it stamped me. Dido was never galled
By passion—when it led her on to steal
Aeneas from his wife, and to betray
Her husband—more than I was when my youth
Had all its hair; nor she of Rhodope,
The Thracian princess, when she heard the truth

About her straying man; nor Hercules
Who died for love of Iole. Here, though,
We don't repent, but rather, unlike these,
We smile—not for the fault that plagued us so,
Back there, but now does not come back to mind—
We smile to thank that Force which, in advance,
Both ordered and foresaw. For here we find
140 The object of our thoughts is in this dance
Of art, this beauty, this sublime result.
We see the good by which the world above
Wheels round the one below, and we exult.
But so you may, out of this sphere of love,
Take satisfaction for the wishes born
When you came in, let me speak more on this.
You'd like a name to fit this burst of dawn
Beside me, sparkling as the sunbeams kiss
The water. In this light, Rahab finds peace,
150 Who gave Christ's envoys, though she was a whore,
Their lodging, so the lights of love's increase
Attain here, as her just reward, far more
Intensity than she once knew, and now
She is with us, and of the highest grade
Our order grants: all other ranks must bow
To honour her, once last but now the first,
Since grateful Christ in triumph wished for it,
She sits up here in state where the dispersed
Last shadow of the earth ends. It was fit,
160 Indeed, some heaven should receive her as
A victory trophy for those sweet palms split
With nails, because she favoured—this cause has
No great place in the Pope's thought—Joshua
And his first glory, Christ's great sacrifice,
There in the Holy Land. But Lucifer
Planted your city, he whose whole device
Was to betray his Maker, and from whom
Hot tears of envy come. Your Florence grows,

And spreads, the florin, the gold flower whose doom
170 Is to mislead the sheep and lambs, for those
Follow the shepherds, who all have the jaws
Of raging wolves. For this, the Gospels sink
Into neglect, and all the holy laws
Of the great teachers. Students, taught to think
Mere canon law important, scrawl their script
In margins. Popes do this, and cardinals,
By self-esteem and scribbling fever gripped.
Their thoughts go not to Nazareth. Gabriel's
Wings were once spread there. But the Vatican,
180 Where Peter died, and all those sacred parts
Of Rome where martyrs served that holy man
With soldiers' deaths, will from those cheating arts
Of profanation be set free, and at
An early date, you may be sure of that."

CANTO 10

As God looked on His son, the Word, with all
The power of Love that both of them exhale,
He, three in one, first and ineffable,
Created everything, fit without fail,
That turns in space and in the mind, and so
No one who looks upon it can but taste
His presence in whatever we can know.
Therefore look up to where the wheels are placed
Aloft, reader. Lift up your eyes with mine
And aim at that point where the sun and moon
And planets cross the equatorial line
There in the stars. Thus you'll enjoy the boon
Of taking pleasure in your Master's art,
Whose eyes are fixed upon it endlessly,
So much He loves that movement in the heart
Of one wheel through another, while we see
The day turn one way, and the way the year
Turns in the other. See the branching out,
Obliquely, of the circle where appear
Planets that answer, as they move about,
The wishes of the world. And if their track
Were not askew, much virtue would be vain
In Heaven, for just let the Zodiac
Be more, or less, divergent from the plane

It turns in—that which governs its straight course—
And, as the virtue there, so would we lose
Potential here, a falling-off of force
In the order of the world, both low and high.
Stay at your bench now, reader, and think through
The first taste that I've given you to try.
You'll tire before it stops delighting you.
The dish set down, now you must eat alone,
For I've been made scribe of a theme that bends
Towards its telling all the care I own.
Measuring everything that starts and ends
With light, and stamping on the world the worth
Of Heaven, nature's greatest minister,
The sun, conjoined with where spring has its birth,
As I have noted, wheeled through dawns that were
Early each time, the spiral of its drift
Towards the summer and its lengthened stay,
And I was there but didn't see the shift
Of its position more than when we say
We have a new thought just before the thought
Appears in our minds. Beatrice is the one
Who leads this instantaneous transport
From good to better so the thing is done
In no time. How they must have burned so bright
Just in themselves, the ones inside the sun,
Distinguished not by colour but by light!
If I had practice, genius and skill
To conjure in the measure of that sight,
My telling would be insufficient still
To give the picture through the power of speech.
We must believe, and long for it, and should
Our poor imaginations fail to reach
Such heights, it is no shame. As if they could!
For no light like the sun was ever seen
By human eye. Thus they were shining there,
The fourth family, of all those who had been

Set on their course by this realm of His care,
The Father on the heights, who satisfies
The theologians and the learned ones,
By showing them the way He breathes, and ties
Three kinds of breath together, His, the Son's
And Holy Ghost's. Then Beatrice: "Praise and prize
The sun that lights the angels, our great Lord,
Who, by His grace, has raised you up to see
His radiance." No heart had ever soared
70 To give itself to God as speedily
As mine at these words, with its whole consent
And all its love so fixed on Him, that she
Who spoke was blotted out. She was content
To be forgotten, and indeed she smiled:
Smiled with such splendour that her glance dissolved
My mind's absorption, so the thoughts compiled
Within it all became far less involved,
Dividing into many subjects. I
Saw many brilliant flashing lights converge
80 On us, the point they were attracted by.
They formed a crown, from which we heard emerge
Voices yet sweeter than their aspect shone.
Sometimes we see the moon, Diana, shine
Yet brighter for the girdle she has on:
That soft and shimmering halo is the sign
The air is charged with water. In the court
Of Heaven I've returned from, many jewels
Are found, more beautiful than can be thought,
And past all price, and, by the kingdom's rules,
90 There they must stay. This song was one of those—
The song of lights. He that does not take wing
To fly up there, it is as if he chose
To hear news from the dumb. The angels sing
To souls whose virtues lift them to the heights.
So, singing thus, three times these burning suns
Had swept around us, as, on starry nights,

Stars near the poles move faster, but these ones
To me seemed ladies, still held by the dance,
Who pause in silence, listening till they sense
100 The new strain, which will take them from their trance.
And so, in one of them, I heard commence
This speech: "The beam of grace that lights true love
And grows by loving, shines so multiplied
In you, that it has brought you here above
By that stair which nobody took a stride
Back down except to mount again. One who
Refused, from his jug, wine to quench your thirst,
Would know the obstacles the rivers do,
Restricted by the rocks they'd like to burst
110 And so resume their unimpeded flow
Towards the sea. You ask, what flowers bloom
Here in this garland whose love-glances glow
Around the lady by the powers of whom
You gain your strength for Heaven. You should know
That I am Thomas of Aquinas. He
Here on my right is Albert of Cologne,
My master. We were both lambs glad to be
Of that flock where, if none strays on its own,
It eats well of the true food, for the soul.
120 We were Dominicans. If, for the rest,
You'd have such facts, then follow round the whole
Wreath with your eyes as I say how it's blessed
With famous names. Next comes the blazing smile
Of Gratian, he who well served both courts:
He worked for truth and went the extra mile
For justice, so for virtue of two sorts
He is in paradise. Next in our choir:
Peter of Lombardy, who gave the Church
All that he had. No tribute can rank higher
130 Than that. His four great books, where we may search
Successfully for truth in dogma, give
A new equivalent for those two coins

The widow gave God, and like them they live,
For everything's the widow's mite that joins
All we possess to heaven. Then there comes
The fifth light, the most lovely in the wreath,
A breath of such love that it still benumbs
The senses of those in the world beneath,
Who starve for news of it. It's Solomon,
140 Given such wisdom in his lofty mind
The learned disputation still goes on
That he might have been saved, for of that kind
Of vision there's been nothing since his rule.
And Dionysius is next in line,
A candle now, that burns in this bright school,
But down there in the flesh, when day was dim,
He still saw into what the angels are
And how they minister. And then, within
The next small light, smiles he who was by far
150 The advocate that best explained how sin
Grew less in Christian times, Orosius,
Whose treatise was such help to Augustine.
And if your mind's eye scans those I discuss
From left to right as you hear what I mean,
You seek the eighth already. There he is,
Boethius. He rose from martyrdom
And exile to this peace. Who knows of his
Vision of goodness knows this light comes from
A body left below the Golden Roof,
160 For so the church in Pavia is now called
Where he was put to rest after the proof
Of how the world deceives, which saw him walled
Into the prison where he wrote his book
On how philosophy consoles. And then,
Beyond a little further, if you look,
You'll see three more flames that were once three men.
There's Bishop Isodore, he of Seville
And the *Encyclopedia*, and there is Bede

Of England and the sermons and the skill
170 In doctrine, and then comes the prior we read
For mysticism, Richard, who was born
In Scotland, but in Paris lived to prove
That contemplation leaves mere man forlorn,
For it is more than man. And then you move
Your eyes to me from that light there, which holds
Brabant's Siger, so coiled and crushed in thought
He thought that death, to free him from thought's folds,
Came slowly, but in Italy was taught,
Through treachery, that it can come too soon,
180 And all he'd talked of in the Street of Straw
In Paris, about how the opportune
Had no role in Creation, for the Law
Determined all: that doctrine played its part
If forming the high truth which turns dispute
Into a driving force. Then, with the art
By which a clock, both early and astute,
Tells us the Church, the Bride of Christ, will sing
Matins to its dear Bridegroom, that He may
Adore her, and one tiny part will bring
190 Another closer so the interplay
Triggers the actuation of a spring
Striking a chime to herald the new day
So sweetly the well-ordered spirit swells
With love, just so I saw the glorious wheel
Rotate, and, voice to voice, like peals of bells,
Give out the harmony no one can feel
Except there, where eternal joy is real.

CANTO 11

Thick-witted mortal cares, how false and vain
Your earthbound reasoning, that keeps your wings
Beating in downward flight! One hoped to gain
Letters in law, one strove to do great things
In medicine, one followed the priesthood,
One set himself to rule, by craft or force,
One studied robbery, one found the good
In state affairs, one signed on for a course
In carnal knowledge—though he understood
10   He would need weary years to graduate—
And one did absolutely nothing. I,
Set free of all these lures, was in a state
Of grace with Beatrice high in the sky,
Received in glory. When each light returned
To where it was before, at the same place—
As if, upon its stand, a candle burned—
It stopped. Within its radiance, the face
Which had already spoken spoke once more,
Smiling and brighter yet. "As I reflect
20   Its beams, so in the Light Eternal I see your
Thoughts and their cause. They intersect
With my gaze. You have doubts, and want my words
Made plain and clear—so you can understand
On your own level—touching on the herds
Of sheep well fed, and on the other hand

My reference to no second Solomon.
Here, in both cases, we must make distinct
The meaning of each word we dwell upon:
Expression and significance are linked.
30   The Providence Divine that rules the course
Of all the human world with its decrees,
Strikes blind, with its unfathomable force,
All eyesight in creation, comes to please
Solely the understanding of that one
Who is the Bride of Him that cried aloud
In agony for what the blind had done.
With sacred blood He married her. Now, proud
In her position and her faithfulness
To Him, she finds her sure way to his side,
40   Her guides, two princes matched in their prowess:
The one, St. Francis, always sanctified
By his seraphic ardour, kept the watch
For faith. The other was St. Dominic,
Who always screwed his knowledge up a notch
And so, in splendour, shook the heretic
With his cherubic light. Two souls, one mind.
I, the Dominican, shall speak in praise
Of Francis, since the way those two combined
Means lauding either one will work both ways,
50   Commending each for working to one end.
There where Perugia feels the heat and cold,
And where poor Gualdo and Nocera bend
Their heads beneath the yoke that they must hold
With weary arms, for they receive less light,
There falls a fertile mountain slope between
Two waters. One comes streaming from the height
Where once Ubaldo's guiding hand was seen.
The other's the Topino. From that hill,
Where, at Assisi, steepness most gives way
60   To level ground, a sun—as this sun will
Rise sometimes from the Ganges—broke like day,

A dawn called Francis. Not 'I rose' but 'East'
Would be a better name for that blessed place.
'*Ascesi*' is a small word. At the least,
We should invoke, to suit a splendid case,
The orient '*ex alto.*' He had not
Yet risen far when first the earth began
To feel strong from his mighty virtue. What
Marked out his course was how, still a young man,
He crossed his father for a lady's sake—
She to whom nobody unlocks the door
Of his free will, but only by mistake,
As he might do with death—and so, before
The bishop, and with his own father there,
He married her. Her name was Poverty,
And he gave her each day more loving care.
Bereft of her first husband, Jesus, she
Could only wait—unknown even by name,
More than eleven hundred years despised—
Without a suitor, loyal till he came.
Not even Amyclas could make her prised
When he stood up to Caesar in his fame,
A fisherman who faced that fearful voice
And only with her spirit; and the same
When she had so much courtesy to show
And courage, as Christ mounted on the cross,
While Mary, full of love, remained below,
But lest my speech should leave you at a loss
With metaphors, let's say, in all I've said,
Francis and Poverty both loved as one,
Their harmony and happy glances led
To wonder among men, and sweet dreams spun
In thought, and holy pondering. And thus
It was, that Venerable Bernard first
Ran barefoot, at a speed which still to us
Seems quick enough, though he thought he was cursed
With slowness. And then, barefoot too, goes Giles,

70

80

90

Barefoot Sylvester, following the groom,
They're so pleased with the bride. Onward for miles
100 That father, subject to a humble doom
It seemed, yet still a master, took the road,
He and his lady and their family tied
Together with a single cord. His code
For being just a merchant's son was pride
Not cowardice, nor was his brow weighed down
For being subject to contempt and scorn,
As if a circus act had come to town.
Instead, as if to royal purple born,
He showed his colours to Pope Innocent,
110 And from that firm resolve came the first seal
Upon his order. And so on he went,
The convoy of his brothers at his heel
Increasing always, so their life was sung
Better by heaven's glory than my voice:
The angels are a choir, and I one tongue.
And so the shepherd who had made his choice
For owning nothing, wore a crown again.
Honorius bestowed it, as envoy
Of the eternal sprit. And then, when,
120 Thirsting for martyrdom, for him a joy,
He'd preached of Christ and his devoted men
In the palace of the Sultan, greatly proud,
And found the Saracens had not begun
To be ripe for conversion, he, unbowed,
But seeing that it could not serve the turn
To stay, went back to where his homeland yields
A surer harvest. There he came to earn—
High on a crag arising from the fields
Between the Tiber and the Arno—his
130 Last seal, received from Christ—and all who know
What Christ's wounds were will know what that seal is—
And for two years his body was marked so,
Until the time came for his great reward

When God, who destined him for so much good,
Raised him at last to heights that would accord
With how he'd kept as lowly as he could.
And to his brothers, as his rightful heirs,
He gave the keeping of his lady dear
And bade them love her and soothe all her cares
140 So she might never more have cause to fear
That they might not be faithful, and then, from
Her bosom his great soul chose to take wing
On his returning flight to its kingdom,
Because bare earth, bereft of everything,
Was all the pomp of his bier. Ponder now
What kind of man was this man's fit ally
To keep the bark of Peter's questing prow
Rightly directed when the seas were high,
And such was Dominic, our patriarch:
150 Meaning his followers, you may perceive,
All carry merchandise of goodly mark
If they obey him. But you must believe
His flock has grown so greedy for new food—
Positions, honours, dignities and such
Distractions—that they're by themselves pursued
To scatter in wild pastures, out of touch
With their first shepherd, and the more footloose
They wander from his guidance, the less milk
They bring back to the fold. So they're no use,
160 And those that stay close are the fearful ilk
Who just seek safety, and get little stuff
To suit their cowls. If now my words are not
Obscure, and you have listened long enough
So there is something you have not forgot,
You will be satisfied in part, and see
The way the plant is wasted, and what's meant
By that correction in the homily:
'Where we eat well' was how the first words went,
But 'If we do not stray' spells discontent."

CANTO 12

The moment the blest flame said its last word,
The holy millstone once again began
To turn, and from where that last word was heard
The ring of light, according to its plan
Of circularity, was turning yet,
Its course unfinished, when another one
Just like it formed around it, so they met
Each other's match in how the thing was done:
All movements mirrored, each song echoed song—
10   Songs which our muses and our sirens here
On earth, though they should play however long
On their sweet pipes, could never quite come near
With their reflection of a splendour. When
Two rainbows, colourful in parallel,
Curve through thin cloud, the inner one again
Born in the outer—Juno bends to tell
Her handmaid Iris what to do—the voice
Of Echo lives again, the nymph whom love
For her Narcissus left without a choice
20   Except to fade, as the bright sun above
Devours all vapours. People here presage
The world, because of God and Noah's pact,
Will not be flooded in a later age
As once it was, and so we saw, in fact,

Those two wreaths of eternal roses turn
Around us, and the way the one within
Induced the outer one to sing and burn
At its command. Then all the joyous din
Of that great dancing festival, its flame
30 And song, its play of light with light,
Its grace, stopped all together at the same
Moment, with one accord. Our human sight
Works just that way, whenever both our eyes
Moved by one impulse, must together close
And open. But then one new light gave rise
To such a voice that, as the needle shows
The pathway to the star, I turned to it.
"The love," it said, "that makes us beautiful
Draws me to hail another master, fit
40 To praise, since in his name we have heard all
The good things said about my leader. Let
Great Dominic be lauded now just as
Francis has been, for both, let's not forget,
Fought for one end. Each sun of glory has
A right to shine, in one great blaze well met.
Christ's army, the Church militant, which cost
So dear to rearm, slowly moved, and few
And full of doubt, and looking next to lost,
Behind their standard. Then the emperor who
50 Forever reigns on high provided for
His soldiers in their peril—not from their
Deserving of his helping hand, but more
From the unbounded mercy of his care—
And, as we said, two heroes He assigned
His Bride, and they inspired, by word and deed,
His scattered troops. And where we look to find
Sweet Zephyr rising to breathe on the seed
And spread new leaves in Europe by which she
Sees herself clothed again, there in the west,
60 Not far inland from where the waves can be

Heard beating behind which the sun will rest
In summer from his long trajectory
And hide from men, lies favoured, in Castile,
The town of Calaruega, by the shield
Protected where we see one lion kneel
As subject, and the other rule the field.
And there the Christian faith's most faithful man,
The holy athlete gracious to his own
And cruel to foes, was born. His mind began,
70 As soon as formed, to show how, all alone,
It had such power that, in his mother's womb,
It made a prophet of her, so she dreamed
About a dog let loose in a dark room,
And, in its mouth, a hot torch that redeemed.
And when the sacred nuptials between
Him and the faith before the holy font
Were signed and sealed, and each of them had been
Dowered by the other with all both could want
Of being saved, his godmother, who gave
80 Assent for him, saw glowing in her sleep
A star set in his brow, which was the brave
Symbol of what would spring from him, and keep
On springing from his heirs, a marvellous fruit,
And, that his name might signal what he was,
A spirit put the Lord's name at the root
Of his name, Dominic, spelt thus because
The form, possessive, showed he was possessed
Completely by his God. Of him I speak
As of the labourer Christ thought the best
90 To help Him in that Garden where we seek
Eternity on earth, our Holy Church.
Herald he seemed indeed, and of the house
Of Christ himself, for if today we search
Among his actions, all of them espouse
Christ's love, even the first, which has the ring
Of Christ's first counsel, which was 'First seek ye

God's kingdom.' And there was another thing:
Often the nuns would find him silently
Awake stretched on the ground, as if to say
100 'For this end am I come.' Happy indeed
His father, with a name fit to display—
Felice—satisfaction, as we read
The grace of God set in his mother's name,
Giovanna. Medicine and common law,
From which bright students take now their world fame,
Had no appeal. He loved true manna more,
Becoming, in so short a time, so great
A teacher, that he tamed the vineyard which
Soon withers if its keeper should be late,
110 Or lazy with his care, or would grow rich
In the wrong way, and to the papal seat—
Not in itself, but in its occupant,
Less kind now to the just poor, yet replete
In favour to itself, blind to its scant
Distance from decadence—he made appeal,
Not for the right to skim funds for good works,
Not for the first free post, not for a deal
To milk the tithes, not for the cosy perks,
But for the chance to fight the erring world
120 For faith, the seed from which they grew,
These twenty-four plants, each a flame unfurled,
The singing fires that here encircle you.
Then, like a torrent from a high spring hurled,
With doctrine, zeal and apostolic force
He went forth, and with mighty strength he fell
Upon those thorn bushes which were the source
Of heresy, and pummelled them pell-mell,
Most vigorously where they best fought back.
From him there sprang the energising streams
130 By which the thirsty saplings, when they lack
Sufficient water, flourish as it teems
In the Catholic garden. If such was one wheel

Of Holy Church's fighting chariot—
With which she saved herself and brought to heel
Her enemies—then surely you are not
In doubt about the other excellence
That Thomas spoke of before I appeared,
And spoke so courteously. In one sense,
However, its top rim is cracked and peeled,
140 Or put it this way: mould has lined the cask
There where a good wine ought to leave a crust.
The wine went bad. His family at their task
Had started on the one path they could trust,
Formed by his footprints, but they turned about,
The one in front thrown on the one behind.
The lax were lauded and the strict cast out
And soon there'll be a harvest of the kind
Where tares, denied the barn, start to complain.
Whoever searched our rule book page by page
150 Might still find on one leaf, after some strain,
'I'm what I once was, even in this age,'
But he would be from neither of the schools
That vie to dominate the order now—
The one that petrifies its hallowed rules
Of poverty, the other that tells how
They count no more. I was the living soul
Of that man born in Bagnoregio
To lead the order and to keep it whole
By always rating worldly matters low.
160 Bonaventura was my name. And these?
Illuminato, early follower
Of Francis, and among the first to please
God with their barefoot poverty. They were
The vanguard of the cord. Here's Augustine,
Another of them. Then the mystic Hugh,
Who at St. Victor wrote the books that mean
So much now; as, you must know, also do
The writings of the Bookworm Peter. Next,

Peter the Spaniard, logic's champion,
170 Who codified it in twelve sheaves of text
That shine below for you to dwell upon.
The prophet Nathan foretold David's sin
With someone else's wife, and Chrysostom
Fought greed and helped the great Church to begin;
And then Anselm, in all of Christendom
The greatest theologian of his time.
And then Donatus, who once set his hand
To grammar, the first art, so we might climb
From verbal chaos and thus understand
180 Expressive form, one of the special fields
Of the Franciscan order. He who wrote
So much of the great library that yields
Our knowledge about everything of note
In exegesis, is Rabanus. See
Him there. And then the abbot Joachim,
Born in Calabria, shines close to me.
In life I quarrelled bitterly with him—
The world envisioned in his prophesy
Granted the spiritual significance
190 Beyond its bounds—but here we're reconciled,
In how the bright connecting circles dance
Of love and knowledge. How St. Thomas smiles
On you with all his courtesy and fine
Judgement of glowing language is what draws
This celebration, from both me and mine,
Of such a mighty soldier for the cause—
Which is ours too, so this was all applause."

CANTO 13

Let him imagine, who would comprehend
What I saw now—and let him hold the thought
Rock solid, while I speak, until the end—
The fifteen stars whose light is never caught
By any barrier in all the air,
Shining in various regions of the sky.
Let him imagine also the Great Bear
Of seven stars—which freely turn on high
Around a pole with room enough to keep
All visible—and add them to the score.
And then let him imagine how the steep
High axle-hub that caps the First Wheel's core
Puts forth the Horn where two more stars stand out
Within the Little Bear. Then think of these
Two dozen stars arranged and turned about
All by themselves in all the right degrees
Into a pair of sparkling garlands spread
In heaven such as Ariadne made
From her wreath when she knew she'd soon be dead,
And Bacchus, loving her, raised her to braid
The Corona Borealis. As I said,
One shines within the other. Both revolve
In such a manner that one goes ahead,
The other after. That way he can solve

10

20

The problem, to a small extent—he'll know
The shadow of the answer, if you will—
Of how that constellated double flow
Danced round the point where I now stood stock-still.
It lies as far beyond where thought can go—
30 Based on experience—as does the speed
In spinning of the Primum Mobile
Beyond the sluggish course through mud and reed
Of some tired Tuscan creek on a hot day.
They sang there, not of false and pagan gods
Like Bacchus or Apollo, but of three
Persons in one, combined against all odds—
And in one person, man and mystery.
The singing circle's measure once complete,
The holy lights now gave us their regard,
40 Rejoicing that they had new aims to meet.
The change to unsung speech might have seemed hard,
But doctrine and their song permit no choice
Between. The light from which I'd heard the tale
Of Francis the Poor, man of God, gave voice.
Breaking the hush of those who never fail
To make God's work their own, he spoke thus: "When
One sheaf is threshed and all its grain is stored—
I mean the line about the straying—then
Sweet Charity next calls me to accord
50 That treatment to the other. You believe
The light that was infused into the breast
Whence came the rib that made the whole world grieve,
Giving us her whose fair face failed the test
Of reining in her hunger—the same light
That shone into another breast, the one
The spear pierced, and which gave us, in the flight
Of past to future, satisfaction
That far outweighs, when balanced and set right,
Our every fault—you think that light, which is
60 The only light allowed to humankind,

Was all instilled by God, and is all his
Who made both man and Saviour. So your mind
Marvels at what I said about the good
Contained in the fifth light not having known
An equal since. When you have understood
The answer you have been already shown
By me, you'll see my words and your belief
Meet in the centre of the circle, where
The truths reside. Of all truths, this is chief:
70 That which dies not and that which dies are there
As nothing but the splendour of our Sire's
Idea, which, loving, he begets. Because
That living light—which, streaming from the fires
Of its bright source, is never, as it pours,
Detached from its first well, nor from the love
Which, with those two, makes three—collects its beams
Through its own goodness, mirrored there above
In nine angelic orders, without seams
Stitched into one forever, it descends
80 To earthly potencies from act to act,
Becoming such that all things have their ends
In brief contingency, the fleeting fact—
Things generated with, or without, seed—
Produced by movements of the heavens. Since
The wax of these, and that which does the deed
Of moulding—what's imprinted and what prints—
Are not always the same, so that the light
Beneath the stamp can more, or less, shine through,
It happens that two trees of one type might
90 Bear better or worse fruit. The same with you:
You're born with different talents. If the wax
Were perfectly receptive and the force
Of Heaven could run truly on the tracks
Of its descent, the seal would match the source
In brightness, but there is a falling short
By nature always, as the artist's craft

Comes from a trembling hand. Yet keep this thought:
If the clear vision of the Primal Draught
Of Power is moved by burning Love, then all
Perfection is acquired up here. The Earth
Was once made fit for the impeccable
Advent of Adam, and our Saviour's birth
Out of a virgin. Therefore I commend
Your judgement when it comes to nature's lack
Of power ever afterwards to blend
With God, and bring that same achievement back—
Human perfection. If I left it there
And said no more, then you would say 'So how
Was he we spoke about beyond compare?'
But just to clarify your mind, think now
Of who he was; and why, when bidden 'Ask,'
He asked for wisdom. I have not concealed
My meaning with my words enough to mask
The fact he was a great king, who appealed
For knowledge suitable to that state. He
Did not ask which forms of the mental moved
This upper realm, how many they might be;
He didn't seek to know how it is proved
Contingency undoes necessity
When any statement harbouring a doubt
Meets one that doesn't; he had no concern
For motion without cause, nor cared about
A triangle that had no room to turn
Inside a semicircle if without
A right angle; or any of those things.
He wished to know only of government.
Note what I say and said, then: for the kings,
It's royal wisdom that is heaven sent,
An unmatched vision. There the arrow lands
Of my intention. It applied to those
Men who wore crowns, and met the fierce demands
Of ruling in the world. Many arose:

Good ones were few, and still are hard to find.
Take my words thus, and they will fit the frame
With what you hold already in your mind,
About the world's first father, and the same
For our Beloved. And let this be lead
To make your feet slow always, like a man
Grown weary, when a 'yea' or 'nay' is said,
140   And you would move as quickly as you can
To either point, although your sight is dim.
For he indeed is a low-ranking fool,
Whichever point of view appeals to him,
Who weighs in, either way, without the rule
Of scrutiny, since often it occurs
That quick opinion swings to the wrong side,
And then the sudden storm of feeling blurs
The intellect, and so he breasts the tide
Worse than in vain when he casts off from shore,
150   For as he sets out he does not return
The same, who, fishing for the truth, is poor
In patient art. And of this you can learn
From minor minds that Aristotle scorned:
Parmenides and others who, confused
As to their course, would not be schooled or warned.
And scholars like Sabellius abused
Their role, and, to the scriptures, they were swords
Reflecting from their blades the natural face
Distorted. So we should be strict towards
160   All people when they judge at too great pace,
Like those who count the corn crop in the field
Before it's ripe. I've seen the briar show
Harsh through the winter and too hard to yield
When touched, and yet when spring comes it will grow
The rose, and on the other hand I've known
A ship to cross the sea for all its course
Straight as a die, swift as a hawk alone,
And, at the harbour's entrance, with full force,

Crack up and drown. Let not just anyone,
And his wife, Mrs. Anyone, assume,
Therefore, that when they witness a deed done
They can be certain of the doer's doom
On the divine scale. One who robs may rise,
And one who makes an offering may sink.
Our judgement isn't made from just our eyes,
And least of all will it be what we think
When we have barely taken time to blink."

CANTO 14

The water moves from rim to centre when
A round container is struck from without.
The water moves, when it is struck again—
But from within—the other way about,
Centre to rim. This proof from science fell
Into my mind the instant that the soul,
So glorious, of Thomas, ceased to tell
His story, because Beatrice took the role
Of speaker, and was pleased to follow thus:
10 "This man requires—he may not tell you so
In words, or thought detectable by us—
To reach into another truth's roots. Go,
You lights, and tell him if you'll keep your bloom
For all eternity as now you glow,
Your substance flowering. Should he assume
That when, at resurrection, you arise,
Made visible, you will not fear the sight,
Seeing yourselves with ordinary eyes
Despite the fact that you remain this bright?
20 Or do you think you won't be able to?"
Just as the singing dancers in a round,
Drawn on by joy, redouble what they do,
Lifting their voices as they spurn the ground
With quickened steps, so these ones, as they flew,

Kindled by the devout oration's spark,
Showed new delight in how they turned and sang.
Whoever grieves that we die in the dark
Down here to live above, would find that pang
Soon put to rest if he could see, up there,
30 Refreshment spill from the eternal source.
They sang of One, of Two, of how Three share
The rule of Two and One, linked fields of force
Uncircumscribed though unified. This theme
Was sung three times by all of them, to such
A melody its beauty would not seem,
For any merit that it praised, too much.
And then I heard from that most sacred blaze
Of all the inner circle, a soft voice
That Mary might have heard with dazzled gaze
40 From the angel sent down to announce God's choice.
"As long as there's a Feast of Heaven, just
So long our love will generate these robes
Around us. For their brightness, you may trust,
Answers our ardour as it first englobes
Our vision, which in turn is amplified
By what divine grace does to merit. When
The flesh, made glorious with sacred pride,
Is put back on to us, our persons then
Will be more worthy, being more complete,
50 So that the light the Great Good freely grants
Will grow: the light that makes us fit to meet
His overwhelming grandeur with our glance.
So vision will increase, and form that flame,
Then ardour too, and then the radiance.
With any coal that glows white, it's the same:
The glow outshines it, but its shape is kept.
So the effulgence that surrounds us will
Be far surpassed by what in earth has slept,
The buried flesh. But we, untroubled still,
60 Will simply have again, to make us strong,

Our bodies' organs to abet the shell
Of light you see around the dancing song
Of our great joy." And so keen, truth to tell,
Did both those choirs appear to say "Amen,"
That they showed very clearly their deep need
To have their bodies with them once again,
Not for themselves alone, perhaps: indeed
It might have been their parents they thought of,
And everybody else they once had known,
70 When they had lived, for whom they had felt love,
Before they changed to endless flame alone.
And then, behold! All round, and more intense
Than what it framed, an unflecked brightness rose,
The lustre that the new day's imminence
Lends the horizon. And as, at the close
Of day, new light starts showing through the sky
Until the real looks unreal, I began
To see the first two rings encircled by
A third, of new souls. Mouth, do what you can:
80 Describe the sparkling of the Holy Ghost.
Eyes could not bear it. Suddenly it glowed
Beyond the prowess that my sight could boast.
To help me see again, fair Beatrice showed
Her smiling face that beggars memory.
My eyes gained strength and lifted, and I saw
Myself moved, with my lady next to me,
Up to a plane exalted even more,
Of whose high ranking I was given proof
By Mars. More rosy-coloured than before
90 It now seemed. With my heart not held aloof,
But fully yielded, I employed the tongue—
Befitting all the loving care and grace
That lit the favours I was now among—
Of one and all when making, in that place,
The burning sacrifice to God, and still
It burned in my breast though I knew it was

Accepted, and propitious. For the spill
Of splendour was so shimmering because
Of two beams, and so roseate, I said
100 "Divine Sun that so glorifies this!" As
The galaxy, by lights inhabited—
Those lights pricked out both big and little—has
A way of whitening between the poles,
Spaced out at each end of the universe,
That puzzles still the very wisest souls—
How did it gather, when will it disperse,
This river in the sky?—the two beams made,
Thus constellated in the depths of Mars,
The venerable sign which is displayed
110 By quadrants in a circle, when crossed bars
Form the Greek cross. And here my skill must bow
To memory, for that cross so said Christ
In flames of glory, that I don't know how
To find comparison. Who follows Christ
By taking up a cross must yet forgive
All that I leave untold, when in that dawn
He sees Christ's outline come alight and live.
Between the peak and base, from horn to horn,
Lights moved that sparkled as they met and passed
120 Brightly, as, here, we see the particles
Of matter in the sunbeam, slow and fast,
Straight and askew, and think a light breeze lulls
Or lifts them, altering how they appear
Inside the shaft that sometimes streaks the dark
That we devise with cunning, from our fear
Of day undimmed. And as we might remark
How harp and viol, strung with many chords
In harmony, touch us with their sweet chime,
Though we don't catch the tune their sound affords—
130 For too much beauty does not give us time—
So from that light a melody emerged
Sent by the cross, to hold me there entranced,

Although the hymn's full meaning, as it surged,
I mainly missed. But as the song advanced
I did perceive how plaudits formed its theme.
The words "Arise" and "Conquer" I picked out:
Piercing suggestions of a general scheme,
Sure hints of what it must be all about,
And I was moved to such love that till then
140 Nothing had bound me with so sweet a chain.
My bold words here might seem excessive when
It is remembered how with might and main
I lavished praises on my lady's eyes,
In which all my desires achieve their rest,
But one who takes the time to realise
That those twin living seals, which so attest
To all of beauty, gained in strength with each
Ascent, and that in Mars I had not turned
To see them once again, will quickly reach
150 The sound decision that I might have earned
Exemption from reproof, having accused
Myself, and see that all I say is true,
For there the holy pleasure is diffused
Unchecked. Far from excluded, it pours through:
As we climbed higher, the more pure it grew.

CANTO 15

The will of grace—into which liquefies
Always the love that breathes in the right way,
As does cupidity, in its own guise,
Dissolve into ill will—now set the stay
Of silence on that sweet lyre, and made still
The sacred strings that Heaven renders taut
And loosens, with its right hand. When I fill
Their ears with my prayers that are justly wrought,
How can the souls be deaf, these spirits who,
To make me beg of them, with one accord
Fall dumb? His grief indeed is always new
That robs himself of love forever stored
Up there, and takes the love that cannot last.
As, through the still and cloudless evening sky,
Sometimes a sudden fire will run so fast
You'd think it were a star attracted by
The notion that it might change place—except
That where it came from no star has been lost
And only for a blink is this one kept,
Before, by vanishing, it pays the cost
Of its velocity—so from the horn
Of that cross, on the right, down to its base,
There streaked a single star abruptly born
Out of the splendid cluster there in place,

10

20

And this gem wasn't from its ribbon torn:
Running across the radial strip it glowed
Like fire through alabaster. So the shade
Of great Anchises, carrying his load
Of fatherly affection, reached, and made
30 Himself known, to Aeneas, deep within
Elysium, and—if I may translate—
The shade, in Latin, said this to begin:
"My blood! The flow of God's grace far too great
To measure! Who but you has ever seen,
A second time, the leaves of Heaven's gate
Swing open?" Thus the light spoke. I had been
Fixed on it. Then I turned my eyes again
To my great lady, and was twice amazed:
By that speech first, and now by her face when
40 I saw her smiling eyes and how they blazed:
I thought I touched, with mine, my deepest grace
And paradise. The soul then added joy
To his first words with words I couldn't place—
But still they gave delight, in his employ,
To sight and hearing—so deep was his speech.
Not from his choice, but from what had to be,
His meaning was concealed beyond my reach,
For his thought far outsoared mortality,
And when at last the bow of burning love
50 Relaxed enough to let his speech descend
To where the subject he was speaking of
Might fall within our scope to comprehend,
The first thing that I understood was: "Blessed
Be You, the Three-in-One, who, to my seed,
Show so much favour." Then there was the rest:
"My son, it is a long and happy need—
Drawn from the reading of the mighty book
Whose black and white are never-changing things—
That you have satisfied here, when we look
60 Through this light and we speak: the light that sings

Out thanks to Him by whose will you are clad
For this high flight with your befitting wings.
You think that any thought you might have had
Comes down to me from Him, the Primal One,
Even as unity must radiate
All numbers, which go forth and get things done
As five, and six, but always illustrate
That first One. Thus you do not ask me who
I am, or why I seem the gladdest soul
70 Of all this happy throng. Well, good for you:
For your belief is right, and here the whole
Of what is thought comes back before you think
Out of the mirror. For both great and small,
This thing is true. But so that I may drink
To quench my sweet wish, satisfying all
The holy Love for which I stay alert
On constant watch, let your strong, fearless voice,
So full of joy and unafraid of hurt,
Sound forth the will to which I have no choice
80 Of answer, the desire I am ordained
To meet with my response." And so I turned
To Beatrice, who without my speech had gained
My mind's import, and smiled, a sign that burned
To make the wings grow on my will. I said:
"Love and Intelligence, after the First
Equality appeared to you, were led
Each to a poise where neither was dispersed
By the other, since the sun that lit and warmed
You both with even heat and light was so
90 Unbiased no imbalance can be formed.
In mortals, will and faculty don't go
Together, for their wings have not the plumes
So equally arranged. I, as you know,
Am mortal. The discrepancy assumes,
In me, the form of feeling. I must give
My heartfelt thanks for your paternal vow

Of greeting. Tell me, topaz, as you live,
Gem of this precious jewel, your name." "My bough,
Who made me joyful just by coming near,
I was your root." His answer thus began,
And went on: "Know this much, now you are here:
We are connected, through a single man.
Around the hill a hundred years and more,
Down there on the first terrace, he has gone.
He was my son, and also he was your
Great-grandfather. His labours have gone on
A long time. It is fit you shorten them
With your good works. Your Florence, in those times,
Knew peace inside its ancient outward hem
Where still at nine and noon they hear the chimes.
But she was chaste then, flaunting not a gem—
No bracelet, no tiara, no fine gown
Rich with embroidery meant to be seen
More than the wearer warranted. The town
As yet lacked daughters certain to demean
A father with the fear they were too young
To marry, and the dowry was too high:
No house that still looked empty shared among
A family, or anyone to try
Outdoing Sardanapalus. Not yet
Did Rome give points to Florence on the rise,
As one day it will see that same sun set,
A fall worse than its own in its own eyes.
Gualdrada's father, old Bellincion
Berti, in humble bone and leather clad,
I saw, and from the glass, with no paint on
Her face, his lady came. Good men were glad
To wear plain buff. Their women spun the flax.
Fortunate women! Then, they all knew where
They would be buried, home ground at their backs
And not the soil of exile. They were there—
Not elsewhere, with their husbands, loading sacks

Of gold in France. While one would tend the crib,
Soothing the new child with the baby talk
Father and mother love, mopping its bib,
Guarding her hatchling like a mother hawk,
Another, from the distaff drawing skeins,
Would tell the servants stories of how Troy,
Through Rome and then Fiesole, remains
140 Alive in Florence. We take little joy
Today in shameless women, or in men
Who are not honest, but in those days they
Would have been freaks. Such things were unknown then.
It would have been as if, the other way,
Great Romans such as Cincinnatus came
To us, or women like Cornelia.
To such a fair and civil life where fame
Was all for peace, the public life by far
More loyal, to so sweet a domicile
150 Mary consigned me when my mother called
Her name in pain, and in the ancient style
Of your old Baptistery I was installed
As Christian and as Cacciaguida both:
Brothers, Moronto and Eliseo.
The future wife to whom I pledged my troth?
Ferrara, in the valley of the Po
Bred her. Her family name lives in your stem,
For it was Alighieri. Currado
Joined France's Louis and then I joined them
160 To go on the Crusade. The emperor
Made me a knight, so greatly did I earn
His favour as we battled that false law
Whose people, because our popes never learn,
Still rob you of your rightful Holy Land,
And there that foul breed disentangled me
From the deceitful world which has unmanned
So many souls for love of it. Set free
By martyrdom, I found the peace you see."

CANTO 16

Our poor nobility of blood! If you
Move men to glory in you here below
Where our affections languish as they do,
It never will cause me to ask "How so?"
Since even there, where appetites run true,
Unwarped, in Heaven, I was brought to know
Glory in you. For truly you wore such
A mantle as will quickly shrink if not
Added to, day by day, at least as much
As time goes round to shear off what it's got.
Thus with the plural "you"—once Rome's polite touch
Of speech to honour Caesar, but which since
Has lapsed (the present Romans use it least,
No doubt because they think it would evince
Some small thought for the empire they have ceased
To pay allegiance to)—I spoke again,
And Beatrice, a little set apart,
Smiled at my honorific word, as when
The lady coughed to warn the hasty heart
Of Guinevere, and him that wooed her then,
That she knew their great secret. I spoke this:
"You are my father, you gave me the nerve
To speak, you lift me up so that I miss
No aspect of myself that goes to serve

The object of increasing me. My mind
Is filled with sheer joy by so many streams
That it rejoices further still to find
It bears up without bursting at the seams.
So tell me then, dear shade from which I stem,
30 Who were your ancestors? Your boyhood, how
Do you recall its years? Remember them
For me. And Florence, not as it is now,
But when it was the sheepfold of St. John,
How big was it? Which were the families
Deemed fit for the high seats that they sat on?"
As coal is quickened by the merest breeze
To flame, just so I saw that light take fire,
At my fond words, and as it grew more fair
In my sight, so I heard its voice acquire
40 Yet more the sweetness of a gentle air,
But not in new speech: from an older store.
"From that first *Ave* till the day that I
Was born, five hundred times and eighty more
Mars came back to the Lion in the sky
To be rekindled underneath its paw,
For two more years. And I was born, like all
My family members who had gone before,
Just where the runners reach the inner wall
In your games every year. Let it suffice
50 To hear this much about my forebears: who
They were and whence they came exacts a price
If spoken of. Silence will have to do:
Just say that they were old stock. All those there
Between the Baptistery and the Old Bridge
And of an age that they had arms to bear,
Beside those who now have that privilege
Were but a fifth, yet still the blood was pure
Even in humble artisans, who now
Reflect in every vein, you may be sure,
60 All the surrounding villages. Yes, how

Much better to have all those aliens
For neighbours, with their place outside your bounds,
Than face the knowledge of their teeming dens
Within your gates, enduring on your grounds
The stink of those two crooks from out of town,
Baldo and Fazio, both lawyers schooled
Elsewhere to skills in how to do you down.
One of those swine, who had the council fooled,
Kept you in exile. If the popes and priests—
70 They who fell furthest short of what they should
Have done—had not behaved like beasts,
Those cruel stepmothers to great Caesar could
Have been real mothers to a son. There's one
Grand name I know up to his neck in trade
Who'd be back home where such stuff's better done,
Although his grandfather went bankrupt, paid
In smaller coin. Pistoia's main street still
Would own the castle that now Florence rules,
And not the Conte Guidi. Names that fill
80 The annals of our strife and leave dark pools
Of blood, might have remained in valleys far
Beyond our walls. Mixture of origin
Has brought us to the point where we now are,
Just as the body's ills often begin
With bolted food. Remember how the bull,
Because too big, more easily will fall
Than any lamb which lives to keep its wool,
And that a single sword—what we might call
A symbol for a people unified—
90 Cuts better and cuts more than any five.
If you recall how other cities died
And others still are only just alive—
Luni and Urbisaglia are quite gone,
Chiusi and Senigallia, almost—
Then you'll see nothing strange to dwell upon
At famous families giving up the ghost,
Since cities do the same. All your affairs

Will have their death in time, like you. But this
Fact is concealed in anything time spares
For any span, and our short lives might miss
Seeing the way it ends. Just as the shores
Are covered and uncovered by the moon
Without cease from her heaven, fortune pours
Its tides on Florence, which are just as soon
Withdrawn, a flux the living eye ignores,
But it occurs. It's not a marvel, then,
That I can speak of the great Florentines
Whose names are faded now, forgotten men.
I could name famous names, but each name means
So little now, that once meant power and wealth.
Some were already in decline, but some
Had all the lustre, dominance and health
That they had always had. How could they come
To nothing? Come they did. Over the gate
Which bears today such an unheard-of load
Of perfidy it's creaking with the weight
And soon must crack up like a barque tight stowed
With rotten grain, where now the Cerchi plot
Their infamies, the Ravignani dwelt,
And of their line came all those who were got
On daughters of Bellincion. Men knelt
Already to the della Pressa. From
The house of Galligaio shone the gold
Sword-hilt and pommel, knighthood's burdensome
But proud insignia. Noble of old,
So long illustrious, they hang their shield
In exile now, the Ghibelline old guard.
The Pigli coat of green pale in red field
Was great, and all the bloodlines that die hard:
Sacchetti and Fifanti (he unreeled
A whole long honour roll) are scattered names
By now, but they were all together then:
Who now are embers once were living flames.
The stock of the Calfucci bred great men:

Sizii and Arrigucci, Guelphs all, sat
In seats of office. Here I saw them grand:
All the Uberti long since fallen flat
Because they heeded pride's obsessed demand.
Chiaramontesi falsified the sale
140　Of salt by short weight. Lordly, rich in land,
Once they were bold, yet now you see them pale,
Blushing forever for one foolish hour.
The golden balls of the Lamberti shone
In Florence when that family had its power,
And now the clan of Mosca is all gone
Into the shadow. I saw the first flower
Of men whose sons seized every chance to leech
On vacant bishoprics and split the take.
The Adimari—honeyed in their speech
150　To him with teeth to bite and claws to rake,
Yet dragons at the back of him that flees—
The Adimari, bred to insolence
And on the rise already, did not please
Ubertino Donati, whose expense,
At marriage, turned out to include a link
Of shameful kinship with their paltry stock.
The Caponsacchi, come down from the brink
Of high Fiesole, had doors to lock
Already near the market. And mark this:
160　Giuda and Infangato were esteemed
As citizens. And here's one you might miss
(Unless I told you, you would not have dreamed):
The inner gate was once named for the line
Of della Pera, and where are they now?
And Baron Hugh of Tuscany's design
Of arms was one with which he would endow
All of his house since then until today,
When still the feast of Thomas signifies
His hour of death. The same coat's proud display
170　Marks Giano della Bella, who denies
The rich the right to crush their underlings,

And turns his words to action. Just the edge
Of his shield differs: all the quarterings
Come down from that one source of patronage—
The Baron, still the captain of his tomb
In the Badia. The Borgo would have stayed
Quiescent, but the Amidei spelt doom
For Buondelmonte. A just price he paid
For jilting their dear daughter, but they spread
180 Their vengeance further, and so all the tears
You weep now sprang from that one watershed,
When that one house had honour. Many years
Of civil strife began there. Happiness,
For you, died then, with clans at daggers drawn.
Ah, Buondelmonte, if you'd listened less
To bad advice, and not held vows in scorn,
And not fled! Many men, since you first crossed
The Ema, on your way into our town,
Would now be glad and not in grief be lost
190 If God had pushed you into it to drown.
But it was fitting that the wasted stone
Of Mars that guards the bridge should see one last
Peace offering—a man cut down alone—
Before all that the city in the past
Had known of harmony was torn to bits.
It was with all these families and more—
I mention only those that time permits—
That I saw Florence as she was before,
In all her plenitude of joyful calm,
200 Her people glorious. Not once in war
The lily on her flag had come to harm,
Turned head to toe to show disgrace and spite,
Or changed in colour. When the Guelphs expelled
The Ghibellines, the lily turned from white
To red, to show the victors held
The field. It was our city. What a sight:
The flag of daylight changed to fly by night."

As Phaethon, when he heard that he was not
Apollo's son, came in confusion to
His mother Clymene, from whom he got
Assurance that he was indeed the true
Heir to the god—and then he asked if he
Could drive the chariot for just one day,
Which led to such complete catastrophe
All fathers with ambitious sons will say
They were made wary by the memory—
10   Just so was I, and so I was esteemed
To be by Beatrice, and also by
The holy lamp that previously had seemed
To alter its position in the sky
Solely for my sake. Then my lady said:
"Put forth the flame of your desire, so it
May bear the mark of what lies in your head
And heart, the inner stamp that shapes to fit
The stuff that forms the sign, not just to swell
Our knowledge with your words, but to secure
20   The process yielding you a truth to tell
About your thirst, so that the draft so pure
May be poured out for you." I spoke just so
To Cacciaguida. "Dearest plot of seed,
You that are raised so high that just as no

Mentalities on earth are not agreed
Two angles, and no fewer, are acute
In any triangle, so you, when you
Gaze at the point where light is absolute
And all times come together, see what's true
Before it is, contingent things before
They are—when I and Virgil walked the hill
That heals the souls, and when we plumbed the core
Of that dead world where souls are always ill,
Grave words about my future life I heard—
Though I feel set four-square against the blows
Of chance, for if, before it has occurred
I know my fortune, all the anguish goes
From my desire, since it is met, just as
An arrow, when foreseen, more gently flies
Our way, as if what's not yet happened has."
Thus, speaking of my wish in the same wise
That Beatrice bade me, I addressed the light
That talked to me before. Not with the dark
Riddles by which fools tied their meaning tight
Before the Lamb of God undid that mark
Of sin he answered me, but in plain speech
And clear-cut terms—paternal love revealed
In words—he granted what he had to teach,
By his own smile both laid bare and concealed.
"Contingency, in your small world confined,
Is part of the Eternal Vision, yet
Does not derive, from that all-seeing mind,
Necessity. Think of the ship that met
Our eyes but later dropped downstream. From this
What lies in store for you in times to come
Comes to my eyes with the sweet synthesis
Of organ notes in their harmonic sum
Striking the ear. Just as Hippolytus,
When he staved off the cruel incestuous will
Of Phaedra, was cast out of Athens, thus

You will be sent from Florence. To fulfil
This aim—which is determined and contrived
In detail and will soon come true—there sits,
As pleased as if the moment had arrived
Already, him the papal crown now fits,
Proud in the hall where Christ is bought and sold
All day. Yes, Boniface. And, as it must,
The outcry of the common crowd will scold
The injured one. Though vengeance, to prove just
70   The truth that sends it, will come, you will leave
All that you love the best, which is the bolt
That exile's bow shoots first. You will achieve
Full proof the bread of others tastes of salt,
And how all stairs are steep when they belong
To other men, to climb or to descend,
And what will weigh you down, however strong
Your shoulders, is the evil without end
Of all the senseless company you keep
In that sad valley into which you fall:
80   Ungrateful, raving even in their sleep
With fury aimed at you. Quite soon they all
Shall have red brows, not you. Their foolish deeds
Will prove their brute stupidity. That you
Are by yourself a party, one that needs
No other membership: that fact will do
You honour. Your first refuge, your first inn,
You'll find by courtesy of that great stem
Of Lombards, the Scaligers. To begin
Your sojourn, you will meet the first of them,
90   Bartolomeo, with his family shield—
The ladder with the empire's eagle spread
Above—held out for you, that it may yield
Protection. His regard will so be wed
With grace, that everything you two exchange
Of asking and of giving will be turned
The other way around: he will arrange

All that you need before you say so. Burned
From birth by this brand of a mighty star,
One you will see whose deeds will be renowned.
The people have not noted him so far:
For just nine years the wheels have circled round
His young head. But before Henry's deceived
By Gascon Clement, this youth will show sparks
Of the heroic. It will be believed,
Even by enemies, this great dog barks
Against mere wealth, and his munificence
Will be part of his military fame.
Such generous bravery, sparing no expense,
You'll learn to look for in his blazing name—
Can Grande della Scala. With his aid
Fortunes will change for many. Many rich
Will be brought low, and beggars raised in grade
To take their place, and these are all things which
You'll carry written in your mind about
This great prince of Verona, but you can't
Speak of them yet." And then he spelled them out,
Things people will one day see, and yet shan't
Believe their eyes. And then he added: "Son,
These are expansions on the several hints
You've had about the things that will be done
To you in just a few short years, which, since
They haven't happened yet, are still, like snares,
Concealed where they lie waiting. And yet you
Should not, when you compare your fate with theirs,
Envy your neighbours. For the deeds they do
Their punishment will come, but far beyond
That date, your life will last." The holy soul
Fell silent, having said this to respond
To my entreaty. So it was made whole,
The woven cloth of which I'd set the weft:
He'd put the woof into the web. Now I
Began again—I still had one doubt left—

Seeking from him, that I'd been counselled by,
The benefit of how he saw, and willed
And loved, all rightly. "Father, I see well
How time, that wants my destiny fulfilled,
Digs in the spurs and heads for me pell-mell
To deal the blow which falls with greatest weight
On him who heeds least. All the better, then,
140 That I am given power to see my fate
So that, if I may not come home again,
I shan't lose other places by my songs.
Down through the world of endless bitterness
And on the fair hill where they purge their wrongs,
Up from the peak from which the eyes I bless
Of my dear lady lifted me to find
Light after light throughout these halls of good,
That journey forms a lesson in my mind
Which, should I tell it, would be sheer wormwood
150 To many. And if I prove, to the truth,
A timid friend, I fear to lose my name
Among all those who one day, in their youth,
Will call these old times." Bright light turned to flame.
Inside, the smiling treasure I had found:
Outside, a golden mirror in the blaze
Of sunlight, saying "Conscience, I'll be bound,
Shamed by its own or someone else's ways,
Indeed will find your words harsh. Still you must
Put lies aside and make your vision plain,
160 And let those scratch who have an itchy crust,
Since if your voice, at first taste, gives them pain,
Yet it will nourish when it's taken in.
For even as the wind, this cry of yours
Will strike the highest peaks, which is to win
No little honour. This has been the cause
That you've been shown, in these wheels here, and on
The mountain, and down in the woeful pit,
Only the souls that fame has fixed upon,

In order that the story you transmit
170   Will capture the attention of all those
Who recognise the names. For otherwise
They'd be shut out as if by doors that close
Ahead of them. The secret of surprise
Lies in a framework that we recognise."

CANTO 18

Already that blessed mirror, in his thoughts,
Rejoiced alone. I was still tasting mine,
Striving to balance their contesting sorts,
The bitter and the sweet, while the divine
Lady conducting me to God on high
Said "Think again. Remember I am near
The One that all wrongs are made weightless by."
My comfort's loving voice, love I could hear,
Caused me to turn, and then I saw her eyes:
10 Love I could see, but whose full force must rest
Untold for now, because its power defies
The saying of it. I can't pass the test
Of putting all that glory into speech,
And, also, memory jibs at the task
Of turning back beyond where it can reach
Without the One's help. It's too much to ask.
Yet, of that moment, this much I can tell:
I looked at her, and my heart was set free
Of all other desires. The light that fell
20 On her was the Eternal Joy. To me
It was reflected from her eyes so fair—
The Second Aspect of divinity,
It satisfied and overwhelmed me there
Through her smile. She said "Turn and listen now,

For Paradise is not just in my gaze."
And as sometimes a human face shows how
The soul is seized by an emotion's blaze,
Just so, in that burst of the holy fire
The sacred furnace towards which I turned,
30 I recognised the signs of his desire
To speak to me of more I'd not yet learned.
He spoke thus: "Here the tree, in its fifth hall—
The tree that lives top down, always in fruit,
Never to shed its leaves—is home to all
Those souls whose living fame was so acute
Before they came up here, poets grew rich
In praise from praising them. Regard, therefore,
The cross's arms, and note the speed with which,
When I name names, each one will travel more
40 Swiftly than lightning through a cloud." A light
Flashed through the cross to beat the spoken sound
Of Joshua's name. Sound yielded to the sight
Of Maccabeus, brightly spinning round
While flying, like a child's top whipped by joy.
Charlemagne and Roland drew my focused glance
Like falcons in their flight. Next to employ
That path across the cross came, not by chance,
William and Renouard, who both once slew
The Saracen, though Renouard was born
50 A Saracen himself. Duke Godfrey flew
The same route, the crusader who had worn
A king's crown in Jerusalem. There, too,
Was Robert Guiscard, founder of the line
Of Normans in our south. These were the knights
Of Christian battle whose brave names still shine
For us today. And now, among their lights,
Shone Cacciaguida, who had said such things
To me, and now had gone to show his skill
At singing, there where everybody sings,
60 In that realm. On my right hand, Beatrice still

Stood waiting to say what my duties were
By word and sign. I saw her eyes so glad
And clear that her whole aspect spoke for her
Of even more delight now than she had
Displayed at any time, even the last,
And as a man delights in doing good,
Aware each day that this day has surpassed
The day before in virtue, so I could
Be certain, when I saw that miracle
70   More fair than ever, that my circling route
Around the heavens had become more full,
The radius making radiance more acute.
Just such a change as strikes the pale white face
Of a woman set free from a weight of shame
Now struck my eyes, as I took up my place
Inside the white light of the temperate flame
Of Jupiter, the sixth star. I saw there,
In Jove's torch, the bright sparkle of the love
Consigned to trace our speech in vivid air
80   To our eyes, and, as birds that rise above
The river bank, well pleased at how they fed,
Are now a round flock, now some other form,
Just so those holy souls by song were led
Within their lights, shaping their shining swarm,
Each one so quick and vivid on its own,
To various figures as they flew, now D,
Now I, now L. First, singing each alone,
They sang their own notes. When combined to be
One of these shapes, however, then they paused
90   In silence. Ah, divine Calliope,
Muse-child of Pegasus, you that have caused
Glory in genius, as it has done
To cities and whole kingdoms, give me aid
With your light so that I may, one by one,
Describe these several figures as I made
Them out. For these lines, give me all you've got.

In five times seven verbs and consonants
They showed themselves. I noted all, and what
They seemed to mean as they combined to dance.
100 "Love justice" said the first words of the lot
(In Latin: I translate) that met my glance,
And "you that judge at home" was the last bold
Phrase written. In the fifth word shone an *m*
And it was silver all pricked out with gold,
And to the summit of this precious gem
Descended other lights, all it could hold,
And they sang of the Good attracting them
Into itself. Then, as rich sparks arise
In myriads when burning logs are struck—
110 Prompting crass auguries from the unwise—
So countless lights appeared to come unstuck
From there and float up, some the more, some less,
According to the impulse of the sun
That kindled them in this way to express
Its love, and when the whole design was done
With each spark settled, then I saw the head
And neck of a great eagle, all picked out
In fire. He that designs this can't be said
To have a guide. He guides. We look about
120 And see a bird's nest, and we know the force
That formed it is from Him. And now the rest
Of those blessed souls, which seemed to be on course
To gild a lily on the *M*, digressed—
Forgetting France or Florence as a source
Of empire, finding Rome was still the best—
And joined their friends in the heraldic scheme.
Sweet star, how many and how bright the jewels
Making it plain to me that all we deem
As earthly justice with its written rules
130 Is Heaven's work, the sky in which you gleam!
Therefore I pray the Mind in which begin
Your movement and your power, that it regard

The place in Rome that makes the smoke wherein
Your beam is dimmed. High time to crack down hard
Once more on trade within the temple walls,
Put there by miracle and martyrdom.
Sky armies upon whom my vision falls,
Pray now for those on Earth, distracted from
The truth by ill example! Once it was
140   The custom to make war with swords, but now
It's done by holding back the bread because
The ones denied that nourishment see how
It can be had again for coin, although
Sweet God decreed that none should be deprived
Of sacraments. But you that traffic so,
Giovanni, you that, grasping, have contrived
To sell indulgences for ready cash,
Take thought of Peter and of Paul, who died
To plant the vineyard that you turn to trash:
150   They are alive. You might say, in your pride,
"I know them not, for I have set my mind
On him who lived alone till Salome
Danced him to bloody death, and whom you'll find
Depicted on the florin. That's the way
Ahead for me, and for the Church today."

CANTO 19

With open wings, the lovely image reared
Before me: those collected spirits, glad
In sweet fruition. Each of them appeared
To be a little ruby the sun had
Instilled with such a flame the light was thrown
Back to my eyes. And all that I have now
To tell, was never yet by tongue made known,
Nor put in ink. No fancy has known how
Even to think of it. I saw and heard
10   The beak talk, saying "I" and "mine" for "we"
And "ours," so lending one voice to each word.
"For being pure and kind I come to be
Exalted here to glory unsurpassed
By any worldly wish, and on the earth
I left behind, such memories now last
That even wicked men concede the worth
Of what I did, though they don't do the same."
In just the way we feel a single glow
From many brands, out of that image came
20   A single sound that many loves made so.
And then I: "Everlasting flowers of bliss
Eternal, who make all your perfumes seem
To me but one, when you breathe forth like this
You save me from the fast no feasts redeem

On Earth, of which my hunger was the proof.
I know that though a mirror for Divine
Justice takes fire beneath another roof
Of Heaven, none the less you see it shine
Without a veil. You must know how intent
30 I am on listening: you know the doubt
I hungered from so long, and what it meant."
Just as the falcon moves its head about,
Freed from its hood, and once more flaps its wings
To show how keen it is, and dips its beak
To preen its feathers, so I saw these things
Echoed by that sign getting set to speak,
Combining all the songs that those up there
Rejoice in. "He that compassed all the bounds
Of this world—and, in it, made some things bare
40 To sight and others hid, so it astounds
With its variety—could not impress
His Power thus throughout the universe
Without his Word, in infinite excess,
Remaining, and this truth we can rehearse
By thinking of the fate of Lucifer,
That first proud spirit, highest of the high,
And how, before his ripeness could occur,
He fell the day he could no longer fly,
Because he had not waited for the light,
50 The Word of God. From which it follows, all
The lesser natures at a lower height
Are too slight vessels for the flood we call
The Good, which has no limits we can find,
And only by itself is measured. Thus
Our vision is but one ray of the Mind
That fills all things, and it is not for us
To blink the fact that our sight's origin
Lies far beyond the furthest we can see,
And so the power of eyesight working in
60 Your world may pierce the sheer infinity

Of Everlasting Justice only as
The eye into the sea, whose bottom shows
Near shore, but in the open deep it has
No bottom to be seen, though the mind knows
Depth has concealed the truth. All light must come
From clear unclouded sky. Else, darkness reigns,
The shadow of the flesh, which is the sum
Of all its sensual errors and dark stains.
But now the place is opened up to you
70 Which hid the Living Justice you have sought
So often, saying 'What good does it do
For some man born in India who's taught
Nothing of Christ by speech or text, and yet
All his desires and deeds, with virtue filled,
In life or speech show nothing to upset
Our human reason. With not one sin willed,
Outside the faith and unbaptized he dies.
Where is the justice that condemns him? Where
Is this man's fault?' But who are you, whose eyes
80 Would judge across a thousand miles of air
From your small bench with short sight? Yes, we could
Dispute the issue, you and I, and were
No scriptures set above you, then there would
Be ample room to cavil and demur,
As if your questions counted. Clods of earth!
Mud brains! Nothing can move the Primal Will.
Good is itself, draws from itself all worth:
Whatever meets that mark can do no ill
And must be just. And no good that is made
90 Can draw it in, because its blazing rays
Create that good as well, and are displayed
In all it makes, and all that meets our gaze."
Just like the circling stork above the nest
Where she has fed her young, and the one fed
Looks up to her, so I below the blessed
And lofty image as its bright wings, led

By many counsels, moved to make it wheel.
It sang, then spoke to me. "The notes I sing
That you can't follow but whose truth you feel,

100   Show you the Holy Word is everything,
To mortals, that they cannot comprehend
About Eternal Judgement." Then they paused,

Those scintillating fires without an end,
Sparks of the Holy Ghost, the sign that caused
The world to hail the Romans still their frame—

Which then began again. "None ever rose
To this realm who did not revere the name
Of Christ, either before the doom He chose

Or after it. The tree, the nails, the death:
110   These they believed. But some who cry Christ! Christ!
Will be less near to Him at their last breath

Than many others who do not know Christ.
Even the Ethiope shall then condemn
Such false Christians, when those two companies

Are parted so there's no more joining them,
The rich and poor, forever. Infamies
Of your kings will be in the open book.

What will the Persians say when they see writ,
Among the deeds of Albert, how he took
120   The realm of Prague from Wenceslas, and it

Was ruined? And the misery shall be seen
Brought to the Seine by Philip when he tore
The value from the coin, stripping it clean

Of worth, and he himself killed by a boar
He hunted. Also will be seen the pride
That maddens men with thirst, so that the Scot

And Englishman can't keep to their own side
Of the drawn line, but think that what they've got
Is nothing without what the other holds.

130   And it will show the way the King of Spain
Was lost to lust and luxury's soft folds,
And that Bohemia shrank from the reign

Of one who knew no worth nor sought it out.
And crippled Charles of Anjou, for his one
Real virtue, liberality, no doubt
Will get a mark, but the evils he has done
A thousand marks. The avarice of him
In Sicily, and also his faint heart,
Will there be shown in words no eye can skim,
140 For they will be abbreviated, part
Serving for whole, so as to fit the news
In a small space. And all the dreadful deeds
Of that same Frederick's uncle will accuse
Themselves in that book, for whoever reads.
His brother, too, will be accounted for:
A pack by whom a noble lineage
Has been dragged through the mud, and what is more—
And here alone is text for a whole page—
Two crowns have been besmirched. And Portugal
150 And Norway too will have kings named. And he
Of Serbia, who forged the means to call
A lead plug a Venetian ducat. We
May cry 'Ah, happy Hungary!' now that
No longer she connives at her own wrong.
Happy Navarre, were she not aiming at
Abject surrender to the siren song
Of a dynastic marriage. Let her trust
In her surrounding mountains, and be warned
By Cyprus, whose twin cities sadly must
160 Live with the loose French ruler they once scorned—
And pray for a new day, which has not dawned."

CANTO 20

When he that lights the whole world sinks from sight
Out of our hemisphere, so that the day
Is spent on all sides, sky concedes to night—
Sky that was lit by him alone gives way
To many lights, all shining with his light.
This scattering in the sky came to my mind
When the world's flag, and flag of all its kings,
Fell silent in its beak, for me to find
That all its shining points, those living things,
Shone still more brightly, and a river flowed
Of songs I cannot now recall. Sweet love
Mantled in smiles, how brilliantly you showed
Yourself in those flutes as they soared above,
Filled with the breath of holy thoughts that glowed!
After the lucid, precious gems with which
The sixth realm was bejewelled had chimed their last,
I seemed to hear a mountain streamlet switch
Its murmuring path from rock to rock, not fast
But falling, softly, proving full the source
It came from, high up; and as sound takes form
At the lute's frets, and as breath shapes its force
At the pipe's vent, so, rising through the swarm
Of lights that made the neck, the murmur welled
As if the throat were hollow. I was kept

Waiting no longer. Clear words were expelled,
Awaited words. Out of the beak they swept,
These words that I'd longed for, and now wrote down.
"That part with which a mortal eagle sees
And turns towards the sun without a frown,
Watch now in me. From fires of all degrees
My shape is made, and those that make the eye
That sparkles in my head outrank the rest.
The one the shining pupil is made by
Is he who brought the ark home like a guest
While always singing of the Holy Ghost.
Now David knows the burden of that song,
As he conceived it, was no idle boast,
Because the recompense is rich and long
For his wise counsel. Of the five who make
My eyebrow's arch, the nearest to my beak
Is Trajan, who joined in the widow's wake
For her son. Now he knows how life is bleak
Without Christ, for he's seen the difference,
Having been pagan once, and later saved.
Next on the upward curve of eminence
Above my eye, Hezekiah shines, who craved
More time, and his repentance helped him there,
For what he asked Isaiah he obtained—
A long life, and now life beyond compare.
And next comes Constantine, the one that reigned
In Rome, and who meant well by moving east
And turning Greek with me and all the laws,
And one good thing came out of it at least:
There was no harm for him, although his cause,
That made the Pope a king, only increased
The chaos in the world. His crop we reap.
William you see next on the downward curve,
For whom now Sicily and Naples weep,
As living Charles and Frederick show they serve
Themselves: but how the power of love runs deep

Up here for the just king, is proved to us
By his face spilling fire. Who would have guessed,
In the erring world below, that Ripheus
Of Troy would be the fifth light in this crest?
The sea of Grace the world finds a deep thing
He sees through now, though not down the whole way."
Just as the soaring lark at first will sing
And then fall silent, by its latest play
Of sweetness satisfied, that image seemed
70   To me. It was the imprint of the Will
Of the Eternal Pleasure, which has deemed
That all which was, and is, and will be still,
Might be. As glass is to its coloured coat
I was to my perplexity, and yet
My question would not wait to play a note,
But weight and pressure forced it from the set
Of my lips. "How can these things be?" I said,
And then I saw a sudden festival
Of lights, and then the bright eye in its head
80   Flashed still more, as the sign replied, lest all
My stunned suspense continue. "If you think
These things are true because I say them, yet
You can't see how they can be, so they sink
From sight although believed, then all you get
From anything is just its name: the pith
Of that thing is withheld from you, unless
It's all set out for you to conjure with.
For Heaven's Kingdom suffers, and will bless,
Violence of vivid love and hope on fire,
90   Which conquer the Divine Will not as man
May conquer man, but out of its desire
Thus to be conquered, and because its plan
Is conquest through its goodness. Yes, the first
And fifth stars of my eyebrow puzzle you
To see the realm of angels thus imbursed.
But here and now you should revise your view

That they were unbelievers when they left
Their bodies. They were Christians, of firm faith,
One that the dear Feet would be nailed and cleft,
The other that they were. Trajan, a wraith,
Came out of Hell to find his bones again,
And since none there are saved by willing good,
This was the prize for that saint among men,
Pope Gregory, whose prayers were understood
And helped by God, so that one damned might then
Be raised to where his will could be so moved.
This glorious soul, returned thus to the flesh
For a short time, believed in Him that proved
Able to intercede. Love flared afresh
From that belief. The emperor lived to face
His next death, and came here to us. And now
Regard the Trojan, saved by God's good grace
Whose fountain goes so deep no one knows how
To see down to its wellspring, its first place,
And yet he came to love the right, his eyes
Opened by God from grace to grace, to our
Future Redemption. Truth that never dies
He found, and so, believing in its power,
He spurned the stench of paganism from
That day, scolding the people in its spell
For their perversity. His baptism
A thousand years too soon? That task befell
Three ladies you saw near the gospel car
At its right wheel: Faith, Hope and Love. Your root,
Predestination, how it stands so far
From that gaze—gaze no matter how acute—
Which sees in parts but can't see how they are
United in the First Cause! Mortals, be
Restrained in judging. We, who see God, know
Not all of the elect as yet, and we
Find the lack sweet, our good perfected so
By His. We will what God wills, willingly."

Thus from the image I got medicine
Sweetly to clear the shortness of my view,
And as a good guitarist will bring in
The notes of trembling strings to make more true
The singer's melody, whereby the song
Grows sweeter still, so, while it spoke, the paired
Exalted lights kept time and played along,
140 Like eyes that blinked together and then flared
Their little flames, moved by the words they shared.

CANTO 21

Already with my eyes fixed on her face
Again—and, with my eyes, my mind,
Which had no thoughts of any other place—
My lady did not smile, but, to be kind,
She said, "Were I to smile, you would become
Like Semele when she was turned to ash
By Jupiter, her lover, in his sum
Of splendour unadorned. It would be rash:
My beauty, which you've seen increase the higher
10   We climb together on the lofty stairs
Of this eternal palace, is a fire
So brilliant that the strength your body bears
Would be, if mine were not restrained, a bough
Split by a thunderbolt. Here we arise
To Saturn, seventh splendour, which is now
Close under Leo's burning breast, a guise
In which the planet sends down mingled rays
With extra powers. So now, behind your eyes,
Let your mind make them mirrors for the blaze
20   Of that shape which will now appear to you."
Great was the joy I took from seeing her,
But when she made me look at something new
The joy was greater still: I could defer
To her desires and could remember too

I had beheld her, so the scale-pans were
Poised in the balance. Bearing the great name
Of that chief who killed off all wickedness
In Crete, and gave the Golden Age its fame,
The crystal Saturn ringed the world. No less
30 Than gold in sunlight flashed a ladder there,
Rising so far its top rungs fled my sight.
Descending it were splendours past compare
And so past counting I thought every light
In heaven had been poured out through the air:
And as the jackdaws, when they rise at dawn
Together, by their natural habit sent
To warm cold feathers, split up, with some drawn
Away not to return from where they went,
And some turn back to where they started from,
40 And some stay wheeling, so it seemed to me
Such movements took place in the maelstrom
Of lights arriving scintillatingly
On any given step. The one that paused
Closest to us became so bright, I said
In my mind: "I see well what love has caused
Your signal." But from her by whom I'm led
To speak or else keep silent, there came not
A word, so that, against my will, I made
No query. She, aware the cat had got
50 My tongue because I'd seen One who displayed
The signs of seeing everything, spoke thus:
"Now satisfy your keen desire." And I:
"I'm far from being meritorious
Enough to hear your answer, but I'll try—
For her sake who grants me the leave to ask
The question—to be worthy in the way
I frame it. Let due reverence be my task.
Blessed living soul, still hidden in the spray
Of light which is your happiness, what brings
60 You near me, and how is it, in this wheel,

Heaven's sweet symphony no longer sings,
Which filled the air with such divine appeal
In all the wheels below?" "The way you hear,"
He said, "is, like the way you see, earthbound.
If you, a mortal, were touched by the sheer
Perfection of the music, then the sound
Would do to you what one look at a smile
From Beatrice would. Therefore I have come down
The sacred staircase for a little while
70   And just this far, still mantled in my gown
Of light, to welcome you with naught but speech.
Nor was it greater love that sped me on
(For just such love and more is felt by each
And all of those above me: look upon
Their flames) but the high Charity which makes
Us prompt in service of the Counsel's will
That makes the world, and freely gives and takes,
As you can see." This while I looked my fill.
"I see indeed," I said, "my sacred lamp.
80   I see how love, set free, serves in this court
For the fulfilment and the final stamp
Of the Eternal Providence. One thought,
However, still confounds me. Why you? How
Were you cut out, to get this labour done,
From all your fellows?" I can see it now:
The speed with which, before I'd said those last
Words of my speech, the light began to spin,
Its axis the smooth axle of a fast
Mill wheel. And then the love that was within
90   Replied. "Focused on me, a light divine
Pierces this glow in which I am encased.
Its virtue, joined to what I may call mine
Of vision, raises me, from where I'm placed,
So far above myself that the Supreme
Essence I see from where it emanates.
From this the joy that forms my fiery beam,

Since to my sight, by perfect estimates
Of clear view, I make that of my own flame.
But not a soul in Heaven, even the most
Alight—no seraph, of whatever name—
Whose eye, of all the highest heavenly host
Is closest fixed on God, will satisfy
Your question. What you ask is far removed
In those high depths of the abyssal sky
Where the Eternal Ordinance has proved
Itself cut off from every vision which
Had been created. In the mortal world,
When you return, make your recounting rich
With this news, so men may no more be hurled
Into futility by setting foot
On such a path, to such an end. The mind
Which shines here, smokes on Earth, and therefore put
Your thoughts to just how, down there, it may find
The means by which it ever could achieve
That which it can't up here." Checked by his words
That scorned a subject it was time to leave,
I only asked him who he was. "The birds
Can't soar to where I came from. Thunder claps
Below. Quite near your birthplace, plumb between
The shores of Italy, a ridge-line caps
The range with crags sharp as you've never seen.
That's Catria. There in the Apennines,
Beneath the ridge, a hermitage once was
To worship, in all true forms and designs,
Entirely given, praise its only cause."
So he began again for the third time.
Then more: "There I became, seeing the Lord,
So constant, that with thoughts on the sublime,
I passed through heat and frost, my bed and board
Poor stuff, thin scraps eked out with oil
Of olives. Yet I was content. The yield
Of prayer to Heaven from that spot of soil—

A cloister doing duty for a field—
Once ached for harvest. But it now lies waste:
Soon everyone will know. My name when there
Was Peter Damian, and when displaced
And made a cardinal, shame and despair
Led me to give myself another style:
Peter the Sinner, for my lasting care
140 Was purity, and power made it vile.
Corruption ruled us even as we reigned
On our high chairs, low down and out of touch
With those dear peaks which in my mind remained
The fortress of frugality. Not much
Of mortal life was left to me when they,
There in Ravenna, dragged me to that hat
Which gets passed on in a progressive way—
From bad to worse. By now we're used to that.
There was a time when Peter and Paul both
150 Were hard and barefoot, eating humble food
At ordinary inns, and nothing loth:
But modern shepherds find such rigour crude.
A pope now needs a man each side to prop
Him up, and one before to clear his trail,
With one behind his awesome bulk to stop
His train from dragging. If his legs should fail
To hold him up, he rides: his cloak will flop
Around two beasts with one skin. Patience, can
You stand all this?" And at his cry, I saw
160 More little flames come down as they began,
Wheeling, from step to step, and they were more
Lovely with every spin. They swarmed around
His light, and stopped, and then they cried aloud:
So loudly that down there on our home ground
Nothing could equal it, a shouting cloud
Of clear lights, and I couldn't understand—
By such sweet thunder deafened and unmanned.

CANTO 22

Still stunned, I turned back to my guide, just as
A child, when scared, will run back to the place
Where confidence resides, the voice that has
The gift of reassurance, the one face
Of comfort for a pale and breathless boy—
His mother. She said "How can you not tell
You are in holy Heaven? All the joy,
All that is done here comes from the true well
Of zeal, and so you've seen the truth appear
Of how that song, and my smile, would have stirred
Your brains, because the truth was in that cry
Which so much moved you, and if you had heard
And understood the prayers within it, why,
You'd know already how the prelates will
Suffer a fate you'll see before you die.
Up here, God's vengeful sword does not fulfil
Its task too early or too late, except
As it might seem to him who, with desire
Or fear, awaits the blow, the promise kept.
But turn now to the others in the choir
That raised the shout, and if you aim your gaze
As I say, countless spirits you will see."
I did her bidding and I saw the rays,
Criss-crossing, of a multiplicity

Of little spheres, a hundred of them, all
Made still more beautiful by their shared beams—
A light-stream interplay, a mirror hall
For fireflies. I stood as one who deems
The prick of wishing must be checked, for fear
30 He'll seem presumptuous if he should pose
A question. So it was that there drew near
The largest and most lustrous of all those
Shivering pearls, intent that I should hear
My inner question answered. Then the light
Unfolded its own nature from within.
"If you could only share my power of sight
You'd see the love we burn in, and begin
To say what's on your mind, but since you might
Be slowed down on your high path if you wait,
40 I'll answer now the thought you closely guard.
The mountain where Cassino has its gate
Was once thronged, on its summit high and hard,
By people both deluded and deceived,
And I was first to bring the name up there
Of Him who brought to Earth, to be believed,
The truth that sublimates us; and so fair
A grace shone down upon me that I drew
The nearby towns away from their old cult
Of worshipping Apollo as the true
50 And only God, in which they would exult
As once the whole world did. These other flames
Were all contemplatives, fired by that heat
That brings forth holy flowers and fruit. Their names?
Macarius, and all my brothers. Meet
The ones who kept their feet and steadfast hearts
Within the cloister." I to him: "You've shown
Affection in your speech, and all the arts
Of kindness, and your fires reflect your tone.
My confidence expands just as the sun
60 Unfolds the rose into its fullest bloom.

And so I ask you—if it may be done
To grant the gift, and I do not assume
Too much in asking—that I may for one
Moment see you with face unveiled." And he:
"Brother, your high desire shall be fulfilled
Above in the last sphere: for you, and me,
The end point of all wishes. All are stilled,
Our long desires. They're perfect, ripe and whole.
Up there alone each part is what it was
70   Always, for that place turns around no pole:
It's not in space. You see, then, by what cause
Our ladder, going up to it, must climb
Out of your sight. Jacob the patriarch
Saw to the hidden top in the sublime
And saw it packed with angels. That high mark
None lifts a foot to reach now, and my Rule
Merely wastes paper. Those walls that were once
An abbey are now thieves' dens. A whole school
Of cowls are sacks of spoiled grain. Nothing affronts
80   God's pleasure—even usury at its worst—
So much as when the monks skim from the flow
Of income from the faithful. Such a thirst
Turns fruit to folly. Surely they must know
All the Church has belongs to those who seek
In God's name, not for kin or cronies. So
Soft is the flesh of mortals, and so weak,
A good beginning made below does not
Last from the oak's birth to the first acorn.
No silver and no gold had Peter got
90   When he began his order. Mine was born
With prayer and fasting. Francis founded his
With mere humility. And if you look
At what each was, and then at what it is—
Where it has strayed from its first open book—
You'll see white turning dark. Nevertheless
The Red Sea gaped, and Jordan was rolled back

By God's will to annul the helplessness
Of Israel's children on the long, hard track
That led to safety. Those were strange events
Down there, but here such succour's everywhere
And nothing marvellous. Common, in a sense."
Having thus spoken, Benedict left us there,
Withdrawing to his company, which drew
Together, pressing close. Then they were swept
Quickly above as if a whirlwind blew.
With just a sign, my dear sweet lady kept
Me climbing after them, so much her force
Conquered my nature, and here in the world
Where natural law will always take its course
To govern how we climb, none has been hurled
Aloft as I was, with so swift a flight.
Reader, as I hope one day to return
To that pure triumph for which, in the night,
I beat my breast until my knuckles burn
With sorrow for my sins, you could not snatch
The finger from the fire that you pushed in
More quickly than the sign that tries to catch
The Bull, which is the Twins—wherein begin
Learning and intellect—was there before
My eyes, and then around me. Stars in flame
With glory, light filled to its pregnant core
With power that drives what I have to my name
Of genius, with you the sun, each May,
Arises, father of each mortal born,
And so sets. Twins, it was when you held sway
That I first tasted the sweet Tuscan dawn,
And later on, when I was granted grace
To enter the high wheel that bears you round,
Your region was my designated place.
To you my soul now utters the profound
Sigh of devotion. May the strength be mine
To make the big step that I now must face

Of being drawn towards itself. The sign
Could not be more propitious. "You're so near
To final blessedness," Beatrice began,
"That you must have your eyes both keen and clear,
And so, before you go—and now you can—
Yet further into it, look down and see
How much already of the universe
Is underneath your feet, put there by me,
So that your heart be ready to disburse—
When you meet the Host Triumphant, finally—
Your full joy as it comes rejoicing through
This rounded ether." With my sight I went
Back down through all the seven spheres anew
And saw the globe, the start of my ascent,
And smiled at its pipsqueak significance.
Whoever has his mind on other things
Can be called just: it's scarcely worth a glance.
I call his judgement best who never clings
To its importance, rating it the least
Of realms. I saw the moon's clean other side:
Diana with her lovely glow increased,
Being without the shadow from which I'd
Believed her, once, to be both rare and dense.
I saw the Sun, son of Hyperion,
In full flame, unrelentingly intense,
And Maia's daughter, Mercury, sailed on;
And Venus, too, Dione's daughter, moved
Close to the sun. Their circles copied his.
All of the spheres were there. I saw it proved
From this, that Jupiter's condition is
Forever to create a tempered blend:
The heat of his son Mars mixed with the cold
Of Saturn, still his father. Without end
The seven change position as they hold
Their places. I could see this, and their size
And speed, and all their distances between

Each other. And this paltry world we prize,
170 This little threshing floor where we have been
Always so fierce, was made plain from its hills
To river mouths, while I was wheeling there
With those eternal Twins. They turned like mills,
And I with them, the universe laid bare.
And then my eyes met hers, my lady fair.

CANTO 23

Just as the bird that in the branches sings—
Branches she loves, the source of her delight,
The nest of her sweet brood with flightless wings
Where she has sat in vigil through the night
That hides things from us—stays put till time brings
The moment, blessed if only for their sake,
When, on the open spray, she'll once more see
Their longed-for looks, and find the food to make
Them grow, the work she welcomes heartily,
Singing, with all her wishes wide awake,
Until dawn breaks, just so my lady stood
Erect, alert, and turned towards that part,
The zenith, where the sun slows. Thus I could
See the suspense and longing in her heart,
And I became as one moved by desire,
Hope satisfied. But the interval was short
Between expectancy and the first fire
That set the sky alight beyond all thought:
First clear, then bright, then blazing. Beatrice said:
"Behold the hosts of Christ in triumph! Hail
The blessed, the fruit that has been harvested
From all the wheeling spheres which never fail
To give the striving soul its just reward!"
It seemed to me her face was all in flame,

Her eyes too full of gladness to afford
My words the chance to give her joy a name.
As, in clear nights that show us the full moon,
Diana smiles among the nymphs that dance
Forever, always decking, late and soon,
30 The sky through all its depths, just so my glance
Was drawn beyond a thousand lamps to meet
A sun which kindled all of them the way
Ours does with every pinpoint that might meet
Our eyes when we look up at the display
Of stars, and, streaming through the living light,
The vital substance which is Christ was more
Than my eyes—for it was so very bright—
Could bear. Ah, Beatrice! More now than before
My dear, sweet guide! "What overwhelms you now,"
40 She said, "is power beyond all defence.
Here is the might and wisdom that knew how
To open up the roads through the immense
Distance dividing Heaven from the Earth,
An age-old dream." As fire breaks from a cloud,
Swelling until it seeks a path for birth,
And falls towards the ground although endowed
Not with that nature, my mind, at that feast
Grown greater, left itself, and what became
Of it, it can't recall now in the least.
50 "Open your eyes and see me not in name
But as I am," she said. "You've gained the strength,
From what you've seen, to bear my smile." As he
Awaking from a dream may seek at length
In vain to recollect it, so with me,
Hearing this invitation. All the past
Is in a book, and how my thanks were great
Can never now, from this day to the last,
Be blotted out. Such was my blessed state,
If all the tongues that Polyhymnia
60 And her Muse sisters fed with milk so sweet

Should sound to aid me now, I would by far—
A thousandfold—fall short of means to meet
The truth in singing of the holy smile
And how that smile lit up the holy face,
And so, to picture heaven in fit style,
This sacred poem, as one leaps the place
That breaks one's path, must cease a little while
To match the facts. But he who gives due heed
To this theme's weight, the human shoulder frail
70 That's burdened with it like a trembling reed,
Will blame me less if I appear to fail.
No easy passage for a little barque,
This is a sea a daring prow must cleave,
Steered by a pilot who would make his mark
With no thought for his comfort, no reprieve.
"Why does my face beguile you," Beatrice said,
"So much you do not turn towards the fair
Garden that flowers in the sunrays shed
By Christ? You'll find his mother Mary there,
80 The Sacred Rose, the Holy Word made flesh.
There are the lilies, the apostles who
Gave out the fragrance that made sweet and fresh
The good path. This is what you're coming to."
She spoke, and I, so keen for her advice,
Struggled to fix my eyelids on the task,
Weak though they were. But it was worth the price.
As I once saw a field of flowers bask
In sunlight streaming through a broken cloud—
Saw them with shaded eyes—so now I saw
90 Whole hosts of splendour, crowd on sainted crowd,
Flash in the brilliant light that seemed to pour
From on high, though I couldn't see its source.
Ah, gracious might that sets your stamp upon
Them all, you climbed to grant scope by your force
To eyes that had no strength for you. As on
The very greatest of those fires I gazed—

Mary, I mean—the name of that fair flower
Which I invoke each morning to be praised,
And in the evening too, took all the power
Of my mind to behold it as it blazed,
And when I pictured the intense extent
And quality of that star in my eyes—
The star surpassing all those who were sent
To be up there, as she in worldly guise
Surpassed all those below—I saw a brand
Descend the sky, and, once it had come down,
Draw circles which I came to understand
As being in the likeness of a crown
Spun for her lovely head. Down here below,
Whatever melody, though it be sweet
Enough to draw the soul into its flow
And drown there with all earthly dreams complete,
Would seem, compared to that lyre's perfect sound
Like thunder in the clouds. But why compare?
This was the melody with which was crowned
The sapphire that made sapphire all the air,
The bright blue sky. "I spin angelic love
Around the joy supreme," sang Gabriel,
"Which breathes from that womb, seeded from above,
That sheltered what we all desired so well,
Both men and angels; and this I will do
Lady of Heaven, till you reach your Son,
Ascending in His path until you, too,
Are in the highest sphere. This will be done."
And so the circling song came to a close,
And all the other lights sang out as one
The name of Mary. Then, as she arose,
The royal cloak, the Primum Mobile,
The sphere that burns the most of any sphere
That spins around the world, was far away,
So far its inner rim did not appear
To my sight even yet—which is to say

The breath of God and His works, far from near,
Seemed nowhere—so I could not follow her
With my eyes as she soared towards the seed:
Her light-crowned flame had left us where we were.
Just as an infant, having slaked its need
For milk, still stretches out its little arms
To mother, while its inner impulse flares
140   To outward flame in its beseeching palms,
So these white radiant beings reached above
Themselves with all their fire, and it was plain
To me how each one felt the deepest love
For Mary as they sang the sweet refrain
Regina Coeli, Queen of Heaven. So
Sweet was their song that it is with me still
As always. Ah, how great the goodly store
In these rich gatherers! They had the will
To sow the seed when they were here before,
150   And there they live in all the wealth they earned,
Rejoicing in it, everything they won
With tears in their long exile, where they spurned
The gold of Babylon. Under the Son
Of God and Mary, Peter reigns in all
The triumph of his victory. The school
Of all the saints whose names we might recall
From either testament approves his rule,
Of which the keys to glory are the sign
His office is eternal and divine.

CANTO 24

Then Beatrice said: "O fellowship elect
To that great supper of the blessed Lamb
Who feeds you so that no desire is checked
But always satisfied, know that I am
In charge of this man who by God's grace has
Foretaste of that which from your table falls
Before the fatal time appointed as
His day of death. Give heed to how he calls
In hunger without measure. Give him dew,
10   If only a few drops, you that may drink
Deep from the fountain he aspires to,
That flow of which he cannot cease to think."
And then I saw the happy spirits flock
In circles on fixed poles, flaring as bright
As comets, and, as wheels inside a clock
Revolve so that it seems the first wheel might
Be stock-still while the last wheel seems to fly,
Just so these choirs at different speeds, some slow,
Some quick, expressed the same resolve that I
20   Should gauge the wealth that they had put on show.
And from the richest one, I saw shoot out
A fire so joyful that none other shone
More brightly, and it wheeled three times about
My Beatrice with a song—I can't go on—

Divine beyond what my words can evoke,
And so my pen lifts, all its powers gone,
And I write nothing suitable. This cloak
Had folds too subtle for my pigments. Bold
Colours cannot paint shades that lie within
30 The indentations fine draped cloth may hold,
And this flame's plainsong was no less rich in
Its intricacy. The song's words went so:
"My holy sister who has prayed to us
So piously, it's by the melting glow
Of your affection you detach me thus
From that fair circle." She then: "O
Eternal light of the great soul to whom
Our Lord entrusted the twin holy keys
Which he brought down to give us the full bloom
40 Of all this glad amazement, may it please
You now to test this man with points both light
And grave, as you see fit, pertaining to
The faith by which you walked, at your full height,
Upon the water. Whether his love is true
And whether his hopes and his beliefs are right—
These outcomes have all been foretold by you,
There where all things are seen depicted. Yet,
Since in this kingdom citizens are made
By the true faith, let's try not to forget
50 The higher justice stands to be betrayed
Should he not speak of this faith, which will be,
By his words, glorified." In the same way
The bachelor, when seeking a degree
By *viva voce*, guards what he will say
Until the master puts the question he
Will argue but not settle, so I armed
Myself with all my reasons while she spoke,
To be prepared and therefore less alarmed
By such a questioner, and not to choke
60 Through awe of his profession. "Christian, speak.

Declare yourself, and tell me what faith is."
At this I lifted up my brow to seek
The light which breathed these sudden words of his,
Then turned to Beatrice, who quickly signed
To me with one look that I should present
The waters of my spring. "May I now find,"
I said, "The proper words of argument
To fit my thoughts, by that same grace that grants
Me leave to make confession to the Chief
70 Centurion, flag-bearer and first lance."
I went on: "As that pen of true belief
Held by your dearest saintly brother Paul
(He who helped you in choosing the right track
For Rome) once wrote, faith is the stuff of all
Things hoped for, and, of all things that we lack
The sight of, is the evidence: and this
I take to be its essence." Then I heard:
"You are correct in your analysis
If you grasp why Paul placed faith, the key word,
80 First among actual things and only next
Among the arguments." And I: "The deep
Occurrences, to me made a clear text
Up here, to eyes below so tightly keep
Their secrets, that belief alone suggests
They might exist. On that, high hope is based,
Which therefore, in the Scripture which attests
To it, takes substance. As we find it placed
In Testaments both Old and New, from those
We take belief, and from belief we must
90 Then reason, seeing no more. So I close
By saying that faith holds, in sacred trust,
The character of evidence." "Well done,"
I heard. "If all the doctrine there below
Were understood so well by everyone
Concerned, the sophists, proud of what they know,
Or think they know, would have less elbow room

For empty cleverness." Thus breathed the flame
Of kindled love. Then more: "We can assume
We have well weighed the coin that bears the name
100 Of faith, whose alloy, too, we have assayed.
Now tell me if you have it in your purse."
And I: "I have indeed, and it's high grade.
So bright and round that I, too, can be terse.
It's fresh out of the mint." And from the heart
Of that deep shining light came this: "This jewel,
Precious with every value in each part,
How did it get to you? Give me the rule."
And I: "The rain the Holy Spirit pours
In floods from those twin parchments Old and New:
110 It forms a syllogism which implores
Me always to believe, and so I do,
Since every other demonstration weighs
As nothing beside that one." He then: "Why
Do you hold what the Old and New Books say
For Holy Word that you cannot deny
Settles all arguments?" I: "For the way
The works that followed proved it to be fact:
The miracles, which nature could not make
With heated iron or struck anvil. Backed
120 By such great things, it could be no mistake."
And he: "Now tell me how you are assured
These works occurred. Surely the very thing
That must be proved is all that can afford
A proof for them." I said: "To this I bring
The words of Augustine, who said the world
Needed no miracle for it to be
Won to Christ's way, and from that fact unfurled
The greatest miracle we'll ever see,
Such that all others put together yield
130 Less than a hundredth part of it. For you
When you were poor and fasting, took the field
To sow the good vine, now degraded to

A thorn. But still with you the pact was sealed:
The written promise was proved true." That said,
The high and holy court, through every sphere,
Rang with the song that they sing overhead:
"We praise you, God." And then the Baron (here
I use the earthly title) who had brought
Me thus from branch to branch in my defence
140 Of how my deepest faith had formed my thought,
Began again: "God's grace, which, in a sense,
Is in love with your mind, has until now
Opened your lips in ways that I endorse,
But finally we reach the highest bough
Of this tree, the completion of the course:
What is it you believe? And tell me how
It came to you. Where from?" And I replied:
"O Holy Father, you that outstripped John,
Whose young feet got there first, to go inside
150 The sepulchre—because he waved you on,
You being senior—you ask the form,
The essence, of my willing faith. As well,
You ask the source of it." Then I grew warm
To that theme. "I've a simple truth to tell.
In one sole and eternal God I place
All my belief, the God who reigns unmoved,
Yet moving all of Heaven with the grace
Of His love and desire. The fact is proved
By physical and metaphysical
160 Proofs I possess, but also by the rain
Of truth that never falters in its fall,
Sent down to us, as spring showers to the grain,
Through Moses and the Prophets and the Psalms,
The Gospels and through you, the ones that wrote
The vital extra texts. His burning arms
Embraced you: you were holy. On a note
Less simple, but essential, I believe
In three eternal persons, and all these

One essence, three in one that interweave
170 Oneness with threeness so the whole agrees
With singular and plural, 'is' and 'are.'
Of this deep, sacred state of which I speak,
The teaching of the Gospel is by far
The stamp that never stops. There you may seek
The start and spark which broadens to a star
Shining within me." As a master hears
His servant out who has brought pleasant news,
Then, when he's fallen silent, gladly nears
The man and gives him the embrace we use
180 With friends, so now the apostolic light,
To which I'd spoken at his firm request,
Encircled me three times in joyful flight—
Because, having survived the spoken test,
I had no more to say, which pleased him best.

CANTO 25

If ever it should come to pass that my
Long sacred poem—to which Heaven and Earth
For many years, twisting my life awry,
Have set their hand—should prove its proper worth
And overcome the cruelty that keeps
Me far from the fair sheepfold of my birth
Where once I lay down as a new lamb sleeps,
Foe to the wolves that war upon it, then,
Clad in an older voice, a tougher fleece,
10   I'll come back as a poet. Once again,
Before that font where infants never cease
To come to be baptised, I, just as when
I took that sacrament, will take the crown
Of laurel. There I came into the faith
That makes souls known to God when He looks down,
And now, on that account, the shining wraith
Of Peter runs a circle of renown
Around my brow. At this, a light moved near
From that same circle out of which had come
20   The first fruit of the line Christ left us here
To reign as pope. My lady, brimming sum
Of gladness, said to me: "See, see! Behold
The Baron for whose grave, down there below,
Galicia is visited by bold

And hardy pilgrims." As the dove will show,
When it alights beside its mate, the love
It holds, and each will bill and coo and go
Circling round the other, so, above,
I saw two great and glorious princes wind
30 Around each other while both praised the feast
They shared up there. Their joy was unconfined,
But when their ceremony of greeting ceased
They both stopped just before me, in such flames
My sight turned blank. And smiling Beatrice said:
"Illustrious living soul, revered St. James,
Who wrote of how our royal chapel spread
Largesse below, make hope resound up here.
You can: for you exemplified it, all
Those times when Jesus showed he held most dear
40 The three of you. Sufficient to recall
That evening in Gethsemane, when you
And John, and Peter, were with Him." Whereat
The second fire said this: "Adjust your view
Upward. Stop looking at your shoes like that.
Take confidence, for all who climb this high
From mortal life are ripened by our rays."
Thus reassured, to those hills in the sky,
The two apostles, I addressed the gaze
They had weighed down before. The second light
50 Went on: "Our Emperor, in his Grace,
Wills that you come, before your fatal night,
To meet his noble cohorts face to face
In the inner chamber, so that, having seen
The truth of this court, you will gain in force
To spread abroad the one hope that can mean
True love below, and is its only source.
All the aforesaid being so, tell me
What hope is, how it blossomed in your mind,
And whence it came to you." But instantly
60 My lady Beatrice, infinitely kind,

Who trained the feathers of my wings to soar
So high, replied for me. "That's quickly done:
The Church in Arms has no child with a store
Of hope like his. It's written in the sun
That radiates through all our hosts. Therefore,
He comes from Egypt to Jerusalem,
To see the way it looks, before his war
Is finished. Two more points—and both of them
You raised, not for your own enlightenment,
But to find out how he will give report
That it is dear to you, this heaven-sent
Virtue of hope—for him, one would have thought,
Will easily be met, nor need he fear
To seem vainglorious. So, with God's Grace
His only help, he'll speak, and you will hear
His answers on these questions in each case."
Encouraged thus, I, like a pupil who
Answers his master, eager and prepared
To show he knows his subject through and through,
Said: "Hope. It is the expectation—spared
From all uncertainty, devoid of doubt—
Of future glory. From the Grace Divine
It springs, although that fact does not leave out
The merit of good works. Hope was made mine
Like light from many stars, but it was first
Distilled in my heart by the singing King
David, in holy numbers so well versed
Our Lord of Hosts appointed him to sing
As sovereign cantor. His divine song goes:
'In you, let them have hope that know your name,'
And this, in my faith, everybody knows.
He made the rain for us. You did the same,
In your Epistle. So I was fulfilled,
To rain your rain on all." I saw the flame
Flash while I spoke, its living heart instilled
With lightning, sudden and repeated. Then

70

80

90

It breathed: "The love, with which I still burn, for
The virtue that stayed with me even when
They put me to the sword, bids me breathe more
100 To you who so delight in it. Now tell
What hope has promised you." And I: "The new
And ancient scriptures set forth very well
The goal that all souls may look forward to
That He befriends. And here, are we not there?
Isaiah says that each, in his own land,
Will be twice clothed, in soul and body. Where
Is that but here? We see on every hand
This land is the sweet life, and if we care
To read your brother John, he tells us of
110 A white-robed multitude, the self-same sight
Made yet more definite." Then, from above,
As soon as I had finished, "That they might
Have hope in you" was heard, and all the choirs
Responded, and among them, one bright light
Shone out, and if the Crab contained such fires,
Winter would have a month without a night,
Lit by that jewel. And as a maiden, glad
To bless the bride, will rise and join the dance,
Not for the reputation to be had
120 Of lightness, but for honour, so my glance
Was caught by that great splendour which had grown
More bright, as it approached the two that wheeled
To that song, matching, to its lilting theme,
Their burning love. He joined them as they reeled,
Singing and dancing, and my lady gazed
Solely on them, a still and silent bride.
"This is the saint the Pelican once raised
Up to His breast to drink blood. The pierced side
Of Christ is that bird's bosom. This is John,
130 The one that was selected from the cross
So Mary's motherhood might yet go on,
With a new son to soothe her for her loss."

So much my lady said, but never moved
The focus of her gaze when she was done,
A fixed intensity already proved
Sufficiently before she had begun.
As one who strives to see—and strains his eyes
Until they lose the power of sight—the sun
When partly its light lives and partly dies
140 Through incomplete eclipse, so, while it spoke,
Had I become before that last fire. "Why
Submit your vision to this dazzling stroke,
Looking for what is not here in the sky
But in the earth, and is earth, and will stay,
With all the other bodies, earth until
Our number tallies, on the final day,
With the eternal aim? Search as you will,
Only two lights, Christ and his mother, wear
The double robe of soul and body still,
150 After ascending to the cloister. Bear
That message when you go back to your world."
And at these words the flaming circle fell
Silent, together with the sound that swirled
And mingled, given out by that sweet well
Of threefold breath. The same way, to avoid
Fatigue or danger, oars that, till then, struck
The water, will, the whistle once employed,
All stop at once. I could have cursed my luck
When, turning to the sight I so enjoyed,
160 My lady, I saw nothing, though I stood
Beside her, there where all things should be good.

CANTO 26

While I was still in fear from my lost sight,
The splendid flame which had extinguished it
Breathed some advice that kept me rapt. "You might,
Until your eyes recover from the fit
Induced by seeing me, find recompense
With speech. To start with, tell me of the aim
Your soul is set on. Be assured your sense
Of sight is just confused. That's not the same
As being ruined: for your lady, who

10   Guides you through Paradise, has in her look
The power of the hand the Lord sent to
The stricken Saul. One touch was all it took:
The hand of Ananias." I then: "May
Healing come soon or late as pleases her
Who brings it to the doors that were the way
She entered with the fire. And those doors were
My eyes: the fire, the one with which I burn
Always." The voice that saved me from my fear
Of sudden dazzle now spoke in its turn,

20   Thus prompting me to greet what I could hear
With further speech. "It's certain that you must
Sift with a finer sieve and say who trained
Your bow to this mark." I said: "Here I trust
The philosophic arguments ingrained

In me on Earth, and the authority
Sent down from here. It's fitting that such love
Should leave its imprint sharply edged on me,
Since good, just by the goodness it's made of,
Must kindle love as soon as it is known,
And all the more the more good it contains.
Towards that Essence, then, in which alone
Such irresistible advantage reigns,
That any good outside is just a glow
Spilled by its radiance, the mind is moved—
Solely by love, and nothing else we know—
Of anyone who sees the truth is proved
On which this logic rests. This argument
Was set forth beyond all doubt, to my mind,
By Aristotle. That was his intent
When he said that the heavens—where we find,
Of course, the angels of intelligence—
Were moved by primal love, or the First Cause,
To use his term. Just so, in congruence,
The truthful Author, God, who gave the laws
To Moses, spoke when of Himself He said
'I'll make you see all goodness.' And you, too,
Told me the same when, in your book, I read—
It's there in Chapter One—of what was true
From when the world was new: that it began
As one Word. A sublime announcement! More
Than any other forecast known to man
It told the world below what lay in store
Above: the holy mystery of this place."
I heard: "On grounds of human reason, then,
And all authorities that match its pace,
The highest of the loves instilled in men
Looks toward God. But are there other cords
That draw you to Him? Name me all the teeth
With which this love that hauls you heavenwards
Bites you." The holy aim at work beneath

These things Christ's Eagle said was not concealed
From me. Indeed, I marshalled from the start
The thoughts I guessed he wished to be revealed.
"All things," I said, "whose bite can draw the heart
To God, are unified within the field
Of what joins them. The world, and I, exist.
The death He bore that I might live. The hope
Of Heaven, which, the living facts insist,
Is shared by all believers. This whole scope
70 Of knowledge draws me safely from the sea
Of perverse love and brings me here to this,
The shore of true love and its equity,
The destination of a synthesis.
The Gardener Eternal has bedecked
His bowers with infinities of leaves.
I love them all, for what makes them connect:
The good He gives, the splendour it achieves."
As I fell silent, a great wave of song
Flooded the heaven, and my lady sang
80 The same sweet melody. She sang along
With all the others, and the welkin rang
To "Holy, holy, holy!" And as sleep
Is broken by a sharp light piercing through
Film after film because a spirit deep
Within the sense of sight will take its cue
To meet the impact, and the awakened one
Shrinks back from what he sees, so unaware
Is he, when the new vision has begun,
Of what it means, until, to help lay bare
90 The truth of it, his judgement comes back, so
The motes in my eyes were all chased away
By Beatrice with her radiance, whose flow
Travelled a thousand miles, and the array
Of lights was clear again, more than before.
I asked her in amazement how it was
The three lights there had been joined by one more.
"These rays," she answered, "are sent out because

The soul within, the first soul ever made
By the First Power, looks with love upon
His Maker." As a branch whose top is swayed
By a gust of wind, springs, when the gust is gone,
Upright again by natural force, so I,
While she was speaking, was at first amazed,
Then once again my confidence was high,
Spurred by the need to speak with which I blazed.
I said this: "You, the one fruit born full-grown
In ripeness, and of old the father to
All brides—each one of whom could be your own
Daughter or your son's wife—I beg of you
To speak with me. I ask with all respect.
You guess my wish. To have it sooner met,
I do not say it." Sometimes we detect
A hidden animal by how its fret
To move disturbs its wrappings. Light unchecked,
This primal soul showed through its coverings
How gladly it had come to gratify
My silent wish. It breathed the following things:
"Without your saying so, I can descry
Your wish more clearly than your own sight brings
Your utmost certainties to mind, for I
See it through God, the truthful mirror which
Reflects all else though not reflected by
A single thing that serves to make it rich.
You want to hear how much time I have shared
With God since He first put me in this place
Your lady brought you to, so well prepared
To see its splendour, by a steep staircase.
You want to know how long my eyes were bared
To its delight, and also the real spur
Of God's great wrath. What was it, the first sin?
What language did I shape and use? These were
Your thoughts, my son. Hear me as I begin
To answer them. The tasting of the tree
Was not, alone, the cause of my exile

For so long. No, we crossed a boundary
Of pride, for that fell serpent had the guile
To say: 'The day you eat this, you will be
Like Gods.' In that place where your lady went
For Virgil, I missed seeing the sun's trail
140 Forty-three hundred times after I spent
More than nine hundred years to see it sail
From point to point, lighting the Zodiac
In its due order, which can never fail
To be fulfilled, for always it comes back
While men can see. As for the tongue I spoke,
It died before the race of Nimrod gave
Their minds to the Babelic tower that broke:
A project no amount of hope could save,
For nothing human reason makes endures
150 Forever, since all human tastes must change
According to the stars. Nature ensures
That men shall speak, but neither is it strange
That how they speak will switch this way and that
As human pleasure—nature's gift—dictates.
Even before I went down to Hell's vat
Of pain, the Good Supreme that radiates
The endless joy that swathes me now was named,
On Earth, in several ways, and that was fit,
For human usage can no more be blamed
160 For changing than a leaf, which does not sit
Forever on its branch, but falls and grows
Again, another one to match the last.
In Eden, on the soaring mount that knows
No hindrance as it rises unsurpassed
Out of the sea, I lived, first pure and then
Ridden with guilt, from dawn till just past noon—
For seven hours. The very moment when
The sun changed quadrants—it was all too soon—
I left that garden, knowing shame and fear,
170 Then exile, death, and Hell. Now, I am here."

"Glory," all paradise began to sing,
"To Father, Son and Holy Ghost!" The sweet
Song held me spellbound. I saw everything
In all creation smile. My joy complete
Came into me by hearing and by sight.
The thrill! The gladness, more than I can say!
The life fulfilled with love, peace and delight!
The riches held secure and there to stay,
More than the soul could crave, try as it might!
Before me the four torches stood aflame.
The one that had come first grew still more bright,
Though in its aspect it became the same
As Jupiter would be if it and Mars
Were birds exchanging plumage. Providence,
Which here rules time and duty and the stars,
Reduced the holy chorus to silence
On every side, whereat I heard: "If I
Change colour, do not marvel. While I speak
You'll see them all do that, and here is why:
It is the way that shame will flood a cheek.
He that on Earth usurps my place, my place,
My place, which now is empty in the view
Of God's Son, turns my tomb to a disgrace,
A sewer of blood and muck, a comfort to

10

20

The twisted one who fell from here, and now,
Down there, lives well." I saw the colour of
The sunrise and the sunset clouds endow
With earthly red light all the world above,
And as a woman, chaste and self-assured
30 In virtue, hearing of another's fault,
Flushes with shame, so I saw my adored
Beatrice change semblance in the same assault
Of anger. Just so, all white light was spent,
I do believe, when Heaven looked down upon
The agony of the Omnipotent
And went into eclipse. Their joy was gone.
Peter continued, in an altered voice
To match his altered looks. "Our Holy Church,
The Bride of Christ, was nurtured in the choice
40 Of martyrdom by men who did not search
For gold. Linus and Cletus shed their tears
And blood to gain this life. And there were more—
Sixtus and Pius, in those early years,
Urban, Calixtus, all our noble store
Of saints—of whom none meant that there should sit,
On our successor's right hand, just one part
Of Christ's flock, or that he should find it fit
To place the rest, by his divisive art,
On his left hand, Guelph split from Ghibelline;
50 Nor that the keys that were consigned to me
Should be his battle standard, meant to mean
His war on the Colonna just might be
A holy one, though they were Christians all;
Nor that my head, carved on the papal seal,
Should lend prestige to an indulgence stall,
As if I gave men leave to cheat and steal—
For which I often turn red and flash fire.
From here above I see the ravening
Wolves dressed as shepherds hunt at their desire
60 Through all the pastures. Why, why do you cling

To sleep, dear heavenly defence? Two popes—
Clement of Gascony, John of Cahors—
Would drink our blood. Ah, founder of our hopes
And fair beginnings, tell me for what cause
You fall so far, to such a paltry end!
Yet Providence, which gave us Scipio
To conquer Hannibal and so extend
Rome's glory to the world, will soon, I know,
Bring help. And you, my son, when you return

70 To your mortality down there below,
Must tell them of the rage with which I burn.
I show it. So should you." Just as our air,
In winter, with the sun in Capricorn,
Is flaked with frozen vapours, so, up there,
I saw—but falling upwards—flakes adorn
The ether in their triumph, all of those
Who had been with us, and I watched them climb
Until the distance brought it to a close,
That sight, though I had watched them all the time,

80 And not once looked away. My lady, then,
Seeing me freed from gazing up, said "Cast
Your sight down, now. Look at your path again
And see how far you've travelled since the last
Time that you looked." I saw how, since then, I
Had moved through all the arc—Jerusalem
To Spain—swept by the stars of Gemini,
So there, beyond Cadiz, glittered the hem
Of ocean on which, sailing out to die,
Ulysses in his madness stitched his track,

90 And over there the sun had set on Crete,
Where Jupiter the bull took, on his back,
Europa as a burden fair and sweet.
All this I saw, and might have seen yet more,
But underneath my feet the sun did not
Stand still: across that little threshing floor
The eastern edge moved west, the bright and hot

Becoming dark and cool. The loving mind
That woos my lady always, without cease,
Was burning to have my eyes reassigned
100 Again to her, the object of release
For all my joy. If Nature ever made
In human flesh, or art in portraiture,
Baits for the eyes so that the mind be swayed
Until possessed, all those together were
As nothing when compared to the divine
Delight that shone upon me when I turned
To see her smiling face look into mine
With holy grace. The impulse that I earned
From that glance pulled me free from the fair nest
110 Of Leda, mother of the Twins, and sent
Me straight to where there spun, without arrest,
That heaven whose sheer speed is never spent,
The Crystalline, the sphere that sets the test
For all the others. High or low, its parts
Are so alike I couldn't tell which one
She chose to put me in, but with her arts
Of divination, how my thoughts had run
Was plain to her. With God's joy in her face
She smiled and spoke. "From here, the universe
120 Begins, unmoving only in this place,
The launching point from which the rays disperse
Of love, which the Divine Mind has instilled
Just here. Only from here the sweet rain falls
Of virtue. A still centre He has willed,
And light and love in circles He installs
Around it, as it does with lesser spheres,
But of this one sphere's girdling, only He
Is the Intelligence. The light, the years,
The spin of all the others come to be
130 By measure from this one, as two and five
Come out of ten, and how time has its roots
In this one's plot, and theirs can come alive

Only as leaves because it puts out shoots,
Might now be clear to you. Covetousness!
You plunge the mortals so deep that none has
The power to lift his drowned eyes. None the less,
Will blossoms within men, but even as
It does, like sound plums in unending rain,
They wither. Faith and innocence are found
140 Only in little children, and remain
Only while cheeks are bare. Both things are bound
To flee. For one who lisps may keep the fasts,
But when his tongue is free, eats everything
In any month: that first pledge never lasts.
Another, lisping too, will gladly bring
Love to his mother, lend her views respect,
But when his speech is perfect he will ache
To see her buried. Just so, the unflecked
White skin of innocence is sure to take
150 A dark tone at the first sight of the sun's
Fair daughter Circe, she that represents
The pleasures of the world. Since no one runs
The Earth, to be astonished makes no sense:
The human family strays. But even though,
Because our calendar has made the year
Too long by an hour's quarter, as you know,
And January must gradually appear
A little later in the season, still,
Before it shifts completely—call the span
160 Less than a thousand years—for sure there will
Be such a shining on the world of man
From these realms on the heights, that the event
So long awaited must turn all the ships
From prow to stern, the fleet again be sent
On its true course, and flowers the bee sips
Will be succeeded by good fruit, as they
Should be. Not now, but soon. Somehow. Some day."

CANTO 28

The truth about the life poor mortals lead
Today, had been expounded by the one
Who turns my mind to paradise. I need
Say only how, after the thing was done,
I was like someone who, lit from behind,
Can see, before he thinks, a torch's flame
There in the mirror, and turns round to find
If glass tells truth, and finds both flames the same,
Agreeing with each other like a song
With its own measure. So, my memory
Records, I did then, gazing deep and long
Once more into the fair eyes that for me
Were love's noose, fashioned for my capture. Then
I turned again, and my eyes were met by
What must appear to the observer when
He looks hard at the spinning in the sky
Of this sphere. There I saw a point that so
Streamed sharp light that the eyes on which it burns
Must close, pierced by its force. No star we know,
Even the least from which our sight returns,
But would not seem a moon if put beside
That brilliant point like star with star combined.
And as a halo closely will abide
With that light which supplies it but refined

10

20

Through air most dense, so, maybe just as near,
About this point a fiery circle wheeled
So fast that even that most rapid sphere
Which girds the world would have been forced to yield
The palm for speed. The Primum Mobile,
30 I mean, was slow compared to this, and this
Was circled by another the same way,
And then both by a third. Analysis
Revealed a fourth and fifth, and then two more,
The seventh spreading so wide that Iris,
The rainbow, Juno's herald, would be sore
Put to contain it even if complete:
And then there were two more again. Yes, nine
All told, and each in movement the less fleet
The more removed it was, in this design,
40 From that first one, flame clear beyond compare,
Because, I thought, less distant from the pure
Initial spark, and thus with the best share
Of all the truth it held. Keen but unsure
I must have seemed, because my lady said:
"The heavens and all nature both depend
From that point. Know the inner ring is sped
So swiftly by the burning, without end,
Of love." And I said: "If the universe
Were set out in the order that these wheels
50 Conform to, then the clean match would disperse
My doubts about the scheme your speech reveals
As heavenly. But in the world of sense
We can't help seeing that the circles are
Always the more divine the further hence
From our own centre, set from near to far
The other way around. If my desire
May gain its end in this most wonderful
Temple of angels—love and light on fire
Its only bounds—then I must hear it all
60 About the reasons that the pattern and

Its copy do not follow the same plan,
Since by myself I strive to understand
Without result." My lady then began
"Nothing to wonder at, that such a knot
Defies your fingers, since it has grown hard
From being left alone." She went on: "What
I tell you about next in this regard
You should take, if you would be satisfied,
As whetstone for your wit. Material spheres
Are large and small according to the tide
Of virtue, as it spreads out and inheres
Through all their parts. An excellence more great
Makes greater blessedness, which in its turn
Must take a greater body if the state
Of all its parts—just look and you will learn—
Is equal in perfection. Thus we see
That this sphere, swept along with all the rest
Of what exists, responds in symmetry
At all points to the circle that loves best
And knows most. So if you apply your gauge
Not to the seeming, but the virtue, of
The spirits that you still think, at this stage,
Are circles, you will see how, here above,
Each heaven marvellously corresponds
With its Intelligence, the small with less,
The great with more, united by their bonds."
Just as the air is cleared of all distress,
Its vault serene and shining, by the breeze
From the northeast, as Boreas puffs his cheek
Most mild, and yet the thickest fog with ease
He thins and drives away, its grip grown weak,
Until the blue sky smiles on us again
With all its lovely pageant, so it was
With me, through what my lady granted then:
In heaven a star shone, and all because,
Her answer clear, the truth was plain. And when

She paused in speech, the circles sparkled just
As boiling iron sparkles, and each spark
Stayed with its fire. And at this point I must
100   Have recourse to the Persian patriarch
Of chess, who asked his king for pay in corn,
One grain for the first square, two for the next,
Four for the third. A hill of seed was born
From just one chessboard, and the king was vexed,
But all that mighty number would not meet
By many thousands this great multitude
Of lights. From choir to choir I heard the sweet
Hosanna sung to that fixed point, imbued
With power that holds them there, and always will,
110   Where they have always been. And she then said
(Aware that, deep down, I was wondering still),
"The first two circles showed you the life led
By Seraphim and Cherubim, held in
Their course by bonds of love, and therefore sped
Swiftly to all the likeness they can win
To that point. By the measure that their view
Exalts them, they do so. Beyond these rings
The spirits circle that are known to you
As Thrones of Sacred Aspect. By three things,
120   Therefore, the primal triad is made whole.
Know also that they all take great delight
In how their vision pierces to the soul
Of truth, in which all minds enjoy the right
To find rest. And from this it may be seen
That blessedness comes from the power of sight
And not of love, which follows. Here I mean
That merit, which goodwill and grace beget,
Measures their vision. That's the process, grade
By grade. The second triad to be set
130   And flower in this spring which has been made
Eternal, with no Ram at night to serve
Autumn and winter, sings without a pause

Hosanna, as three ranks pursue their curve
In bliss, and form the triad. By the laws
Of hierarchy the next orders come:
First the Dominions, then the Virtues, then
The Powers. Next to last in this great sum
Of circles—three times three, one less than ten,
And each one by the next in girth surpassed—
140 The Principalities revolve, ringed round
By the Archangels, and, not least, but last,
The Angels play their games on holy ground
Of open sky. And all the orders gaze
Above, and so prevail below, that all
Draw, and are drawn, to God. In early days,
When Paul still lived, I'm sure you will recall,
His convert Dionysius worked out
The plan in every detail, large and small,
With zeal presaging what I've talked about,
150 Though later Gregory thought otherwise,
And when he got here he was forced to smile
At what he'd said by that which met his eyes.
But if one mortal saw it well the while
He was on Earth, there's no cause for surprise,
For Paul had told him of it. Paul was here
Before his death, and saw all this and more
Of Heaven's truth, so he knew how to steer
The mind of Dionysius to shore
Across the sea of doubt. Now what Paul knew
160 While he yet breathed is known again, by you."

CANTO 29

When, at the time of our spring equinox,
The Sun, Apollo, rises in the Ram
And the Moon, Diana of the lovely locks,
Is sinking in the Scales—when, to the gram,
The two are balanced, so that each one wears
The world's horizon for a belt, both west
And east, loads that the zenith bears—
For just the time between that point of rest
And when the two of them change hemisphere,
10   Unbalanced from that girdle, Beatrice kept
Her silence, smiling with her face a sheer
Cascade of light, and on the point that swept
My senses from me, her own gaze was fixed.
"I tell," she said, "I don't ask, what you ache
To hear, for I can see it there unmixed
Where all dimensions meet with no mistake
And every time and place is centred. Wrong
To think that He might for Himself gain good:
That cannot be, in short term or in long.
20   Right, though, to think that His great splendour could
Shine back and say, from His eternity,
'I am.' Beyond time and all other bounds,
The everlasting love was pleased to be
Revealed as who He is, one who astounds

With all His new loves. Nor did He, before,
Lie still and sleeping, as we now might say.
'Before' and 'after' were mere words that bore
No meaning, not until He made our day,
Moving upon the waters. Substance, form,
Both separate and united, then could come
To life, three arrows flying in a swarm
From one bow with three strings: a life, in sum,
Without flaw. As a ray shines into glass,
Amber, or crystal so that from the time
Of its arrival no more time will pass
Before it is complete, just so the prime
Threefold creation happened in a flash,
Sent by its Lord in one burst with no sign
Of demarcation, one thing with no clash
Of lesser things or even their outline:
Whole from the start. And with that, there began
Order, the frame created and ordained
For all the angels, summit of the plan
Which is the universe. From them it gained
Pure Act, and the pure Potency was placed
Lowest, and in between these purities
The bond that knows no bounds was interspaced
To join them. Your Jerome wrote fantasies
About the course of ages that it took
To make the angels, the world not made yet:
But what I say comes from another book,
A truth on many pages firmly set
In writing by the scribes whose guiding voice
Outranks Jerome. I mean the Holy Ghost.
Just read it carefully and make your choice,
Helped by the written source that matters most,
Although your reason, too, to some extent
Should see it, for no logic can allow
The heavenly movers ever could be meant
To wait for their perfection. You know now

The where and when of their creation, and
On top of those two things you know the how:
The three flames of what you would understand
Are thus already spent. Then, sooner still
Than you might count to twenty, a small part
Of that angelic total took ill will
To your world, but the rest stayed with this art
That you see now, and circled in delight,
Never to leave. The signal for the fall?
70 The accursed pride of him who, in the night,
You saw imprisoned down there, crushed by all
The world's weights. But the angels you see here
Humbly acknowledged that they had been made
By Goodness, fit, in being kept so near,
To know so much, and to the highest grade
Their virtue was exalted by God's grace
And their own merit, so that they have full
And firm minds. Nor should you allow a place
For doubt, but be convinced, immovable,
80 On this point: it's a merit to receive
Such grace, by just as much as the heart stays
Open to let it in. Only believe
My words, and you're at liberty to gaze
Without my help on this community.
But since your schools on earth say that the sort
Of angels is to have a memory,
To understand and will—all this is taught—
I shall go on, that you might clearly see
The truth, which is, down there, so sadly fraught
90 With ambiguity. Not since the day
That they were made glad by God's face from which
Nothing is hidden, have they turned away
Their eyes from it, so nothing new is rich
Enough to reach their sight. They have no need
To recollect the past by any scheme
Of abstract thought. Down there where mere men breed

And die, while they're awake they only dream,
Believing they speak truth or that they lie,
But in that second thing's the greater blame
And shame. With no one path to codify
Your thinking, you get caught up in the game
Of showing off, and even this is borne,
Up here, with far less ire than when divine
Scripture is slighted or misread to spawn
Perversion. There is never any sign
Of thought among you of the blood it cost
To sow the world with it, or how he earns
Respect who comes to it with all pride lost.
Each flaunts originality, each burns
To put in something clever, gaily tossed
Into the text from which he never learns.
The price goes up when preachers add their share
Of footling comment, and the Gospel runs
A distant second, silent in despair.
One says that at Christ's agony, the sun's
Light was blocked out because the moon turned back,
And others say the light, all on its own,
Went into hiding, so the sky turned black
From one end to the other of the zone,
So Spaniards and Indians as well as Jews
Were in the dark. Florence has fewer boys
With names so many families seem to choose—
Lapo and Bindo—than these bags of noise
Proclaiming from their pulpits cocksure views—
Year in, year out, the pleasure never cloys—
To poor sheep who return from pasture fed
On pure wind. That they do not see their loss
Doesn't excuse the pundits peddling lead
For gold. Christ didn't say 'The crowd wants dross:
Spin them a line' to his first regiment.
He gave them a true basis. Nothing less
Was on their lips than gospel when they went

Into the world to battle faithlessness:
It was their shield and spear. But now they preach
With jokes and taunts, and if they get a laugh
Their cowls puff up, as if the stuff they teach
Were not just too much cleverness by half
But all that counts. They bask in the acclaim
And ask no more. The devil, that sleek crow,
140 Nests in the hood's tail to wrap up his fame,
Yet if the people saw him they would know
They're trusting in a swindle, from which such
Folly has grown on earth that they will flock
To any promise, and without so much
As one hint of a warrant. Thus the stock
Of hogs that were St. Anthony's wax fat,
Which once were sacred. Others more swinish still
Wax fatter. And the coin they pay for that
Is counterfeit: pardons exchanged for swill.
150 But we've digressed enough. Time for your eyes
To once more meet the straight road, so it may
Be shortened, with the time. Here in the skies,
These angels number, in their vast array,
Beyond what mortal thought can well devise
A figure for, or mortal speech can say,
For Daniel spoke of thousands but could not
Be definite: ten thousand squared, and then
That number cubed, and . . . he just meant a lot
More than the mind could hold. Unknown to men,
160 The sum is yours to see. The primal light
Irradiating all of them is caught
By them in many ways, in all the bright
Splendours from which that central blaze is wrought.
Therefore, since the affections follow on
From their conception, the initial act,
Love's sweetness, streaming from the paragon,
Shines variously in them, by that one fact
Impelled to all the numberless degrees

And kinds of brilliance, pinpoint strength unpacked
170 Into the myriad intensities
Of its expression. Look at how it glows,
The height, the width of the Eternal Good:
So many mirrors where it breaks and goes
On breaking, yet remains the one thing. Could
One and the many show more harmony?
It stuns you, doesn't it? It still stuns me."

CANTO 30

Six thousand long miles eastward it is noon.
Here, night is ending. The Earth's shadow lies
Level in bed, and in the mid-sky, soon,
Deep up above us, to our searching eyes,
A change will come: the odd star disappears,
The handmaid of the sun approaches. One
By one the sky's lights shut down as she nears,
Even the loveliest, and it is done:
The new day dawns. Exactly in that wise
10 The triumph that has always been at play
Around that point, and will be though time flies
Forever—the pure point that took away
My senses and which, to the reeling mind,
Includes that which includes it—bit by bit
Retreated from my sight, so, being blind
And full of love, there was no help for it:
I turned my eyes to her. If all I've said
Of Beatrice up to now were gathered in
One song of praise, it would be left for dead
20 By this task. I scarce know how to begin.
Not only is the beauty that I saw
Beyond our measures, but I do believe
Only its Maker can express the store
Of joy in it. For me, I can't conceive

The first phrase, and I must admit defeat.
Comic or tragic, poet never met
A point, in any theme he chose to treat,
More dizzying, for, as weak sight is set
Wavering by the sun, the memory
30   Of that sweet smile undoes my mind. In all
The time from that first day I came to see
Her face in life to this incredible
Moment of seeing her again, my song
Has gone on, but from now I must desist
From singing of the beauty that so long
Has drawn my verse, unable to resist,
Through many cantos, since the point must come,
For any artist, when his powers give out.
Therefore I leave her to a mightier sum
40   Of heraldry than mine: the final shout
Of my poor trumpet falters and falls dumb
As its hard theme comes winding to an end.
With voice and bearing of a patient guide
Whose work is done, no hard way left to wend,
She said "We have come through to the far side
Of Heaven's largest realm, to which you lend
The name of Primum Mobile, and here
We rise into a heaven of pure light—
Of intellectual light, light full of sheer
50   Pure love, love full of goodness true and right,
Love full of joy, joy so sweet as to shame
All other sweet things else. Here you will know
By sight, the holy soldiers that you name
Angels and saints, and those saints will be so
As they were in their lives, and thus the same
As they will be when you see them again
At the Last Judgement." Thus, exactly as
Our visual spirits are soon scattered when
A bolt of lightning strikes, because it has
60   Such power our power to see it is outrun

And even the clearest objects lose their place,
Just so a vivid fiery light was spun
Around me like a veil that made all space
Invisible to me, with every one
Of its particulars eclipsed. "The love
That calms this heaven," she continued, "will
Always so welcome one who comes above,
Preparing the cold candle thus to fill
Its cusp with flame." When these brief words arrived
In my mind, I was instantly aware
Of powers within me that had never thrived
So much, or so far risen through the air:
New powers of vision, such that there could be
No light, however strongly brought to bear,
My eyes could not have borne. And suddenly
I saw light with a river's form that poured
Its splendour in between two banks bedecked
With all the colours our spring days afford:
A marvellous spring, though one you might expect,
Except this living flood sent sparks abroad
To settle on the flowers of either bank
Like rubies set in gold. As if their heads
Were dizzy from the perfumes that they drank,
They rose again out of the flower beds
And plunged back, scintillating rank on rank,
Into the stream, to be replaced by more
That soared from the same ripples where they sank,
And so it all continued as before.
"The high desire," she said, "that flames within
Your mind to know just what is happening
Delights me more the more it swells to win
More space to burn. But now to the first thing
You need to do before you can begin
To slake your great thirst. First you have to drink
From that stream." Thus the sun who ruled my eyes
Addressed me, and continued: "Look and think:

The river and the topazes that rise
And fly from it and then return to sink,
And how the flowers laugh, are the forecast,
100 In shadow, of the truth. They don't fall short
Of being perfect. It is you, at last,
That has the defect. Still less than it ought
To be, your vision is outmatched as yet."
No infant that has slept too long could throw
Itself so suddenly, its sure aim set,
Towards the milk, as I, who thirsted so
To make of my eyes better mirrors still,
Bent down to where I saw the waters flow,
With all the sparkling interchange they spill,
110 For our perfecting. When my eyelids' eaves
Were wet, it seemed that instantly the stream
Transformed its length to roundness. What deceives,
Reveals, once done away with, how a dream
Holds more than we had thought. As people who,
Having worn masks, when they remove them seem
Not quite the same as those we thought we knew,
For me the sparks and flowers now had changed
Into a greater festival, in which
Both courts of Heaven clearly stood arranged.
120 Splendour of God that let me see the rich
High triumph of truth's kingdom, help me tell
Of what I saw! There is a light that spreads
So wide that its circumference would fall well
Outside the girdle of the sun. It sheds
The sight of their Creator, as He is,
On all whose peace depends on seeing Him,
For He is with them all, and they are His.
And all the flood of light within that rim
Is made by no more than a single ray
130 Reflected from, with all its wealth and force,
The summit of the Primum Mobile,
And as a hillside looks down to a course

Of water at its foot and sees itself,
Adorned with its spring flowers and its green grass,
Exactly pictured in that mirrored shelf,
I saw, above this light, one tier surpass
Another for a thousand tiers, and there
Were all of us who ever have returned
On high, and if the lowest level's share
140 Of incandescence that within it burned
Was so great, what could be the full extent
Of this rose in its furthest petals? Here
The breadth and length did not exhaust my glance,
Since there was no increase from being near
Or loss from being far, in this extent
And quality of joy. For where God's law
Directly rules His unmixed element,
The law of Nature can apply no more.
Into the yellow everlasting rose,
150 Rising and spreading in its serried ranks,
Exhaling heady perfumes that disclose
Praise to the sun, extending its deep thanks
For a perpetual spring, Beatrice drew me
As one who, silent, still would speak. "Behold!"
She said, "How great, how great the company
Of these white robes! See, see now and be told
How great the city! See our seats so filled
That few souls are still lacking. And in that
Great chair on which your eyes are held and stilled
160 By the crown poised over it, there will be sat—
Before you come to join the nuptial feast—
The soul of Henry, who shall be, below,
Made emperor, to get Italy released
From her wrong course, but she will be too slow
To heed him. Ah, too soon, too soon deceased,
Your one hope and the hopes of your fair land!
For your blind greed will only be increased,
Driving the Guelphs to take their senseless stand

And break his noble heart. Greed makes you like
170 The hungry infant who drives out his nurse,
For at that time a two-faced pope will strike
With his forked tongue. Yes, Clement, who will curse
Henry in secret while he speaks aloud
In praise of him. God will not suffer long
That pope in office. Mantled in a shroud,
He will go down to share the prize for wrong
With Simon Magus. A still deeper place
Awaits his predecessor, Boniface."

CANTO 31

The form, then, of the saintly host of Christ
Was shown to me as being a white rose,
A perfect rose which, with His own blood, Christ
Has made His bride. But also there are those—
The other host—who, flying, see and sing
The glory of the Lord who holds their love
And goodness that has made them everything
They are, and there they are, at large above.
Just like a swarm of bees that first will dive
10 Into the flowers and then go back to turn
Their toil to nectar, treasure of the hive,
These ones I watched—for I was here to learn—
Descend headlong into the mighty flower
Of many petals, and then re-ascend
To where the love abides in all its power
Forever, and then, flying without end,
They swoop again, their faces living flame,
Their wings of gold, and for the rest, so white
Our fresh snow couldn't hope to seem the same.
20 When they again went back down from the height
Into the bloom, they gave it, tier on tier,
The peace and order they had gained from how
They fanned their sides with wings. Nor did the sheer
Abundance of their flying—marvel, now—

From height to flower, in any way impede
The sight in all its splendour. The divine
Light penetrates, with instant spread and speed,
The universe to every part, in line
With what it's worth. Nothing can intercede.
30   Serene and joyous kingdom, thronged with all
These people old and new, where love and sight
Without a break, shared one field and no wall!
Ah, look upon our tempest, Threefold Light,
Sent outward from a single star to fall
On everyone in equal measure! Think
How the barbarians, born where the Bears—
Great Bear and Little Bear—both wheel and blink,
Were so reduced to slack mouths and dumb stares
When first they saw the mighty works of Rome,
40   The Lateran outsoaring any roof,
By ten times, that they'd ever seen at home.
Then think of me, when faced there with the proof
Of how far I had come, the human plane
To the divine, time to eternity,
The Florentines to people just and sane.
Amazement added to my joy made me
Content to hear no sound and to remain
Silent. And as a pilgrim looks around
The temple of his vow refreshed, and hopes
50   To tell again some day of what he found,
So I took my eyes upward through the slopes
Of living light, and I surveyed the ranks,
Now up, now down, and now around again,
Through all the faces so evoking thanks
For Charity. With Another's light, and then
With light from their own smiles, their faces shone,
And every move with dignity and grace.
Thus I had seen, but not yet lingered on,
In any part, the structure of that place.
60   And for those points my mind had paused upon

I turned to ask my lady if she'd make
Them clear to my rekindled eagerness.
My expectation, though, was a mistake.
Instead of her, I saw I must address
An old man, in the radiant attire
Of that exalted company. His eyes
And cheeks suffused with reassuring fire
Of gracious joy, his aspect kind and wise,
He seemed a tender father. I, in haste,
70 Said "Where is she?" And gently he replied
"Beatrice, from her concern you would not waste
Your longing, sent me down here to your side
From my seat. If you'd know how she is placed,
Look up there to the third tier from the peak
And you'll see her again, set on the throne
Her merits suit her for." I did not speak,
But lifted up my eyes and saw her where
She made herself a crown fit to reflect
The everlasting beams. Here in our air,
80 The highest region, thundering unchecked,
Is not so far from mortal eye—not when
The eye is in the deep sea lost—as was
Beatrice in glory from my vision then,
And yet it made no odds to me, because
Her image was undimmed as it came down
To my eyes, since the air was pure between.
"Lady, aloft beneath your fitting crown,
In whom my hope found strength, and who has been
To Hell and left her footprints there for my
90 Salvation, let me say I recognise
Such grace and virtue was made actual by
Your power and goodness. You gave me the prize
Of loosened bondage, lending all the ways
And means at your command. In that same wise,
Preserve in me, until I end my days,
Your bounty, so the spirit you made whole

May leave the body you were pleased to know."
That was my prayer, delivered from the soul,
And she, who seemed so far off, smiled, and though
100 She looked at me awhile, she turned once more
To the Eternal Fountain. The saint said
"In order that the path which lies before,
Your journey to the end, which you now tread,
Should be familiar to you and complete,
Fly with your eyes, and thus prepare your sight,
Through this tall garden, so you're set to meet
The Radiance Divine as you gain height.
The Queen of Heaven, who has all my fire
Of love, will surely grant us every grace,
110 For I am Bernard, her most faithful squire,
Rewarded with the vision of her face."
As some Croatian pilgrim who is shown,
In Rome, the Veronica (the handkerchief
That once, when Christ climbed his last hill alone,
A woman used to bring him some relief,
Mopping his brow), will say, within his mind,
"Lord Jesus Christ, true God, was this you?" such
Was I, since Bernard, when with humankind,
Had known, by contemplation, how to touch
120 On this peace. "Child of grace," he said, "This state
Of joy you will not see if you should keep
Your eyes down here around the entrance gate.
You must look up as far as the most steep
Of circles till you see the Queen to whom
This realm is subject and devoted." I
Lifted my gaze, and as there is more room
For light on the horizon where the sky
Is touched by sunrise in the morning than
There is where the sun sets, just so, when my
130 Eyes, from the valley where their climb began,
Attained the mountain top, I saw one part
Of the extreme edge far outshine the rest

Of that rim with its light. As at the start
Of sunrise, we see one place the more blessed
With fire, and on each side of that it shades
Away, just so that peaceful oriflamme—
Not the French flag for battles and parades—
Showed brighter in the middle, with a dam
To hold it back on either side. And at
140 That middle point, I saw, with outspread wings,
A thousand angels—no, far more than that—
In festival, each, in specific things
To do, and in its brightness, quite unique.
And smiling on their sports and songs, there reigned
A beauty, joy to all. If I could speak
As I imagine, yet I'd be constrained
To silence on the subject of the least
Suggestion of her splendour. Bernard saw
My eyes on her from whom he never ceased
150 To draw warmth, and he turned to her once more
His own eyes, with a love that made the thrill
Of my first sight of her more thrilling still.

CANTO 32

Absorbed in pleasure, that contemplative
Freely became a teacher, and began
His lesson. He had holy words to give.
"The wound that brought death to the Son of Man,
Which Mary closed with ointment, was first prised
Apart and then pierced through by that one there,
Seated below her feet. You've realised
That it is Eve, because she is so fair,
And here she is, redeemed. In the third row,
Below her, Rachel sits with Beatrice,
As you can see. Then Sarah you must know,
And then Rebecca. Judith has found peace,
And Ruth, great-grandmother to him that so
Grieved for his sin he didn't sing, but cried
'Have mercy on me.' (Yes, King David.) Then,
You see there, as I name the sanctified,
The way they sit below and then again
Below, the holy women line by line
Down through the rose, all duly ranked from one
Soft petal to the next. See how they shine.
And from the seventh grade, as they have done
Above, the Hebrew women rank by rank
Divide the tresses of the flower, for they
Are like a wall, the wall we have to thank

For how it parts the sacred stair. The way
They looked on faith in Christ is what decides
The matter. On the one side, where the flower
Is in full bloom and not one space abides,
Sit those with faith that Christ, in all his power,
30   Would one day come. The other side holds those
Who saw he had. Not all of them as yet
Are there, so some half-circles of the rose
Are cut by vacant places. Like the set
Of tiers that comes down from the glorious seat
Of Heaven's Queen, to constitute one edge
Of the divide, so, downward from the feet
Of great John, comes the other, ledge to ledge.
He, holy always, braved the wilderness
And martyrdom, and then, for two years, Hell,
40   Until Christ crucified eased his distress.
Below him, reading downward, we can tell
These seats were well assigned, for there we see
Thomas and Benedict and Augustine
And others in their multiplicity—
So many of these great ones there have been—
All the way down to here. Behold how deep
The sacred foresight was, for both aspects
Of faith shall equally take up the steep
Slopes of the garden, not as separate sects
50   But as two halves of one whole. Also note
How, anywhere below that level grade
That cuts the two lines of the upright moat,
Those have their seats who have not been arrayed
On their account, but for their parent's worth,
Conditions being met: they were absolved
From their small bodies too close to their birth
To have a choice, or know what was involved,
And this you will yourself deduce from how
Their faces look, and how their voices sound
60   So childish, if you concentrate your brow

To look and listen. I see I astound
You with these words, for you are sore perplexed,
And in perplexity are silent. Thought—
One subtlety criss-crossing with the next,
So no clear line emerges as it ought—
Has made a hard knot you are trapped within.
I'll loosen it. Nothing of any sort
Can here exist or even can begin
Subject to chance, which simply finds no place
70 In all this kingdom's breadth, not any more
Than hunger, thirst or sorrow. All you face
Is soundly based upon eternal law:
The fit of ring to finger is exact.
It follows that all those who hastened here
To have their true life are not ranked, in fact,
As high and low, however it might appear.
The King through whom this realm rests in such love
And sheer delight that no desire may dare
To do more—making all minds, here above,
80 In His glad sight—bestows his gracious care
According to his wish. The facts fulfil
The proof of this, but Scripture tells you, too,
That, in the womb, the twins did not lie still,
But fought in anger, just as they would do
In later life. Esau and Jacob had
Their different colourings of head to prove
The guiding light that chose how each was clad
In hair, chose also how their souls would move
From birth to death, not by themselves inspired.
90 It's not the merit of their doings, but
The keenness of the vision they acquired
In their first instant, that sees each one shut
Into the certain path—by Him desired,
Not them—that leads to the particular
Rank they hold here. In early times it was
The innocence of their young character

Abetted by their parent's faith, gave cause
For their salvation, earned by those two things.
First age completed, males were circumcised,
Strength being lent to their unknowing wings
Solely by that, as if they'd been baptised;
But when the age of grace came, innocence
Was held below, unless it had been blessed
With baptism in its full Christian sense.
That said, look now on that face you think best
Resembles Christ, for only its intense
White light can show you Him." I saw such joy
Rain down on her, borne in the holy minds
Created for those heights where they deploy
Their flight, that all the many different kinds
Of gladness I'd seen up till then had not
So held me in suspense and wonder, nor
Evinced such likeness to the Lord, and what
That loving spirit who had flown before
With his announcement did now was to spread
His wings before her and to sing again
"Hail Mary, full of grace." On every side,
The blessed court sang their response to this
Divine song, every face filled with the tide
Of brightness in this canticle of bliss.
"My saintly father, bearing for my sake
The task of stepping down from that sweet place
Where you by lot eternal rightly take
Your seat, give me the name to match the face
Of that one angel gazing on the eyes
Of our Queen with such rapture, so enthralled
He seems on fire." As you might surmise,
I well knew what that cavalier was called,
But wished more lessons from the man who drew
Beauty from Mary as the morning star
Draws beauty from the sun. He knew I knew,
But answered anyway. "Because you are

Still hungry, hear this. He is Gabriel
The herald. Every confidence that can
Exist, and every courtly ease as well,
Whether in angel or the soul of man,
Is found in him, and we would have it so,
For he's the very one who brought the palm
To Earth for Mary, so that she might know
140　The son of God had sought her inner calm
To put the burden on of human flesh.
But follow with your eyes as I denote
Some you have seen but now will see afresh
In their right place: great nobles, though their coat
Of arms attests, in this empire of peace,
To mercy and to justice. Those two there,
Whose happiness no blessing could increase
Because it is the Empress that they share
For neighbour, are the two roots, as it were,
150　Of this rose. On her left, the father whose
Rash tasting first instilled in humankind
The bitter taste of all they stood to lose
Through sin, and on her right, the father of
Our Holy Church, to whom Christ gave the keys
Of this resplendent flower and all its love.
Beside him sits the one whose prophecies,
In his Apocalypse, foretold the grief
Of Christ's fair bride, won with the lance and nails:
John the Evangelist, spurred by belief,
160　While still alive, to see beyond the veils
Of his own time. Beside the other rests
That leader whose weak, thankless, fickle flock
Were given manna though they failed all tests.
Opposite Peter in that central block
You can see Anna, mother of the Queen,
So well content to see her daughter, she
Still keeps her eyes where they have always been
While singing her hosannas constantly.

The first great family father sits across
170 From Lucy, she who sent your lady down
To help you when you were at such a loss
Your brow was not just furrowed with a frown,
But beaten to destruction. Since the time
Is flying now that holds you in your sleep,
We should pause to take stock here, as a prime
Tailor will cut his cloth so as to keep
The outlines of a coat within the bounds
Of what he has to work with. Let's direct
Our eyes to where the Primal Love resounds
180 In silent light, so that your intellect
May enter, insofar as it's allowed,
His mighty fire. But lest, perhaps, you fall
Short of that aim, recoiling with head bowed,
Yet still with beating wings, in spite of all
Still hoping to advance, grace must be won
From Her who has the power to see you through.
So follow me with love while this is done.
Lend your heart to my words, for they are true."
And what he said next, I'll now say to you.

CANTO 33

"Our Virgin Mother, daughter of your Son,"
St. Bernard prayed, "So low of birth and yet
Exalted so much more than anyone
On Earth or in the sky, forever set
As goal of the Church council, you are she
Who so ennobled human nature's state
Its maker deigned to have His majesty
Made in its making. God's love incarnate,
The same fire that first made this flower bloom—
10 The warmth pervading its eternal peace—
Was kindled once again within your womb.
Up here, for all of us, you never cease
To be the charitable torch of noon,
And down below you are hope's living spring
For mortals. You, great lady, late and soon,
Are so supreme, he would be floundering
Who sought for grace and did not turn to you,
His wish without wings, without everything,
Despite whatever he might strive to do.
20 Your kind love comforts all who ask, and may
Often anticipate the asking. Through
Your goodness, all the good in any way
In every creature is combined. You are
All mercy, pity, bounty, joined in one.

This man, who comes to see you from so far
Below, the sky has never known the sun
In that pit of the universe, has seen
The spirits each and all. Now, by your grace,
He seeks the power to say his eyes have been
30 Still higher, even to the final place
Of his salvation. Never for my own
Great vision did I burn as now I burn
For his, but now I pray for him alone
That your prayers, prayers divine, will in their turn
Divest him of his every mortal cloud,
So that the joy supreme may be disclosed
To him. My Queen to whom all is allowed,
I pray that if you do what I've proposed,
You afterwards keep his affections pure,
40 The vision splendid having been achieved;
That you will guard him thenceforth to ensure
By human impulse he is not deceived
And led astray again. But now see how
Beatrice and all the others clap their hands:
It must be for my prayer." The Queen's eyes now
Made clear to us how well she understands
And cherishes our prayers. The eyes revered
And loved by God beheld her courtier
For long enough to prove his prayers endeared
50 Him further to her, but then went elsewhere—
Towards the Light Eternal, where no gaze
Other than hers so deeply penetrates,
As I, my own desires in their last phase
Where steady craving finally abates,
Already did what Bernard asked me to
By signing with a smile. I looked up. More
And more my sight, becoming pure and true,
Was entering the beam of that high store
Of light, itself true. From that moment on,
60 My vision outsoared all our powers of speech,

Which quail at such a sight and then are gone,
And memory fails, the task beyond its reach.
As he who sees all in a dream, but when
He wakes, finds just the passion has remained
In mind, and all the rest will not again
Come back to him, a spectacle retained
Only in feeling, such am I. It fades,
My vision, and yet still, within my heart,
The sweetness that was born from it cascades
70 In drops, a distillation, the last part
To melt, just as the snowdrift in the sun
Blurs outlines, and the Sybil's oracle
That she wrote on the leaves, when she was done,
Was lost along the wind. Ah, if not all,
Give me at least a little, Light Supreme—
You that are raised above all mortal thought—
Of how you looked, so I might give a gleam—
And lend my tongue the power to report—
Of your great glory for those yet to come,
80 For if it comes back to my memory
At least in part, and some part of the sum
Lives in these lines, then so much more will be
Your triumph realised. I think that by
The sharpness that I suffered from the force
Of that ray's vividness the chance was high
My eyesight, had it been turned from that course,
Would have been dazzled. Such, indeed, was why
I dared, I now recall, to face the light
Straight on, so long that all my sight was spent
90 Upon it. In its depths I saw, packed tight,
Bound in one book by love, all that is sent
Abroad throughout the universe as leaves
Torn out and scattered: single, separate things,
And any kind of quality that cleaves
To them and enters, and whatever brings
A partial framework to some area

Of all that multiplicity. But here
All things and links that ever were and are
Were fused together so they might appear
100 To me as one pure light. I know I saw
The universal form of this intact
Complexity, because my joy, the more
I tell of it, expands to mark the act
Of speaking. Thus a single moment holds
Me in a trance far deeper than those five
And twenty centuries have kept their folds
Around King Neptune, who must always strive
To comprehend what crossed his upward glance:
The shadow of the Argo. Thus my mind,
110 Held fast, gazed fixedly and not askance,
By thoughts rekindled of what it might find
Plumbing the crucible of happenstance.
For at that light, no man can turn aside—
Not by consent—to see aught else: the good,
The object of the will and our best guide,
Is gathered into it, and nothing could
Exist apart from it and not be called
Defective, for perfection can be sought
Only where all perfections are installed,
120 In that light. But my speech must now fall short
Even of what I can remember still.
An infant's tongue still bathing at the breast
Could say more. As my eyes yet drank their fill
Of that light, things did not remain at rest:
Not that the light did not remain the same—
It always had one aspect, as before—
But as my sight, in gazing at the flame,
Gained strength, the single aspect the light wore
Was changing in my eyes as I was changed.
130 In that high flame's deep and unblemished field
Three circles of three colours were arranged,
All of the same extent. One seemed to yield

Its lustre—as a pair of rainbows may—
To the other, and the third was made of fire
Breathed forth by the first two. What can I say?
Was this the trinity of my desire
Or was it not? Alas, how scant is speech,
Failing my concept by so very much!
And what I saw, that concept failed to reach
140   By such a distance, was so out of touch,
To call it "little" scarcely would suffice.
Eternal light, known to yourself alone,
Knowing yourself alone, once, twice and thrice,
In loving company yet on your own,
The self-renewing well of paradise
Forever! All the circling thus unloosed
Reflected light, which my eyes dwelt upon
And saw the way those swirling tints produced
A painted likeness that my eyes fixed on
150   Completely, for that likeness was of us.
Like the geometer who sets his soul
To square the circle and will not discuss
One thing besides, and yet—although the whole
Of what he knows is poured into the task—
Can't find the necessary principle,
Just so was I when faced with that strange mask.
How was the image fitted to the full
Activity within the circle? Why
Should it be placed there? But my wings were not
160   Sufficient. It took faith's flash to supply
My mind with that sharp blow by which it got
Its wish. Imagination, there on high—
Too high to breathe free, after such a climb—
Had lost its power; but now, just like a wheel
That spins so evenly it measures time
By space, the deepest wish that I could feel
And all my will, were turning with the love
That moves the sun and all the stars above.

ABOUT THE TRANSLATOR

Born in Australia, Clive James lives in Cambridge, England. He is the author of *Unreliable Memoirs*; a volume of selected poems, *Opal Sunset*; and the best-selling *Cultural Amnesia*. He has written for the *New York Times Book Review*, *The New Yorker* and *The Atlantic*. He is an Officer of the Order of Australia (AO) and a Commander of the Order of the British Empire (CBE).